PUBLIC ECONOMICS

PUBLIC ECONOMICS

by

LEIF JOHANSEN
University of Oslo

NORTH-HOLLAND PUBLISHING COMPANY – AMSTERDAM • OXFORD
AMERICAN ELSEVIER PUBLISHING COMPANY, INC. – NEW YORK

North-Holland ISBN: 7204 3022 4
American Elsevier ISBN: 0 444 10075 X

This book was originally published under the title
"Offentlig Økonomikk" by Oslo University Press
It was translated from the Norwegian
by Mrs. M.C. Brown and R. I. Christophersen

PUBLISHERS:
NORTH-HOLLAND PUBLISHING COMPANY – AMSTERDAM
NORTH-HOLLAND PUBLISHING COMPANY, LTD. – OXFORD

SOLE DISTRIBUTORS FOR THE U.S.A. AND CANADA:
AMERICAN ELSEVIER PUBLISHING COMPANY, INC.
52 VANDERBILT AVENUE, NEW YORK, N.Y. 10017

First edition 1965
Second printing 1968
Third printing 1971
Fourth printing 1975

PRINTED IN THE NETHERLANDS

Contents

Preface to the English Edition

This book is based upon a series of lectures given to students of economics at Oslo University in recent years.

The book was originally published in two parts in the Norwegian language, the first part in 1962, covering the first five chapters, and the second part in 1964. Some figures have been brought up-to-date, but apart from this only a few amendments have been made in the present translation.

The exposition treats economic theory in its relation to the problems of public economy and lays emphasis on principles and applications of theory rather than on description. Thus a complete description of national institutions, fiscal system and policy, and any systematic comparison between countries has been avoided; facts and figures from Norway and other countries are used mainly to clarify points of principle, and to illustrate the practical importance of the problems which are treated.

The economic models which are employed are all quite simple. Generally I have tried to avoid lengthy theoretical arguments that do not lead to any definite conclusions. A prior knowledge of some basic macro-economic theory and economic welfare theory is probably necessary for the reading of some of the chapters since I do not spend time and space on critical examinations of basic points of theory which are thoroughly discussed in most text-books on general economic theory.

References to literature are given where the present exposition can be fairly directly followed up by reading literature on special points.

L. J.

Introduction

1.1. The public sector

The public sector in the Norwegian economy includes the state, the municipalities and the counties.

The state sector in a country can be subdivided in various ways. In the Norwegian national accounts, the following classification is used:

1. Government institutions

A. Government in a narrow sense (administration, judicial system, education, defence, etc.).
B. Government funds. Some of these have independent legal status, and are kept separate from the Treasury.
C. Social insurance.

2. Enterprises

A. State enterprises directly under the government (Norwegian State Railways, the postal service, the telegraph service, etc.). The institutions in this category do not have independent legal status. They are included in the state accounts, and their financial resources make up part of the Treasury. They cannot raise loans on their own, and they require grants from the state budget to undertake, for instance, building activity. Considerable social interests are usually involved in the activity of these enterprises, and as a rule they do not compete with private firms.
B. Government joint stock companies. These are separate juridical persons. They often compete with private firms and therefore need

greater independence and freedom of management. This is the reason why they have been given the form of a limited company.

C. The state banks. These are banks established to serve special purposes which are not sufficiently attended to through private banking.

The institutions included in 1A and 2A above constitute the central parts of the state sector. Their income and expenditure are included in the state budget and the state accounts.

A division similar to that shown above for the state can also be made for the municipalities and the counties.

The expression "the public sector" will be frequently used in the text, without it being clearly stated what this includes on each occasion. Wherever necessary, however, the expression will be defined.

The public sector during the last 50–100 years has been a growing sector, and has made up an increasing proportion of the total economy of the country. Consider, for instance, employment in the public sector in proportion to the total working population. It was well over 5% in the year 1900, well over 8% in 1920, a little under 8% in 1930, almost 13% in 1946, and almost 14% in 1950. In 1960 it had passed 16%. These figures cover state administration inclusive of defence, local administration and public enterprises, but excluding the government joint stock companies.

This trend is not confined to Norway. In the U.S.A., for instance, the equivalent figures were about 4% in 1900 and have been well over 12% since the second world war.

Another measure of the size of the public sector can be obtained by considering public revenue in proportion to the gross national product. This has been done in table 1. The greater part of the revenue comes from taxation.

It will be seen from the table that a considerable part of the increase in public revenue has been absorbed by the increase in transfers from the public to the private sector, in the form of subsidies, social benefits and interest payments. (A smaller part of the transfers relates to foreign countries.) But that part of the public revenue which has been disposable for public consumption and public saving has also shown a considerable increase.

During this period, the revenue and expenditure of the state have grown relatively somewhat faster than those of the municipalities.

Table 1

Public revenue in percentages of the gross national product in Norway

	Revenue before transfers	Transfers (subsidies, insurances, interest)	Disposable revenue
1900	9.1	1.7	7.4
1910	9.8	2.0	7.8
1920	12.5	4.2	8.3
1930	15.6	5.9	9.7
1939	18.6	6.1	12.5
1950	28.3	12.0	16.3
1962	30.7	12.0	18.7

This growth in the extent of the public sector conforms to Adolph Wagner's so-called "law of increasing expansion of public activities". This "law", which was put forward about 1880, was founded on the claim, amongst others, that social progress necessitated a growth in the public share of total income. Such a growth might encounter financial obstacles, but in the long run these would always be overcome, in Wagner's opinion.

Others have been less far-sighted than Adolph Wagner. In 1906, for instance, the economist Leroy-Beaulieu wrote*:

"We believe that it is possible to fix an empirical lower and upper limit to taxation. The limits are not inflexible, they are only approximate. We consider that taxation is very moderate when the sum of national, provincial and municipal taxes does not exceed five or six per cent of private incomes. Such a proportion should be the normal rule in countries where the public debt is small and whose politics are not dominated by the spirit of conquest. Taxation is still bearable, though heavy, up to ten or twelve per cent of the citizens' income. Beyond twelve or thirteen per cent the rate of taxation is exorbitant. The country may be able to bear such a rate, but it is beyond doubt

---

* Quoted from *Classics in the theory of public finance,* eds. R. A. Musgrave and A. T. Peacock (New York – London, 1958) p. 164.

that it slows down the growth of public wealth, threatens the liberty
of industry and even of the citizens, and hems them in by the vexa-
tion and inquisition necessarily entailed by the complexity and height
of the taxes."

There have also been more recent attempts at determining limits to total
taxation. Particular attention and discussion have been provoked by
Colin Clark's contention that a level of total taxation of 25% or more of
the national income will have an inflationary effect. There is, however,
hardly anything more absolute about the limit Colin Clark sets than there
was in those Beaulieu tried to set up.

This section is meant to serve only as a preliminary sketch helping to
identify the public sector from the beginning. We shall return to a closer
consideration of the extension and growth of the public sector in Chapter 6.

1.2.   What distinguishes the public sector from other sectors in the economy?

The question posed in this title can, of course, be answered from many
points of view. The interest here is in those things that distinguish the
public sector from an *economic* point of view. Some of these things are
perhaps quite obvious, especially in our own times.

1.   The public sector is nowadays a large sector partly directed from
     a central authority. Owing to its size it will exercise influence on the
     whole economy of the country. (This occurs whether it is intended
     by the authorities or not.) One result of this is that in public econom-
     ics the focus must be on the effects on the entire economy of the
     actions taken by public authorities.
2.   The public authorities can set up types of objectives other than those
     possible for the private sectors. A private producing or trading unit
     must to a certain degree make it its aim to gain a large profit, oth-
     erwise it would not survive in competition with other private units.
     This is not a question of "social conscience". A system with com-
     peting private units makes such an objective a necessity for the indi-
     vidual unit. The public sector, however, is not subject to any such
     necessity.

3. The public authorities have other types of means of action than those available to the private units in the economy. This is due to the fact that the public authorities have power to direct or regulate the actions of other sectors, to impose taxes, etc.

4. The public authorities have financially a much freer scope than the private units of the economy. It could be said that the public authorities are in theory not subject to any budget restriction at all, inasmuch as they can always provide all the money they might wish for simply by printing it. On the other hand the Legislature can choose to lay down institutional and legal conditions which prevent this. In Norway, for instance, it is the Bank of Norway that has the right to issue notes, and the Bank is subject to provisions of an Act considered to prevent it from granting loans directly to the State.

With such possibilities of setting up other objectives than those open to the individual private unit, and with the large range of means available to the public authorities, the latter can be seen as a tool for "collective actions". By this is meant a tool for realizing such activities and projects as cannot, or will not, be carried through by the actions of individuals or single firms, but which need co-ordination in some form or other.

From the above it follows that one must be careful about applying to the public economy conclusions based on principles relevant only to private economy. Such conclusions have formerly resulted, amongst other things, in the public authorities contributing towards amplifying trade fluctuations instead of levelling them out.

1.3. The necessity of applying economic theory

It has been mentioned that the public sector of the economy is now so large that its actions must necessarily have far-reaching consequences for the economy as a whole. When discussing essential questions of public economy it is therefore always necessary to bear in mind the interplay between the public sector of the economy and the rest of the economy. This cannot be done in a satisfactory way without applying economic theory. In this book a relatively heavy emphasis will be laid on those questions that especially require such an application of economic theory.

The ideal, naturally, would be to have a universal economic model which would answer "all" questions. Recent research at the Institute of Economics at the University of Oslo in connection with economic decision models has to a great extent aimed at the building up of such universal models. In certain other countries research has shown somewhat different trends. In Holland, for instance, a number of smaller models have been constructed, each of them able to answer only a limited number of special questions, in place of attempts at building a large model which would answer a wider range of questions.

The question of which of these lines is the more fruitful cannot be answered generally. In teaching, however, it is necessary to use simple and clear models. Here, therefore, to a large extent the course will be taken of making a new model for every type of question asked.

These models will not go very far in the direction of theoretical perfectionism. The models used will mostly be so simple that the conclusions will be relatively clear and unambiguous. Many things must then be considered given, even if they can be made the subjects of doubt. The models are most of them well known and much used in theoretical economics, and it is left to theoretical economics to discuss these theories thoroughly; this is not considered the task of public economics.

1.4. *Two ways of dealing with the public sector*

The public sector, both in general theoretical economics and in public economics in particular, can be treated according to two different principles.

One can firstly limit oneself to trying to answer questions of the following types: if the public authorities do this and that – what will be the consequences of these dispositions? Or: if one wants to obtain this and that, what means are then at the disposal of the public authorities, and how should they use these means to obtain the desired objectives? By this view we regard the public sector as autonomous, i.e., we do not try to build up any theory in explanation of the factual actions of the public authorities in various situations.

But it is possible to go further and to consider the public sector in another way. One then tries to explain the actions of the public authorities as determined by, for instance, such things as the various influences of social classes and pressure groups, the social mechanism of selection of leaders of state and municipal institutions, their knowledge or lack of knowledge when taking decisions, etc. This will be a theory *about* politics.

It cannot be said that *one* of these views is right and the other wrong. Both views lead to interesting fields of problems. Here, however, the first view will be stressed the most. This is without doubt the simplest: it makes possible a relatively technical analysis of the problems within public economics. The second view requires a far greater element of political and sociological theory.

There is, however, no doubt that an understanding of the role of the public sector throughout the ages would require an analysis of the type mentioned under this second point of view.

Targets and instruments

2.1. *Targets and instruments in general*

The following general discussion of targets and instruments properly belongs under what one might call general theory of economic policy. It is, however, of such great importance for the understanding of public economics that I find it useful to include the main features here.

The presentation will appear rather abstract; so if it seems difficult to associate economic realities with this discussion during the first reading, it is better to continue without spending too much time on this section. It is then recommended to return to it again after reading the next chapter, which deals with the macroeconomic effects of fiscal policy.

2.1.1. *General description of the economic system*

Let us assume that the mechanism of the economic system under observation can be described by the following set of conditions:

$$
\begin{aligned}
f_1\,(x_1 \ldots x_I;\; t_1 \ldots t_J) &= 0 \\
\vdots \qquad\quad \vdots & \\
f_I\,(x_1 \ldots x_I;\; t_1 \ldots t_J) &= 0
\end{aligned}
\tag{2.1}
$$

$$
\begin{aligned}
&t_1 \\
&\;\vdots \quad \text{are determined directly by the government.} \\
&t_J
\end{aligned}
\tag{2.2}
$$

The variables included in this system are divided into two groups. The variables $t_1...t_J$ are variables which the government controls directly. They can be tax-rates, public expenditure of different kinds, etc. These can be utilized by the government in economic policy, and we can call them the government's means of policy or instrument variables. The variables $x_1...x_I$ are all the other economic variables which it is found necessary or useful to include in the analysis.

When the government has decided which values it will give its instrument variables $t_1...t_J$ the equations (2.1) will generally determine the values of the variables $x_1...x_I$. The x's are thus not directly determined by the government, but it is obvious that the values the x's will assume generally must depend on which values the government has given the t's. We can thus consider the t's as instruments by which the government can indirectly influence the values of the x's. This further explains the term "instrument variables" for the t's.

The system (2.1) can generally be solved in such a way that we get the x's expressed in terms of the t's. This can be written in the following way:

$$x_1 = g_1(t_1 ... t_J),$$
$$\vdots$$
$$x_I = g_I(t_1 ... t_J).$$
(2.3)

The above system is so general that it prompts the question whether it can convey any information at all. It does, however, make clear an important connection between the number of instruments the government has at its disposal and the number of targets wihch it can set up without the set of targets and instruments becoming contradictory. This connection is of importance in clarifying almost any problem in economic policy.

2.1.2.   *The number of targets and the number of instruments*

Let us assume that the government has certain targets which can be formulated by demanding that K of the variables $x_1...x_I$ shall take on certain values. This is marked thus:

$$x_1 = \bar{x}_1$$
$$\vdots$$
$$x_K = \bar{x}_K$$
(2.4)

assuming that the variables are numbered in such a way that it is the K first variables for which the government has targets*.

The question is now whether the goal expressed by (2.4) can be achieved within the system described by (2.1) and (2.2). To examine this we insert the values from (2.4) in the equations in (2.1), now regarding $t_1 ... t_J$ as variables which can be adjusted so that the equations are satisfied with the desired values of $x_1 ... x_K$. This way of regarding $t_1 ... t_J$ does not conflict with what has been expressed in (2.2). It only means that we wish to calculate which values the government must determine for $t_1 ... t_J$ in order to achieve the targets (2.4). While doing this calculation one must, of course, consider $t_1 ... t_J$ as unknown variables.

The insertion mentioned can be expressed by (2.5):

$$f_1(\bar{x}_1 ... \bar{x}_K, x_{K+1} ... x_I; t_1 ... t_J) = 0,$$
$$\vdots \qquad \vdots$$
$$f_I(\bar{x}_1 ... \bar{x}_K, x_{K+1} ... x_I; t_1 ... t_J) = 0. \qquad (2.5)$$

In this system there are now in all $I - K + J$ unknown quantities, viz., $x_{K+1} \; x_I$ and $t_1 ... t_J$. The number of equations is I. If we assume that the equations are independent and – in those cases where we have fewer, or as many, equations as unknowns – that they are not contradictory, we can have the following different cases:

a) $I - K + J > I$, i.e., $J > K$: more unknown quantities than equations.

b) $I - K + J = I$, i.e., $J = K$: as many unknown quantities as equations.

c) $I - K + J < I$, i.e., $J < K$: more equations than unknown quantities.

$$\qquad (2.6)$$

---

* The above formulation includes the case where the government might have targets which are expressed by the variables $x_1 ... x_I$ being subjected to certain requirements in the form of equations, for instance that certain variables shall assume certain proportions to each other, or that there shall be a given difference between certain variables, etc. Such constraints can generally be expressed in this way: $F(x_1 ... x_I) = 0$. If, however, we have such a constraint we can only introduce a new variable x_{I+1} defined by $x_{I+1} = F(x_1 ... x_I)$ and introduce this equation of definition in addition to those already included in (2.1) while simultaneously introducing $x_{I+1} = \bar{x}_{I+1} = 0$ among the targets in (2.4).

In the case of a) we have more unknown quantities than equations and there will usually be several ways in which to satisfy (2.5) with the given values of $x_1...x_K$. In the case of b) we have as many equations as unknown quantities, and there will usually be one and only one set of values for the unknown quantities which satisfy the equations. This means that there is only one set of values for the instrument variables $t_1...t_J$ enabling the targets concerning the variables $x_1...x_K$ to be achieved. In the case of c) we have more equations than there are unknown variables, and the system cannot be fulfilled. This means that there does not exist any set of values for the instrument variables $t_1...t_J$ such that they will lead to all the targets in (2.4) being achieved simultaneously.

We see from the arrangement (2.6) that what determines which of the three cases we shall have, is whether the number of instruments J is greater than, equal to, or smaller than the number of targets K.

We can formulate the above conclusions almost like a catchphrase, in the following way: to achieve a given number of targets the government must have at least the same number of instruments. Or: the government cannot set more targets than the number of instruments available to it.

With special forms of the equations describing the system it may happen that one target is automatically achieved with the fulfilment of another target. Or it may happen that two proposed targets are incompatible, even if one has the sufficient number of instruments according to the rules given above. These special cases will not be further treated here. A discussion of such cases is provided by Bent Hansen*.

2.1.3. *The efficiency of an instrument with regard to a target*

Consideration of the relationships between the number of targets and the number of instruments must be supplemented by consideration of the efficiency of the instruments. It will be of little use to have a great number of means of policy at one's disposal if they are not efficient.

Assume that we are in a situation where $x_k = x_k^0$ and that we wish to get into a situation where $x_k = \bar{x}_k = x_k^0 + \Delta x_k$. It is then natural to turn to an instrument which is such that only a small change in the value of the

---

* See Chapter I in: *The economic theory of fiscal policy* (London, 1958).

quantity expressing this instrument is sufficient to produce the wanted change in the value of x_k. Here, of course, it is not clear what is to be understood by a "small" change in t_j. We can suppose that there exists, for institutional reasons, only a certain finite range of variation for t_j; and when we say that a change in t_j is "small" we see the change in relation to this range of possible variations.

From such a way of thinking we could say that the instrument t_j is more efficient with respect to the target variable x_k the bigger the derivative

$$\frac{\partial g_k(t_1 \ldots t_J)}{\partial t_j}, \tag{2.7}$$

where g_k is one of the functions introduced by (2.3). If this derivative is great a certain change in t_j will, of course, produce a great change in the value of x_k; or differently expressed: a certain change in the value of x_k can be produced by a small change in the value of t_j.

In (2.7) we observe a change in t_j while all other t's are kept constant. But here an important question is raised. If we change one t_j while others are kept constant, then not only will x_k change its value, but usually *all* the x's will be changed. If we then have many targets which we wish to keep while we change the value of x_k from x_k^0 into the new, desired value, then the x's expressing these other targets will also be changed.

In this situation we could then proceed in such a way that we not only change the one t_j, but also the values of a series of the other instruments, so as to arrive at a new situation where the one x_k is changed as desired, while the other x's for which we have targets are kept constant. The other t's which we now have changed do, however, also affect the one x_k whose value we were interested in changing. The result of this is that we must now also change the value of the instrument t_j – the one we first thought of using – by more or by less than we intended when we did not worry about the values of the other x's. From this point of view we could define the efficiency of an instrument with respect to a variable in a new way, viz., the efficiency of an instrument with respect to a variable is expressed by that change in the value of this instrument which is necessary to produce a certain change in the value of a target variable, when other instruments are used in such a way that the values of other target variables are kept constant*.

The line of thought here indicated does, however, also lead to certain difficulties. The measure of efficiency which we get by this way of thinking will, for instance, depend on which other set of instruments we have at our disposal. Moreover, it is somewhat arbitrary to attach the effect on x_k to a certain instrument t_j, when we actually change a whole set of instruments.

This discussion shows that generally it is necessary to consider all instruments in connection with all targets. It is as a rule hardly possible to define in a satisfactory way a concept such as we have tried to find, viz., a concept expressing the efficiency of *one* instrument with respect to *one* target variable.

It can, however, be the case with certain instruments and certain target variables that a given instrument affects a given target variable considerably, but only has small effects for other target variables. Formally this will be reflected in the following way:

$$\frac{\partial g_k(t_1 \ldots t_J)}{\partial t_j} \quad \text{is "great",}$$

$$\frac{\partial g_h(t_1 \ldots t_J)}{\partial t_j} \quad \text{is "small" for } h \neq k. \tag{2.8}$$

In such a case we can say that t_j is a *selective* instrument with respect to x_k, and then the measure (2.7) will be a suitable measure of the efficiency of this instrument.

A more thorough formal discussion of the concept of efficiency of an instrument has been carried out by Jan Tinbergen**.

2.1.4.   *Can the use of the instruments be decentralized?*

Within the formal framework outlined above we shall consider the

---

* The greater the efficiency of the instrument, the smaller this number will be. It would therefore, perhaps, be more natural to use the inverse of this number.

**See especially Chapter VII in: *On the theory of economic policy* (Amsterdam, 1952).

question of delegating to different institutions the power to take decisions as to actions involving the various instruments.

Let us assume that we have $J=K$, i.e., that we have as many instruments as we have targets. Can we then "share out" these instruments to various institutions and instruct the institutions to see to the achievement of their particular target? In the case now under consideration we shall have

$$x_1 = g_1 (t_1 \dots t_K)$$
$$\vdots$$
$$x_K = g_K (t_1 \dots t_K)$$

(2.9)

which can be solved with respect to $t_1 \dots t_K$:

$$t_1 = h_1 (x_1 \dots x_K)$$
$$\vdots$$
$$t_K = h_K (x_1 \dots x_K).$$

(2.10)

In the form (2.9) the equations indicate which values we shall get for the x's with which we associate targets if $t_1 \dots t_K$ are given certain values. In the form (2.10) the equations indicate which values we must give $t_1 \dots t_K$ if we want certain values for $x_1 \dots x_K$. Generally the value of every single target variable will depend on the values of all the instruments $t_1 \dots t_K$. And conversely, the necessary value for an instrument variable will generally depend on all the targets. This complicates a decentralization of targets and instruments. The value of the target variable given to a certain institution to "look after" will depend on what all the other institutions do; and to determine the necessary value of the instrument assigned to that particular institution does in principle require knowledge also of the targets which come under other institutions.

In certain cases, however, it can happen that a target variable is virtually independent of all save one, or one definite group of instruments, and simultaneously that this instrument (or these instruments) has (have) only a small influence on other target variables. Expressed differently, it could be said that we then have one selective instrument, or a group of these, with respect to one target variable, while at the same time other instruments are neutral with respect to this target variable. In such a case we can delegate this target and the appurtenant instruments to a separate institution without disturbing other targets. This institution may then only be notified of the target, but does not need information from any central authority about how the instruments are to be used.

In practice a complete neutrality and selectivity will hardly occur. On the other hand, it seems unthinkable that all instruments at the government's disposal should be centrally determined and co-ordinated. As a rough principle we could say, then, that instruments affecting many targets ought to be employed centrally, while instruments affecting only one or a small number of targets can to a larger extent be decentralized*.

In connection with the question of centralization and decentralization so many other considerations also, of course, assert themselves that this rule will not always hold. We return to some of these considerations in Chapter 8.

2.1.5.   Maximization of a preference function

To determine targets as in (2.4) one must combine two different things. Firstly, the targets expressed by (2.4) must reflect what we *want*. But next they must also reflect what we judge it *possible* to obtain. The latter condition involves considerations as to how the economic system actually works and the limitations to which it is subjected, and to this extent it is a question of matters that in principle are objectively recognizable. It would be more satisfactory were it possible to separate these two matters. On the one side could then be set out one's preferences, in some form or other, while on the other side could be set out a model containing all available information about the workings of the economic system and its limitations.

This can be obtained in principle by operating with a preference function, which we could write as

$$W = W(x_1, ..., x_I).$$
(2.11)

This function should then be maximized within the range of existing possibilities, that is, under the conditions, in the form of equations and

---

* Problems of the type here touched upon are thoroughly treated by Jan Tinbergen in: *Centralization and decentralization in economic policy* (Amsterdam, 1954).

inequalities, to which the system is exposed. In such an analysis there would be no rules of the type we have had before, as to the number of targets and of instruments. With this last formulation there is one target, viz., to maximize W, and for that target all the instruments present are used.

A realistic preference function will have to be a function of very many variables, and with a complicated structure. One can choose a somewhat simpler way, by letting W express the most essential aspects of the preferences, while letting other aspects be expressed in the form of equations and inequalities of different kinds. Such questions, together with the question of how the establishment of a preference function could be imagined, are thoroughly treated in connection with the work on decision models carried out by Professor Ragnar Frisch at the Institute of Economics at the University of Oslo.

2.2. The most important targets considered in public economics

Many of the targets considered in public economics are quite obvious. For the sake of order it can, however, be useful to set up a list of the most important of these targets.

2.2.1. High current private consumption

In itself, this target is obvious. Some people may perhaps say that it is important to keep a relatively low current consumption, thereby being able to save and invest and thus securing a higher consumption in future. This is, however, a thought that only asserts itself when we look at the question of co-ordinating a series of different targets which partly oppose each other. Otherwise it is clear enough that *in itself* high consumption now is a desirable thing.

2.2.2. The satisfaction of collective wants

The concern here is with satisfaction of the need for goods which are of such a nature that they cannot be split up and sold to some individual buyers, while other people are excluded from consuming these goods. The production and distribution of these goods can therefore not be regulated through the usual markets. The clearest examples of such goods are those that have to do with the maintenance of law and order, but there are also such things as, for instance, the regulation of watercourses to protect against flooding, expansion of communications, etc. Purely collective goods in this sense hardly exist, as many of those things that usually come under the heading collective goods *could be imagined* split up and sold to individual buyers. This is the case, for instance, with education, and one might also imagine police protection being individualized and sold in a market. But although there are thus many border-line cases, it is yet convenient to operate with the expression 'collective wants' as a term for certain types of requirements. Accounts often give the impression that the satisfaction of such wants has been the original task of the state. Historically this may perhaps be somewhat dubious, but there is no doubt that for a long time it has been, and still is, one of the government's most important tasks.

2.2.3. *The ensuring of economic growth*

Since economic growth demands net investments, this target may to a certain degree conflict or compete with the target of high current consumption. The question might then be asked whether it is the business of the government to set up targets in these two fields. Could not the government leave it to separate individuals to strike a balance between present consumption and economic growth, through their choice between saving and consumption? The answer to this (without treating it in greater detail here) is that existing market mechanisms are hardly suited to ensure a result which is in any precise accordance with the inhabitants' own preferences about present consumption versus economic growth. There is also the observed fact that the citizens often vote for a policy giving a higher investment rate than the same citizens would produce were all investment to be decided by voluntary private saving, without any actions on the part of the government with a view to maintaining high investment. Finally, as already mentioned, the government now constitutes such a large part of the entire economy that its actions must have consequences for almost all economic units or circumstances whether this is intended or not. This makes it difficult to imagine a policy purporting to be neutral with regard to the question of present consumption and economic growth. And this, then, also means that the government cannot avoid giving a certain consideration to this issue.

2.2.4. Influence on the distribution of income

Here, too, it might be asked whether it is a "natural" objective for the government to influence the distribution of income. There is no need, here, to discuss this question, only to bear in mind the fact that there are very few countries where the citizens accept the income distribution that comes into existence of itself in the markets. They usually wish to interfere in various ways, through the government, to adjust this distribution. The question of distribution of income does, however, have different aspects. One could look at a) the distribution of individual earnings, b) distribution according to family type, c) distribution among industries, and d) distribution over geographical areas. Even though instruments of fiscal policy can be used, and are used, in connection with the last two aspects here mentioned, only the first two are traditionally considered as belonging to the field of public economics.

2.2.5. High employment

The target of high or full employment can be based on two different considerations. Firstly, high employment can be set up as a target because high production is desirable. If so, it is really unnecessary to set it up beside the targets we already have set out above. Secondly, however, the target of high employment can be set up from social and political considerations which count *in addition* to the importance of employment for the sake of production. In this case there is reason to note it as a target on a par with those noted above.

The employment target is often formulated as a demand for *full* employment. This is not yet a completely unambiguous formulation because different definitions have been put forward as to what is to be understood by full employment. How, for instance, should one regard purely "frictional unemployment" which is caused by the fact that it takes time for the labour force to move between sectors, and how should one regard seasonal unemployment? Also, there is reason to take note of the circumstance that it is quite possible to have full employment on different levels of employment. Depending on wage- and tax-conditions, etc., a greater or lesser number of people may choose to offer their services. Furthermore, there may be full employment with either long or short working hours, and consequently full employment with different levels of production.

2.2.6. *Satisfactory external trade balance*

This target will not be precisely formulated here. In certain situations a country may want to import capital, while during other periods it may wish to manage without, etc. The point here is only that the government must give attention to external trade and set up certain objectives in this field.

Actually, a target concerning the balance of external trade is a reflex of the other targets already mentioned. When a country wishes to avoid an unfavourable payments situation, this may, for instance, be because such a situation might lead to difficulties with respect to the import of raw materials necessary for the country's production; or it may be because such a situation might limit freedom of manoeuvre in economic policy. This will then reflect back on the targets already mentioned. To this extent it should be unnecessary to set up this as an independent objective. But one might also wish for a particular development in external trade on the more political grounds that one does not want to develop a relationship of dependence vis-à-vis foreign countries. In such a case, this is a factor on a par with those mentioned above.

2.2.7　*A stable price level*

This, too, is not a fundamental objective such as the targets of high consumption, the satisfaction of collective wants, etc. If the targets previously mentioned could be achieved at any time, regardless of how the price level developed, then there would be small reason to concern oneself about the latter. When a stable price level is, nevertheless, set up as a target, this may be because it is considered that a rising price level, *due to effects which are not allowed for by the model in use,* may complicate the achievement of the above-mentioned targets. The following factors are probably the most important: (a) A rising price level may undermine the possibilities for rational calculation. (b) A shifting price level will lead to a trans- ference of wealth between persons and groups who have net monetary claims, and persons or groups having net debts. This may be con- sidered unjust. (c) A rising price level can lead to export difficulties.

If we have a model which allows for the effects mentioned under (a)–(c) it is unnecessary to introduce a stable price level as a target in the model. Conversely, if we have a model not allowing for these effects, we can "correct" this imperfection in the model by introducing a stable price level as a separate target. A similar argument applies under 2.2.6.

The target of a stable price level can be understood in several ways. It can apply to the price level for the entire national product, or it can apply to the price level for consumer goods; it can apply to the price level in- clusive of sales tax and net excises or the so-called factor price level, i.e., prices exclusive of sales tax and excises. It can be of some importance in these matters which particular price level is referred to in wage negotia- tions, for instance, or is involved in wage agreements.

2.2.8.   *Efficient use of national resources*

In various situations state interference or direct governmental manage- ment may effect a more efficient use of a country's resources than would result from leaving things "to themselves". Such situations may occur, for instance, when the real social costs of a production are not fully expressed in the private cost-accounting, or when a certain production or activity affords a utility which cannot in its entirety be sold to buyers in the ordi- nary way. This is what in the theory of welfare economics is called "indirect effects", or is characterized as deviations between private and social marginal costs or marginal utilities. (If the divergence between private and social utilities makes itself strongly felt, we may approach the field of what were earlier called collective goods.) As another example, there may be cases where a certain production activity, under unregulated market conditions, leads to monopoly and thus to less efficient use of resources. This can, *inter alia,* apply in cases with strongly declining average cost curves. In such cases optimal output will be impossible under private production without state subsidies, or interference of some other kind, because a price in accordance with the marginal costs would create a deficit.

The target of efficient use of a country's resources is also derived from the more primary objectives mentioned earlier. But if we are working within the framework of a model which is not sufficiently detailed to consider various kinds of factors bearing on efficiency, there are grounds for setting this up as an independent target in the same way as in the previous instance.

In sections 2.2.1. to 2.2.8. the various targets have been quite loosely described. It is unnecessary at this point to enter into more precise definitions, neither shall we adopt any particular attitude to these different targets. The purpose of the list is only to point out the most important factors usually included in the setting up of economic targets in a country like Norway. We shall return later to more careful discussions of most of the issues raised in the above survey of targets.

It is not certain that all the targets mentioned can be simultaneously achieved if they are set up as absolute demands. In principle, the most satisfactory thing would be, as mentioned before, to establish a preference function depending upon magnitudes which express the factors in this list. Failing that, one must set up targets concerning these magnitudes, taking into account what one thinks can actually be obtained. Through a process of trial-and-error, experimenting with different targets, one might then perhaps approach a solution in the vicinity of what one would have obtained by setting up a preference function and maximizing it.

One main concern of the following chapters will be to discuss the extent to which the targets mentioned here might be combined, and to what extent they might conflict with each other under various conditions. These questions cannot, of course, be answered without stating, for every situation, precisely which instruments are available. Targets conflicting with each other when *one* set of instruments is available, might be consistent if one has *another* set of instruments at one's disposal.

2.3. Instruments in public economics

The instruments at the government's disposal can be said to come under

the following main headings:
1) instruments of fiscal policy,
2) instruments of monetary policy,
3) direct interference through orders and prohibitions,
4) the government's own business activity.

The difference between monetary policy and fiscal policy is not clear and unambiguous. The distinction can, for instance, be drawn according to the following criteria:

(a) According to the institutions making the decisions. One might, for instance, say that the political decisions made by the central bank belong to monetary policy, while those made by particular state institutions belong to fiscal policy (*other* state institutions than the central bank if, as in Norway, this is owned by the state). Such a distinction may, however, be somewhat arbitrary. When these state institutions and the central bank are closely co-ordinated, it will often be quite practical matters which decide who is to make the various kinds of decision.

(b) One might imagine drawing the distinction according to the objectives being pursued. One might, for instance, say that that which aims at influencing the value of money, currency conditions, etc., is monetary policy, while fiscal policy is that which seeks to meet the collective wants and influence employment. It is, however, apparent from the previous general discussion of targets and instruments that it is hardly possible to draw any rational distinction along these lines.

(c) One can draw the distinctions according to which markets the various measures have a *direct* bearing on. Consequently, one might say that monetary policy is that which primarily influences the markets for financial claims, while fiscal policy comprises all other state receipts and payments. This is more or less equivalent to another definition sometimes applied: fiscal policy determines the development of the government's net debt (inclusive of central bank money in private hands), while monetary policy determines its composition.

We shall here largely keep to the criterion given under (c). Fiscal policy will then be a principal part of public economics. In addition, we shall deal with parts of what comes under point 4 in the list above. Similarly, we shall concern ourselves with that which lies on the borderline between fiscal policy and monetary policy. This applies, *inter alia,* to some problems concerning the public debt. Instruments coming under the head of direct interference, will only be dealt with in so far as they relate to fiscal policy.

Considering the division of the instruments of the state given above, one might ask where is the place of industrial policy, social policy, and so on. The reply might often be that matters concerning various *total* sums are matters of fiscal policy, while the question of the use of these total sums in various fields can be a question of industrial policy, social policy, etc. For the rest, it is hardly fruitful to speculate further on the subdivisions of the political sphere.

Should one wish to subdivide the instruments of fiscal policy into categories, it may be done by the following arrangement:

Fiscal policy
- Payments to the government.
  - Taxes. / Excises. / Duties. } Taxes in a broad sense.
  - Sale of goods and services.
- Payments from the government.
  - Purchase of goods and services.
  - Payment of subsidies and social benefits (transfers).

How are we to envisage the number of instruments in such a context? Can we, for instance, say that *one* tax constitutes *one* instrument? Not necessarily. If we have an income tax where the tax makes up a certain percentage of the taxpayer's income beyond a certain tax-free minimum, we can say that we are dealing with two instruments, viz., the size of the exemption and the tax rate. These can then be used to meet two groups of considerations, viz., considerations concerning the over-all demand level, and considerations concerning the distribution of disposable income.

From this point of view, one might imagine acquiring just as many instruments as one could wish for, by framing complicated forms of taxation including many kinds of allowances, tax percentages, brackets of progression, etc. This is schematically correct, but there remains the question whether the instruments provided in this way are efficient with respect to the targets.

In principle, we ought to count as an instrument only that over which the government has direct control. Accordingly, the *amount* brought in by a particular tax, for instance, should not be regarded as a public instrument, as this will, of course, depend on the dispositions of the private sector. What the government directly controls, are tax rates, allowances, etc., and it is these which are really the government's instruments. For the sake of convenience, we shall, however, often treat the incoming tax yields themselves as instruments. If the government possessed complete information as to the reactions of the private sector to various kinds of interference, it would always be able to work out a definite correspondence between tax rates and tax yields,* and the simplification we make in considering the tax yield as the instrument would then not be of a serious kind. In certain situations this issue can, however, be of great importance. This applies especially in dealing with situations which involve great uncertainty of some kind or other.

It may seem somewhat difficult to fit the municipalities into the formula of targets and instruments which has been discussed. One way to regard this, might be to say that the state here chooses to undertake a decentralization based on the kind of considerations we made in section 2.1.4, as the municipalities have the responsibility for achieving targets of a local character, and have been given instruments which, when used within the limits drawn up by the state, through its legislation on local government and taxation, do not complicate the government's policy in other respects. Other ways of regarding this, however, also present themselves. We shall return to some problems concerning municipal economy in the final chapter.

---

* This correspondance would involve also the other instruments.

Macroeconomic analysis of problems in fiscal policy

In this chapter we shall analyse the connections between the main categories of public revenue and expenditure on the one side, and economic macro-concepts like national product, private consumption, etc. on the other. This will be done within the framework of simple macro-models of the Keynesian type. By and large the public sector will be considered as one unit. Only in some cases shall we touch upon the problems arising from the fact that we have the state on one hand and the municipalities on the other, with different scope for their economic policies*. We shall assume that all income is being earned by the private sector of the economy, with the government getting all its revenues from taxes. This view is most realistic if we exclude the state enterprises from what we shall now understand by the public sector.

A part of the income which is "being earned by the private sector" consists of wages and salaries earned from the public sector.

We shall proceed step by step, first considering quite simple models for cases with constant prices and with exogenous investment. Later, we shall look at cases where these greatly simplified assumptions are modified.

3.1. Models with constant prices and exogenous investment

3.1.1. Relationships in national accounting

We shall first look at some aspects of the interaction between the public sector and the private sector of the economy purely from the point of view of national accounting. For the sake of convenience we shall dis-

---

* An analysis of some problems of this kind is given at the end of Chapter 8.

regard gifts between the home country and foreign countries, and the balance on interest and other transfers. The main macroeconomic magnitudes which we shall consider are then the following:

R = the net national product, A = total exports,
C = total consumption, B = total imports,
I = total net real investment, S = total saving.

The magnitudes C, I and S can be split up into one component for the private sector and one component for the public sector. We indicate the private sector by adding the index p to the symbols, and the public sector by adding the index o to the symbols. Thus we have:

C_p = private consumption, C_o = public consumption,
I_p = private net real investment, I_o = public net real investment,
S_p = private saving, S_o = public saving.

Between these magnitudes we have the connections

$$C_p + C_o = C,$$
$$I_p + I_o = I, \tag{3.1}$$
$$S_p + S_o = S.$$

We further introduce the following magnitudes: T = net tax yields paid by the private sector to the public sector (i.e., transfers from the public to the private sector are deducted); G = the public sector's purchase of goods and services from the private sector.

The latter magnitude is equal to*

$$G = C_o + I_o. \tag{3.2}$$

By the help of the magnitudes introduced above we can define the disposable income of the private sector:

---

* One might ask whether we should not here have the gross instead of the net investment as a component in the total public purchase of goods and services. However, the depreciation of public consumption capital is included in the magnitude C_o. This is a component which is not bought from the private sector. By adding together public consumption inclusive of this depreciation and public *net* investment we therefore get the total public purchase of goods and services. (We have excluded public enterprises from what we now call the public sector. Consequently, there exists no other real capital in the public sector than that which is called public consumption capital.)

$$R_p^* = R - T = \text{private disposable income.} \qquad (3.3)$$

With the simplifying assumptions introduced above the government's disposable revenue is simply equal to the tax yield:

$$R_o^* = T = \text{public disposable income.} \qquad (3.4)$$

If we add the private disposable income and the public disposable income, we get the country's total disposable income, which with the simplifications we have made is equal to the national product.

We shall then consider savings in respectively the private and the public sector. Saving is generally defined as disposable income minus consumption expenses. We thus get the following for the savings of the two sectors:

$$S_p = R_p^* - C_p = R - T - C_p, \\ S_o = R_o^* - C_o = T - C_o. \qquad (3.5)$$

If we add the private and the public saving we get the country's total saving. This will, of course, be equal to the national product minus total consumption:

$$S = S_o + S_p = R - C_p - C_o = R - C. \qquad (3.6)$$

We shall then consider the connections between saving and investment in terms of national accounting. We start with the basic equation

$$R = C + I + A - B, \qquad (3.7)$$

which together with (3.6) gives

$$S = I + A - B. \qquad (3.8)$$

If we here split up the saving and the real investment between the private and the public sector we have

$$S_p + S_o = I_p + I_o + A - B \qquad (3.9)$$

which says that private saving plus public saving equals private net real investment plus public net real investment plus the export surplus. If the latter equals zero it means that total saving must equal total real investment. A corresponding equality does not, however, necessarily hold for the private sector and the public sector *considered separately*. It is possible to have larger investment than saving in one of these sectors, this being balanced by larger saving than investment in the other sector. In such a case financial claims will arise between the two sectors. This can be further clarified by deducing a new expression for private saving from (3.5). If we insert from (3.7) for R in the expression for private saving, splitting the magnitudes C and I into private and public components and also using (3.2) we obtain:

$$S_p = C_p + C_o + I_p + I_o + A - B - T - C_p = I_p + (G - T) + (A - B). \qquad (3.10)$$

It will be seen from this that private saving can be interpreted as consisting of three components: firstly I_p which represents the increase in the private sector's real capital; secondly $(G-T)$ which represents public expenses in excess of public income, and which involves an increase in the private sector's claims against the public sector (interpreting here central bank money as claims against the public sector); thirdly the component $(A-B)$ which stands for the export surplus, and which involves increased claims against foreign countries.

The content of (3.10) could also be regarded from a different angle. The equation is then re-written in the following way:

$$I_p - S_p + (T - G) + (B - A). \qquad (3.11)$$

In this form the equation says that the private real investment can be larger than the private saving if there is a public budget surplus on current account and/or an import surplus.

For the public investment one has correspondingly

$$I_o = S_o + (G - T).\qquad(3.12)$$

The public net real investment can thus be covered either by public saving or by a deficit in the transactions with the private sector which manifests itself in increased private net claims against the public sector.

In recent years in Norway there has been greater saving than net real investment in the public sector. This means that public saving has helped to finance some of the real investment which has taken place in the private sector. This has happened mainly through loans from the state to the state banks, which again grant loans to the private sector. The figures for 1962 are given in the table below.

Table 2

Saving and investment in Norway, 1962, in
millions of Norwegian *kroner*

Private net real investment	4384
Public net real investment	2239
Total net real investment	6623
Private saving	2210
Public saving	2888
Deficit on the external balance	1525
In all	6623

This table corresponds to equation (3.9), re-written in the form $I_p + I_o = S_p + S_o + (B - A)$.

The receipts and payments of the public sector expressed in the magnitudes T and G will influence liquidity in the private sector of the economy. We shall return later to the national accounting relationships which are relevant in this connection, see section 3.3.2.

3.1.2.   A model for a closed economy

The model we shall first consider is the simplest multiplier model for a closed economy. The important point here is that we explicitly introduce taxes and public expenditure on goods and services into the model.

We shall first examine a closed economy. Two interpretations are possible here. Firstly, the model for a closed economy can be seen as a model for a country with negligible external trade. Secondly, such a model can be seen as a model for what will happen in a country which has an external trade regulated in such a way that exports and imports balance each other at any time.

In this section we shall first and foremost aim at arriving at relations of the type we have in a general form in the formulae (2.9) and (2.10) in Chapter 2. We shall first regard the tax yield T as the instrument. Moreover, we suppose, for the time being, that all tax is gathered as direct tax and that it does not influence the market prices. (It will later be seen how the formulae we develop under this assumption can also be used as an approximation when dealing with indirect taxation.)

Using the symbols introduced in the previous section, we get the following simple model:

$$R = C_p + I_p + G$$
$$C_p = a(R - T) + b \qquad\qquad (3.13)$$
$$I_p = \text{exogenously determined.}$$

The magnitudes T and G are instruments for the government.

The second equation in the model (3.13) is a consumption function which, for the sake of convenience, is written in linear form with a and b as constants. We have assumed that it is the private disposable income $R - T$ which determines the private consumption*.

---

* In theoretical economics, the consumption function is often justified on the grounds of considerations as to the behaviour of the individual personal income recipient. However, business savings actually play so great a role in a country like Norway that this way of justifying the form of the consumption function can be somewhat unsatisfactory. Let us therefore consider how the consumption function can be substantiated when account is taken of business savings. Firstly, we divide the income into the components L, which consists of wage earnings and incomes of persons in independent occupations, and P, representing business profits. We then have

$$R = L + P.$$

(Footnote cont.)

Interest now mainly centres on the effects on the national product of changes in T and G. If we solve (3.13) with respect to R we get

$$R = \frac{1}{1-a}G - \frac{a}{1-a}T + \frac{I_p + b}{1-a}. \tag{3.14}$$

We have here an expression of how the national product depends on public expenditure and on the tax yield. (3.14) is an example of an equation of the type (2.9) in Chapter 2, as R is to be understood as a

---

(Cont.)

We assume that we have a constant structure of income, so that we can write

$$L = gR + h,$$

where g can be called the marginal wage share. We further assume that the distributed profits from business enterprises can be written as a linear function of the business profits:

$$U = uP + v.$$

If a constant fraction of the business profits is distributed to the owners, u will be positive, while v will equal zero. (By investigations in various countries, values of u have been found between 0.3 and 0.5.) On the other hand u will equal zero, while v will have a positive value, if the companies stabilize distribution of profits independently of the level of income. (Such a tendency is also observed in many countries.)

We now assume that private consumption can be written as

$$C_p = a_L L + a_U U + b,$$

where a_L and a_U are marginal propensities to consume for the two categories of income. By insertion, we then obtain

$$C_p = a_L\{gR + h\} + a_U\{u(R - gR - h) + v\} + b,$$
$$C_p = \{a_L g + a_U u(1 - g)\}R + \{a_L h + a_U(v - uh) + b\}.$$

If the coefficients which enter into the functions we have introduced are constant, C_p is here expressed as a function of the national product with a marginal propensity to consume equal to $a = \{a_L g + a_U u(1 - g)\}$. As can be seen, this is a somewhat complex quantity. It can be important to bear this in mind when judging its stability, but it does not prevent us from operating with it in the model as an "ordinary" marginal propensity to consume.

If we now wished to introduce taxes into this picture, we ought to distinguish between taxes on business profits and on the incomes of individuals. We would then only under special conditions come out with such a simple result as in the consumption function in (3.13). See further section 3.3, where a simple model is used in which distinctions are made between the taxes on persons and on firms.

target variable, i.e., as an x in formula (2.9) in Chapter 2, and G and T are to be understood as t's in the formula.

Already from (3.14) conclusions of a certain interest can be drawn. As a is the marginal propensity to consume which is positive and less than one in value, we see that an increase in public expenditure leads to an increase in the national product, while a greater tax yield leads to a decline in the national product. Or, expressed in a different way: public expenditures on goods and services have an expansive effect, while taxes have a contractive effect. We also see that the effect of a certain increase in the public expenditure G is greater than the effect of an equivalent sum in tax reduction. Let us for an example suppose that the marginal propensity to consume a equals 0.75. Then, an increase in the public expenditure of 100 million *kroner* will lead to an increase in the national product of 400 million *kroner*. A reduction of the total tax yield of 100 million *kroner* will, however, lead to an increase in the national product of only 300 million *kroner*. The reason for this can be said to be as follows: the increase in public expenditure is at once used, in its entirety, to buy goods and services. A tax reduction of 100 million *kroner* does not give direct results in the same way. If the consumers have an extra 100 million at their disposal only ¾ of this will, in the first instance, be used in purchasing goods and services.

From the difference observed in the multiplier effect of public expenditure and of tax reductions, follows a further conclusion of considerable interest. Let us assume that we make a change ΔG in the public expenditure and a change ΔT in the total tax yield, while the private investments remain unchanged. Let us further assume that ΔG equals ΔT, which means that increased public expenditure balances exactly with increased taxes. We then get the following change in the national product:

$$\Delta R = \Delta G \quad \text{when} \quad \Delta G = \Delta T . \tag{3.15}$$

This shows that the change in the national product will be exactly equal to the change in public expenditure. This conclusion may be called the theorem on the multiplier effect of a balanced change in the budget*.

---

* See Trygve Haavelmo, Multiplier effects of a balanced budget, *Econometrica* (1945). Reprinted in: *Readings in fiscal policy,* published for the American Economic Association (1955).

This conclusion is important because it seems so natural to think that an increase in public expenditure will have a neutral macroeconomic effect when taxes are increased correspondingly.

Differently expressed, the conclusion can be formulated as follows: the question of whether the budget shows a surplus or a deficit is not a sufficient criterion determining whether it will have an expansive or a contractive effect. The *size* of the budget is in itself of importance; as a large, balanced budget has a more expansive effect than a smaller budget which is also balanced.

In the model we have now considered, the government has two instruments, G and T. If one only considered the one target of obtaining a certain value of the national product R, this could be done in different ways. It is clear, however, that most of what is comprised in the quantity G directly serves the goal which in Chapter 2 was called satisfaction of collective wants. If we, then, consider both the targets of a certain size of national product and of a certain volume of collective consumption, the situation will be that the quantity G is directly determined by the latter target, and the quantity T is used to regulate the total demand so that this will be of the size necessary to obtain the target for the national product.

Suppose that there exists a definite capacity limit for production in the country and suppose again that the target for the national product aims at using this capacity to the full. The total demand must then be so large that this capacity is used, but not larger as this would bring on inflation. (The formal model under consideration here does not, of course, say anything about what would happen in such a case, but this follows from the usual extensions of the model.) The line of argument above shows that, within such a framework, the task of taxation is the following: the public expenditure, G, in itself has an expansive effect; taxation has to counteract this expansive effect just sufficiently to ensure that the total demand does not exceed what is permitted by the production capacity.

There is no obvious reason why these demands should result in T being approximately equal to G. In the years between the world wars, especially in the U.S.A., there were many who thought that full employment or full utilization of capacity would demand a considerable permanent deficit in the public sector. In post-war years, conditions in several countries have seemed different. It has in fact in some countries seemed as if the avoidance of inflation has demanded a permanent surplus in the public sector. Which of the two cases will arise depends, of course, on the development of the labour force, on private investments, on technical progress and its effect on the production capacity, and on the propensity to consume.

The result reached here, that G ought to be adjusted so that the desired level of the public or collective consumption is obtained, while T ought to be used to regulate the total demand in order to get a high level of capacity utilization, though not inflation, will be too schematic in a world exposed to "disturbances" and "frictions" of various kinds. In this case there are many things which support the idea that certain types of public expenditure ought also to be used to regulate the level of demand. This will be further discussed later.

So far, we have considered the total tax yield T as the government's instrument. As mentioned earlier, this is not really quite satisfactory. What the government can determine directly, are tax rates and the like, while the volume of tax revenue depends on the reactions of the private sector. We shall now take this into consideration in a simple way by assuming that the tax yield is a linear function of the national income. Thus we let the assumption that T is decided by the government, be replaced by the equation

$$T = tR + k \qquad (3.16)$$

where t and k are constants within the region of variation under consideration. The quantity t can be called the marginal tax rate in macro. The relationship (3.16) will depend on corresponding relationships for the single individual in a similar way to that in which a macro-consumption function depends on individual demand functions.

Let us now combine equation (3.16) with equations (3.13). If we insert from (3.16) and the second equation in (3.13) into the first equation in (3.13) we get:

$$R = a(R - tR - k) + b + I_p + G \qquad (3.17)$$

which gives

$$R = \frac{1}{1 - (1 - t)a}(G + I_p + b - ak). \qquad (3.18)$$

The government's instruments are now considered to be G, t, and $k*$. Let us first discuss the effects of changes in G, tax rates and tax rules being kept unchanged, so that t and k in (3.16) are constant. We then see at once that the multiplier effect of an increase in public expenditure will now be smaller than it was in terms of the considerations which formed the basis of (3.14). If we set as a plausible numerical example $t = 0.20$ (and, as before, $a = 0.75$) we get, for instance, the multiplier

$$\frac{1}{1 - (1 - t)a} = \frac{1}{1 - 0.80 \times 0.75} = 2.5 .$$

The multiplier for public expenditure will now be only 2.5, while in the equivalent case it was 4 when the tax yield was kept constant. The reason for this difference is, of course, that increased income resulting from increased public expenditure through (3.16) leads to increased taxes which, to a certain degree, neutralize the expansive effect of the increased public expenditure.

One could ask how great a change in the tax yield will result under these assumptions. Is it, for instance, conceivable that the increased tax revenues would be so great that they completely "financed" the increased expenditure? From (3.16) and (3.18) we get

$$T = \frac{t}{1 - (1 - t)a} G + \text{etc.} \tag{3.19}$$

where "+ etc." stands for various additive items in which we are not interested here. With the same numerical example as above, i.e., with $t = 0.20$ and $a = 0.75$, this gives

$$T = 0.50\, G + \text{etc.}$$

---

* Even t and k are, of course, not in practice determined by the government, but they are more closely and directly connected with government decisions than the tax yield T. For instance, a "disturbance" through a shift in private investment will influence T, but not t and k.

This means that an increase in public expenditure of a certain amount leads to an increase in the government's tax revenues of exactly half that amount. Thus the increased expenditure does not completely finance itself, but it half does so. (The problem is here being discussed within a static model. We do not consider the time lapse before the increase in expenditure leads to increased tax revenues.)

It is easily realized that "complete self-financing" is impossible. The fraction preceding G in (3.19) will only equal 1 if $t = 1$, i.e., if the marginal tax rate in macro equals 100, which is hardly conceivable.

As to the effect of changes in taxation, we must here distinguish between two different cases. Firstly, we can have the kind of changes which work through the constant k in (3.16). If, for instance, we increase certain social benefit payments which are independent of the receiver's income, this will be the same as a reduction in k, since we consider such transfers to private persons as negative taxes. The effect of such a change appears in (3.18). We see that we get a multiplier effect in a similar way as from tax reductions in (3.14), but the multiplier is now smaller because part of the derived increase in income is automatically reabsorbed through t. Secondly, we can have changes in taxation via t. This will, for instance, be the case when the ordinary rates for the taxation of income are changed. The effect of a change in t can be studied by differentiating the solutions for R and T with respect to t. We shall not pursue this further here, but only note the following: a reduction in t will reduce the tax yield by less than one would expect if one only considered (3.16) and assumed that R remained constant. A reduction in t will result in an expansive effect leading to an increase in R, and thereby to an increase in the tax revenues, which to a certain extent will balance the decrease caused by the smaller tax rate. Correspondingly with an increase in the tax rate: the increase in the tax yield will be less than what one would get through a simple consideration based on (3.16), because the tax-base, R, will be smaller. Within the model now considered, however, the secondary effects arising via changes in the tax-base will not be able to balance completely the primary effect which is the result of the change in the tax rate. The total tax yield will, accordingly, always go up when the tax rate is raised, and down when the tax rate is lowered. It might be different within a model where we had reactions via private investment. If these reactions were strong, it might be conceivable that a reduction of the tax rate t

resulted in such a great increase in the tax-base R that tax yield would go up: and vice versa with an increase in the tax rate*.

As has been mentioned, a relationship between tax yield and national income such as the one which in (3.16) has been expressed by a linear approximation, will depend on corresponding functions for the single individuals or income receivers. These micro-relationships will be relatively stable. With changes in total income the distribution of income will, however, usually be altered, and the relationship will therefore not be so stable in macro. Moreover, the concept of income which forms the base of taxation will not accord with the concept of income used in the national accounts. This also tends to prevent the relationship in macro being very stable. This will apply even more if we bring into the picture other types of taxation, where the base of taxation is something other than income. There is thus an econometric problem involved in the study of such relationships as (3.16). Such studies have been carried out in some countries. In the USA it was found that, with the tax-rules and -rates of the mid-fifties, the elasticity of the federal tax yield with respect to the national income was about 1.5. Such an elasticity greater than 1 is to be expected with progressive taxation of income. (That the elasticity is greater than 1 means that k is negative in the linear approximation.) When state and local taxes are considered, the elasticity will be less**.

3.1.3. *A multiplier model with a general sales tax*

In the model which has so far been considered we made the simplification of assuming that all tax was gathered as a direct tax on income. We shall

---

* A dynamic analysis would perhaps show that in such a case the system would be unstable.

** See R. A. Musgrave: *The theory of public finance* (New York, London, 1959), p. 511. See also, for instance, L. Cohen: Measurement of the built-in flexibility of the individual income tax, *The American Economic Review,* Papers and Proceedings (1959). In Cohen's study the problem, which there concerns income taxes, is split into two: first he discusses how the tax-base for income taxes varies with the national income (actually a somewhat different concept is used); next he studies how the tax yield varies with the total tax-base for the income taxes. The co-variation between total tax yield and national income will be found by combining these effects. More detailed relationships of the type (3.16) of course also enter into many econometric macro-models, as, for instance, the well-known Klein-Goldberger model.

now see how a similar model can be used as an approximation when we have a general sales tax besides the direct tax. We assume that the sales tax is imposed with a rate τ on all sale from the retail level, including goods and services which are bought by government itself. This latter is a pure formality; one could without difficulty, and without changing the line of argument, also have allowed for no sales tax being levied on the goods and services the state itself buys. We further assume that the sales tax manifests itself completely in the market price level. We must now distinguish between the values of consumption, investment, and so on, calculated in the final market prices inclusive of sales tax, and the values of the same magnitudes calculated in the prices which would be current if there were no sales tax. Accordingly, we shall let the values first mentioned, i.e., the values inclusive of sales tax, be indicated by R, C_p etc., while we indicate the corresponding magnitudes calculated at prices without sales tax $\bar{R}$, $\bar{C}_p$ etc. We then have the relationships

$$R = (1 + \tau)\bar{R}, \qquad C_p = (1 + \tau)\bar{C}_p \text{ etc.}, \tag{3.20}$$

assuming that the sales tax rate τ applies on the values exclusive of the sales tax *.

The total amount brought in by the sales tax is noted T^{ind} ("ind" standing for "indirect tax"). This amount will be

$$T^{\text{ind}} = \tau\bar{C}_p + \tau\bar{I}_p + \tau\bar{G} = \tau\bar{R}. \tag{3.21}$$

We then have

$$R = \bar{R} + T^{\text{ind}}, \tag{3.22}$$

i.e., the national product calculated at market prices inclusive of sales tax equals the national product calculated at the prices which would apply if there were no sales tax, plus the amount brought in by the sales tax.

---

* In practice, the rates for sales taxes and different kinds of excises are often given as a percentage of the price or value *inclusive of* the tax or excise. This applies, for instance, for the Norwegian sales tax. This is, however, a purely practical matter which has no importance for the argument above.

The quantity $\bar{R}$ is often called the national product calculated at factor prices. It is the income left over for remuneration of the production factors and profit in the private sector after the sales tax has been paid in to the state.

Let us then consider how the consumption function, which is the central relation in a multiplier model of the type we had in the previous section, can be formulated in the case where we have both direct and indirect tax of the type which has just been described. We shall let the amount coming in through direct taxation be T^{dir}. The disposable income of the private sector is then, nominally calculated, $\bar{R} - T^{\text{dir}}$. The price level facing the consumers in the market, however, is now raised. If we let the price level exclusive of sales tax be represented as 1, the price level inclusive of the tax will be $1 + \tau$. The disposable *real* income for the private sector of the economy will then be $(\bar{R} - T^{\text{dir}})/(1 + \tau)$. It is now reasonable to suppose that $\bar{C}_{\text{p}}$, which can be considered a measure of the volume of private consumption, is a function of this disposable real income:

$$\bar{C}_{\text{p}} = f\left(\frac{\bar{R} - T^{\text{dir}}}{1 + \tau}\right). \tag{3.23}$$

This consumption function could, if desired, be formulated as a linear function, as was done in the model (3.13).

Together with the relation

$$\bar{R} = \bar{C}_{\text{p}} + \bar{I}_{\text{p}} + \bar{G}, \tag{3.24}$$

an assumption that $\bar{I}_{\text{p}}$ is exogenously determined, and the fact that the quantities τ, T^{dir} and $\bar{G}$ are determined by the government, we now have a model for the case where one has both direct and indirect taxation. It does not, however, appear to be such a simple multiplier model as (3.13). We cannot, for instance, as a matter of course here make a calculation to find something which might be called the multiplier effect of the total tax yield. Let us, however, see whether it is possible to arrive at such a concept by an approximation.

We then use the following approximation, which is permissible if τ is quite small:

$$\frac{1}{1+\tau} \approx 1 - \tau. \tag{3.25}$$

The disposable private real income can then be written as

$$\frac{\bar{R} - T^{\mathrm{dir}}}{1+\tau} \approx (\bar{R} - T^{\mathrm{dir}})(1 - \tau).$$

Using (3.21) we further have

$$\bar{R} - T^{\mathrm{dir}} - T^{\mathrm{ind}} + \tau T^{\mathrm{dir}} = \bar{R} - T + \tau T^{\mathrm{dir}}.$$

We have here introduced T as total tax yield, thus

$$T = T^{\mathrm{dir}} + T^{\mathrm{ind}}. \tag{3.26}$$

If we now write the consumption function as a linear function in a similar way as in (3.13) we have the following model:

$$\begin{aligned}
\bar{R} &= \bar{C}_{\mathrm{p}} + \bar{I}_{\mathrm{p}} + \bar{G} \\
\bar{C}_{\mathrm{p}} &= a(\bar{R} - T + \tau T^{\mathrm{dir}}) + b \text{ (approximation)} \\
\bar{I}_{\mathrm{p}} &= \text{exogenously determined.}
\end{aligned} \tag{3.27}$$

This model now shows great formal similarity to the one used in the case where one had only direct taxes, the model (3.13). Two things must, however, be noted. Firstly, we have now calculated the quantities deflated, so that we get them expressed in the prices which would be current exclusive of sales tax. Moreover, there appears in the middle formula in (3.27) a term which combines the effects of direct and indirect taxes, viz., the term τT^{dir}. This term has a positive effect on private consumption demand and can be interpreted from two angles. Assume that we have a certain direct tax amounting to the total yield T^{dir}. Then an indirect taxation is imposed at a rate τ. This sales tax will reduce disposable private real income by the tax yield. This is taken into account through the quantity T in the consumption function. But there is an additional effect, in that the raising of the price level in itself reduces the real value of the nominal tax revenue from the direct tax. This is expressed in the term τT^{dir}. From another angle the matter can be seen as follows. Assume that we have a certain sales tax expressed by the rate τ and that we change the nominal amount of the direct taxation. This will effect a smaller reduction of private consumption demand than it would have done if there had been no sales tax, because the real value of the amount of the tax change will be smaller. Therefore, the term τT^{dir} appears in the model (3.27), in addition to such items as were included in the relationships of the model (3.13).

We could transform the model (3.27) into a form which was even more like the one in (3.13) if we introduced the quantity

$$\bar{T}^{\mathrm{dir}} = \frac{T^{\mathrm{dir}}}{1 + \tau}, \qquad (3.28)$$

which is the real value of the direct tax yield T^{dir}, i.e., this tax yield deflated, so that it becomes comparable with quantities expressed in the prices which would be current without the sales tax. By the help of this quantity the disposable real income could be expressed as

$$\frac{\bar{R} - T^{\mathrm{dir}}}{1 + \tau} = \frac{\bar{R}}{1 + \tau} - \bar{T}^{\mathrm{dir}} \approx \bar{R} - T^{\mathrm{ind}} - \bar{T}^{\mathrm{dir}}.$$

The total tax yield could then be defined as the sum of T^{ind} and $\bar{T}^{\mathrm{dir}}$, thereby avoiding a term of the type τT^{dir}. The model would in that case appear exactly like (3.13), except that we operate with deflated quantities. With direct tax it is, however, more natural to operate with the nominal tax yield than with the deflated one.

In a model of the type now considered, the state has three instruments, viz. purchase of goods and services, direct tax, and indirect tax. One might accordingly imagine three targets here. Firstly, a certain level of collective consumption; secondly, a certain level of total production;

thirdly, a certain market price level. The subject of price level will, however, be returned to in a later chapter. The purpose of this section has only been to show how a model of the type used earlier, when only direct taxation was considered, can, with certain adaptations, also be used for the case when we have both direct and indirect taxation.

It has been assumed here that the sales tax is levied on all kinds of goods and services in the last stage of distribution. Actually, such an extensive sales tax hardly exists in any country. As a rule certain types of services, and usually also some goods, are exempted from this taxation. For a more precise analysis of such a case, one would have to make a certain disaggregation of the quantities, and not operate only with such pure macro-quantities as in this chapter.

3.1.4. *A model for an open economy*

Equivalent questions to those dealt with for a closed economy will now be dealt with for an open economy.

We employ the following model:

$$
\begin{aligned}
R &= C_{\mathrm{p}} + I_{\mathrm{p}} + G + A - B \\
C_{\mathrm{p}} &= a(R - T) + b \\
B &= \beta_C C_{\mathrm{p}} + \beta_I I_{\mathrm{p}} + \beta_A A + \beta_G G + \beta \qquad (3.29)\\
I_{\mathrm{p}} &= \text{exogenously determined} \\
A &= \text{exogenously determined.}
\end{aligned}
$$

The first formula here expresses the fundamental relationship in national accounting which we have in (3.7), but with consumption and investment split into a public and a private part as in (3.1), and with the introduction of the quantity G defined by (3.2). The second equation is a consumption function of the same kind as in the model (3.13). We now assume, as in (3.13), that all taxation is direct. With this open model, we can, in a similar way as with the formulae (3.20)–(3.28), also introduce indirect taxation without any great complications. It is now important to note that the quantity C_{p} in the consumption function comprises all private consumption, whether what is consumed is produced at home or imported.

The third equation in (3.29) expresses the imports as a function of the total private consumption, the total private investment, total public expenditure on goods and services, and the exports, assuming that the β's are constant. The coefficient β_C depends on demand functions for consumer goods not produced at home. It also depends on market conditions and the degree of utilization of home capacity for the production of such goods as are both imported and home-produced. It further depends on the need for imported raw materials for the production of consumer goods at home. The coefficient β_I will be more technically determined. Here, too, there will be some goods which are both imported and produced at home, and the size of β_I may therefore depend on capacity utilization in home production. The coefficient β_A will be determined by such things as the need for raw materials in export production. The quantity β_G may have a somewhat different character from the other β's as it will depend on the nature of the public expenditures on goods and services, and to a certain degree this composite can be decided by the government in view of the politico-economic targets it has set up. It is perhaps not natural to call β_G an instrument of the government, but certainly it does have some control over it*.

The supposition that the private real investment is exogenously determined, corresponds to the assumption made in the earlier model.

The assumption that the export A is exogenously determined is a common assumption in models for "a small country". It is not quite obvious that this is a reasonable assumption. If, for instance, the exporters of a country consider prices as given in the world market, and adjust the exported quantities accordingly, which might very well be the case for some goods, the assumption is not correct. A realistic treatment of exports will probably demand a division of exports into various types of commodities with different market conditions. The essential factor

---

* Instead of expressing the import function as we have done it in (3.29) one might make the imports a function of R. This is just as usual in the macro-economic literature. It gives simpler formulae, and those wishing to make this simplification can work out the following calculations with such an import function. It is, however, probable that the function as we have it in (3.29) is more precise. On various ways of expressing the import function, see Tore Thonstad: *Produksjonsstruktur, import og sysselsetting* (Structure of production, imports and employment) (Samfunnsøkonomiske Studier 8, Central Bureau of Statistics, Oslo, 1959), especially pp. 25–31.

in this connection is that we assume exports to be determined by conditions – and we do not discuss which conditions – that are independent
of the fiscal policy.

If we solve the model (3.29), by insertions from the second and third
equations in the first equation, we get for the national product

$$R = \frac{1}{1 - (1 - \beta_C)a} \{(1 - \beta_G)G - a(1 - \beta_C)T + (1 - \beta_I)I_p$$
$$+ (1 - \beta_A)A + (1 - \beta_C)b - \beta\}.\tag{3.30}$$

Let us here study the effects of changes in public expenditure and tax
yield, comparing it with the results reached in the case of the closed
model.

For the effects of changes in public expenditure, we have

$$\frac{\partial R}{\partial G} = \frac{1 - \beta_G}{1 - (1 - \beta_C)a}.\tag{3.31}$$

In the closed model, the equivalent multiplier was $1/(1-a)$. The multiplier
in (3.31) is smaller for two reasons. Firstly, the numerator is reduced by
the fraction β_G which expresses the direct effect on imports of public
expenditure. A certain proportion of an increase in public expenditure
will be aimed at foreign countries, thereby causing a correspondingly
smaller increase in the demand for home-produced goods. Secondly, the
denominator is larger because of the quantity β_C. The effect causing this
reduction of the multiplier, is that a certain part of the private consumption demand induced by the increased public expenditure, will leak
out to foreign countries. Thereby a smaller demand will, in turn, be
directed at home production. Let us, for a numerical example, set $a=0.75$
as we did in the closed model, and $\beta_C=0.2$. This latter means that for
every *krone* of increased private consumption demand, a demand of
20 *øre* will be spent on imported goods. The multiplier will then be

$$\frac{\partial R}{\partial G} = 2.5(1 - \beta_G).$$

Thus, the multiplier will now at most be able to take a value of 2.5. This it will do if public expenditure does not directly have an import content, i.e., if $\beta_G=0$. If $\beta_G=0.1$ the multiplier will be 2.25*. If we compare with the value of 4, which the multiplier had in the corresponding example for the closed economy, we see that the fact of the economy being open results in a substantial reduction of the multiplier. This means that an increase in public expenditure in an open economy has a considerably smaller effect on activity or employment than is the case in a closed economy.

As already mentioned, the quantity β_C may depend on the degree of a country's utilization of capacity. It is therefore probably approximately constant only over limited ranges of variation. If we are in a situation with high utilization of capacity in many trades, the quantity β_C can easily be greater than 0.2. If we have $\beta_C=0.4$, we get, instead of the above.

$$\frac{\partial R}{\partial G} = 1.8\,(1 - \beta_G).$$

Thus, the multiplier could conceivably drop considerably below 2 in value in an economy with an extensive foreign trade, like that of Norway.

Let us now consider the effects of changes in the tax yield. We have

$$\frac{\partial R}{\partial T} = - \frac{a\,(1 - \beta_C)}{1 - a\,(1 - \beta_C)}. \tag{3.32}$$

As with a closed economy, an increased tax yield will lead to a reduced national product, but the effect will here be relatively smaller. If we assume $a=0.75$ and $\beta_C=0.2$ as in the first example above, we now obtain $\partial R/\partial T= -1.5$. If we instead set $\beta_C=0.4$, as in the second example above, we get $\partial R/\partial T= -0.8$. In the case of a closed economy the equivalent figure was -3.0. For an open economy like the Norwegian one, a tax

---

* If we here, instead of with a constant T, had calculated with a tax function like (3.16) the multiplier would have been still further reduced. For realistic values of t, it might have gone below 2 in value.

relief of, for instance, 100 million *kroner*, may thus give an increase in the national product which is not very much larger than this amount, and it is even conceivable that the effect will be so weak as to give an increase in the national product of less than the amount of the tax relief.

Let us now consider the effect of a balanced change in the budget, i.e., a change in the public expenditure which corresponds exactly to a change in the tax yield. Let these changes be ΔG and ΔT, so that $\Delta G = \Delta T$. In the closed model, such a budgetary change resulted in a change in the national product which was exactly equal to the change in the amount of public expenditure. On the basis of formula (3.30) we now obtain

$$\Delta R = \left[1 - \frac{\beta_G}{1 - (1 - \beta_C)a} \right] \Delta G \quad \text{when} \quad \Delta T = \Delta G. \qquad (3.33)$$

It is seen here that the theorem about the multiplier effect of a balanced budgetary change no longer holds in exactly the same form as in the model for the closed economy. But if the quantity β_G, which expresses the direct import effect of public expenditure, is small, the square bracket in (3.33) will be near to 1 and thus the result of a balanced budgetary change will be approximately as in the closed economy.

Let us next consider the effects of fiscal policy on imports. We then insert from the consumption function into the import equation in (3.29) and use the solution we already have for the national product in (3.30). For imports this gives,

$$B = \frac{1}{1 - (1 - \beta_C)a} \{ [a\beta_C + (1 - a)\beta_G] G - a\beta_C T + H \}, \qquad (3.34)$$

where the quantity H is a term depending on I_p, on A, and on the coefficients in the model, but not depending on the quantities G and T. Since we shall here only consider the effects of variations in G and T there is no need to specify the solution in more detail.

Since all the coefficients a, β_C and β_G are equal to or larger than 0, and less than 1, we see from (3.34) that an increase in public expenditures on goods and services leads to an increase in imports, while an increase in the tax yield leads to a decline in imports. If we take as a numerical example the one used earlier, with $\beta_C = 0.2$, $a = 0.75$ and $\beta_G = 0.1$, (3.34) is reduced to

$$B = 0.44G - 0.38T + 2.5H . \qquad (3.35)$$

Thus in this case an increase in the public expenditures on goods and services of 100 million *kroner* will lead to an increase in imports of 44 million *kroner*, while an increase in the total tax yield of 100 million *kroner* will lead to a decrease in imports of 38 million *kroner*. A simultaneous increase in public expenditure and tax yield by the same figure will only make a small difference to imports. If, instead of $\beta_C = 0.2$, we had set a somewhat higher value, which would be reasonable when capacity is almost fully utilized in a number of industries, the effects on imports of both expenditure and taxes would have been greater than those expressed in (3.35).

Let us next consider the effects on the national product and on imports jointly. We shall use the same numerical example as in (3.35), and assume that the quantities I_p and A are constant. The changes ΔR, ΔB, ΔG and ΔT will then be connected by the following relations.

$$\begin{aligned}
\Delta R &= 2.25 \,\Delta G - 1.50 \,\Delta T \\
\Delta B &= 0.44 \,\Delta G - 0.38 \,\Delta T .
\end{aligned} \qquad (3.36)$$

This can be considered an example of the type of relation which was generally discussed with reference to formula (2.3) in Chapter 2. Accordingly, ΔR and ΔB are considered quantities for which we have certain targets, while ΔG and ΔT are the government's means of policy.

We really ought also to consider the target for public consumption, but we may assume this to be implied in (3.36) through there being *one component* in G which directly satisfies this target. In addition to this component in G we can have a component which can be determined with more regard to the targets for the national product and for imports.

As already seen, the quantities ΔG and ΔT can be said to be relatively efficient instruments with respect to ΔR, when the target for R is considered in isolation. However, as was discussed in Section 2.1.3, the question of the efficiency of an instrument with respect to a variable is more complicated than it may at first seem when having several targets. Let us pose the following question in connection with (3.36): how great a change in the public expenditure is necessary to obtain a certain change in the national product *when we simultaneously wish to use taxation in such a way as to keep the level of imports unchanged?* This corresponds to the alternative way of considering the efficiency of an instrument, as was mentioned after we had found (2.7) in Chapter 2 somewhat unsatisfactory.

To get the change in imports to equal 0, we must, according to the second equation in (3.36), have the following relation between the changes in the public expenditure and in the tax yield:

$$\varDelta T = 1.16 \, \varDelta G \, .$$

Thus, we must actually make an "over-balanced" change in the budget.

Inserting this in the first equation in (3.36) we get:

$$\varDelta R = 0.51 \, \varDelta G \, . \tag{3.37}$$

The effect on the national product of a change in public expenditure will, consequently, here be of the order of magnitude of only half the increase in public expenditure.

Thus we may draw the following conclusion: public expenditure is a relatively efficient instrument with respect to the national product if no account is taken of the fact that there is also a target for imports. On the other hand, if this latter factor is considered and changes are made in taxation so that the level of imports is kept unchanged, then a change in public expenditure will be a relatively inefficient instrument with respect to the national product.

In economic policy it is generally not difficult to find efficient means when only one target is being considered. It is usually far more difficult when we recognize that we have several targets which we wish to obtain simultaneously. The formulae and the numerical examples above illustrate this fact.

3.2.   A discussion of alternative forms of stabilization policy

3.2.1.   Problem presentation

In the previous sections of this chapter we have sought to clarify the connections between the government's expenditure and revenue and such quantities as national product, import, etc. We shall now imagine that we face situations where various kinds of "disturbances" occur, which displace the target variables from their target values, and that we wish to counteract these disturbances through the fiscal policy.

The disturbances can, within the framework of our models, arise
1. through private investments,
2. through exports,
3. through a shift in private consumption demand,
4. through a shift in the import function.

Through variations in G and T, we wish to counteract the effects of these shifts, thus maintaining a stable total demand and, if possible, also a stable balance in the external trade.

From the models it is easy to see that a shift in the consumption function has on the whole the same effects as a change in private investment. Furthermore, it is easy to see that a shift in the import function has roughly the same effects as a change in exports. It will, therefore, suffice here to bear in mind the problems arising through changes in private investment and in exports*.

When it is a question of a fall in employment and production, the two cases will present quite different problems. If it is private investment which fails there is no immediate worsening of the balance of payments – there is rather an improvement. If, on the other hand, it is exports which fail there is an immediate worsening of the balance of payments. The problems of balance of payments will therefore be far more acute in the latter than in the former case if one is trying to re-establish the desired level of activity.

---

* What has been said in this paragraph applies, of course, only within the framework of a short-run macro-model.

3.2.2. Active fiscal policy

We have in our models clarified connections between the quantities R and B (and thereby also $B–A$) and the instruments G and T. To the extent that the models are realistic, we ought therefore in principle to be able to neutralize the effects of any disturbance of R and B, as long as they are not too large. A policy which tries to watch the development of those quantities which are target variables (for instance, R and B or $B-A$) as closely as possible; and which, as soon as these show an unwanted development, interferes by changes in G and T, will be called an active fiscal policy.

We have seen that in a closed economy the multiplier effects of G and T are relatively large. There ought, then, to be a good chance of neutralizing tendencies for quite considerable fluctuations in R.

For an open economy, the multipliers are smaller. Also, measures designed to stimulate demand, and through it home production, will simultaneously have a stimulating effect on imports, so that the problems of balance of payments will increase. This is apparent from formula (3.36). It is therefore more difficult to counteract great disturbances in the case of an open economy. This is apparent, *inter alia*, from the argument relating to (3.37).

For an open economy where total demand becomes deficient, leading to unemployment and decline in production, there are then the following possibilities for restoring production and employment:

(a)   One can introduce a direct regulation of imports, and in its shelter pursue an expansive policy resulting in high demand and home production. However, to the extent that imports are technically conditioned (they consist, for instance, partly of raw materials necessary for home production), the increase in imports cannot be fully prevented unless one tries through selective means to reduce the importation of less essential goods in order to ensure importation of essential raw materials. One must, also, consider the possible political and commercial effects of such a policy on exports.

(b)   One can avail oneself of the fact that the various uses of the national product do not have the same marginal effect on imports. For instance, that part of the national product used for public consumption and investment has a relatively small marginal effect on import. This fact is made use of in such a policy as was discussed in connection with (3.36) and (3.37). Here, the use of the national product is turned somewhat away from private consumption, which has a relatively high import content; to public use, which has a relatively smaller import content, thereby saving on imports. As already seen, however, such great changes are needed in the amounts of G and T to achieve any significant effect on the national product, that one can hardly conceive of counteracting considerable disturbances in this way.

(c) One can let imports increase, and finance this by using the foreign exchange reserves. This, of course, is only possible if the reserve is large enough for this to be done without serious risks, and it is equally clear that this policy can only be pursued for a limited period.

d) One can finance an increase in imports by raising loans abroad, provided it is possible to obtain such loans. Here, of course, the immediate advantage must be balanced against the inconvenience of future repayment and interest payments on the loans.

The most satisfactory solution of the problems which an expansive policy in an open economy will lead to is, of course, for several countries to start an expansive policy simultaneously. Then the fact that the expansive policy of one country leads to increased imports for that country, can be compensated for by other countries' expansive policies leading to increased imports for these countries, and thus increased exports from the first country. This increase will in itself have a stimulating effect on the economy and make it possible to achieve a given effect on the national product with measures involving smaller changes in G and T than would otherwise have been necessary.

It may be of some interest to consider in more detail the size of the changes in public expenditure and tax revenue which might be necessary. The Norwegian net national product in 1960 was about 28 thousand million *kroner*. If there is, for some reason, a deficient demand resulting in a 10% failure in the national product, measures must consequently be found which have an effect on the national product of about 2.8 thousand million *kroner*. If we have a closed economy (which we can "provide" by a strict regulation of imports), a change in public expenditure of about 700 million *kroner* will be necessary, using the orders of magnitude for the coefficients with which we have operated earlier. For an open economy we can reckon with a multiplier of the order of magnitude 2. The increase in the public expenditure would then have to be of about 1.4 thousand million *kroner*. If production were to be restored through tax relief an even larger amount would be necessary, because the multiplier effect of any given tax relief is less than the effect of an equivalent increase in public expenditure. For a closed economy a tax relief of about 900 million *kroner* might be necessary, and for an open economy a relief of about a couple of thousand million *kroner*.

These demands for change in the public expenditure or in tax yields can be compared with the following figures: public consumption in Norway in 1960 amounted to about 4 thousand million *kroner*, and public net real investment to about 1.8 thousand millions. The direct taxes totalled about 4 thousand millions, of which about 1.4 thousand million *kroner* were state taxes. The general sales tax brought in about 2 thousand million *kroner* to the state. If we assume that it is only the state who can conduct an active fiscal policy, we see that it is in practice difficult to imagine such large short-term changes in public expenditure or revenue as the figures arrived at above on the assumption that the national product fails by 10%.

If, on the other hand, the deficiency amounted to only 1% of the national product, the measures necessary to counteract it would be of a more reasonable order of magnitude. Then even a policy of a balanced budgetary change might be sufficiently effective. 1% of the Norwegian national product in 1960 would be about 280 million *kroner*. As the multplier effect of a balanced budgetary change is 1 in the case with a closed economy, and probably near to 1 in the case with an open economy (see formulae (3.15) and (3.33)), a budgetary change of 280 million *kroner* or something a little over that would be required. This is not an unthinkable change. It can be mentioned that in the winter 1958–1959 something over 100 million *kroner* were allocated for extraordinary employment measures, and there is no reason to believe that this is the maximum that could be used to stabilize employment or production.

An active policy of stabilization of the type discussed above does, however, also raise many problems which are not reflected in a static macro-model such as the one we have used.

1) Firstly, there is the question of timing, i.e., of starting the measures at the right time. In any economy there will always be certain upward and downward movements in production, employment, prices, and so on,

without these being signs that the whole economic situation is undergoing a change. An attempt to be especially prompt in applying remedies may therefore involve the danger of misinterpreting an "accidental" change as the beginnings of something bigger. Instead of contributing towards stabilization, one might then apply measures which were contributing either to inflation or to unemployment and a decline in production. On the other hand: a desire to guard against this danger may involve the risk of frequently waiting too long before interfering. This implies a danger that dynamic processes may be set in motion, and once started these may be difficult to stop. Such dynamic processes may have an effect via the expectations as to future development and thereby through investment, something which is not expressed in the models here considered.

2) Next, there is the question of the right "dosage", i.e., of applying measures of the right strength or volume. There are two difficulties here. In the first place information available about the existing situation is often incomplete, and secondly there is often incomplete knowledge of the "model" in operation, that is, incomplete knowledge of the reaction mechanisms which are in operation.

3) The two problems mentioned above will be present even in the absence of administrative problems. But in fact, the administration always needs time to make decisions.

4) Special problems arise in connection with public expenditures of the kinds current in the measures against unemployment. It is, of course, possible at short notice to start fairly primitive undertakings of the "relief work" type, that is, the sort of enterprise for which manpower and other resources would not be used unless there was extensive unemployment. For more "sensible" enterprises preparations of various kinds will always be necessary. The work must be technically planned, and where construction work is concerned, there are often legal arrangements to be made about the site. Such matters can take a long time. The best way of dealing with this problem is to have a special emergency budget. This budget would cover work which it was planned to carry out in any case, sooner or later, at public expense. Should the employment situation require it, those of the enterprises having highest priority can then be carried out. Should there prove to be no need for such measures to stimulate employment, top-priority measures in this emergency budget can eventually be transferred to ordinary budgets, and the emergency

budget be constantly supplied "from the bottom" with new projects, There have been budgets of this type in use in Sweden. In Norway there has been an "enterprise reserve" in the Directorate of Labour serving similar purposes.

5) It can also be difficult to interrupt work already under way at the times best suited to stabilization of the economy. If the original move consisted in an increase of taxes, a reduction may be fairly easy: the opposite might prove more difficult. If public expenditure is being directed to "sensible" projects, it can often be difficult to interrupt the work at a suitable time without causing waste and without some of the values already created being lost. Road construction may be relatively straightforward in this respect, while on the other hand many other kinds of construction activity, once started, must be completed if losses are not to be incurred. If, however, one keeps such works going beyond the time when they were necessary for the sake of stabilization, they may contribute towards an inflationary development. Instead of letting this inflation develop one should then, of course, interfere with contractive measures which, for instance, reduce private investment. Yet this would entail inefficient management if the private investment works thereby hampered had a higher priority in the national economy than the public works which were continued after they were no longer necessary to stabilization.

6) Lastly, there are frictional problems of various kinds. There are many who consider intermittent economic decline a necessary feature of development because a setback results in a redistribution of labour, a weeding-out of inefficient firms and so on, thus clearing the way for new economic growth on a "healthier" basis. A policy aiming at continuous full employment would, in the opinion of some, therefore act as a brake on economic growth in the long run, by preventing the mobility created by economic setbacks. A special problem in connection with the use of public building and construction projects as a means of stabilization is that through such work manpower will be tied to these particular industries; since, as wages in building and construction are often relatively high, labour which has entered this field may not easily leave it again when it is desirable to reduce this type of activity. This may result in a public construction activity originally started as an "extraordinary" regulator of employment becoming difficult to interrupt, so that new activities continually have to be started because labour has been tied to the industry.

Let us then, in concluding, consider the question of which would be the more useful to a stabilization policy: to apply taxes, or to apply public expenditure. It has been mentioned earlier that the most natural approach would be to let public expenditure be determined by the need for collective consumption and public investment, taxes being used to regulate the level of total demand. Some considerations do, however, favour public expenditure as being, after all, the more useful regulator in certain situations.

As already mentioned, public expenditure can to some extent be so arranged that it has a relatively small effect on imports, because the quantity β_G in our models is to a certain extent controlled by the government. This may result in public expenditure becoming the more useful method in situations where one must take into consideration the effects on the balance of payments.

Some of the practical considerations already mentioned also make a case for the use of public expenditure, at least when well planned and prepared beforehand, as described under point 4 above. Public expenditure can be especially useful when unemployment is not evenly distributed over regions and industries, but is concentrated in certain districts and certain branches. Expenditure can be injected where unemployment is highest. Taxes, on the other hand, must usually be formulated quite generally and will therefore affect the economy in a far less selective way.

If there is a general depression, a combination of means will probably appear the more useful. One might then give tax reliefs up to a point, i.e., to the point where bottlenecks begin to make themselves felt in some parts of the economy. In addition, public works could be started in those industries or those districts where unemployment persisted after such bottlenecks had arisen.

Some authors maintain that taxes are the best means of regulation, on the grounds that tax reliefs leave it to people themselves to decide what the extra resources will be used for. This argument does not, however, carry much weight in the case of unemployment which is concentrated in a few regions or industries; because tax relief is then too unselective a method. Moreover, when the public works projects are well planned, through an enterprise reserve of the type mentioned earlier, it should be high-priority tasks which they perform.

From a social point of view, public works will seem the better means.

Tax reductions* will, in the first instance, benefit only those who pay state tax of some significance, that is, people who have a considerable income, while the unemployed will get their income raised only gradually as the indirect effects of the tax reductions lead to increased employment. Public works, on the contrary, immediately bring income to those who have had their income reduced through unemployment.

A policy of stabilization via adjustment of public revenue and expenditure, such as has here been discussed, may imply that the state incurs debt. The problems raised by public debt will be dealt with in a later chapter.

We have touched upon the problems of timing and "dosage" of public measures for purposes of stabilization. If the government's measures are inadequately based it is obvious that they can contribute towards destabilization instead of stabilization. This problem is analysed in an original and interesting way by Milton Friedman **. It can loosely be said that Friedman shows the following: consider the accuracy obtainable in the timing of measures as a datum. The poorer this timing is, the smaller must be the scale of the measures if they are to be as stabilizing as possible.

3.2.3.   *Automatic stabilization*

An active fiscal policy such as has been discussed here presupposes a constant re-appraisal of the situation, and interference in accordance with the results of this re-appraisal. Since such valuations present great uncertainty, and the continuous risk of destabilizing instead of stabilizing through the policies they suggest, it is natural to ask whether stabilization could not be achieved more automatically, without such continual re-appraisals of the situation.

The model examined in connection with (3.16)–(3.19) provides a basis for a discussion of this problem. Through (3.16) we found that the tax yield automatically increases when national income increases and decreases when national income decreases. This should have a restraining effect on the fluctuations in the national product.

---

* What is meant here is reduction in taxes in the ordinary sense. It does not, of course, apply to increase in transfers to the population, which we have considered as a "negative taxes".
** Milton Friedman: The effects of full-employment policy on economic stability: a formal analysis, in: *Essays in positive economics* (Chicago University Press, 1953).

Let us imagine that the "disturbance" comes via private investment activity. If there was no automatic reaction in the tax yield the change in national income per unit of change in private investment would be

$$\left(\frac{\partial R}{\partial I_{\mathrm{p}}}\right)_0 = \frac{1}{1-a}. \tag{3.38}$$

This formula follows from (3.14). The index 0 on the left side in (3.38) has been added to distinguish this case from the case where we do have automatic reactions in the tax yield.

Two forms of policy may be implied in (3.38). Firstly, it may be that one has forms of taxation such that the tax yields are not automatically changed when the national income changes. If, for instance, taxation of general property is particularly important, (3.38) will be relevant. Secondly, if the forms of taxation are such that the tax yield is related to income it may be possible that the state adjusts tax rates when the national income changes in such a way that the tax yield is kept constant. Then, too, (3.38) will be relevant.

Let us now consider the case where one has such forms of taxation that the tax yield, with unchanged tax-rules and -rates, is automatically changed with the national income in agreement with (3.16). A shift in private investment activity then gives a reaction in national income which is indicated by

$$\left(\frac{\partial R}{\partial I_{\mathrm{p}}}\right)_t = \frac{1}{1-(1-t)a}. \tag{3.39}$$

The index t on the left side is here added to mark this as a case where we have a "macro marginal tax rate" t.

If the macro marginal tax rate t is greater than zero, we see that we have

$$\left(\frac{\partial R}{\partial I_{\mathrm{p}}}\right)_t < \left(\frac{\partial R}{\partial I_{\mathrm{p}}}\right)_0. \tag{3.40}$$

A disturbance occasioned by private investment will, consequently, cause a smaller reaction in the national product when the tax yield is automatically changed with national income than when it is not. We have, therefore, a certain stabilizing effect which may be called automatic because the state does not actively interfere in any way, but only maintains the tax-rules and -rates which were previously decided.

As can be seen, (3.39) will not under any circumstance equal 0. Consequently we will not obtain complete stabilization.

As a measure of the degree of stabilization which is obtained, we could take

$$\gamma = \frac{(\partial R/\partial I_p)_0 - (\partial R/\partial I_p)_t}{(\partial R/\partial I_p)_0}. \tag{3.41}$$

The numerator in this expression is the reduction in reactions in the national income due to the presence of automatic stabilization. This reduction is next measured as a proportion of those reactions which would appear if there were no automatic stabilization. If we insert here from (3.38) and (3.39) we readily get

$$\gamma = \frac{ta}{1 - (1 - t)a}. \tag{3.42}$$

For a numerical example we can take $a = 0.75$ and $t = 0.30$. We then get a value for γ of 0.47. If we instead set $t = 0.20$, as we did in the numerical example following (3.18), we get a value for γ of 0.375.

No thorough statistical examination of this relationship is available for Norway. In the U.S.A. certain investigations have been carried out which suggest that taxation leads to an automatic stabilization effect which gives a γ of about 0.40[*].

For a really thorough study of the relationships bearing on automatic stabilization, one must study individual types of taxation separately. Many forms of public expenditure ought also to be included in the

---

[*] See R. A. Musgrave, *The theory of public finance* (New York, London, 1959) pp. 510–12. See also A. S. Goldberger, *Impact mutlipliers and dynamic properties of the Klein-Goldberger model* (Amsterdam, 1959) pp. 37–48 and 127–29.

analysis. Expenditure on various social insurances has a tendency to rise when incomes generally decline. This effect is especially clear in the case of unemployment insurances. These therefore play a not inconsiderable role as automatic stabilizers*.

A policy based on automatic stabilization will lead to fluctuations in public revenue. The change in the tax yield T when private investment is altered (while both the public expenditure G and the macro marginal tax rate t are constant) is given by

$$\frac{\partial T}{\partial I_\mathrm{p}} = t\left(\frac{\partial R}{\partial I_\mathrm{p}}\right)_t = \frac{t}{1 - (1 - t)a}. \tag{3.43}$$

With such numerical examples as have been employed earlier, this magnitude will reach a level of 0.50 or higher. Thus, very considerable reactions will result from disturbances due to private investment. This means that such a policy involving automatic stabilization will imply a fluctuating balance in the budget. If the situation is such that the budget is just balanced at a sort of middle level of activity in the economy, there will automatically be a budgetary surplus during a boom and a budgetary deficit during a depression. There is, however, nothing to suggest that one must get a balance on just such a medium level. Therefore it may also be that such a policy implies an average surplus or deficit in the long run.

In connection with this automatic stabilization policy it might be necessary to reconsider the function (3.16) in more detail. Such a function with undated variables can be relevant in two cases. Firstly, it can be relevant if we discuss alternative stationary levels. This is, however, of no great interest to the problem of automatic stabilization. Secondly, the function (3.16) can be relevant if the pay-as-you-earn system of taxation is everywhere in force. The tax revenue will then depend on income earned in the same year. There is, however, hardly any country where such a system is fully realized. The system has only lately been introduced

---

* A relatively thorough study based on a quite detailed model for the USA is provided by J. S. Duesenberry, O. Eckstein and G. Fromm, A simulation of the United States economy in recession, *Econometrica*, No. 4, 1960.

in Norway and has not been applied to all forms of income. Norway has, therefore, still a considerable element of tax which depends on income earned in past periods. To cover such a case, one would – instead of (3.16) – have to introduce a function where the tax revenue for one particular year depends on income in the same year and one or more earlier years. And the whole question of automatic stabilization must then be analysed dynamically*.

3.2.4.   A destabilizing policy

A policy which has been followed in some countries at various times has roughly consisted in accepting the automatic fluctuations one gets in the tax revenues, while keeping a balanced budget by letting public expenditure undergo equivalent fluctuations. Such a policy will have a destabilizing effect, unlike the stabilizing policy discussed in the previous section. This follows from the fact, already noticed, that the multiplier effect of a change in public expenditure will be larger than the multiplier effect of a change in the tax yield. Let us, however, consider this kind of policy a little more directly.

Instead of (3.16) with G kept constant, we now have

$$G = T = tR + k.\tag{3.44}$$

If this is combined with the equations in (3.13) we get

$$R = \frac{1}{(1 - a)(1 - t)}\left[I_p + b + (1 - a)k\right].\tag{3.45}$$

Since we have

$$\frac{1}{(1 - a)(1 - t)} > \frac{1}{1 - a},$$

---

* For an example of such an analysis see Musgrave, op. cit., pp. 512–15. Stabilization is discussed within a dynamic model also in the article in *Econometrica* mentioned in the previous foot-note.

a certain reaction in private investment will now lead to a greater reaction in the national product than would be the case if T and G were kept constant. In this sense, then, this policy will indeed have a destabilizing effect.

3.3. *The effects of fiscal policy via investments. Interactions with monetary policy*

In all the arguments so far, I_p, the private investment, has been taken to be exogenously determined. Either it has been considered as constant, or we have considered given variations of I_p. But in fact fiscal policy can, in various ways, influence the level of private investment. One can distinguish between three ways in which these influences make themselves felt.

1. Via effects on disposable business profits.
2. Via effects on availability of credit.
3. Via effects on the rate of interest.

The two last points border on monetary policy. From the way they will be discussed below, one might perhaps regard them as consequences, for monetary policy, of fiscal policy.

We shall consider each of these three points separately, and in so doing, apply alternative theories or models. One can, however, regard these alternative theories not as competing theories, but as theories which can be applied to *different situations*. In a model where several sectors are specified it might also happen that different alternatives are applied simultaneously in different sectors.

3.3.1. *Effects via disposable profits*

Let us imagine an economy with the following simple features. All production is undertaken by private enterprises. The income created by this production is divided into wage income and business profits. We assume that the ratio of this division is constant and let the wages share be represented by g. We further assume that all wage income, after deduction of taxes, is spent on private consumption, and that this makes up the entire private consumption. As to the behaviour of enterprises, we assume that investments depend on disposable profits, that is, the total revenue after deduction of wage payments and taxes. No difficulties would present themselves in modifying this model in various ways: for instance, by assuming that not all disposable wage income is spent on consumption, and that a given part of the business profits is distributed to the owners who use some of this on consumption, and so on. (Cf. the footnote on the consumption function on page 32.)

We introduce the following symbols: L=wage income; T_L=tax on wage income; T_B=tax on business profits. With g, h and k as constants, and with the assumptions made above, we have the following model:

$$
\begin{aligned}
R &= C_\mathrm{p} + I_\mathrm{p} + G \\
C_\mathrm{p} &= L - T_L \\
L &= gR \\
I_\mathrm{p} &= h(R - L - T_B) + k.
\end{aligned}
\qquad (3.46)
$$

In what follows we shall call the quantity h the marginal propensity to invest.

À propos of this model, it can be mentioned that several econometric investigations have pointed to disposable profits as being a more important factor in an explanation of private investment than are rates of interest or such explanatory factors as are used in connection with the acceleration principle.

From this model we get the following solution for the national product:

$$
R = \frac{1}{(1-g)(1-h)}[G - T_L - hT_B + k]. \qquad (3.47)
$$

The quantity g is here relatively straightforward. It can be expected to be on a level of 0.6 to 0.7. The quantity h is far more uncertain. If the entrepreneurs are "pessimistic" and wish to use any increased profits to lay up financial reserves, h will be near 0. If they are more "optimistic" they will put more emphasis on providing production equipment than on laying up financial reserves. Then, h will be nearer to 1. It will be seen that the model collapses in the case with h exactly equal to 1. In itself, a relation like the last equation in (3.46) is possible also with $h=1$, but this would require changes elsewhere in the model. This will not be further treated here.

If we consider the multiplier effect of public expenditure we see that it can now take on very different values according to the size of h. With $h=0$ the multiplier will be $1/(1-g)$, and with an h approaching 1 in value, the multiplier will approach infinity.

With regard to the effects of changes in the tax yields, we see that a given amount of tax relief on wage income will now have exactly the same effect on the national product as the same amount of increased public expenditure on goods and services. This is connected with the assumption that all disposable wage income is spent on the purchase of consumer goods. The effect of an equivalent amount in tax relief for business profits will, however, be smaller when we assume that h is less than 1. If h equalled zero, the tax reliefs for business profits would not manifest themselves in the national product at all. This means that in this case the enterprises would use the whole amount saved by the tax relief on building up financial reserves, so that there would be no increased demand for goods and services which could bring about an increase in the national product.

In the model now under consideration it is of special interest to look at the solutions for private consumption and private investment separately. From the second and third equations in (3.46) we have

$$C_p = gR - T_L.$$

By insertion from the solution (3.47) we get the following solution for private consumption

$$C_p = -\frac{gh + 1 - h}{(1 - g)(1 - h)} T_L - \frac{gh}{(1 - g)(1 - h)} T_B$$

$$+ \frac{g}{(1 - g)(1 - h)}(G + k). \tag{3.48}$$

It can here be seen that the value of the fraction in front of T_L is greater than the value of the fraction in front of T_B. This means that taxation of wage income has a greater effect on private consumption than the taxation of business profits. In the extreme case of h approaching zero taxation of business profits will have practically no effect on private consumption.

The solution for private investment is most easily obtained by insertion from the first and second equations in (3.46) into the last equation in (3.46). This gives

$$I_p = -\frac{h}{1-h}(T_L + T_B) + \frac{h}{1-h}G + \frac{k}{1-h}. \qquad (3.49)$$

The most striking thing in this solution is that a change of taxation of wage income will have exactly the same effect on private investment as an equally large change in taxation of business profits. A tax relief for wage income will in the first instance here only be reflected in an increase in the purchase of consumer goods. This increase will, however, cause a rise in national income which will be divided between wages and business profits. The latter of these components affects investment, while the former will again cause an increase in purchases of consumer goods which creates revenue for enterprises, and so on. Altogether, the total effect amounts to the same as with a tax relief given directly to business. This result is dependent upon the simplification made above that all disposable wage income is used in the purchase of consumer goods. One might say that in the model no income "leaks out" in the form of savings by the wage-earners, all their income being spent in buying from the enterprises.

We have thus seen that, while the two types of taxes have a different effect on private consumption, they have – under the assumptions made – the same effect on private investment. This opens a possibility of regulating the ratio between private consumption and private investment. Let us consider a shift in taxes such that the national product is kept unchanged. We then see from (3.47) that we must change T_L and T_B with the quantities ΔT_L and ΔT_B so that

$$\Delta T_L = -h\,\Delta T_B. \qquad (3.50)$$

If we imagine a reduction in T_B, i.e., a ΔT_B which is less than zero, we see that it is unnecessary to increase T_L by an equally large amount in order to neutralize the effect on the national product. (As earlier, we assume that h is smaller than 1.)

With a change in taxation which satisfies (3.50) we get the following effects on private consumption and on private investment:

$$\Delta C_p = \quad h\,\Delta T_B (\text{when } \Delta T_L = -\,h\,\Delta T_B) \qquad (3.51)$$

$$\Delta I_p = -\,h\,\Delta T_B (\text{when } \Delta T_L = -\,h\,\Delta T_B). \qquad (3.52)$$

If, for instance, $h = 0.5$ here, and a tax relief of 100 million *kroner* is granted to the enterprises, we must increase taxation of wage income by 50 million *kroner* to keep the national product unchanged. The effects on consumption and investment will be that private consumption goes down by 50 million *kroner* while private investment goes up by 50 million *kroner*.

Thus, we apparently have here a means to influence the division of the national product between consumption and investment. We can imagine having targets for private investment, for private consumption, and for public purchase of goods and services. These three targets are achieved by the help of the three instruments T_L, T_B and G. We cannot, of course, set any target for the national product independently of these three, as $R = C_p + I_p + G$. However, there are many elements of uncertainty in the application of this set of instruments for the regulation of investment. Firstly, it is possible that changes in the taxation of business profits may manifest themselves in the prices of products and thereby not affect the disposable profit in quite such a way as might at first appear. We shall later return to this point in more detail. Secondly, the behaviour of investors involves a large element of uncertainty.

On the other hand, it must be stated that changes in the taxation of enterprises can take many different *forms,* and some appropriately formulated changes might affect investment more than a pure macromodel of the type now used seems to suggest. For instance, changes in the rules for tax treatment of depreciation might show up greatly in investment in certain situations. This, too, will be returned to in a later chapter.

3.3.2. The effects of fiscal policy on money supply in the private sector

It was mentioned in the introduction to this section that fiscal policy can influence private investment via availability of credit and via interest rates (as well as via disposable profits in private enterprises). Both these effects are connected with the fact that fiscal policy influences the money supply in the private sector. We shall, therefore, look at how this influence works before treating these two factors separately.

Any payment from the public sector increases the money supply in the private sector of the economy, and any payment from the private to the public sector reduces the money supply in the private sector. Let us indicate the money supply with the symbol M. Let M without any index indicate the money supply (as a stock) at the end of the period we are looking at, while M^0 indicates the money supply at the beginning of the period. The money supply is in this connection considered to consist only of cash and current-account deposits in the central bank. If the public sector does not undertake any transactions other than buying goods and services from current home production on the one hand, and collecting taxes on the other, and if all purchases of goods and services are paid in cash, we simply have the following connection between the factors characteristic of fiscal policy, namely, G and T, and the change in the money supply in the private sector:

$$M - M^0 = G - T .\qquad(3.53)$$

We have thus found that a deficit in the current transactions of the public sector leads to an increase in the money supply, and that a surplus in public current transactions leads to a reduction of the money supply. As before, T indicates the net tax revenue, i.e., taxes minus transfer payments from the public to the private sector.

Besides buying goods and services from current production, the public sector can also buy real property from the private sector or sell real property to the private sector. Under this heading we can also include such an item as the buying and selling of shares. Such transactions will not effect a direct increase or reduction of income in the private sector, but will only imply a change of the balance sheet for the private sector.

On the other hand, they will influence the money supply in the private sector, as they will, of course, involve payments and receipts. If we introduce the symbol $F=$ public net purchase of real property from the private sector, we can now instead of (3.53) write

$$M - M^0 = G + F - T. \tag{3.54}$$

In this connection it is important to note that those transactions included in the quantity G and those included in the quantity F will have quite different economic effects. While G has such effects via incomes as have earlier been analysed, F will have effects only to the extent that changes of the balance sheet for the private sector – amongst them changes in the amount of money in the private sector – affect the behaviour of private enterprises and individuals. Similarly, it is important to be aware that payments to the state in the form of taxes, and payments when the state sells real property or shares (equivalent to negative components in F) also have different effects.

Apart from influences through such transactions as introduced in (3.54) the public sector has influence on the money supply through its loan transactions. Let H be the private sector's claims against the public sector at the end of the period we are considering, and let H^0 be the claims against the public sector at the beginning of the period. Thus

$H - H^0 =$ the increase of the private sector's claims against the public
     sector = the increase in public debt.

We are reckoning with net quantities, so that $H - H^0$ represents public borrowing plus repayments from private persons to the public sector, minus private borrowing from the public sector, minus public repayments to the private sector. We then get as the general formula for the effect on the money supply in the private sector

$$M - M^0 = G + F - T - (H - H^0). \tag{3.55}$$

According to the distinction made earlier between fiscal policy and monetary policy, it is reasonable to include the component $H - H^0$ under the heading of monetary policy, while the other components represent fiscal policy.

Besides being influenced by the transactions of the government sector, the money supply in the private sector is, of course, also influenced by the transactions of the central bank. Taking account of this would call for still more terms in (3.55). We shall not enter upon that here, but it is easy to see how it could be combined with the present analysis.

The money supply is thus affected both by those transactions which come under fiscal policy and those coming under monetary policy. So it is clear that these two aspects of economic policy are closely interlocked. If one, for instance, wishes for a particular development of the money supply in the private sector, it is impossible to decide which monetary policy this calls for without knowing and taking account of the fiscal policy which is being followed.

For an illustration of the relationship (3.55) some figures can be given showing the effects on the money supply of the dispositions of the Norwegian state during the years 1957–1962.

Table 3

Effects of state transactions on money supply in the private sector. (Mill. *kroner*)

	1957	1958	1959	1960	1961	1962
Net increases in money supply through other transactions than loan transactions $[G + F - T]$	− 528	− 772	− 354	− 446	− 245	− 287
Net increases in money supply through loan transactions $[-(H - H^0)]$	288	177	69	431	292	392
Total increase in money supply through state transactions	− 240	− 595	− 285	− 15	47	105

As can be seen, state transactions have up to 1960 led to net *decrease* in the money supply, but this has changed in later years. On the other hand the transactions of the Bank of Norway, mainly purchases of foreign currency from banks and from the public, have in the years 1957–1962 contributed towards an increase in the money supply.

3.3.3. Effects on private investment via availability of credit

Let us now return to the simple model we had in (3.13) with the solution (3.14). With the numerical example $a = 0.75$, it gives

$$R = 4I_p + 4G - 3T + \text{const}.\tag{3.56}$$

When we employed this model earlier, we considered I_p as exogenously determined. Let us now, however, consider I_p as consisting of two components: a component I_p^* which is exogenously determined, and a component I_p' which is determined by new credit possibilities. Consequently, we assume that there are in the private sector of the economy such extensive investment plans that it is the availability of finance which sets the limit to what can be realized.

Let us next compare two alternatives for the fiscal policy.

$$\begin{aligned} &\text{Alternative 1}: \quad G = T = 3.5\\ &\text{Alternative 2}: \quad G = 4.0, T = 3.5.\end{aligned}\tag{3.57}$$

The figures here can, for instance, represent thousand millions of *kroner*.

Let us first imagine that we have no effects on private investment, i.e., that $I_p' = 0$. Then we shall have the following solutions for the national product in the two alternatives:

$$\begin{aligned} &\text{Alternative 1}: \quad R = 4I_p^* + 3.5 + \text{const}.\\ &\text{Alternative 2}: \quad R = 4I_p^* + 5.5 + \text{const}.\end{aligned}\tag{3.58}$$

where "const." represents the same constant as in (3.56). Setting public expenditure at 4.0 instead of 3.5 gives an increase of 2 in the national product, corresponding to the multiplier value of 4.

Let us next look at the case where private investment increases by a value equivalent to the increased availability of credit which one gets in the second alternative. In this alternative the public deficit will be 0.5. We are not reckoning with any other transactions than those implied in the quantities G and T. This deficit will give an increase in the money supply of 0.5 in the private sector. It is well known that a certain increase in the money supply can lay the foundation of a considerably larger credit increase through an expansion of credit in private banking*.

It is difficult to give any definite estimate of the size of the "credit multiplier", but it is not unthinkable that in some situations it might take a value of about 2. If we use this for the sake of argument, then the expansion of credit based on an increase in liquidity of 0.5 will make new credit available to finance an investment of 1.0, i.e., $I'_p = 1.0$. The solution for the national product will then be

$$R = 4(I_p^* + 1.0) + 5.5 + \text{const.} = 4I_p^* + 9.5 + \text{const.} \qquad (3.59)$$

These results can be summed up as follows: to increase G from 3.5 to 4.0 while T is kept equal to 3.5, effects an increase in the national product of 2.0 if private investment remains unchanged. The increase in G from 3.5 to 4.0 leads to an increase in R of 6.0 if the "credit multiplier" equals 2, and if private investment increases in step with the increase in the opportunities for credit financing resulting from a fiscal policy which increases liquidity in the private sector. Thus in this example the "side-effect" on liquidity of fiscal policy has become of greater importance to the national product than the effect which was studied before.

However, one must be careful in drawing a conclusion from such a numerical example. As already mentioned, the behaviour of investors is often unstable and difficult to predict, and it depends on many other factors than those now dealt with. But effects *of the type* we have described here probably make themselves felt during periods of extensive investment plans but limited opportunities for financing.

3.3.4. *Effects via the rate of interest*

In the previous section we considered a situation where investment plans

---

* This has been treated, for instance, in Leif Johansen, The role of the banking system in a macro-economic model, *International Economic Papers* No. 8 (London, 1958).

were so extensive that it was the availability of finance which set the limit
to what actually was realized of investment. Let us now deal with the
situation where it is the considerations of profitability which set the limit
to what is realized. Such a situation can be described by the following
model;

(a) $$R = C_p + I_p + G$$
(b) $$C_p = f(R - T)$$
(c) $$I_p = g(r) \qquad\qquad (3.60)$$
(d) $$M = h(R, r)$$
(e) $$M - M^0 = G + F - T - (H - H^0).$$

Equation (b) is here the consumption function written in general form.
Equation (c) expresses demand for investment goods as a function of the
interest level r. Implied in this function are the calculations of profitability
in investment decisions. Equation (d) is a liquidity preference function of
the type found in Keynsian models. The fact that the national product is
included here expresses the need for money for transaction purposes.
Equation (e) is the national accounting relationship introduced in (3.55).

Certain problems arise here because of the fact that M represents the
money supply at the close of the period in question. However, we can
imagine that the public expects the interest- and income-levels prevalent
in a given period to continue into the next period; and that it therefore
aims at keeping in hand, at the end of any such period, liquid funds which
are determined by the level of income and interest during its course.

The quantities M^0 and H^0 are given from the previous period. The
policy instruments of the public sector are now H, G, T and F. When
these quantities are determined all other quantities included in the model
will be determined by the five equations in (3.60).

With regard to the quantities included in the model, we see that F and
H are only included in the last equation and in such a way that it is only
the difference $(F - H)$ which is of any importance. We can therefore say
that we really have only three instruments with respect to the quantities
included in the model, namely G, T and $(F - H)$. The choice between
using F or H to influence the money supply must be taken from consider-

ations which are not expressed in the model, – for instance, the consideration of what kind of property one thinks the state should own.

One could now undertake a complete analysis of the effects of changes in the various instruments by means of implicit differentiation of the system (3.60). However, we shall not here go as far as that, only point out certain possible effects.

Let us first consider the effect of an increase in G, the public expenditure on goods and services. This change will, firstly, add to the total demand for goods and services, and will therefore have effects such as those analysed in the previous, simple multiplier models. The resulting increase in the national product will, however, through equation (d) involve a greater need for liquid balances for transaction purposes. Then, if the total cash balance was given, one would have a certain increase of the interest level, which would lead to decreased investment. However, it will be seen from the national accounting equation (e) in (3.60) that increased public expenditure will add to the money supply in the private sector. In itself, this will point to a lower interest level and thereby increased investment. What the net effect of these opposing tendencies will be, can be found only through such an implicit differentiation in the system as was mentioned above, and the answer will depend on the values of the derivatives of the functions f, g and h.

In a similar way we can deduce the effects of changes in T. We get multiplier effects such as those which have been analysed earlier; and we get effects on the need for liquid balances for transaction purposes, but also simultaneous effects on the money supply in the private sector.

As for the quantities F and H, we have already noted that these are included only in equation (e). Thus, they affect the economy only via changes in the money supply. Then, if the money supply does not affect the level of interest rates, and/or if the level of interest rates does not affect the level of investment, the effects on such things as national product, consumption and investment will fail to appear. If, on the other hand, the functions g hand h are such as to include interest levels as effective arguments, we shall get effects on investment, and furthermore through the multiplier effect of the investments, effects also on other variables.

We shall not here discuss further the theoretical basis for each particular relation in (3.60). That comes under general economic theory. Here it will suffice to mention that, to the extent that the level of interest will affect investment it will probably first and foremost apply to investment in inventories and housing. Many investigations indicate that, beyond this, the level of interest has relatively small or, at any rate, rather unpredictable effects on investment.

To the extent that the money supply affects the level of interest and hence investment, we are in the same situation as in section 3.3.1 when it comes to the number of targets which can be set. The quantity G can be determined from the target for public consumption and public investment. Taxation and the money supply can then be adjusted with regard to total employment and the desired distribution of resources between private consumption and investment. However, I may remind the reader that in section 3.2.2 we found that there may be conditions necessitating the use of components in G for employment purposes, and the uncertainty of effects of M on I_p via r, which is mentioned above, should be emphasized.

In situations like the one we have had in post-war Norway, the effects treated in the previous section relating to (3.58) and (3.59) are probably more important than what has been considered here in connection with (3.60).

We might have applied all these arguments to the case of an open economy. It is, however, quite clear how this could be done, using (3.29) as a basis.

3.4.   Some concrete illustrations from the 1930's

As concrete illustrations of the subject as treated so far, we shall now consider the problems of unemployment in some countries in the years between the wars, and what was then done – or not done – to solve these problems. However, what follows must not be taken as an attempt at an analysis of the problems of that time. That would require far more thorough studies of the actual conditions in each country, as well as far more exhaustive statistical illustrations of those conditions, than are possible here*.

---

* More detailed information can be found in many works. See, for instance, Erik Lundberg, *Business cycles and economic policy* (London, 1957) and P. Mendès-France and G. Ardant, *Economics and Action* (New York, 1955).

3.4.1. The U.S.A. in the 1930's

The great economic depression in western countries in the 1930's started with the collapse of the Stock Exchange on the 24th of October 1929. All industrialized states in the western world were hit by the depression, but the U.S.A. was one of those hardest hit. The decline of industrial production is shown by the following figures:

1929	1930	1931	1932
100	81	68	54

Thus, industrial production fell in the course of a few years to about half of what it had been. Unemployment showed the following development:

1929	1930	1931	1932
429 000	3 809 000	8 113 000	12 478 000

This crisis surpassed any earlier experience. The American authorities, however, thought the depression would be of short duration and that it was unnecessary to intervene in any way. At least, they publicly expressed this view.

The authorities' view implied that the federal budget was to be kept balanced to the greatest possible extent. However, the attempt failed: the budget ran to large deficits. In the first years the expenditure and revenue of the federal authorities were as follows, in thousand million $:

	Expenditure	Revenue
1930	3.4	4.2
1931	3.6	3.1
1932	4.6	1.9

As can be seen, a considerable increase in expenditure took place despite the declared goal of keeping a balanced budget. This increase in expenditure consisted in relief work and other emergency measures which the situation virtually made inevitable in spite of any "philosophy". On the other hand tax revenue automatically declined as the level of income in the private sector of the economy fell catastrophically. There was thus a certain element of active policy in expenditure, while as regards revenue there was an automatic effect which in itself should be stabilizing.

Some writers think, however, that this large deficit which was built up contributed towards a worsening of the crisis, because psychologically it had the effect of emphasizing that "society was on the verge of collapse". Whether there is anything in this notion or not it ought in any case to be observed that the situation would have been different had the authorities. and professional economists declared already *before* the crisis that public finances would be used for regulating trade cycles, and that a deficit on that account did not imply any such danger of collapse.

This view of the deficit may, however, form part of the reason why the new Roosevelt administration which took office did not at once make any conscious decision to accept a deficit as part of a policy of regulating trade fluctuations. Instead of expressing such a view Roosevelt began after he had been elected with the following declaration:

"Revenue must cover expenditures by one means or another. Any government, like any family, can for one year spend a little more than it earns. But you and I know that a continuation of that habit means the poor-house."

Roosevelt had also built his election campaign on slogans about re-establishing the balance in federal finances.

Gradually, however, the Roosevelt administration more consciously initiated an economic policy meant to restore employment and production. But the effects were not as great or as rapid as had been expected. This was partly because the local and state authorities' reaction to the crisis was largely to cut down their expenditures step by step with the decline in incomes. This had an effect of the type which was analysed in section 3.2.4. In the circumstances this was difficult to avoid. The states were subject to budgetary conditions in a similar way to private entities in the economy: each one of them must ensure its own solvency.

Moreover, the law set strict limits to the amount the states might borrow; and even if such limits had not existed it would have been difficult, in the atmosphere of economic distrust then prevailing, for the local and state authorities to raise loans for purposes of regulating trade cycles.

The local and state expenditures on investment works fell from 2.5 thousand million dollars in 1930 to 0.6 thousand million dollars in 1935. These authorities also imposed new taxes during this period. It seems clear that this to a considerable extent counteracted the stimulative measures which the federal authorities had started.

The development up from the slump is illustrated by the following figures, which are a continuation of those given above:

	Index for industrial production	Number of unemployed
1933	64	12 744 000
1934	66	10 400 000
1935	76	9 522 000
1936	88	7 599 000
1937	92	6 372 000

Besides the fiscal policy which has been mentioned, an expansive monetary policy was also conducted in this period through market operations. The effects of these on employment and production depend, however, on the willingness of private enterprises to undertake investment, cf. the discussion in section 3.3.4. If there is no such willingness, an expansive monetary policy will only result in increasing liquidity in the private sector and not show up in real investment and production*.

---

* The inadequacy of monetary policy in the situation as it then was, is discussed by Ragnar Frisch in: *Statens plikt til sirkulasjonsregulering,* Memorandum of January 11th, 1951, from the Institute of Economics at the University of Oslo. (Originally written in December 1932.)

The figures above show that the depression was far from overcome in 1937. And in 1938 a new crisis set in as unemployment then rose again to over 10 million. However, this crisis was more quickly overcome than the one from 1929. To what extent this is connected with the international situation and the threats of war which had begun to make themselves felt, is a question to which it is not easy to give any definite answer.

3.4.2. *Britain in the 1930's*

Developments in Britain in the 1930's ran a much more moderate course than in the U.S.A. Industrial production fell from 100 in 1929 and touched bottom at 83.5 in 1932. From there it rose, and in 1935 topped 105, so that by then the level of production prior to the beginning of the crisis had been restored. The number of unemployed in 1929 reached almost 1 million. The summit was reached in 1932 with 2.25 million. From there unemployment fell gradually, and in 1937 was between 1.2 and 1.3 million.

The lesser severity of the crisis in Britain is connected with, *inter alia,* the development of external trade. On the 20th of September 1931 Britain gave up the gold parity for the pound which the British had re-established in 1925. This involved an actual devaluation of the pound which saved Britain from a strained external economy. She had a far more favourable development of exports and imports than those countries which continued to try to keep up gold redemption and the old parities.

Developments in Britain were further influenced by the fact that conditions were favourable for an expansion in building activity. A monetary policy aiming at low interest was conducted, and this had a considerably stimulating effect, especially on housing. Expressed in terms of the model (3.60) we can say that the conditions in Britain were such that the derivative of the function g had so great a numerical value that the monetary policy had a considerable effect on investment activity and thereby on production in general. An index for building activity in Britain shows the following development from 1929 to 1935:

1929	1930	1931	1932	1933	1934	1935
100.0	105.7	91.5	105.9	140.8	157.2	177.2

As regards fiscal policy, an approximate balance was kept throughout the period between revenue and expenditure. One may thus say that British recovery policy was pursued mainly by monetary means.

3.4.3. Germany in the 1930's

Germany was one of the countries hardest hit by the crisis. In March 1932 the number of unemployed had reached 6 million. The index for industrial production had fallen from 100 in 1929 to 53.3 in 1932.

After Hitler's usurpation of power in January 1933, Germany conducted a more expansive economic policy than any other big western country. Great public works were started, financed by the issue of new currency. (This issue took place in various camouflaged ways, so that it was not clear to the public what really happened.) Simultaneously, control of foreign currency was introduced, making possible an expansive policy at home with less worry about external trade. Price control and freezing of wages were also introduced. Then, gradually, re-armament was added as a powerful mainspring for economic expansion. The results of this policy showed in unemployment falling from its top level of 6 million to 2.7 million in 1934, 1.6 million in 1936, and 0.7 million in 1938. The index for industrial production rose, reaching 106 in 1936 and 126 in 1938.

3.4.4. Sweden in the 1930's

Sweden suffered a milder crisis than many other countries. In 1932 the industrial production index was down to 89 (taking 1929 as 100): thereafter production rose, and by 1937 the index had reached 149.

This is partly connected with the fact that monetary policy in Sweden was aimed at achieving low interest rates, and supplemented by considerable public works. From 1934 onwards, public works were especially extensive: a concern with the balance-of-payments situation having hindered their earlier expansion. The effects of the policies followed in Sweden have been much discussed; the question being whether the monetary and fiscal policy there adopted was responsible for the rise in production. Many think it was, but Professor Ohlin, among others, maintains that this was not the most important cause, and that the rise was due to exports, which in 1934 were already rising significantly. No attempt will be made to decide this question here.

An interesting point, as regards Sweden, is that in 1937 the Swedish parliament *(Riksdag)* expressly agreed that there should be no attempt to balance the state budget over a twelve-month period. It was explicitly declared that a surplus or deficit in the state budget for individual years would be accepted as a necessary consequence of a policy aimed at levelling out the trade cycles.

3.4.5.   *Norway in the 1930's*

Judged by production, the crisis took a relatively mild course in Norway. The following figures show the production index from 1929 to 1938:

1929	1930	1931	1932	1933	1934	1935	1936	1937	1938
100.0	101.0	78.4	92.8	93.8	97.9	107.8	118.3	129.7	129.2

Judged by unemployment, however, the development was less good. There has been some discussion of how great unemployment really was in Norway in the 1930's; a question which raises many problems, partly because not all the unemployed register themselves as seeking work, and partly because of statistical problems in Norway arising from combinations of employment in agriculture and/or forestry, fishing, and industry. The figures given here are the percentages of total trade union membership reported as unemployed:

1929	1930	1931	1932	1933	1934	1935	1936	1937	1938
15.4	16.6	22.3	30.8	33.4	30.7	25.3	18.8	20.0	22.0

That the development of production in Norway became as favourable as shown above was largely due to the currency policy. As noted above, Great Britain abandoned the gold standard in 1931 and devalued the pound. Norway followed suit immediately afterwards by abolishing the gold redemption duty; and, as to devaluation, went further than Britain. This gave Norwegian exporters favourable terms, and exports recovered rather quickly while imports declined.

The effect of the fiscal policy was rather to intensify the crisis. State accounts had not shown such low expenditure since the first years of the war of 1914–1918 as they did in the years from 1931–1932 till 1933–1934. The current accounts showed a surplus during all these years. From 1934 emergency grants for relief work were considerably enlarged, and new increases came with the Labour party government of 1935. These hardly had any significant multiplier effects as they were financed by the introduction of a general turnover tax.

That the development in employment was as shown above despite the relatively favourable development in production, is, *inter alia,* connected with trends in population. A considerable increase in population of employable age took place; and at the same time emigration, which had played a considerable part earlier, altogether ceased.

From the Norwegian figures, as from the figures for several other countries, it can be seen that a new crisis was developing in 1938. However, more or less from the influence of the international situation at the approach of war, this crisis turned quite quickly into a new recovery.

3.4.6.　Summing-up

An attempt to sum up the experiences of the depression of the 1930's involves a considerable difficulty. Experiences from earlier periods have shown that trade cycles always have turned "by themselves". One cannot, therefore, take it for granted that the recovery from 1932, 1933, 1934 – it varies for different countries – was caused by the economic policy which was followed. But if one compares the experiences of various countries as a "cross-section study", the policy adopted does appear to have been of importance.

Such a comparison between countries also illustrates one of the greatest difficulties in any policy aiming at regulating total effective demand through monetary and fiscal means. It concerns the difficulty discussed in connection with the open model (3.29) where it was seen that a policy stimulating economic activity almost automatically leads to an increase in imports. Among the European countries a significant difference arose, with respect to the course of the crisis, between those countries which "followed the pound" (and partly went further in devaluing), on the one hand, and those countries which held on to the old gold parities on the other. The first group of countries enjoyed a more favourable external trade and could therefore follow a more expansive economic policy: in that way, they got through the crisis more easily than the countries in the second group. Apart from this, states instituted varying degrees of control of their external trade by means of direct regulation. As mentioned above, Germany went furthest in this respect; and, as a result of achieving the most complete control of her external economy was able to follow the most expansive policy at home.

A comparison between countries further illustrates something else which has been pointed out, especially in section 3.3, namely that the efficiency of a policy may vary considerably according to prevailing conditions. As has been seen, building activity in Britain was sensitive to changes in the interest rate, and monetary policy could therefore work quite efficiently. In the U.S.A., on the other hand, this was not the case.

Experiences from all countries further show that considerable inertia prevailed in getting an expansive policy started. No country started an expansive policy immediately after the crisis had become a clearly established fact. This was partly connected with those difficulties of external trade which have already been mentioned. It was further connected with institutional conditions in individual countries. Lastly, it was also connected with the fact that the potentialities of monetary and fiscal policy in such situations were not always known or recognized by the authorities.

As regards the new crisis which began in 1938, it is difficult to say whether the rapid turn to recovery here justifies any evaluation of the effects of the economic policies of the time. As has been mentioned, recovery may have been due to the prevailing international situation.

3.5. Have the problems of unemployment lost their actuality? Some reflections on the post-war years

In Norway, unemployment has been considerably less during the post-war years than it was between the wars. For most of the years after World War II it has been so low that it is usually characterized as frictional and seasonal unemployment only. (One may, of course, make it one's goal to reduce or eliminate these forms of unemployment also.) The same applies

more or less to many other countries. Might one draw from this the conclusion that the problems of trade cycles and unemployment now have
lost their actuality? In that case, part of the material so far discussed
would be of mainly historical interest.

There are several reasons why this question cannot be answered in the
affirmative. Let us first see to what degree unemployment still exists
in individual countries. The following figures give average unemployment
for the years from 1948 in the U.S.A. (in thousands):

1948	1949	1950	1951	1952	1953	1954	1955
2064	3395	3142	1879	1673	1602	3230	2654
1956	1957	1958	1959	1960	1961	1962	1963
2551	2936	4681	3813	3931	4806	4135	4163

This table shows clearly that unemployment still plays a part in the
American economy. It appears there was a peak in unemployment in
1949–1950, then a peak in 1954, in 1958, and in 1961. There has thus been
a cyclical movement with periods of 3–5 years' duration. Production has
shown corresponding fluctuations. The production index for industry fell,
for instance, from 100 in 1953 to 94 in 1954; from 110 in 1957 to 102 in
1958. It also fell from 121 in the first quarter of 1960 to 113 in the first
quarter of 1961, but for the whole year 1961 it was nevertheless slightly
higher than in 1960 because the recession in 1960–1961 was of such a short
duration. (The production index had in 1963 reached 136.)

The western European countries have, by and large, had smaller trade
cycles than the U.S.A., but here, too, some countries have had considerable unemployment: for instance Italy, Belgium and Denmark. The
recession of 1958 in particular broke through in many western European
countries, although not as strongly as in the U.S.A. In a good many
countries unemployment rose; in some, production declined; in others, –
Norway among them – it kept constant; while in most of the remainder
production rose considerably more slowly than had generally been the
case in earlier post-war years.

The following are the unemployment figures for Norway from the year
1948 (in thousand workers, yearly average):

1948	1949	1950	1951	1952	1953	1954	1955
9.0	7.7	9.0	11.1	11.6	14.4	12.7	12.5

1956	1957	1958	1959	1960	1961	1962	1963
13.9	14.7	23.6	22.6	17.1	13.0	15.2	17.7

It will be seen that unemployment in 1958–1959 rose to a new level compared to the previous years. Fiscal policy played a special role in Norway in connection with the recession of 1958. From January 1957, the "pay-as-you-earn" system of taxation was introduced for a large proportion of personal incomes. It was foreseen that with the existing tax rates this would somewhat increase tax revenue, but in fact the increase was far larger than had been calculated*. There was also a greater surplus in state accounts than had been foreseen. As apparent from table 3, the withdrawal of liquidity by the state in 1958 was also considerable. So altogether, the policy had a more contractive effect than was planned, and this probably contributed to the recession in Norway becoming somewhat more extensive than in many other countries.

During 1958 some stimulative measures were employed, though rather cautiously, because of fears about the balance of payments. Funds from accounts frozen in the first years after the war were released; stimulus was given to municipal building of schools and hospitals, through exemption from sales tax on investment projects; the state banks had their lending quotas somewhat increased; and in the winter 1958–1959 an extra 138 million *kroner* were spent on public works. From the 1st of January 1959, there was also a reduction in state income tax. This relief was calculated to equal an amount of about 250 million *kroner*. Altogether, the policy in 1959 was more expansive than in 1958.

All in all, then, it must be concluded that unemployment and the phenomena of trade cycles are still current problems, especially in the U.S.A., but also in western Europe.

In evaluating the economic developments of the whole post-war period, it is worth bearing in mind the following factors:

---

* This situation illustrates what was said at the end of section 2.3 about the tax-rules and -rates being the real instruments, rather than tax revenue.

1. After the war there was a great need for reconstruction in many countries. This applied first and foremost, of course, to European countries. The U.S.A. had no real need for reconstruction, but there, too, a large part of the nation's industrial equipment had suffered abnormally heavy wear. This helped in keeping up the demand for investment during the early post-war years.

2. As regards demand for consumer goods, it is clear that by the end of the war private households had worn out their stocks of durable consumer goods, such as clothes, shoes, etc. At the same time, many households had built up quite large liquid holdings. This applied both to the U.S.A. and Europe and helped to keep up demand for consumer goods.

3. For several years after the war, most countries had quite strict direct regulation of various aspects of economic activity, among them investment works and external trade. These regulations have been more or less abolished in many countries; a fact which – one might expect – would gradually give the mechanism of trade cycles a freer course.

4. The trend of trade has been strongly influenced by international events. Perhaps of special importance was the Korean War, which came at a time when many people expected that the American economy was about to enter a quite serious crisis.

Altogether, it is thus easy to find reasons why trade cycles should not make themselves felt with "normal" strength immediately after the war. The factors mentioned should, however, point to a gradual "normalization" of trends as the years passed. It is a matter of judgement whether one should say this has been the case.

On the other hand there are reasons to expect the trade fluctuations to be less strong than they have been previously. This is mainly connected with the fact that the public sector in the economy has grown considerably since the years between the wars. Higher taxation, higher public expenditure, and a more extensive system of social insurance exist in many countries. This contributes towards an automatic stabilization such as was discussed in section 3.2. To what extent an active fiscal policy – such as was also discussed in section 3.2 – is likely to be used, is, of course, difficult to say. That depends very much on political factors. In several countries, either the authorities or powerful political groups officially dissociate themselves from the use of government expenditure and revenue as a means for regulating trade cycles, maintaining that such regulation is within the province of monetary policy and not that of state finance. But in general there is no doubt that views are different now from what they were between the wars. There is now hardly reason to expect anywhere the kind of destabilizing policy shown in section 3.2.4, which was not uncommon in the years between the wars; and many countries have shown that they are willing to employ an active fiscal policy at least to *some* extent.

Some may perhaps consider that the degree of unemployment seen in western European countries after the war is "nothing to worry about", and that one therefore might say that the problems of unemployment are not now current. However, it would be quite wrong to conclude from this that theoretical study of the problems of unemployment is unnecessary. There is hardly any doubt that the economic development which has taken place since the war has, at least to some extent, been influenced by the economic policy which has been pursued. Accordingly, one might say that the fact that there has not been such extensive unemployment after the war in most countries as there was before the war, is to some extent due to the economic policy followed. Then to conclude from this that it is now unnecessary to study the problem of unemployment, would be quite as wrong as to suppose that if we lived in a valley rescued from regular flooding by the construction of a dam, there would be no need to bother about the maintenance of the dam, or to think about floods any more, since we had not experienced flooding for some time.

As foreign trade has been freed, those problems which were discussed in connection with model (3.29) have become more pressing. On account of the effects on imports, several countries have refrained from pursuing such an expansive policy as they otherwise might have done. This applies not least to Britain, which has had periods of stagnation or of only very slow increase in production. In the recoveries from the last recessions in the U.S.A. it has been clear that a concern for the balance of payments, and with it a wish to prevent a flow of gold from the country, has caused the U.S.A. to pursue a less expansive policy than would have been done had only internal conditions been taken into account. The considerable unemployment which Denmark had for many post-war years was also to some extent connected with problems of foreign currency. As was mentioned above, Norwegian caution in 1958 was also partly motivated by the consideration of the balance of payments.

In addition, the problems since the war have been largely connected with movements in price levels. In several branches of manufacture, production has moved closer to the limits of capacity, and in most countries the price level has risen more or less rapidly. It has become a key question whether or not it is actually possible to combine full employment and the full use of capacity with a stable price level. This central problem is not only one of fiscal policy, and it will not here be discussed in all its aspects. However, some of its aspects will be dealt with in the following sections.

3.6. A model with variable price level

We shall now consider a model for a closed economy where the price level is explicitly included as a variable. It will then also be necessary to take more explicit account of the structure of production and the behaviour of the producers than has been done earlier.

In the model we shall assume that the public authorities have three instruments of policy: the public expenditures on goods and services, a tax rate for direct taxation, and a tax rate for sales taxation.

We now let symbols with a bar above them represent real quantities, i.e. quantities calculated as values according to a set of constant prices, similarly to what was done in section 3.1.3. Further, we introduce the symbol N for employment, P for the market price level, and w for the wage level. We are here considering a short-term model and assume that the national product reckoned as a real quantity is a function of employment only:

$$\bar{R} = \varphi(N). \tag{3.61}$$

This production is sold in the market at the price P, i.e. its market value is $P\bar{R}$.

The revenue for the producers after the sales tax is paid, will be $P\bar{R}(1-\theta)$, where θ now is the rate for the sales tax reckoned as part of buyer's price. For the present purpose it is simplest to express the tax in this way, but we could also have reckoned the tax rate as part of the price exclusive of tax*.

Expenditure on wages in the production will be wN. The producers' profit will thus be

$$\pi = P\bar{R}(1-\theta) - wN. \tag{3.62}$$

We further assume that the producers maximize their profits, regarding the price level, the wage rate and the tax rate as given. This gives the following condition:

$$P(1-\theta)\varphi'(N) = w. \tag{3.63}$$

Here $\varphi'(N)$ is the marginal productivity of labour, i.e., the derivative of the production function (3.61).

Let us next consider the demand for consumer goods. We must then take as a starting point the disposable incomes of consumers. These are made up of the profit π and the wage sum wN; to be deducted is the amount for the direct tax T^{dir}. The disposable incomes are thus

$$R_p^* = \pi + wN - T^{\text{dir}}. \tag{3.64}$$

From (3.62) it will be seen that $\pi+wN=P\bar{R}(1-\theta)$. If we insert this into (3.64) we get

---

* The tax yield calculated by means of the rate θ will be $P\bar{R}\theta$. Let us next calculate the tax yield by means of a tax rate τ which is applied on the value exclusive of the sales tax. The tax yield expressed in this way must be $P\bar{R}(1-\theta)\tau$. If we now make the two expressions for the tax yield equal, we get the following connection between the rates θ and τ:

$$\tau = \frac{\theta}{1-\theta} \quad \text{or} \quad \theta = \frac{\tau}{1+\tau} \quad \text{or} \quad \frac{1}{1-\theta} = 1 + \tau.$$

$$R_p^* = P\bar{R}(1 - \theta) - T^{\text{dir}}.$$

For the sake of simplicity we shall in this model reckon with a proportional income tax with the rate t. We then get

$$T^{\text{dir}} = t(\pi + wN) = tP\bar{R}(1 - \theta). \tag{3.65}$$

If we further insert this into the expression for R_p^* we get

$$R_p^* = P\bar{R}(1 - \theta)(1 - t). \tag{3.66}$$

We now assume that the demand for consumer goods depends linearly on the disposable real income. This we get by dividing R_p^* by the price level P. We then get the following consumption function:

$$\bar{C}_p = a\bar{R}(1 - \theta)(1 - t) + b. \tag{3.67}$$

As in some of the earlier models, we shall assume that private real investments are exogenously determined. The same assumption is made about the wage rate. These assumptions, together with the equations (3.61), (3.63), (3.67) and the national accounting equation (3.24), and with θ, t and $\bar{G}$ as policy instruments, give us a determinate model. For the sake of convenience the equations are collected below:

(a) $$\bar{R} = \varphi(N)$$
(b) $$P(1 - \theta)\varphi'(N) = w$$
(c) $$\bar{C}_p = a\bar{R}(1 - \theta)(1 - t) + b \tag{3.68}$$
(d) $$\bar{R} = \bar{C}_p + \bar{I}_p + \bar{G}$$
(e) $\bar{I}_p$ and w exogenously determined.

This system has the special property that one can solve equations (c) and (d) with respect to $\bar{R}$ and $\bar{C}_p$. The solution for the national product will be

$$\bar{R} = \frac{\bar{I}_p + \bar{G} + b}{1 - a(1 - \theta)(1 - t)}. \tag{3.69}$$

When $\bar{R}$ has been found, we get the employment N from the first equation in (3.68), and next get the solution for the price level P from equation (b) in (3.68), w being exogenously determined and the marginal productivity $\varphi'(N)$ being given when we have determined the employment N. If we are interested in the balance for the public sector, it can be obtained in the following way:

$$\text{Public budgetary surplus} = P\bar{R}\theta + P\bar{R}(1-\theta)t - P\bar{G}$$
$$= P\bar{R}(\theta + t - \theta t) - P\bar{G}. \tag{3.70}$$

Let us consider how each of the instruments of the public sector works in this model.

We see at once that an increased $\bar{G}$ with constant θ and t gives an increased national product in a similar way as was seen in the earlier multiplier models. However, the value of the multiplier is reduced through the existence of the two types of taxes with constant rates. The increase in the national product leads to increased employment through the production function. Increased employment usually implies a decline in marginal productivity. From equation (b) in (3.68) we then see that the price level P must rise, as we have presupposed that the wage level w is exogenously determined.

Let us next look at the effect of an increase in the tax rate t. From (3.69) it follows that such an increase will result in a reduced national product. From equation (a) in (3.68) it consequently follows that employment is reduced. With constant w and constant θ it further follows from equation (b) that the market price level also falls. In the corresponding way, a reduction in t will result in increased national product, increased employment and a higher price level.

Let us next look at the effects of an increase in the rate for the sales tax θ. From (3.69) we find that an increase in the sales tax leads to a reduced real national product. Further it follows from (a) that employment declines. Thus, the line of reasoning so far is wholly analogous to that concerning the effect of an increase in the income tax rate t. However, it will be a different matter when we are dealing with the effect on the price level, by means of equation (b) in (3.68). A decline in N results in the marginal productivity φ' going up: but on the other hand the value of $(1-\theta)$ declines. We cannot, then, immediately say in which direction the expression $(1-\theta)\,\varphi'(N)$ will change. If, overall, this expression rises, the price level P will decline, while if it falls in value, P will go up. Which of the two cases will arise, depends on how steeply the curve of marginal productivity will fall in the range in question. In either case, it remains clear, however, that if we compare changes in t and in θ giving the same reduction in employment, it is increases in θ that will prove to lead to the highest price level. For it follows immediately from equation (b) in (3.68) that the higher the value of θ for a given value of N and with constant w, the higher will be the price level.

In the special case where – roughly speaking – the marginal productivity φ' is approximately constant, independent of employment, the model we have now considered will assume the same character as the model used in section 3.1.3. The price level would then be unchanged by variations in the income tax t. By variations in the sales tax θ we would produce such reactions in the price level as would keep the product $P(1-\theta)$ unchanged. The magnitude $w/\varphi'(N)$ is the same as the marginal costs in the production. Thus we would have

$$P = \frac{\text{const.}}{1-\theta} = (\text{const.})(1+\tau), \qquad (3.71)$$

where τ is the sales tax rate as a proportion of the price exclusive of tax, and where "const." indicates the constant marginal cost. One may have approximately such a case when there is considerable unused production capacity.

Irrespective of whether one has this limiting case or the more general case, the government will have three instruments in this model, i.e., G, θ and t. It is, then, possible to set up three targets. It would be natural to let G correspond directly to a target for collective consumption. The combination of θ and t can then be chosen in such a way as to obtain the levels for the national product (or employment) and for the prices which have been aimed at. Suppose, for instance, that one wishes to obtain a certain reduction in the price level while keeping constant employment. It can be seen from equation (b) in (3.68) that to obtain this the sales tax rate θ must be reduced. If nothing more was done, however, demand for labour would increase. To keep demand unchanged, we would have to increase the rate of the direct taxation t, enough to keep the product $(1-\theta)(1-t)$ unchanged. Thus, the intervention would as a whole consist in reducing the sales tax and increasing the direct taxation.

The model used here is almost the simplest imaginable where the price level is explicitly brought in. It is in many ways unsatisfactory; for instance, because the capacity limit is not yet taken account of as explicitly as is desirable. True, we might say that the capacity limit is represented through the production function being included, and that we may have a steeply falling marginal productivity of labour when approaching what is called the capacity limit. But we have not formally included anything which prevents the volume of demand from exceeding this limit, cf. (3.69). To include this we would somehow have to bring in an element which would cause demand to decrease when the price level rises. We might obtain such an element if we said, for instance, that it was the value, and not the real magnitude, of the private investment which was exogenously determined. Some similar notion may be applicable to some part of the public expenses. We might further bring in the effects of the distribution of income in the demand for consumer goods. When the price level rises while the wage rate is kept unchanged and employment increases only a little, a redistribution of real incomes in favour of profits will take place. It is reasonable to assume that the propensity to consume is lower for this type of income than for wage incomes. Thus in this way one would get a situation where an increase in the price level would, via income redistribution, lead to reduced demand for consumer goods.

Such factors as have been mentioned here might be explicitly brought into the static model. There are many variants to choose between here, so it would be a somewhat arbitrary choice to work out only one of them in more detail. It is, however, doubtful whether what happens when one operates in the vicinity of the capacity limit can be satisfactorily analysed within a static model. Later we shall return to some questions requiring dynamic analyses, though without really carrying out such analyses.

The model used here may be considered a simplified version of a model put forward by Bent Hansen in his book *The economic theory of fiscal policy* (London, 1958, see especially Chapter XIII). Bent Hansen here operates with two production sectors, one for consumer goods and one for investment goods. He further distinguishes between sales tax or production excises on means of production (produced in the investment goods sector), and on consumer goods. An investment demand function is also included in the model, in which investment is supposed to depend on the level of interest, the level of prices for investment goods, and the demand for consumer goods. Because the state here has separate taxes for consumer goods and investment goods, and because the demand for investment goods depends on the price level for these goods, it becomes possible for the state to set up a target also for the distribution of production between pro- duction of consumer goods and production of investment goods. The target for the price level is supposed to concern the price level for con- sumer goods.

3.7. Some reflections on the possibility of keeping the price level stable during full employment

The model treated in the previous section was static, and could therfore illustrate only those problems which have to do with the *height* of the price level. However, the central problem of the post-war years cannot be said to be that the price level has been *high*: the problem has been that the level has been constantly *rising*.

Let us for an illustration give the development of the Norwegian index for the cost of living from 1949 onwards.

1949	1950	1951	1952	1953	1954	1955	1956
100	105	122	133	135	141	143	148

1957	1958	1959	1960	1961	1962	1963
152	159	163	163	168	177	181

Some part of this increase may doubtless be attributed to the influence, through imports, of the development of prices in the world market. During the years of the Korean War especially, a considerable price increase occurred in the world market, and this also had repercussions in

Norway*. However, prices have also risen in periods when foreign influences cannot be said to have been responsible. In such a case, assuming
that one was attempting to explain *all* price developments as a result of
foreign influence, one would have to say that influences from abroad
generate impulses which cause a continuous rise in home prices over a
somewhat longer period.

Naturally, it is a difficult statistical problem to sort out the part of the
rise in prices which may be due to foreign influence, and that part which
we may say is generated at home.

To take an example where foreign influence plays a lesser part, let us
consider price developments in the U.S.A. One has there the following
figures:

1949	1950	1951	1952	1953	1954	1955	1956
100	101	109	111	112	112	112	115

1957	1958	1959	1960	1961	1962	1963
118	121	122	125	126	137	143

(The index really has its base in 1953, but has here been converted so that it
equals 100 in 1949, as for the Norwegian figures above.) It will here be
seen that the rise in prices has been quite steady, although of a lesser
extent than in Norway. The rise has slackened in those years when
there has been increased unemployment. Really full employment has not
existed in any year in the U.S.A., apart from the years during the war.
These are less interesting in this connection, as many forms of direct
regulation of the economy were in use during the war.

One may also attempt to make a comparison between countries for a
given period after the war. By and large it will be found that the price
level has risen more rapidly in countries with very high or full employment, and somewhat more slowly in countries with higher unemployment.
One cannot, of course, from this immediately draw any conclusion about

---

* This in addition to the effect of the devaluation in September 1949.

a conflict between the targets of full employment and of a stable price level, because so many factors other than the degree of employment or unemployment also vary from one country to another. Besides, there are exceptions to this relationship.

Even though the experiences from the post-war period cannot alone give any absolute answer to the question about a conflict between the targets of full employment and a stable price level, they do, at least, give good grounds for *asking the question* whether such a conflict exists. Let us, therefore, consider in more detail the various conditions which may create such a conflict, and let us simultaneously see whether fiscal policy can in any way be used to lessen or eliminate this possible conflict.

3.7.1.   *Conditions on the labour market. The "wage-price spirals"*

In our static model in the previous section, the wage rate was assumed to be constant. However, some of the most important problems pertaining to the question of stability of prices during full employment are connected with conditions on the labour market and the determination of wage levels. For employers as well as for trade unions, the situation during full employment will seem different from when there is a certain amount of unemployment: or at least it will do so *if they count on a policy which will also maintain full employment in the future.* Under such conditions the trade unions will not reckon with any difficulties in employment resulting from increased wages. This may influence the demands put forward in wage negotiations.

On the other hand the employers know, firstly, that demand for goods and services will be kept at a high level which will offer a good chance of covering any increase in costs by an increase in prices: something less easy to do in a situation of low demand. Secondly, they know that it would not be easy to find new workers, should they fail to keep the ones they already have.

These circumstances may contribute to the rise in wages (partly in the form of agreements, partly through "wage-drift") being, by and large, more rapid under conditions with full employment than under conditions with unemployment. An econometric investigation for England by Professor Phillips is of interest in this connection. He claims to have found a quite stable relationship between the percentage of unemployment and wage increase per year over the whole of the period from 1861 to 1913, and he considers this correspondence to fit later periods as well, with the exception of the war years *.

A special mechanism will be in operation if the wage rates, either through agreement or through custom, are bound up with the price level in such a way that the workers automatically get compensation in the form of a wage increase when prices rise. Then one might get a so-called "wage-price spiral" where both prices and wages rise. Such a spiral needs an initial price- or wage rise to get started. The impetus for such a development may, for instance, come as follows: taking a starting-point in the model we had in the previous section, we assume that employment is below the desired level. Then, either a relief is granted in income taxation, or the public sector increases its expenditures on the purchase of goods and services, with a resultant increase in employment and production. As has already been seen, this can only take place with increased prices if the marginal productivity curve is falling and the wage rate is kept constant. Thus, as a first step, we imagine that both production and employment rise, and that the price level rises accordingly, as the model in the previous section suggests it will. If now the wage rate is bound up with the price level, (and with this we leave the assumptions of the static model in the previous section) the wages will rise in the second round. This, again, pushes up the marginal cost curve, and if the producers are to be willing to continue producing the quantity equivalent to the new level for employment, the price must rise accordingly, and so on. In this way prices and wages can continue to rise.

Such a process may either continue unlimitedly, or may gradually cease, so that the price level does not rise above a certain point. Three things may cause prices to converge on such a final level, instead of rising indefinitely: (a) It is possible that not all groups partaking in production may get full compensation for the price rise, and for this reason there will be some elements in the production costs which do not follow the upward development. (b) In an open economy it may be that the prices of imported goods are constant on the world market and that these therefore enter the country at constant prices. These goods are to be accounted for partly under cost of production and partly under cost of living, and they

---

* A. W. Phillips, The relation between unemployment and the rate of change of money wage rates in the United Kingdom 1861–1957, *Economica,* November 1958.

will then constitute an element which does not follow the upward spiral.
(c) It may be that the compensation agreements are such that full compensation is not given every time prices rise*.

The question now arises whether fiscal policy can be used in any way
that will prevent such a wage-price spiral.

The state could stop such a spiral by a restrictive policy which drives
down employment, and, through it, the marginal costs. However, the
point of the problem as presented here is that this will not be done. The
state must make provision for a demand level that is always high enough
to keep employment on the high level it has already reached. There seems
to be only one way, then, to intervene by the help of fiscal policy. The
intervention must at some stage prevent increased costs from resulting
in increased prices. That can be achieved, firstly, by increasing subsidies
or reducing sales tax, and secondly, by an increase in direct taxes which
will neutralize the effects on total demand of the increased subsidies or
the reduced sales tax. If we have a model like (3.68) with an added
equation expressing the determining of wages, we would need an intervention where θ is reduced and t increased in such a way as to keep the
expression $(1-\theta)(1-t)$ unchanged. (Subsidies can here be considered
as negative sales tax.)

3.7.2.   *Excess demand as a "pull" for production growth*

With positive net investments the rate of production achievable at any
given level of employment will constantly rise. This means that, to
maintain that level of employment, one must have a continuous rise in
production. Suppose that the producers have a tendency always to plan
for the same quantity to be produced in the next period as in the present
period, unless they know that demand surplus prevails. To keep full
employment under such conditions the state must see to it that such a
demand always exists. Since an excessive demand may easily pull the
price level upwards, we shall thus be in the situation that a rise in production must necessarily be accompanied by a rise in prices.

It will not here be possible to use income taxes as a means to check

---

* A further analysis of the conditions for a "convergence" of the wage-price spiral
can be found in Ragnar Frisch: *Notat om pris-lønns-spiralen,* Memorandum of November 13th, 1956 from the Institute of Economics at the University of Oslo.

the rise in prices, since if we increased income taxes in order to restrain the excess demand, we would simultaneously restrain the rise in production and thereby get unemployment. For a short period, one might employ a policy similar to that mentioned in the previous section, namely a reduction of sales tax with corresponding changes in income taxes to keep total demand on a given level; but since the problem here is not one of stopping a process with a once-and-for-all intervention, but of something which must take place continually, it is obvious that this is not a policy which can solve the problem over a longer period.

The only thing which may help if the producers behave in this way, is a progress in techniques which tends to cause a continuous decline in production costs.

On the other hand, it will naturally change the problem if the producers are so used to increases in production that they always plan for this, even if supply and demand are equal at the moment and stocks are of the desired size. This latter may, of course, very easily be the case. It is not here intended to claim that the circumstances pointed out in this section necessarily create a conflict between the targets of full employment and a stable price level. The intention has been merely to draw attention to a mechanism which *may* have an effect in certain periods. It can, for instance, be of importance in an economy which for a long time has been almost stagnant, because the producers may then have acquired a behaviour pattern like the one described in the introduction to this section.

3.7.3. *The dependence of demand on price expectations*

We have earlier assumed that the demand for consumer goods depends only on the disposable real income. As for the demand for investment goods, we have either assumed that it is exogenously determined, or that it depends on the level of interest, or on the profit of business concerns and the availability of credit. Let us now assume that demand also depends on the rate of change of prices. For total demand, which includes both demand for consumer goods and for investment goods, we might then, for instance, write:

$$X^D = a\left(\frac{R_p^*}{P}\right) + b\frac{\dot{P}}{P} + c \qquad (3.72)$$

where R_p^*/P is disposable real income and $\dot{P} = dP/dt$, i.e., the derivative of the price level with respect to time. Both for the demand for consumer goods and for investment goods it is natural to assume that a rapid increase in prices contributes to high demand. From the consumers' point of view, rapid price increase makes it profitable to buy now instead of postponing purchase to the future. As for investments, it is clear that expectations of rising prices contribute to prospects of great profit, and these expectations simultaneously make it less risky to incur debt in order to finance investment. On the basis of such considerations we may assume $b > 0$ in (3.72).

It is obvious that when the demand X^D is large, this in itself is a factor contributing to the rise in prices. Now suppose that we wanted to try to increase taxation in order to reduce the disposable income R_p^* and thus, through it, the total demand. If this succeeds there will be a fall in $\dot{P}$, i.e. a slower rise in prices than before: the rise might even cease altogether. But thereby one gets a reduction in total demand, through the term $b\dot{P}/P$ in (3.72), which goes beyond the effect of the increase in taxation through disposable private income. This effect may be difficult to foresee; in any case it may be difficult to foresee how important it will be. If the effect is great, demand may easily fall below what is necessary to the maintenance of full employment. For this reason it may be "dangerous" to intervene with increased taxation in order to reduce demand in a situation with rising prices.

This factor is probably of greatest importance where the demand for investment is concerned. However, it may also be important to larger groups of buyers. It may be mentioned that American journals carry big advertisements with headlines such as, for instance: "How you can get inflation working for *you*." These advertisements are inserted by special firms which, either through personal contact, or through brochures and in various other ways, offer guidance to people about how they must dispose their money in order to earn, or at any rate, not lose, on the inflation. Naturally, the guidance consists of recommendations to buy real values of different kinds instead of engaging in ordinary saving in monetary terms. To the extent that such recommendations are followed, the effect here expressed through the term $b\dot{P}/P$, will be in operation.

3.7.4.   Limited mobility

We have so far discussed the problem as though we had only one production sector. Actually, the economy consists, of course, of many different production sectors. Between these, there will in practice be only a limited mobility of production factors. This applies first and foremost to labour.

A process of growth will require a continuous redistribution of labour between the production sectors. This is due to various circumstances, *inter alia* changing composition of the consumers' demand, changes in production methods, changes in the composition of foreign trade, etc.

Suppose that we have two industrial branches A and B. Suppose that we first have a balance between the production factors associated with branch A and branch B on the one side, and the demand for products from branch A and branch B respectively, on the other side. Then a shift takes place in demand for reasons such as have just been mentioned. This shift reduces demand for products from sector A and increases demand in sector B. If things were "left to themselves", a fall in prices would then occur on products from branch A with a reduction in production and employment in that branch. Thus, a certain temporary unemployment would arise. On the other hand we would get increased prices on products from sector B; and this sector would try to attract labour in order to increase production. Since mobility is limited, there will, however, be unemployment, at least for a certain period, among the workers associated with sector A, while at the same time there will be shortage of labour in sector B.

This might perhaps be accepted as "frictional unemployment", and one might leave things to run their own course during the time necessary for labour to move over. But suppose that the unemployment which has arisen in sector A is not accepted. In that case, one might try to intervene by stimulating the total demand level, for instance by giving general tax reliefs. In this way, one might manage to increase demand for the products of sector A so much that the labour in this sector will continue to be employed to the same extent as before. Then, having neither an excessive demand nor a deficient one in this sector, the prices of the products of sector A may remain constant. If we next look at what happens in sector B it is clear that we now get a large excess of demand there. In the first place, we already had an excess of demand in this sector as a result of the shift in the composition of demand, while in the second place we now have a still further increase in demand there which is due to the tax relief. Since the production here cannot immediately be increased because of a lack of labour, it is probable that we shall get a rise in prices for the products of this sector. If we consider the average price level, that, too, will of course rise.

Besides the rise in the price level, an objection against such a policy is that labour will not be transferred between the production sectors as it should do in order to correspond to the shifting composition of demand. We shall under this policy get a transfer of labour from sector A to sector B only to the extent that sector B can *attract* labour by offering better conditions, either through wages or in other ways. Such a process may require a long time.

On the other hand it is also possible that full employment may give greater mobility than one would have with a certain amount of unemployment. Conditions will actually be far less transparent than the illustrative discussion here suggests, simply because there are many production sectors and many firms in each sector. For the individual worker it will seem far less risky to leave a production sector or a trade if he knows that there is full employment and perhaps shortage of labour at various points in the economy, than if he knows that there is unemployment.

The type of inflation illustrated here is described in American literature as "demand-shift inflation". It may be said to be caused by regulation of the general level of demand for goods and services in order to try to keep full employment even in those branches where there is really excess capacity and too large a labour force, relative to other branches. Should one try to regulate demand in such a way as to avoid situations with unemployment in some branches and a simultaneous excess of demand in other branches, more selective means would be required than a regulation of the general level of demand merely through a regulation of the general level of taxation. The employment of special subsidies and production excises would be necessary. All possible measures which facilitate and stimulate the movement of labour will of course help to reduce the problem of "demand-shift inflation".

3.7.5.   Concluding remarks

Not all the factors considered above will be in operation continually. But is is probable that if one tries to utilise fiscal policy to maintain very high or full employment, one will usually come up against one or more of them.

There are also, of course, certain circumstances which will counteract the tendencies described in the subsections above. Firstly, there is the possibility of continuous improvements in productivity through rationalization and improved technical knowledge. This is something which may apply continually and in all countries. It may also be possible for some countries over certain periods to have their problems of prices eased through a fall in prices of raw materials which they import for use in their own production.

Nevertheless, very many economists who have studied the problem of full employment and a stable price level, now seem to have reached the conclusion that a conflict between these targets really exists. On the one side, studies have been made of the developments over long periods. Of these, only a work by Paul Samuelson and Robert M. Solow will be mentioned here*. On the basis of statistical investigations, they present a "menu" for different degrees of unemployment and price stability for the American economy. This "menu" contains such possibilities as, for instance, 2% rise in prices per year and 4% unemployment, 4–5% rise in prices per year and 3% unemployment, etc. Complete stability of prices would only obtain at 5–6% unemployment.

Others put great emphasis on the experiences of the economic setback in 1958–1959 in the U.S.A. and Western Europe. This setback came partly as a result of a restrictive fiscal policy which aimed at curbing demand and thereby the rise in prices. The rate of the rise was checked to a certain extent, and in some countries price stability was, perhaps, attained. However, this policy led to an intensification of unemployment and a lowering of the rate of increase of production, and in some countries even to a fall in production, as mentioned above. Thus, it appears difficult to meet the problems discussed in this section by means of a fiscal policy which regulates only the general level of demand.

---

* Paul A. Samuelson and Robert M. Solow, Analytical aspects of anti-inflation policy, *The American Economic Review, Papers and Proceedings* (May 1960).

As has been pointed out, the possibilities are greater if one can follow a more selective policy. In this connection some writers have put forward suggestions about quite novel ways of framing taxation. The point of these suggestions is usually in some way or other to tie taxation of the individual firm to the increase in the price of the firm's products, from the previous period to the period for which the tax is levied, in such a way that increased profits through higher product prices are treated less favourably than increased profits through increased production*.

It should also be made clear that this discussion has been concerned only with the question of a possible conflict between the targets of full employment and price stability when the instruments used in economic policy are mainly of a monetary and fiscal nature. We have not dealt with the possibility of avoiding this conflict if different forms of more direct intervention in the economy are employed.

---

* See, for instance, M. F. G. Scott, A tax on price increase, *The Economic Journal* (June 1961).

The public debt

In this chapter we shall consider mainly the debt of the central government, which is usually referred to as the "national debt". We shall follow this usage, although the terms "government debt" or "state debt" might have been preferable in order to distinguish it clearly from the total private and public debt of a country to foreign countries.

Some of our considerations, however, also apply to other public debt than the debt of the central government. We shall in such connections use the general term "public debt".

4.1. Why the state raises loans

The question of why the state raises loans must be answered somewhat differently in the case of loans raised abroad from that of loans raised in the private sector at home.

The state may raise a foreign loan in order to finance a surplus of imports, cf. the discussion in the sub-section on active fiscal policy in section 3.2. This surplus may be planned, for instance, with aims of expansion in mind. It may also be that the import surplus is unintentional, and that a loan must be raised to prevent the surplus becoming too heavy a drain on the currency reserves.

For internal loans, other conditions prevail. It has earlier been said that the purpose of taxation is to counteract the expansive effects of public expenditure to the extent this is desirable. Something similar might be said about internal borrowing by the state. As has been seen earlier, the fact that the state raises loans has a contractive effect, except in special cases. In choosing whether to obtain a certain contractive effect through taxation or through borrowing, the state must decide this from, *inter alia,* a consideration of those effects of fiscal policy which were discussed in Chapter 3. It was there seen, especially in section 3.3, that taxes and loans respectively have different effects on consumption and investment. While taxes in the first instance have the effect of reducing private consumption, state borrowing has an effect of reducing investments, either through a reduction in the money supply and in lending by the banks, or through raising the level of interest. It will therefore be, *inter alia,* a balance between private consumption and private investment which must decide whether to raise loans or levy taxes. If the state wishes, for instance, to expand its own investment at the expense of private investment, borrowing will probably be a more effective means than an increase in taxation. Should the state wish to increase its expenditure at the expense of private consumption, an increase in taxation will be more appropriate.

However, it is not necessarily just *preferences* about the distribution of private expenditure between consumption and investment which are decisive. There is also production capacity to be considered, since production equipment is to some extent "rigid", so that enterprises adapted to the production of investment goods cannot immediately shift to the production of consumer goods, or vice versa. If therefore the state wishes to increase its investment in the short run it must release capacity in the investment branch, and this can be done only through measures limiting private investment. Here then, borrowing may be the more appropriate means.

From such considerations one can see that there might be a certain accord between borrowing and public investment. One has something more or less equivalent to the "old-fashioned" view that the state should finance current expenses with taxes, while loans should be used only to finance investments (and only such investments as might be expected to be "profitable"). This traditional doctrine was previously grounded on the consideration of the "financial soundness" of the state. We now find that a similar conclusion can be drawn from economic considerations in more real terms.

This doctrine, however, has in no sense any absolute validity. The industrial capacity situation may not necessarily subject the policy to such absolute restrictions as were mentioned above, and it may well be that the state may wish to increase its investment at the expense of private consumption rather than at the expense of private investment. Furthermore, there are special forms of intervention through taxes which affect invest-

ment almost directly, so that it is unnecessary to use borrowing to influence private investment. An example of this was discussed in section
3.3.1. We shall return to other taxation measures which influence private
investment in Chapter 7.

In addition to such considerations as have so far been pointed out,
there are also considerations of a more political nature to be borne in mind.
These relate to the question of whether or not the state ought to increase
its assets in the long run. This question will not be further treated here.

4.2. Different types of national debt

The national debt can be subdivided in many different ways. We shall here
look at some of the most important distinctions.

4.2.1. Administrative debt and financial debt

For technical reasons, a certain amount of debt to the private sector
must arise almost automatically because of the current transactions of the
state, without the borrowing here being planned or intended in any way.
This debt is called administrative debt. It is to some extent offset by
corresponding claims.

Debt incurred by the state not directly connected with its current
administrative transactions, is called financial debt. This is often considered as the national debt proper. In Norway, such debt can be contracted by the Government only after it has been authorized by the
national assembly, according to § 75 of the Constitution.

4.2.2. Internal and external debt

This distinction has already been mentioned. Obviously, it is of great
importance. The most essential difference between internal and external
public borrowing can be briefly characterized by saying that while external
loans increase the supply of resources because they make an import

surplus possible, internal loans create room for the public disposition of a
country's resources by limiting internal private dispositions. The choice
between internal and external borrowing must be made on this basis.
This essential difference does not come out clearly in older text-books.
Oskar Jæger says, for instance, in his *Finanslære* (Oslo, 1930): "Whether
it is more desirable to raise loans at home or abroad, may usually be
decided in each individual case according to the terms ... Where no considerations other than purely financial ones make themselves felt, one can
therefore lay down the rule that it is best for a country to raise its public
loans in that market where they are cheapest."

4.2.3. Floating and funded debt

This distinction concerns the duration of the loans. Floating public debt
consists of various sorts of short-term loans, i.e., loans which are meant
to be of a transitory nature and which can be terminated either immediately or at very short notice. The funded national debt, on the other hand,
is contracted for a long, or perhaps even indefinite, period.

The distinction between floating and funded debt is, of course, not a
sharp one. Through funding, floating debt can be changed to funded debt.
This usually takes the form of the state raising long-term loans in order
to meet short-term debt.

When choosing between short-term and long-term debt, the question
of the terms will be of considerable importance. In some text-books a rule
is laid down that the state should choose that way of contracting the debt
which, with the least possible interest burden for the state, leads to a given
reduction in the liquidity of the private sector. This rule does not, however, give any clear guidance, and must be supplemented by other considerations. There might, for instance, be a question as to what kind of
investments in the private sector the state wishes to limit. Since the
different kinds of private investments depend on different kinds of credit,
the state can to some extent influence the composition of private investment through adjusting its borrowing in certain ways. The state also
raises loans which have purely monetary-technical purposes, for instance
to help to level out seasonal variations in the liquidity of the private
banking system. Such guiding rules as the one quoted above do not, of
course, apply when these goals are being sought.

4.2.4. *Other distinctions*

The more technical aspects of government borrowing will not be treated here; but a few additional distinctions may be briefly mentioned.

The loans may differ according to the way in which they are going to be redeemed. Any dictionary of economic terms will explain a great number of different types.

The loans can further be distinguished according to the degree of transferability of the claims. Government bonds may be either quite freely transferable; or they may be freely transferable only in the country of issue; or it may have been decided that they can be held, for instance, only by banks; or else they may be completely non-transferable. Through such restrictions government borrowing may be made into a more selective instrument of policy than would otherwise be the case.

One may also make distinctions according to whether or not the state has conversion rights. This right applies especially when the level of interest in the credit market is sinking. Conversion consists in the state exchanging existing debt for new debt on better conditions from the state's point of view. Conversion right usually applies only after a certain period has elapsed since the issue, and on certain conditions.

4.3. *The effects of internal national debt*

In discussing the effects of national debt, it is important to distinguish clearly between the effects of the *raising of the loan* and the effects of the *existence* of the debt.

The effects of the raising of the loan have already been discussed in previous sections, especially in section 3.3. The effects of the existence of national debt will now be furthered considered. This is an issue which is quite extensively discussed in the literature of financial theory, and which may be of great importance when the level of national debt is very high.

4.3.1. *Effects on demand*

It is customary to assume that the greater the wealth of a private person, the higher will be his demand for consumer goods at a given level of income. For the individual private person, his claims on other people or institutions will be included in his wealth. Altogether however, claims within the private sector will not influence the level of demand in this way because a claim there will always be offset by liability.

In the case of public debt, conditions are different. Private persons here have claims which are reckoned as part of their assets, and this may stimulate their demand. The corresponding debit items, however, are entered only with the state, and the state cannot be supposed to react on the existence of the debt in a way similar to that of a private person.

Altogether we may say that such debt makes the private sector "feel richer" and thereby keep up a higher demand than it would have done without this public debt.

The existence of public debt may also have the effect of *stabilizing* the level of demand. Since the private sector has funds to its credit, it may prefer to let fluctuations in income show up less in the demand for goods and services than it otherwise might have done. Because public debt leads to interest payments to the private sector, one also gets a relatively stable element in the incomes of the private sector. This may also have a stabilizing effect, although it is hardly a very important factor.

On the other hand the existence of public debt may have a destabilizing effect in situations where people's expectations about the future may change radically. A shift in expectations may result in a sudden decision to spend. This may lead to abrupt changes in the demand for consumer goods, changes which would not have taken place if the private sector had been more restricted to keep within the budgetary limits set by current incomes.

4.3.2. *Effects on the behaviour of the state*

It is sometimes maintained that the existence of a large national debt makes the state "inflationary". This may happen, because the existence of such debt makes the state interested in keeping down the level of interest, since high interest on a large public debt will lead to great expense for the state. Naturally, this is not a *necessary* effect of national debt, but it is certainly a factor which one may expect the state to consider. Neither is there anything irrational in this. The state cannot, of course, increase taxation indefinitely. Increased interest payments cannot, therefore, always be matched by an increase in taxation in order to maintain other public expenditures. A high level of interest which gradually results in high interest payments for the state, will therefore be a hindrance to the performance of the various tasks of the state.

One might, of course, go further and say that the state will not only consider the cost of interest payments, but that it might simply wish for inflation in order to reduce the real value of its debt. Whether such considerations have been consciously at work in any country, is not easy to say. But there is no doubt that many countries have had their public debt considerably eased through inflation.

4.3.3. Effects on the distribution of income

A large public debt leads to large interest payments. These are usually covered by taxes. The incomes from interest will ordinarily be taxable so that some of the interest payments are met by the same groups in society which receive the interests as income. But it is clear that this will concern only a part of the total amount of interest. One might examine the effect of interest payments and the corresponding taxation by looking at the net interest and tax payments, including in the calculation a fraction of personal taxation which is equal to the state expenditure on interest payments as a fraction of total expenditure. Such investigations in the U.S.A. indicate that the high and the low income groups profit by these transfers of income, while the middle groups suffer a net loss. The high income groups profit, of course, because it is they who receive the bulk of the interest payments. The lowest groups derive some benefit because they pay little or nothing in taxes while at the same time some of their members (perhaps especially among the old) draw a certain amount of income from interest.

4.3.4. The "distribution of the burden in time"

Let us imagine that the central government is going to undertake a great investment project, and let us consider in this connection the two alternatives either of raising a loan or of levying taxes.

In older literature and still in public debate it is often maintained that the alternative of borrowing implies that the burden of the investment is shifted over to the future, while on the other hand by levying taxes, the state lets the burden of the investment be carried by the present population.

It is here important to distinguish between external and internal borrowing. By borrowing abroad one may increase imports so that it is unnecessary to limit current consumption in order to carry out the investment. In return, the loan must be repaid in future instalments out of the then current production in the country itself. Altogether, the project will be advantageous for the future population if it is economically profitable enough to contribute a larger amount to the country's national income than that needed for interests and redemption of the debt. But it would clearly have been even more advantageous for the future population had the investment work been carried out by the help of internal resources which would then have been drawn away from consumption uses. In this case, the future population would continue to have the income of the project, but it would be freed from the burden of the debt. In this sense the burden of a project might be said to be shifted over to the future by borrowing abroad.

With internal borrowing, the situation is different. Let us assume that exports and imports now and in the future always balance. We cannot then escape from that equation which says that private consumption plus private investment plus public expenditure on goods and services together must equal the national product. If labour and capital equipment are fully employed, the size of the national product in the current period may be considered given. An increase in public expenditure on goods and services – for instances, in connection with a public investment project – may then occur at the expense either of current consumption or of current private investment. It is this which, in real terms, will decide the question of the distribution of the burden in time. If the public project is carried out at the expense of private consumption in the present period, we may say that the burden of the project is carried *now*. If the project is carried out at the expense of private investment, we may say that the burden will fall on the future, as we shall enter the coming periods with less private capital equipment and thereby lesser possibilities of earning than we would otherwise have had.

As already has been seen, however, there is not necessarily a connection between the fact that the public sector draws on loans or taxes on the one side, and the fact that the public project may be undertaken at the expense of private investment or private consumption on the other. As has been pointed out earlier, there *may* be a certain connection, but in any case it is the question of how consumption and investment in real terms are affected in the current period, which is decisive in the matter of the distribution of the burden in time.

What we have considered here is only the cost side of the public projects. We shall return to some questions concerning the benefit side and its comparison with costs in Chapter 6.

4.3.5.   *The interest burden of a steadily increasing public debt*

In the years between the world wars, it seemed as if economic development in several countries was going to stagnate completely, unless the government pursued a policy which would involve great permanent deficits in the budgets. The question then arose whether such a policy of deficits, financed through the constant raising of new loans, would gradually result in the cost of interest payment getting completely out of hand. We shall consider this question in the light of an analysis by Domar*.

We make the simple assumption that the government always borrows a certain fraction α of the national income, and that the national income then grows by a rate of r. We let R be the national income and D the public debt. $U = iD$ is the interest payments per year, where i is the rate of interest. The private incomes will consist of the national income plus the income from the interest, U. We designate this by

$$Y = R + U = R + iD.$$

This concept of income forms the base for taxation. The amount needed to meet the interest payments on the public debt will make up the fraction U/Y of private incomes.

---

* See essay II in E. D. Domar: *Essays in the theory of economic growth* (New York, 1957). (Originally published as an article in *The American Economic Review* (1944), under the title: The burden of the debt and the national income.)

We are mainly interested in the long-run development of the relationship D/R, i.e., the national debt in proportion to the national income, and of the tax burden for the interest payments U/Y.

That a fraction α of the national income is borrowed, is expressed by

$$\dot{D} = \frac{dD}{dt} = \alpha R.$$

That the national income grows by a rate of r, is expressed by

$$R = R_0 e^{rt}.$$

For the development of the public debt we get the following:

$$D = D_0 + \int_0^t \dot{D}\,d\tau = D_0 + \alpha R_0 \int_0^t e^{r\tau}\,d\tau = D_0 + \frac{\alpha R_0}{r}(e^{rt} - 1).$$

The public debt in relation to the national income will then develop in the following way:

$$\frac{D}{R} = \frac{D_0}{R_0} e^{-rt} + \frac{\alpha}{r}(1 - e^{-rt}).$$

The first component in this formula will tend towards zero as t approaches infinity. The other component will approach α/r. Thus we have

$$\frac{D}{R} \to \frac{\alpha}{r} \quad \text{when} \quad t \to \infty.$$

For the development of the interest burden, we have

$$\frac{U}{Y} = \frac{iD}{R + U} = \frac{i}{RD^{-1} + UD^{-1}} = \frac{i}{RD^{-1} + i}.$$

Since we already have the development of R/D we can from this easily determine the development of the interest burden. We see especially that we have

$$\frac{U}{Y} \rightarrow \frac{i}{r\alpha^{-1} + i} \quad \text{when} \quad t \rightarrow \infty .$$

From the formulae we have developed here, we see that the public debt in relation to the national income approaches a certain limit, α/r, which can be greater than 1, equal to 1 or less than 1. The proportion of interest payments to private incomes, reckoned as inclusive of this amount, will approach a certain limit which must, of course, be less than 1 in value. Let us for a numerical example say that the rate of interest $i=0.03$, that the national income growth-rate $r=0.03$, and that the state borrows a share of 6% of the current income, i.e., $\alpha=0.06$. Then the public debt in relation to the national income will approach the value of 2. The ratio of interest payments to private incomes will approach 0.057, which means that a tax of 5.7% on private incomes (inclusive of the incomes from interest) will be necessary in order to meet the cost of interest payments.

4.4. A note on the development of the Norwegian national debt

During the latter part of the last century and around the turn of the century, the Norwegian state raised large loans for the financing of railway construction. In 1914 the national debt had reached 357 million *kroner*. The bulk of this debt was incurred abroad as permanent loans.

During the first World War, large loans were raised in connection with defense expenses. These loans were raised at home and consisted for the main part of temporary loans. In 1918 the total national debt had reached 737 million *kroner*, of which over half was internal debt. Of this, 246 million *kroner* were floating debt.

Loans in connection with the war continued for a while after the year 1918. Loans were also raised to help municipalities which had run into difficulties. The growth of the national debt must further be seen against the background of the inflation which blew up all monetary values. In

1925 the national debt topped 1732 million *kroner*, of which well over 700 millions were raised abroad, while well over 300 millions were floating internal debt.

The total national debt then made up about one third of one year's gross national product. Of the state administration's total expenses of 398 million *kroner*, the expenses on interest made up 104 million *kroner* and were thus a very heavy item.

From 1925 up to 1940 no great changes took place in the national debt. Taken overall, there was a certain reduction, and a funding took place so that the floating national debt was considerably reduced. Even though the summit was passed in 1925, the national debt was yet so large during the whole of this period that it played a considerable part in the shaping of the state's policy. It is probable that, with a smaller debt, the state would have pursued a more active policy in the 1930's to counteract the economic depression.

During the second World War, Norway had considerable incomes in exile from shipping. With the help of these incomes, some of the external national debt was paid off. The internal debt in Norway, however, increased greatly during the war, so that the total national debt in 1945 had reached 6.5 thousand million *kroner*. Of this, more than half was floating debt contracted in the form of the issuing of treasury bills.

Most of the floating debt was paid off by 1950. Since then it has somewhat increased again. Both the permanent internal national debt and the external debt have increased during almost the whole post-war period. The internal borrowing has taken place partly to finance loans from the state banks to the private sector of the economy. The borrowing abroad has partly been connected with especially large investment projects.

On various occasions loans have also been raised purely for the purposes of regulating the liquidity situation.

The total national debt had in 1962 reached 10 thousand million *kroner**, while the gross national product this year was 42.1 thousand million *kroner*. For the same year the state spent nearly 400 million *kroner* on interest, of a total expenditure of 8.4 thousand million *kroner* on the state budget. (The level of interest rates was lower at this time than

---

* Of this, a little more than 2 thousand million *kroner* was debt to other state institutions and funds under state administration.

for the debt in the record year of 1925. Besides, the expenditure of the state now makes up a far larger share of the national product than in 1925. Relatively, therefore, the interest burden for the state was far lighter in 1962 than in 1925, even though the national debt, in relation to the national product, was of an order of magnitude which was not much less.)

Some of the features shown by developments in Norway are found also in many other countries. It has been quite common for the internal national debt to increase considerably during, or in connection with, wars. It has also been common that a great part of the debt contracted under such circumstances has been temporary, and that it has been funded later. Further, it was the case in many countries in the 1930's that state debt and interest expenditures acted as a brake on economic policy.

The national debt has also been of some importance in the economic policies of various countries since the war. The U.S.A., for instance, was cautious in pursuing an expansive policy in 1958, because it was thought, *inter alia*, that an increase in federal debt might in the long run lead to difficulties in following an efficient monetary policy.

The state budget and the state accounts

The technical problems connected with the setting up of a state budget will not be treated in any detail in this text. We shall mention only some points of principle related to the material dealt with in other chapters.

5.1. The purpose served by the state budget and the state accounts

A state budget is an arrangement of the state's estimated or planned incomes and expenditures in a coming period, usually one year.

In Norway the state budget is prepared by the Government which presents its proposed budget to the national assembly. According to the Constitution, it is this body which has the authority to decide on spending and the authority to impose taxes, as well as authority as regards the raising of loans. Thus it is the national assembly which makes the final decisions as to the state's income and expenditure. This applies in most countries where national assemblies exist in some form or other.

The state budget serves many purposes. Among these, the following are, perhaps, the most important:
1. It shall make possible a reasonable evaluation of the total state income and expenditure.
2. It shall make possible a sensible balancing between the various items of expenditure and between the various components of income.
3. It shall make possible an evaluation of what effects the state's incomes and expenditures will produce on the economy as a whole, i.e., an evaluation of the macroeconomic effects of the fiscal policy which is implied in the state budget.

4. The state budget shall enable the national assembly to check that the
   Government follows that policy on which the assembly has decided
   via the budget. This control is effected by the keeping of accounts
   corresponding to the arrangement of the budget, so that by comparing accounts with budget it can be seen whether the Government
   has followed the resolutions of the national assembly.

5.2.   The extent and form of the budget and the accounts

In order to meet the purposes mentioned above, the budget must satisfy a
series of different requirements.

From all the considerations mentioned, it is important that the budget be
as *complete* as possible. If we return to the survey of the public sector
given in section 1.1, it might be desirable to include in the state budget all
the parts of the state sector mentioned both under point 1 and point 2.
Norway, however, has gone only as far as including in the state budget
that which belongs to "government in a narrow sense" and to "state
enterprises directly under the government". Other considerations have
worked against that of completeness in the budget. Many government
funds, for instance, have been set apart precisely in order to make them
independent of yearly grants from the national assembly. Similarly, the
government joint stock companies are separate juridical persons, and
these are also kept outside the state budget. The decisive element here has
been that these companies ought to have great independence and freedom
of management. As for social insurances, it may be useful to keep these
too outside, since one here has statutory rules and rates to be followed.
It should therefore be unnecessary for the national assembly yearly to go
through these incomes and expenditures.

Further, it is necessary to have *specifications* of various kinds in the
budget.

One may make an *administrative* grouping of expenditures and incomes,
i.e., a grouping according to which ministries or other institutions the
money goes to or comes from. This grouping is in itself not particularly
interesting, but it is of importance for administrative control.

One may further make the grouping according to *purposes*. This will
apply only for the expenditure side. Here, then, the grouping is made

according to the purposes served by the various expenditures, such as education, health, various cultural activities, defence, etc. This grouping is of decisive importance for the balancing of the different items of expenditure in the budget from the point of view of making the best use of resources.

Furthermore, it is important, from the point of view of evaluation of the effects of the budget on the national economy, that there be a grouping according to *kind*, i.e., a grouping of expenditures on such items as transfers to consumers, purchase of goods and services for consumption purposes, purchase of goods and services for investment purposes, etc. It may be said that this is the grouping which gives the quantities one would wish to employ in a model designed to investigate the macroeconomic effects of a given budget.

With the new arrangement for the state budget employed in Norway from the financial year of 1961 onwards, it must be said that these requirements for specification are well met. As well as such specifications of expenditure and revenue, the budget also contains some figures which are important for an estimate of the effects of the state budget on the money supply. Particularly important in this respect are the loans from the state to the private sector through the state banks. However, new loans to be raised by the state in the coming year are not specified in the budget.

As for the principles of accounting, the situation for the state is quite unlike that of a private firm. The important thing for a private firm is to be able to calculate as correctly as possible the results for a given period and to work out a balance sheet which reflects its wealth and liquidity. These considerations are not so important to the state; and they were therefore not listed in section 5.1 above. The budget and accounts can therefore be set up according to the so-called cash principle, under which one enters in the budget and the corresponding accounts only cash receipts and payments which are expected or are planned to occur in the course of the year. (This applies with certain exceptions.)

5.3.   *Different types of items in the budget*

The items in the state budget vary with respect to the possibility of estimating them exactly, and with respect to the possibility of estimating exactly the point of time or the period when it is appropriate to put them into effect.

In the Norwegian state budget various types of items are characterized by the use of certain 'catchphrases'.

Firstly, there are the so-called "estimated appropriations". This term is used for items of expenditures which are based on uncertain calculations, and where the indicated sum may, if necessary, be exceeded. The term is particularly used where there is a certain project or activity which is to be carried out in any case, regardless of whether it will cost more than has been estimated beforehand. If we wish to relate this to the models used in previous chapters, we may say that such items usually concern cases where it is the volume of purchase of goods and services which is autonomously determined by the state, while the nominal sum will depend on the prices. But there may of course also be cases where it is difficult to say in advance what volume of goods and services is necessary to serve a given objective.

Other items are marked by the catchphrase "can be transferred". This is used in connection with grants for construction works and purchase of materials, to indicate that they will also be available for use in the two following financial periods, to the extent that they are not used up in the period for which the appropriation is really made. This particularly applies where it is difficult to determine beforehand the most suitable time to carry out work, or to say how long a particular project will take.

Finally, there is the catchphrase "may be used under", which is employed with appropriations of expenditure where any saving may be transferred to other, specified items of expenditure in the budget for the same period.

On the revenue side there are some items, such as income from interest, where one can say quite definitely beforehand what sums will come in. But for the more dominating items on the revenue side, i.e., taxes and excises, it is clear that the figures set out in the budget must be based on more uncertain estimates. What is really fixed, is, of course, the tax-rules and -rates adopted by the national assembly in connection with the passing of the state budget. This is connected with what has been touched upon a few times earlier, namely that the amounts yielded through taxation are not really the policy instruments of the state.

The extent of collective consumption and public activity

6.1. Some observations on the way of posing the problem

In previous chapters we have studied the connection between public expenditure and revenue on the one hand, and the level of general economic activity on the other. In doing so, we saw how, in many cases, the situation is such that a definite level of activity can be achieved with a high level of public expenditure and a correspondingly high level of public revenue, or with somewhat lower public expenditure and revenue. Consequently, even though it is intended, by means of fiscal policy, to achieve a high level of income and employment in the country, a certain range will still exist within which the level of public expenditure can be determined. We have previously pointed out that this determination should be based on the need for public consumption and public investment. Our chief concern in this chapter will be to consider this in greater detail.

In section 3.2.2 we indicated certain factors which also favour the use of public expenditure – viz., not only tax revenue – as a means of regulating employment. To the extent that fluctuations occur in the economic life of the nation, and the intention is to counter this by means of an active fiscal policy, some fluctuations will also occur in public expenditure of various kinds. This factor, however, will not be dealt with in this chapter, as we shall concentrate on the *level* of public expenditure.

If a situation existed involving idle production capacity and idle labour and assuming that the balance of foreign trade was not a problem, it would be possible to increase public expenditure without adversely affecting private consumption or private investment. In this case, one would not be faced with any choice between the alternative uses of available resources. If, on the other hand, full employment existed, and it was thus possible on a short-term basis to regard the gross national product as a given magnitude, one would be faced with the choice of using resources either for public consumption and investment, or for private consumption and investment. We shall here consider ourselves faced with this latter type of choice, which by its nature will have to be made on the basis of certain evaluations which are bound to contain strongly subjective elements.

It is here possible to propose two different aims for a theory on the determination of public expenditure. In the first place the attempt may be made to establish a theory as to how public expenditure is in fact determined in an economic set-up such as, e.g., the contemporary Norwegian one. In the second place it would be possible to aim at formulating a more normative theory as to how one might achieve an optimal determination of the level of public expenditure. (See in this connection section 1.4.) Economics textbooks contain no generally accepted theories of either of these types. For this reason, and on account of the subjective elements which are bound to colour any theory on public expenditure, the contents of the following sections may possibly appear somewhat less coherent and more speculative than the contents of previous chapters.

The problem of balancing public and private consumption of goods and services has been the subject of intense discussion in recent years. John Kenneth Galbraith's analysis in his book *The affluent society* (London, 1958) has proved particularly stimulating. Here the author maintains, *inter alia:* "The line which divides our area of wealth from our area of poverty is roughly that which divides privately produced and marketed goods and services from publicly rendered services. Our wealth in the first is not only in startling contrast with the meagreness of the latter, but our wealth in privately produced goods is, to a marked degree, the cause of crisis in the supply of public services. For we have failed to see the importance, indeed the urgent need, of maintaining a balance between the two."

Views similar to those which Galbraith has adduced with regard to the USA have been ventilated in other countries, even though conditions there are hardly as striking.

6.2.   *Satisfying collective wants through public consumption*

6.2.1.   *Observations based on economic welfare theory*

In section 2.2.2 we have indicated the satisfaction of collective wants as one of the most important aims to be considered in public economics. In this connection we also gave a definition of the concept of collective wants.

Ignoring for a moment all marginal cases between collective and personal or private wants, we shall raise the question of an optimal determination of the extent of public use of resources to satisfy collective wants. Let us imagine that we have two groups, persons or parties A and B. Furthermore, let us imagine that we are faced with a situation in which the gross national income R can be regarded as given on the basis of such considerations as those set out in the previous section. The national income R can be allocated in three different directions: it can be made available for private disposal to group A, or for private disposal to group B, or for joint disposal to satisfy collective wants. Let the component allocated to A privately be X, the component allocated to B privately be Y, and the component available jointly be G. We then have the following accounting equation:

$$X + Y + G = R. \tag{6.1}$$

Let us now consider the two groups' preference structures. We assume that one group's utility or welfare can be expressed as a function of the group's private use of goods and services and the joint use G. We express the utility functions of the two groups in the following manner:

$$U_A = F_A(X, G), \qquad U_B = F_B(Y, G) \tag{6.2}$$

where the first function refers to group A, and the second function refers to group B.

We assume that the utility functions (6.2) have similar properties to the utility functions with which one operates in the ordinary theory of demand. They can thus be represented by indifference curves in the usual way. The only novel feature of the formulation here used, is that G occurs as an argument in the utility functions of both persons or groups. This expresses the fact that G satisfies a collective want.

For each group, the indifference curves in a goods diagram will provide the answer to the question: How does the group weigh satisfaction of private against the satisfaction of collective wants? Thus, the slope of an indifference curve will express how much private consumption the group is willing to forego, per unit increase of joint expenditure used for the satisfaction of collective wants.

Let us then put the question whether we can arrive here at a Pareto-optimal constellation of magnitudes X, Y, and G. That is to say, we make the minimum demand that we should arrive at a constellation which is such that, from this constellation it will be impossible to make changes which will be advantageous to one of the groups, without damaging the interests of the other group. Mathematically we can arrive at constellations of such a kind by maximising the utility function of group A, under two subsidiary conditions: the subsidiary condition which is given in the accounting equation (6.1) with R as a given magnitude, and the subsidiary condition that the utility for group B is to reach a specified level. For this purpose we introduce the function

$$\Phi = F_A(X, G) - \lambda[X + Y + G - R] - \mu[F_B(Y, G) - U_B], \qquad (6.3)$$

where the magnitudes λ and μ are Lagrange multipliers.

If we differentiate the function Φ partially with respect to the magnitudes X, Y, and G, set the partial derivatives equal to zero, and eliminate the Lagrange multipliers from the resulting system, we obtain the following condition:

$$\frac{\partial F_A/\partial G}{\partial F_A/\partial X} + \frac{\partial F_B/\partial G}{\partial F_B/\partial Y} = 1. \qquad (6.4)$$

The partial derivatives entering into formula (6.4) are marginal utilities of private and joint disposal implied by the preference structures of the two groups. The two ratios in (6.4) express marginal rates of substitution between the goods in the two preference functions. The figure 1 on the right in (6.4) may be said to express the marginal substitution condition between the goods in the "transformation function" (6.1). The types of magnitude entering into (6.4) are thus the same types of magnitude as the ones occurring in the usual optimisation problems in the economic welfare theory. The new element introduced by the magnitude G, which is an ingredient of both persons' utility evaluation, is that in (6.4) we have to *add* marginal rates of substitution.

In the problem we are now considering, we have three variables, X, Y, and G. The accounting equation (6.1) and the optimum condition (6.4) furnish two equations, so that we have a degree of freedom in the problem after the condition for Pareto optimum has been imposed. It would be possible for us to select one constellation among all those satisfying the Pareto-optimum condition, by prescribing the line of indifference at which one of the persons should arrive, as we actually did in the maximisation that led to condition (6.4). A more satisfactory method of selecting the particular one from among the Pareto-optimal points, is to introduce a social welfare function

$$W = W(U_A, U_B) \qquad (6.5)$$

which is dependent on the utility levels of the two groups. By maximising W subject to condition (6.1), we would determine a special point among those satisfying the Pareto-optimum condition (6.4).

The above is sufficient to establish that the existence of collective wants in no way alters the basic logic of the welfare maximisation problem, compared with the situation when only private needs are involved. It is possible formally to establish a set of Pareto-optimal points, and furthermore it is possible to select one of these, if we introduce a social welfare function expressing how one should balance the interests of the two groups against each other.

Before discussing the problem of how to realise an optimum point of the kind for which we have here established the conditions, there may be grounds for submitting a few critical observations on the foundations for the above analysis. In this connection there are in particular two points that are worth emphasising.

In the first place it is more doubtful in the case we are now considering than in cases where we merely consider a balance between various goods in private consumption, if relatively permanent scales of evaluation exist for the various individuals or groups, as demanded by the introduction of utility functions. The evaluation of the factors entering into joint consumption is often far more difficult than the evaluation of goods that individuals use privately. Nevertheless, the set-up above may perhaps be somewhat more acceptable, if we consider the functions in (6.2) as preference functions for groups that have their *representative spokesmen*. Yet even so serious doubts will arise. One might, for instance, consider the important component of joint consumption associated with education and cultural life. There is hardly any doubt that this *in itself* will over a period of time help to alter people's preferences. One might then have to deal with such questions as, e.g., is it the preferences which are valid *before* certain measures are put into operation that are to be considered, or should one also consider possible prognostications as to how people's preferences will change *as a result of* such measures? It may easily be seen that problems will arise here which are difficult to solve, even on an entirely abstract and logical plane. (The circumstance here indicated also applies, of course, to a number of goods in private consumption.)

In the second place it may easily happen that the authorities of a country ascribe to public use of goods and services a value beyond what is expressed through individual preference scales. This might be expressed by operating, not with (6.5), but with a welfare function, where the magnitude G appears as a separate argument beside the individual utility-levels:

$$W = W(U_A, U_B, G).\qquad(6.6)$$

Maximising the welfare function (6.6) subject to the subsidiary condition (6.1) produces a solution which will not satisfy condition (6.4).

Such a direct evaluation of public expenditure as is expressed in (6.6), instead of an indirect evaluation exclusively via individual utility functions, can of course be motivated on the basis of the observations mentioned in the previous paragraph.

6.2.2. *Erik Lindahl's theory for determination of public expenditure*

From traditional welfare theory we are familiar with the way in which the price mechanism, under certain conditions, can lead to the realisation of a market point that satisfies the conditions for Pareto optimality. For public use of goods and services no such price mechanism exists. As previously indicated, this is due to the fact that goods and services in joint consumption are precisely of such a kind that they cannot be split up and sold to individual purchasers. Once a good of this kind is supplied, it can be enjoyed without let or hindrance by all members of the community.

Yet, in the literature on fiscal theory, the question has often been raised whether a mechanism to determine public expenditure, operating in a manner *similar* to the price mechanism applicable to private consumption, does not all the same exist, or can at any rate be established. The first relatively clear treatment of this problem was provided by the Swedish economist Erik Lindahl in 1919*.

The fundamental point in Lindahl's theory is that he regards the determination of public expenditure in connection with the distribution of the corresponding tax burden among the groups within the community. The distribution ratio for this burden will then play a role similar to that of prices in the adjustment between supply and demand in an ordinary market. We shall consider this theory in greater detail.

Let us suppose that the incomes of the two groups concerned, prior to taxation, are respectively R_A and R_B. The total income of the community is the sum of these components:

$$R = R_A + R_B. \tag{6.7}$$

Let us next introduce the magnitude h, which represents the distribution ratio for the reduction in the private disposal of goods and services

---

* See Erik Lindahl: *Die Gerechtigkeit der Besteuerung* (Lund, 1919). The relevant section is printed in English in *Classics in the Theory of Public Finance,* eds. R. A. Musgrave and A. T. Peacock (New York-London, 1958). Cf. also Leif Johansen, Some Notes on the Lindahl Theory of Determination of Public Expenditures, *The International Economic Review* (1963).

which must correspond to the magnitude of public disposal of goods and services, the total income R being taken as given. The magnitude h may be taken as an expression of the way in which the fiscal system distributes the burden among the two groups, in such a way that h indicates the share of the joint expenditure G borne by group A, and $(1 - h)$ the share borne by group B. We then get the following budget conditions for the two groups:

$$X + hG = R_A, \qquad Y + (1 - h)G = R_B. \tag{6.8}$$

By adding these two budget equations together, we get the accounting equation (6.1), using (6.7).

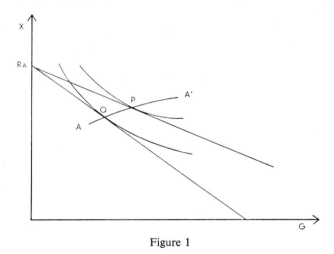

Figure 1

Let us now consider group A, and examine its preferences with regard to private use and joint use of income when the budget condition (6.8) is imposed. We shall assume that the group considers the magnitude h as given. We can then consider a diagram, where we draw in the indifference curves corresponding to the utility function F_A, and a line corresponding to the budget condition in (6.8), in the same way as we do when we study an individual's demand for various consumer goods, see fig.1.

In the figure, two budget lines are drawn in, corresponding to two different values of h. (The steepest budget line corresponds to the highest value of h). The combination of private and joint use of income which group A will prefer, for a given distribution ratio h, can be found by following the budget line corresponding to this value of h, until we reach the point where the budget line is tangential to a curve of indifference. The points P and Q in fig. 1, for instance, are points of this kind. In the figure, we have drawn a curve joining together all such points corresponding to various values of h.

The left terminal point of this curve corresponds to the case when $h=1$, viz., the case when group A, through the medium of taxation, is charged with the whole burden of public expenditure G.

On the basis of fig. 1 we can construct a new diagram which more directly shows the connection between the distribution ratio h and the

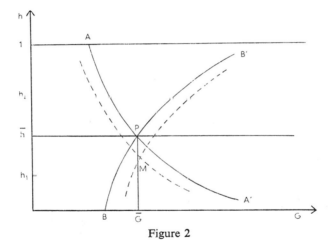

Figure 2

magnitude of public expenditure desired by group A. This is done in fig. 2. The curve AA' corresponds here to curve AA' in fig. 1.

In fig. 1 we see that the desired magnitude of G increases as h decreases, i.e., when the budget line descends less steeply. This corresponds with the plausible idea that the smaller the share of public expenditure imposed on group A, the greater will be that group's desire for public expenditure. In fig. 2 this is expressed by the fact that the curve AA' descends in a similar manner to an ordinary demand curve in a price-quantity diagram.

We can carry out precisely the same construction for group B, as we carried out for group A. The only difference will be that the role played by magnitude h, when we constructed the diagram for group A, will be taken over by $(1-h)$ when we construct the curve for group B. This means that we can include group B's "demand curve" in the same diagram in which we drew group A's "demand curve". Group B's curve will then be shaped as shown by curve BB' in fig. 2.

In fig. 2 we can now read off, for every value of h, how much public expenditure the two groups will desire. If we try a low value of h (e.g., h_1), i.e., if we impose on group A a small share of expenture and impose a large share of expenditure on group B, we see that group A will desire a large amount of public expenditure, whereas group B will desire a small amount of public expenditure. In other words, the two parties will not agree on how great public expenditure should be. On the other hand, if we endeavour to impose a large share of expenditure on group A, and a small share of expenditure on group B (as, e.g., for the value h_2 of the distribution ratio), disagreement will take the opposite direction. Between these values there exists a value $\bar{h}$ which is such that the two parties will desire the same magnitude of public expenditure, that is to say, a magnitude of the distribution ratio such that the two parties will agree on the magnitude of public expenditure. In the figure, this point is marked by P, and the corresponding public expenditure is $\bar{G}$.

We can see that magnitude h plays a similar role as the price in an ordinary market with quantity adjusters* both on the demand side and on the supply side. The equilibrium price in a market of this kind is the price which is such that the supply side and the demand side will "agree" on the quantity to be sold.

This analogy with an ordinary market in which both suppliers and demanders consider the price as given, reveals a difficulty, however, in connection with determination of the solution point in fig. 2. We have seen that a distribution ratio h exists, which is such that the two parties will agree on G, when they both consider the value of h as given; but

---

* In this chapter we shall occasionally use the expression "fixed-price quantity adjustment" or simply "quantity adjustment" to indicate a situation in which producers (consumers) determine quantities produced (consumed) so as to maximize profit (utility) while considering prices as given.

we have not discussed how to arrive at this distribution ratio. Roughly, we might conceive of a process more or less as follows: suppose that the parties first consider a distribution ratio as h_1; in that case group A will desire a larger amount of public expenditure than B is prepared to accept. In this situation it is reasonable to suppose that group A, in order to induce group B to accept a larger amount of public expenditure, will offer to assume a somewhat larger share of the burden of expenditure involved. This will involve an increase of h from h_1. This will mean a movement in the direction of the point of equilibrium P. Correspondingly, if the parties considered a distribution ratio h_2, we might suppose that group B would offer to carry a somewhat larger share of expenditure, in order to get group A to agree to an increase in public expenditure. This means that group B would offer to accept a lowering of the value of h. Thus we see that from values of h lying outside the equilibrium value $\bar{h}$ we may get tendencies to pull in the direction of $\bar{h}$, and consequently the h,G-point in the direction of P.

In an explanation of this nature, as to how the point of equilibrium may be supposed to be reached, we have abandoned the presupposition that the two parties consider h as absolutely given. The difficulties of a logical nature which this involves correspond to the difficulties which also exist in the usual theory of price formation, and we shall not discuss them in greater detail*.

It is, however, worth noting here that with two parties the situation in fig. 2 is more like what in economic theory is usually called isolated barter or bilateral monopoly than a competitive market with many suppliers and many demanders. This brings the question of "power" and negotiation mechanism into the picture. When Lindahl expressed the opinion that in fiscal policy it was possible in negotiations between the parties to arrive at a solution point like P in fig. 2, it was on the assumption that in one sense or other an equal power and ability "to defend its own interests" existed on both sides. We may note that it would actually not help if there were a greater number of parties involved, as it does generally in the case of an ordinary market for a particular

* See Trygve Haavelmo, Hva kan statiske likevektsmodeller fortelle oss? (What can static equilibrium models tell us?), in: *Festskrift til Frederik Zeuthen* (Copenhagen, 1958).

commodity. Whenever the indifference law applies, there will still be only *one* price in the market for the commodity, whereas in the case we are now considering we are compelled to introduce a new distribution ratio for every additional group.

We know from the ordinary theory of welfare economics that a system, in which all parties behave as if they consider the prices as given magnitudes, will under certain conditions result in the conditions for Pareto-optimality being satisfied. It is easy to show that the "Lindahl solution" P in fig. 2 similarly satisfies the condition for Pareto-optimality. To do so, let us consider the formulas for curves AA′ and BB′ in fig. 2.

The curve AA′ expresses the value of G which maximises the utility for group A for a given value of h. We shall obtain a formula expressing this condition by first solving the first equation in (6.8) for X, and then substituting it in the utility function for group A. This gives us

$$U_A = F_A(R_A - hG, G).$$ (6.9)

This formula expresses how the utility of group A depends on h and G, when the budget condition is taken into consideration. We get the desired value of G for a given value of h by setting the partial derivative of (6.9) with respect to G equal to zero. This gives us

$$\frac{\partial F_A}{\partial G} = h\frac{\partial F_A}{\partial X}.$$ (6.10)

This formula tells us that group A achieves maximum utility when marginal utility of public expenditure for this group is equal to the distribution ratio h multiplied by the group's marginal utility of private consumption of goods and services. In fact, group A, since it does not pay the entire joint expenditure G, desires an allocation such that its marginal utility of joint expenditure is less than the maginal utility of the private use of income.

Thus formula (6.10) corresponds to curve AA′ in fig. 2. In precisely the same manner, we can deduce a formula corresponding to curve BB′ in the figure. We then take our starting point in Group B's utility function and budget condition, and obtain

$$\frac{\partial F_B}{\partial G} = (1 - h)\frac{\partial F_B}{\partial Y}.$$ (6.11)

In the last two equations X, Y, and G enter as arguments in the various marginal utility functions. After substituting for X and Y from the budget conditions, as we did in (6.9), then (6.10) and (6.11) will be two equations for two unknowns h and G. The values satisfying this system will be $\bar{h}$ and $\bar{G}$, corresponding to the point of intersection P in fig. 2.

From (6.10) and (6.11) we can now show that this solution satisfies the condition (6.4) for Pareto-optimum. By solving (6.10) and (6.11) for the value of h, we obtain the two expressions:

$$h = \frac{\partial F_A/\partial G}{\partial F_A/\partial X}, \qquad h = 1 - \frac{\partial F_B/\partial G}{\partial F_B/\partial Y}. \tag{6.12}$$

These two expressions must be equal when (6.10) and (6.11) are satisfied at the same time. That means that when we are at the point of solution P in fig. 2, the Pareto-optimum condition (6.4) will also be satisfied. This applies, irrespective of what the income distribution before taxation, expressed by R_A and R_B, may be.

Thus the Lindahl solution is a Pareto-optimal solution. It does not, however, follow from this that this solution will produce maximum welfare, in the sense that it gives the maximal value of a welfare function as that given in (6.5). This could apply only by pure coincidence. In fact, at that time Lindahl and other writers only maintained that a solution, such as the one we have considered, would be a good solution *provided that the distribution of income before the parties concerned are subjected to taxation for covering public expenditure, is acceptable or equitable.*

On this basis, one might imagine a sort of division, into two different categories, of decisions concerning taxation and public expenditure. In the first place, one might carry out a "pure" redistribution of income between the two groups, i.e., in such a way that what is taken from one group is paid out to the other group. One might then deal with the question of public expenditure and a division of the corresponding burden among the two groups, leaving this question to be determined by a mechanism such as the one studied by Lindahl. Thus at this "stage" one would simultaneously deal with questions of the extent of expenditure and the division of the corresponding burden, and no decision on expenditure would be made before agreement had been reached. (In an attempt to give more practical form to this idea, Wicksell and others have referred to "approximate unanimity".)

The term Pareto-optimality was not used in former discussions about these problems, but the line of argument above shows that by using the mechanism under consideration one would arrive at a result which is "good" in the Pareto sense of the word. If one had previously carried out a suitable redistribution of income, the result should by and large approximate to the best possible.

In practice, however, a division of this kind is naturally difficult to achieve, as neither of the parties involved can be expected to have its wishes entirely fulfilled, as far as redistribution of income is concerned when dealing with the first question, and for this reason it must be expected that distribution considerations of this nature will also vitiate the treatment of the other question. Furthermore, it is doubtful whether the Lindahl solution can be described, without further qualification, as an equitable one, even if we start off with an equitable distribution of income before public expenditure and the corresponding distribution of the tax burden are determined. In order to illustrate this, let us consider in greater detail a specific example.

The example in question applies to the case in which public use of goods and services is an "inferior" good, as evaluated from the point of view of individual utility functions. That a good is inferior means in the ordinary demand theory that a consumer will use less of this good when his income is increased and prices remain constant. In the case now under consideration, G represents an inferor good, if one group would prefer a *lesser* value of G, in the event of the group having an *increase* of income (prior to taxation), while the distribution ratio h remains constant.

Let us in a case of this kind see how the Lindahl solution depends on distribution of income before taxation. We shall then be comparing the solution P which we have in fig. 2, and which corresponds to the income distribution R_A, R_B, with the solution we should get with an income distribution with $R_A + \Delta$ for A and $R_B - \Delta$ for B. Assuming $\Delta > 0$, this alternative distribution is more advantageous to A than the one we considered first.

How will the curves now lie in the figure, assuming this alternative distribution of income?

In the case of group A, which with the alternative distribution has a higher income, the "demand curve" AA' will be shifted to the left, as the group will now for every value of h prefer a lesser value of G than before. The new curve is represented by the broken line to the left of the old one in fig. 2. The income of group B will be lower in the new situation. As the good G is also inferior from B's point of view, the result of the lower income will be that the group, for any value of h, will "demand" a greater amount of public goods. This means that the new curve will be situated to the right of curve BB'. This, too, has been dotted in, in fig. 2. The new point of equilibrium will then lie at M instead of at point P in fig. 2. In this new situation of equilibrium we see that the amount of public consumption of goods and services is somewhat increased in relation to the old equilibrium situation. This, however, is not important. It is also conceivable that the value of G at point M might have been less than $\bar{G}$. What is interesting in connection with the new equilibrium situation is that the value of distribution ratio h is lower than in the first situation, this being an effect which will necessarily occur, provided merely G is an inferior good in both utility functions. Thus the fact that group A is in a more advantageous position before the "Lindahl mechanism" has been applied, has also resulted in the group covering a smaller share of the burden involved in public expenditure. Correspondingly, group B, which is now in a less advantageous position, will have to make a larger contribution to cover joint expenditure.

By way of emphasising what this entails, we might imagine that we have a distribution of income before taxation which is given by $\frac{1}{2}R+\Delta$ for A and $\frac{1}{2}R-\Delta$ for B, where R is the total income. Furthermore, let us assume that the two groups have the same preference structure. If the income distribution had been $\frac{1}{2}R$ for each group, we should then have had $h=\frac{1}{2}$, i.e., joint expenditure would have been equally shared among the groups. But because A now has a *larger* income than B, the result of the Lindahl solution will give $h<\frac{1}{2}$, i.e., A will now pay a smaller share of joint expenditure than B. Even a person who was prepared to accept the income distribution $\frac{1}{2}R+\Delta$, $\frac{1}{2}R-\Delta$ as equitable, would possibly not accept the result here arrived at by the Lindahl mechanism.

The effect which here emerges is due to the property of the Lindahl solution whereby the two groups contribute to cover their joint expenditure in proportion to the *marginal* utility of public expenditure, cf. formula (6.12). On the other hand, a great many people will consider that the question of a just distribution of the costs corresponding to joint expenditure is one of *total* utility and not a question of marginal utility. This point is particularly emphasised by Gunnar Myrdal in a critical treatment of the Lindahl theory*.

The intention here is not to maintain that the case we have now considered is the most realistic. As a whole, public expenditure is hardly inferior within the preference scales of the individual groups. The object has merely been to select an extreme case, in order to illustrate an important point in connection with Lindahl's theory. But it is by no means unthinkable that *many components* of public expenditure are inferior in the sense we have now considered. The larger the income one has, the more likely one is to buy a car, and to be independent of public transport. (On the other hand one will naturally be relatively more interested in expenditure on public roads.) The higher one's income, the less dependent one is on a number of public measures of a social nature. The higher one's income, the larger will be the private garden one will acquire and maybe the less will public expenditure on parks weigh in one's preference scale.

This consideration, which involves looking at components of the magnitude G, brings us to another point of some importance in connection with the type of theory we are now dealing with. In order to illustrate this, let us consider the division of the magnitude G into two components, G_1 and G_2. Instead of the previous utility functions, we must now introduce utility functions with both G_1 and G_2 as arguments:

$$U_A = F_A(X, G_1, G_2), \qquad U_B = F_B(Y, G_1, G_2). \tag{6.13}$$

If once again we put the question of the conditions for Pareto optimality, we shall, by proceeding precisely in the same manner as previously, have *two* conditions of type (6.4):

$$\frac{\partial F_A/\partial G_1}{\partial F_A/\partial X} + \frac{\partial F_B/\partial G_1}{\partial F_B/\partial Y} = 1, \qquad \frac{\partial F_A/\partial G_2}{\partial F_A/\partial X} + \frac{\partial F_B/\partial G_2}{\partial F_B/\partial Y} = 1. \tag{6.14}$$

---

* See Chapter 7 of *Vetenskap och politik i nationalekonomien*, (Stockholm, 1937) (English edition, *Political element in the development of economic theory*, London, 1953.)

In order to arrive at a solution which satisfies (6.14) with the aid of a similar mechanism to the one we have considered above, it is now necessary to introduce a separate distribution ratio for each of the two components G_1 and G_2 in public expenditure. We may call these two distribution ratios h_1 and h_2, so that the budget conditions for the two groups will now be

$$X + h_1 G_1 + h_2 G_2 = R_A, \tag{6.15}$$
$$Y + (1 - h_1) G_1 + (1 - h_2) G_2 = R_B.$$

If we now assume that group A considers both ratios h_1 and h_2 as given, and maximises its utility under the condition which is given by the first equation in (6.15), we get the conditions

$$\frac{\partial F_A}{\partial G_1} = h_1 \frac{\partial F_A}{\partial X}, \qquad \frac{\partial F_A}{\partial G_2} = h_2 \frac{\partial F_A}{\partial X}. \tag{6.16}$$

This corresponds to (6.10) in the case when we did not consider any disaggregation of G.

Correspondingly, we get for group B:

$$\frac{\partial F_B}{\partial G_1} = (1 - h_1) \frac{\partial F_B}{\partial Y}, \qquad \frac{\partial F_B}{\partial G_2} = (1 - h_2) \frac{\partial F_B}{\partial Y}. \tag{6.17}$$

Equations (6.15), (6.16), and (6.17) now give us a total of six equations for determining the six variables X, Y, G_1, G_2, h_1, and h_2. In the same way as above, it is easy to show that this solution satisfies conditions (6.14) for Pareto optimality.

If on the other hand we had merely proceeded with one distribution ratio h, likewise in the case where we have two components of joint expenditure appearing as separate arguments in the utility functions, we should obtain too many equations compared to the number of variables. The budget conditions would then have appeared as follows:

$$X + h(G_1 + G_2) = R_A, \qquad Y + (1 - h)(G_1 + G_2) = R_B. \tag{6.18}$$

By carrying out utility maximisation for the two groups, we should obtain conditions precisely as (6.16) and (6.17), merely with the difference that h_1 and h_2 would now have been the same variable h. We should then have just as many equations as above, but one variable less, and thus in general no solution of the system. This means that we should not be able to arrive at any distribution ratio h which could enable us to achieve agreement between the two groups on both the components G_1 and G_2, when this distribution ratio is applied to the entire burden corresponding to the sum of $G_1 + G_2$. The line of thought here illustrated may be interpreted as an argument in favour of dealing separately with fiscal arrangements (i.e., methods of distributing tax burdens) in connection with each one of the public expenditure items. As we have seen, this may be necessary in order to arrive at a solution which is Pareto-optimal. Dealing with fiscal arrangements separately, for each expenditure item, is however not particularly practicable, in view of the considerations dealt with in Chapter 3 on economic stabilisation through fiscal policy. In various ways it may make it difficult to attain a proper over-all view of the fiscal effects of government transactions as a whole. There may consequently be a certain conflict between what is desirable on the basis of such considerations, and what may be desirable from the point of view of an optimal determination of individual expenditure items, of the kind dealt with in this section. In most countries, in fact, we find a certain mixture which can be regarded as a compromise between these considerations. One has a fundamental taxation system, which provides the bulk of public revenue, but on the other hand one has certain special financial arrangements for a number of different types of public expenditure, e.g., various insurance schemes, often for expenditure associatedwith motoring, and occasionally in connection with the maintenance of churches, etc.

Below, we shall return to various other considerations which support separate financial arrangements of this kind for individual components of public expenditure.

6.2.3 Some observations on the principle of majority as a means of making decisions

We have seen above that, in principle, the problem of determining public expenditures and the distribution of the burden these involve, can be divided into two, as is customarily done in other sections of the economic welfare theory. In the first place one may consider the question of the conditions necessary for Pareto-optimality: subsequently the question of selecting one of the Pareto-optimal points as "the best" may be considered.

A method generally used for making decisions in economic policy, as in other kinds of policy, is the majority decision, either on a vote taken from among all the citizens of the community, or from among their representatives. We shall now consider some of the problems that arise in connection with this principle.

It is clear that by majority decisions it should be possible to arrive at a Pareto-optimal solution; for, assuming that we consider a proposal which is such that it is possible to arrive at another proposal, which improves the situation for one or several parties, without making it worse for any other party, then no-one would have any motive for preferring the first-mentioned proposal in preference to the second. Thus there would be a unanimous transition from the first proposal, involving a solution which is not Pareto-optimal, to the second solution, which is an improvement in the Pareto sense. Thus, in using majority decisions we would not acquiesce in a solution that is not Pareto-optimal.

However, this reasoning presupposes that all the aspects of the matter are being considered simultaneously. If, for example, one splits up decisions on public expenditure and decisions on systems used for financing them, making decisions in one field without connecting them with decisions in the other field, there is no guarantee that the majority mechanism will produce a Pareto-optimal result.

It is difficult to decide to what degree it may be said that the treatment of expenditure and income is separate, e.g., when the Storting deals with the Norwegian state budget. For practical reasons the various items on this budget are dealt with separately (to some extent in special committees), and these are then voted on separately. But a general debate on the budget as a whole precedes this, and votes taken on the separate items in the budget are provisional. When the budget is finally accepted, this is done on a vote which applies to the budget as a whole. The final vote, however, is something of a formality, as it is customary for the parties to vote finally for the budget, even though they may have voted against the contents of a number of the items it contains. The reason for this is that the final acceptance of the budget is constitutionally interpreted more or less as the all-clear signal for the Government, which would not be able to function without a state budget having been passed.

On the basis of the formal procedure adopted, it is consequently difficult to say whether the above-mentioned demands are satisfied, viz., that "all the aspects of the matter are being considered simultaneously". In the final analysis the decisive point must be to what extent the individual members of the Storting, in their deliberations, and by their formal and informal debates and the feelers they put out, succeed in "keeping all the balls in the air at once".

A circumstance frequently commented on in Norway and a number of other countries with a similar economic set-up, is that *approximate agreement* seems to exist *on the actual level* of public expenditure. Hardly anyone moots the idea of halving public expenditure, and few favour doubling it. The same can probably be said even if, for instance, we consider a 20% change, instead of the question of halving or doubling. Correspondingly there is also fairly close agreement on the level of total tax revenue. This approximate agreement on the level involved can be seen if, for example, we summarise the proposed amendments that are submitted to the Government's state budget proposition in the Storting.

On the other hand there is probably a greater measure of disagreement on the way of raising taxes.

An explanation of this *may* be that a mechanism similar to the one described in the previous section is effective as far as the main outlines are concerned: disagreement may exist with regard to *redistribution* of income, but a Lindahl mechanism may be responsible for approximate agreement on the level of public expenditure. There is, however, no entirely convincing evidence on which to base a conclusion of this nature, and there are many other possible interpretations than the one here mentioned. The above-mentioned "approximate agreement" on the level of expenditure may *inter alia* be regarded in the light of the following: In the first place it may be due, as far as the parties are concerned, to tactical considerations in connection with the elections. By approaching close to the middle-of-the-road alternative, parties may hope to catch the "marginal" voters without losing the voters they already have, and whose views are further away from the middle-of-the-road alternative. Thus agreement may be more apparent than real.

In the second place, for the decisions involving every single year, one does not have a free hand to change the level of expenditure. Activities which have been set in motion cannot be stopped willy-nilly, and a great many items in the budget for a certain period are the result of decisions made during previous periods. The result of this may be that by looking at the proposed amendments which are submitted for the budget proposal for any particular year, one gets a picture of approximate agreement, even though a continuous majority for different parties, *on a long-term basis*, would have resulted in entirely different levels of public expenditure.

Whatever may be the position of the questions dealt with here, it is a fact that many questions – great and small – are decided by a majority, without unanimity. There are therefore grounds for considering in greater detail this method of reaching a decision, in cases where conflicting interests or evaluations obtain.

Two instances in particular have attracted attention in the theoretical investigations on the principle of majority decisions.

In the first place, it can be shown that majority decisions will not always satisfy the demands one makes for logical consistency in an individual who has to choose between alternatives. As an example, let us consider a case where we have three persons who all have to give their votes, and three alternatives for the policy on which they are to vote. We shall call the three alternatives $a, b,$ and c. The sign $>$ indicates that an alternative is considered better than another. Let us assume that the preferences of the three persons concerned can be expressed in the following manner:

person no. 1: $a > b > c$ (and consequently $a > c$),
person no. 2: $b > c > a$ (and consequently $b > a$),
person no. 3: $c > a > b$ (and consequently $c > b$).

Here we have three persons who disagree as to which alternative is best: person no. 1 considers a to be best, person no. 2 considers b to be best, and person no. 3 considers c to be best.

Let us see what will be the result of a majority decision in this case.

In the first place it is clear that if all three alternatives are voted on simultaneously, none of them will be accepted, as each will obtain only one vote.

Let us now consider the case where voting is on two alternatives at a time. If alternatives *a* and *b* are to be voted on, we can see from the above that person no. 1 and person no. 3 will vote for *a,* while person no. 2 will vote for *b*. In other words, alternative *a* will be accepted on a majority basis. If the alternatives to be voted on are *b* and *c,* we shall find similarly that alternative *b* will obtain a majority. And finally, if we have alternatives *a* and *c* to be voted on, we shall find that there will be a majority in favour of alternative *c*.

We have, in fact, come to the conclusion that the majority decides as follows:

$$a > b, \qquad b > c, \qquad c > a.$$

This is a surprising result: the majority declares that *a* is better than *b*, and furthermore that *b* is better than *c*. We should then expect that *a* would be considered better than *c*, as would normally be assumed in the case of an individual who is faced with a choice between alternatives. However, the majority declares that *c* is better than *a*. The explanation of this apparent paradox is, of course, that "the majority" does not consist of the same individuals for all decisions.

In a case of this kind the final result of a voting process, where the alternatives are voted on two at a time, will depend on how one starts the voting process. In our particular example we can start in three different ways: either by coupling *a* and *b* together, *b* and *c,* or *c* and *a*. The alternative that wins on the first count is then opposed to the remaining alternative, and the one that wins here is the final decision. According to how we start, we shall get the following results, as *a>b* is now interpreted as indicating that *a* is accepted and *b* is rejected, and so on:

1st count	$a > b$	$b > c$	$c > a$
2nd count	$c > a$	$a > b$	$b > c$
Result	c	a	b

Actually, voting in, e.g., the Norwegian *Storting* (the National Assembly) is carried out somewhat differently from the method on which the above table is based. When there is a series of alternatives, the proposals are generally subjected to voting *one by one*, and members then in each case have to vote for or against. If it it possible to indicate which is the most "*extreme*", a start is made with that proposal. If it is obvious that one of the proposals must be adopted, and if no proposal has been accepted when there are only two proposals left, the last count is in reality an alternative count. (One could, too, consider "no resolution adopted" as one of the alternatives.)

In the example above it is not possible to select one alternative as the most extreme. Let us therefore consider what would happen if we start voting with, respectively, *a, b,* and *c.* If we start with *a*, two persons, viz., no. 2 and no. 3, must be expected to vote against, as each of them is of the opinion that one of the remaining proposals is a better one, from their point of view. For this reason, proposal *a* will be rejected. This leaves *b* and *c*, and voting in this case will actually be an alternative vote where *b* is accepted by two votes to one. Similarly, it will be seen that *c* will be accepted, if we start with *b*, and *a* will be accepted if we start with *c.*

Using this approach, too, the result is, therefore, dependent on how we start voting. Any one of the three possible alternatives can be adopted.

Great care must be taken in interpreting conclusions such as those we have arrived at here. It cannot, for instance, be said that a majority mechanism is incapable of arriving at the correct result. The point is that such a large measure of disagreement exists between the three persons that we cannot say what is "the right result"*.

As far as the problems that arise in determining the extent of public expenditure are concerned, the example adduced above is perhaps somewhat too specifically chosen. The difficulty encountered in this example will not occur if various alternatives for the policy to be pursued can be arranged along an axis, and in such a way that the representatives voting have preferences which can be expressed by their considering one alter-

---

* In this connection see the discussion in section IV, part 3, of Trygve Haavelmo, *Innledning til høyere kurs i økonomisk teori* (Introduction to advanced course in economic theory), Memorandum of 1 July 1962 from the Institute of Economics at the University of Oslo.

native best, while other alternatives are worse, the further away from this best alternative they are situated on the axis in one or the other direction. (If we were to describe this by means of a utility function, we might say that the total utility could be thought of as a unimodal function along the axis mentioned.) In order to illustrate this, let us consider the alternatives *a, b,* and *c* above as "big", "medium", and "small". Person no. 1 in the above table prefers alternative *a* to *b*, and considers *b* in turn as better than *c*. This means that he considers "big" as better than "medium" and "medium" as better than "small". There is nothing peculiar in a preference-order of this kind. Nor can the preference-structure of person no. 2 be said to be strange; he prefers the middle alternative *b*, and of the other two alternatives, he considers alternative "small" best. Person no. 3, on the other hand, has a somewhat strange order. He prefers the alternative "small" to both the other alternatives, but if the alternative "small" is not accepted, then he prefers the alternative "big" to the alternative "medium". Let us see how majority mechanism works if person no. 3 shows a more natural order, preferring "small" to "medium" and "medium" to "big". We then arrive at the following preferences:

$$\text{person no. 1: } a > b > c \text{ (and consequently } a > c),$$
$$\text{person no. 2: } b > c > a \text{ (and consequently } b > a),$$
$$\text{person no. 3: } c > b > a \text{ (and consequently } c > a).$$

If we now group the alternatives two and two, and consider what the majority decide, we shall get the following results:

$$b > c, \quad c > a, \quad b > a.$$

These results reveal no "self-contradiction" of the kind we got in the case shown above.

With this alteration in the example, the result will also be that a definite alternative, viz., alternative *b* or "medium", will be adopted. This applies, no matter which alternatives one starts with, if we employ a procedure in which votes are always taken on two specified alternatives. If we employ a procedure, whereby only one proposal at a time is voted for or against, *b* will be adopted, if one starts with one of the extreme proposals, that is to say *a* or *c*. This extreme alternative will then be rejected on the first count, and *b* will be adopted on the second count. If, on the other hand, we had started by proposing the medium alternative *b*, then this might have been rejected, as person no. 1 would consider it as "too small" and person no. 3 would consider it as "too big". On the second count alternative *c* would then have been accepted, as person no. 2 would then have changed over to it.

We see here how the rule of first voting on an extreme alternative helps to ensure that the process produces an unambiguous result, and in a compromise being adopted when none of the extreme proposals heads the preference scale of a majority of those giving their votes.

In cases involving decisions concerned with the magnitude of public expenditure for various purposes, and the way of distributing the burden of expenditure between groups, etc., it will as a rule be possible to imagine the alternatives as arranged along an axis, as we have done in the last example. Furthermore, it will probably be possible as a rule, for every group to identify an alternative as the best, and the others as worse, the further away from this alternative they are situated. For decisions of this kind, therefore, where questions of degree are involved, it should be possible to choose between Pareto-optimal points, without running into the sort of difficulties we illustrated in the first example.

We then come to the second difficulty in connection with the majority principle, viz., that this principle takes no account of the *degree of preference*. For example, in the last example we considered, the position might be that person no. 3 considers it entirely decisive that *c* should be adopted instead of *b*. At the same time, we might envisage the possibility that for person no. 1 and person no. 2 the choice between alternatives *b* and *c* does not matter very greatly. It would then be reasonable for alternative *c* to be adopted instead of *b*, even though *b* is actually the alternative that would command a majority, in the event of a vote between *b* and *c*.

This difficulty cannot be avoided with a purely formal consideration of the majority principle, when all those voting do so from purely selfish considerations. In practice, in the sort of cases we are interested in, it may probably be assumed that the various parties have some sort of consideration for the force of other persons' preferences. But even then we shall run up against difficulties. What we have just said with regard to person no. 1, person no. 2, and person no. 3, may after all involve their preferences *after they have taken into consideration what they believe to be other persons' interests.* In other words, the preference sequences that are set up need not involve purely "selfish" preferences, but may involve what every single person assumes to be best on the whole, after duly weighing his own interests and other people's interests.

An attempt to overcome this weakness of the majority mechanism might be made by introducing a system involving "weighted" votes. Every person might, for example, have at his disposal ten points, which he would have to distribute among the three alternatives (as is done, for example, when judging a pop-song competition). Anyone with a very strong preference for a particular alternative would then allot a great many points to this alternative, and only a few points to the other alternatives. However, even a system of this kind would result in difficulties, as it would be possible for a person to allot a great many of his points to his most highly preferred alternative, even though he might not consider this alternative very much better than the other alternatives. Thus he would be able to use his points in such a way that there would be the greatest possible probability that the alternative he preferred would be adopted, even though the others were *almost* equally good in his opinion. A points system of this kind has not been tried out in any national assembly or similar body where decisions regarding fiscal policy have been made*.

Another way out of the difficulty we have now considered is to introduce "purchase of votes". In the case of person no. 3 it was a matter of great importance that alternative *c* should be adopted instead of *b*, whereas person no. 1 and person no. 2 merely considered alternative *b* a *little* better than *c*. In this situation person no. 3 could pay the other two a compensation, in return for their accepting alternative *c*, and in that way one would arrive at a solution which all parties would consider better than the adoption of *b*. This means that adopting *b* would not be a Pareto-optimal solution, as another arrangement would exist, which everyone would prefer. But to arrive at this arrangement, we should

---

* For a more detailed discussion of a voting mechanism of this kind, see Richard Musgrave, *The theory of public finance* (New York, London, 1959) pp. 130–132.

have to permit payments between the persons concerned. We called it above "purchase of votes", but we could equally well regard it as an expression of the fact that all sides of a situation must be dealt with simultaneously, if we are to ensure that the majority principle results in a Pareto-optimal solution; this means, *inter alia,* that one must deal with questions involving the distribution of tax burdens and modifications in distribution of income in connection with measures involving public expenditure. In this way, using a somewhat different approach, we have arrived at a conclusion which we intimated at the beginning of this subsection.

Finally, with the aid of a special example, we shall illustrate certain problems arising when the utility effect of public expenditure is very unevenly distributed among groups within the community. Let us imagine that a national assembly is discussing the problem of building a main road and a number of secondary roads leading off from this main road. There might be a clear majority in favour of building the main road, which would serve all groups in a more or less equal degree. There may of course be disagreement as to how good the road should be. If one deals with the distribution of expenditure at the same time as one deals with the question of how big and good the road is to be, it is possible that one might reach a solution more or less similar to the one which is implied by the Lindahl mechanism dealt with above.

We then come to the question of subsidiary roads. Every single subsidiary road will, to an overwhelming extent, serve the needs of a certain subgroup within the community, viz., those who live in the vicinity of the projected subsidiary road. Others will also derive some benefit from the road, but not to the same extent. We are assuming here that since it is the national assembly that is dealing with the question of these subsidiary roads, their construction will nevertheless be financed on a national basis, i.e., by means of a tax that is similar for all, no matter what district they live in.

Here several kinds of behaviour are possible on the part of individual representatives when they vote. In the first place, one might imagine every representative voting entirely selfishly: that is to say, he will vote *for* the construction of the road situated in his district, and will vote against the building of all other subsidiary roads. With this behaviour, t is quite obvious that no resolution whatever to build subsidiary roads will be adopted. The reason for this may be said to be that by financing all the roads on a national basis one compels everyone to contribute to paying for things from which they will derive no corresponding benefit. And they will then, prompted by a "selfish" behaviour of the kind we have here presupposed, vote against.

An alternative behaviour is for every single representative to make up his mind on the quality of the road he considers should be built in his own district, and vote *in favour* whenever other representatives propose corresponding roads in their own districts. We could then imagine expenditure for roads being decided in the following manner: representatives are arranged, from the one who is in favour of the least expenditure (this might equal nought) to the representative who wants to vote the largest sum for road-building. Counts would then start with the most extreme proposal, that is to say the one demanding the largest grant. If this is rejected, the proposal involving the next largest grant would be taken, and so on. The final decision would then be the amount which is such that it just manages to carry a majority.

If all the representatives now follow the rule, that they vote in favour of a road in another district which is as good as the one they would consider reasonable in their own district, it is obvious that we shall get more or less equal subsidiary roads in every district.

The solution we arrive at in this way, however, will not generally be Pareto-optimal. People in the various districts may, after all, have different preferences when the choice between roads and other goods is involved, and it is perfectly possible that in some districts one might have improved the situation by building somewhat poorer roads, and in return imposing somewhat lower taxes on the population, while on the other hand in other districts having somewhat better roads built and imposing higher taxes on the citizens, and this could have been carried out in such a way that no-one, taken all round, would have been worse off, in his own evaluation. Here we are once again back to something which we also touched on in connection with the Lindahl theory, viz., that it may prove necessary, if we are to arrive at Pareto-optimal solutions, to consider special fiscal arrangements for every item of public expenditure. In a case like this it might be necessary to introduce a geographical differentiation of taxation; but it would be difficult to do this in the case of a tax payable to a central government.

On the other hand, the problem with which we are here involved can be solved by undertaking a decentralisation of decisions, i.e. by delegating authority, where the construction of subsidiary roads is involved, to local units such as municipalities or counties. This has to a large extent been done in a country such as Norway. However, very often "regional interests" and "local interests" will be so interwoven with one another, that it will not be possible to divide all projects into two clearly distinguished groups. In the example treated above the preferences concerning the main road and the subsidiary roads may for many reasons be mutually dependent, and the advantages of decentralized decisions therefore to some extent obtained at the cost of breaking this connection.

The discussion on the possible behaviour patterns in voting on such problems as we have here mentioned could be dealt with in much greater detail. For example, some representatives might in the case we have just considered "break out" and hope that *other* representatives would continue to follow the behaviour pattern mentioned. The "breakaway" members would then manage to secure certain benefits by voting for good roads in their own districts, and poorer roads in other districts. If a great many carried out a breakaway, one would eventually approach the situation we first described, in which no subsidiary roads at all would be built. This again would be a situation which all of them would consider as being not particularly good. It might be assumed that some of the representatives would then endeavour to form coalitions, in order to have their projects carried out. If a majority agreed on the formation of a coalition of this kind, they could of course by ruthlessly exploiting this coalition have their own projects carried out, while at the same time managing to block all other projects. And they could also get those who did not have their projects carried out to assist in carrying the burdens. However, coalitions of this kind would be apt to prove very unstable, since what was originally a minority would always be in a position to offer some of those in the majority coalition certain advantages by seceding*.

Finally, we shall tentatively summarise various conclusions on the majority principle as a decision mechanism in connection with the sort of questions we have here considered.

---

* For a more detailed discussion see G. Tullock, Problems of majority voting, *The Journal of Political Economy* (1959).

1. If all questions which in one way or another are interrelated are dealt with simultaneously, one should in principle arrive at solutions that are Pareto-optimal. In practice, however, it is impossible to deal with all the questions simultaneously and maintain an overall view. For this reason the conclusion is perhaps not particularly illuminating.

2. In a choice between points that are Pareto-optimal, the majority principle will be able to provide answers that do not satisfy the demands for logical consistency which we make of an individual's preference order. In such cases the final result of a voting procedure may depend on the actual approach adopted for casting votes, and to this extent might be fortuitous. In cases involving such things as the magnitude of certain types of public expenditure, one is not, however, likely to run up against cases of this kind. These might primarily arise where a choice between alternatives that are qualitatively different, and consequently cannot be arranged along an axis according to quantitative measures, is involved.

3. Wherever the majority principle may result in decisions which are not fortuitous in the sense mentioned in para 2 above, the objection may be made on the principle that it fails to take into consideration the strength of the individuals' or groups' preferences, and is therefore capable in certain situations of resulting in non-optimal decisions. A solution of this problem can be obtained if one introduces the possibility of some form or other of income transfer among the groups, in connection with cases where a constellation of preferences of this kind exists. The problem we have here indicated will naturally be somewhat reduced if the individuals taking part in the voting bear in mind the interests of "the whole", and do not vote merely on the basis of purely selfish interests. However, though in practice the problem will be less acute, logically it will continue to exist if individual representatives evaluate the interests of "the whole" in different ways. Furthermore, a system where every person endeavours to evaluate the interests of "the whole" raises additional logical and philosophical problems, which it would be out of place to discuss here in greater detail.

4. Special problems arise where the utility of each item of public expenditure accrues to a minor and limited group of the community. A great deal can be done here by decentralising decisions, if geo-

graphically limited groups are involved, although "general interests" and "local interests" are often so interwoven that it is difficult to solve the problems involved satisfactorily, either by means of purely central decisions or by complete decentralisation. In such cases negotiations and joint measures between various bodies or administrative levels will in practice play an important role.

6.2.4. Some figures showing public expenditure on goods and services in Norway and other countries

In section 1.1 we have already given various figures to illustrate the relative growth of the public sector within the total economy of Norway and other countries. We shall here consider in somewhat greater detail various figures which illustrate the expenditure used for the purpose of satisfying what we have called joint wants or collective wants. We shall get the most direct gauge of the total disposal of goods and services for covering joint needs by considering *public consumption**. If we consider the development over a longer period of time, we shall naturally observe that the nominal amount has increased very greatly. It has also increased very markedly even if we consider deflated figures. We shall possibly get the clearest idea of the development that has taken place by considering the amount of public consumption in proportion to the gross national product. This has been set out in the case of Norway for selected years from 1900 up to the present in table 4.

Table 4

Public consumption in Norway shown as a percentage of the gross national product
for selected years

	1900	1910	1915	1919	1925	1930	1933	1935	1939	1946	1950	1955	1960	1961
Civilian	4.5	4.6	3.9	6.3	6.9	6.6	6.9	6.7	6.6	8.0	7.1	6.8	8.0	8.1
Military	2.0	1.3	2.2	1.2	0.8	0.8	0.8	0.8	1.8	4.2	2.1	3.4	3.0	2.9
Total	6.5	5.9	6.1	7.5	7.7	7.4	7.7	7.5	8.4	12.2	9.2	10.2	11.0	11.0

---

* For a closer definition of this term, see *National Accounts 1930–1939 and 1946–1951* (Central Bureau of Statistics of Norway, Oslo, 1952) pp. 19–20.

A distinction has been made in table 4 above between civilian and military consumption.

Investment in public consumption capital is not included in the above table. On the other hand, *depreciation of public consumption capital* has been included in the figures above, so that the actual use of public consumption capital to satisfy collective requirements is in principle reflected in the figures shown in the table. We shall return to the question of investments below.

During the years prior to the First World War the figures showed no marked development. During the First World War a certain increase in total public consumption took place, and naturally within this framework a certain redistribution took place, in favour of consumption for military purposes. After the First World War total public consumption showed marked fluctuations from year to year, although the level was clearly somewhat higher than in the prewar years. As expenditure for military purposes declined, there was greater scope for an increase in civilian public consumption. Thus, expressed as a share of gross national product, it showed throughout the entire interwar period a considerable advance on the period prior to the First World War. On the other hand, no considerable increase took place in the course of the inter-war years; even during the depression in the 'thirties civilian public consumption remained remarkably constant, in relation to national product.

In 1939 military expenditure once again started to increase, so that total public consumption increased. Norway emerged from the Second World War with a higher level, for both civilian and military public consumption, than had been the case in the inter-war years. During the postwar years a certain wave motion has taken place in these figures: first a certain tendency to fall, and later a tendency for public consumption, expressed as a share of the national product, to increase.

Taking the long-term view, we may consequently say that there has been an increase in the share of the national product which is allocated to satisfy collective wants. The development, however, has not shown an even trend, but has taken place step-wise. First the level was raised somewhat in connection with the First World War, after which it remained relatively constant throughout the whole inter-war period.

Subsequently the level rose in connection with the Second World War.

During certain periods *investments in public consumption capital* have shown somewhat greater fluctuations than public consumption, especially during the inter-war years, when investments in public consumption capital were more markedly influenced by trade cycles than public consumption. If we consider the investments in public consumption capital as a share of the total gross investments, we shall find that they were on a level of from 7–9% during the period prior to the First World War. The level was somewhat lower during the war. During the inter-war years fluctuations occurred, and for several years it was in excess of 10%. In most of the postwar years gross investments in public consumption capital have constituted 8–10% of total gross investments, but have been somewhat in excess of this from 1959.

Thus all in all investments in public consumption capital have over a long period increased somewhat, reckoned as a share of total gross investment. When, in addition to this, we take into account the fact that total investments have increased in relation to the national product, particularly if we compare the postwar years with previous years, then it will be clear that investments in public consumption capital have increased markedly as a share of the gross national product. (By public consumption capital we mean roads, schools, public administrative buildings, and other capital equipment for non-military purposes which is not used for business purposes.)

The development in other countries often shows the same features as the development in Norway. The step effect which we noted in connection with the figures in table 4 is to some extent still more marked in other countries. In England a similar rise in level occurred in connection with the First World War and the Second World War. In the USA, apart from these two steps, there has been a rise in the level of public expenditure in connection with the depression in the 'thirties, especially if we consider the expenditure of the federal authorities. This difference between the USA and England is connected with the different form that anti-depression policy took in these countries. As described in section 3.4, the policy in the USA made greater use of public expenditure as a remedy, whereas the policy in England was carried out rather with the aid of monetary instruments.

This step-wise increase in public expenditure as opposed to an even trend-like increase, has been dealt with in considerable detail in a book by Alan T. Peacock and Jack Wiseman*.

If the question of the amount of public expenditure necessary to satisfy collective wants were at all times decided by mechanisms such as those we have discussed more theoretically in the foregoing subsections, there would not be any particular reason to expect a step-wise development of this kind. That a step effect nevertheless occurs, is, in the opinion of Peacock and Wiseman, bound up with the fact that, in a society which is not exposed to extraordinary pressure or events of any kind, a certain conception will form as to what is a reasonable or acceptable level of taxation**. As long as an opinion of this kind obtains, one can achieve an increase in public expenditure pari passu with an increase in the general level of income, but it would be difficult to achieve any considerable increase in public expenditure as a share of the country's total income. "In settled times, notions about taxation are likely to be more influential than ideas about desirable increases in expenditure in deciding the size and rate of growth of the public sector." During a period when public expenditure is not increasing as a share of the national product, a tension may arise between the needs for public expenditure and the limit that taxation sets on what can be realised in the way of expenditure. Should a "shock" then occur, in the form of a social upheaval, an economic crisis, or a war, the customary notions about taxation level will dissolve, and a new level will be reached, which will be maintained until the next time a major "shock" occurs.

Maybe another factor should be mentioned, in addition to these observations, viz., the following: in periods with a steady rise in nominal price and wage levels, the public authorities, by maintaining tax rates unchanged, would be able to have an increasing share of the national income canalised to the public sector. This applies at least to some forms of taxation, though not to all forms. (We shall return to this question in a later chapter.) In such periods, therefore, there should be opportunities for a more even increase in public expenditure as a share of the national product. Something of the sort may have taken place

---

* *The growth of public expenditure in the United Kingdom* (The National Bureau of Economic Research, Princeton, 1961).
** In this connection see the observations at the end of section 1.1.

in the postwar period in Norway, apart from the very first years, cf. the figures in table 4.

The special features in the development of the level of public expenditure we have here considered, need not necessarily mean that the considerations dealt with previously in this chapter are irrelevant. It is perfectly possible that at the bottom of it all is a mechanism similar to the one we described in the section on Lindahl's theory, but that the notion of a reasonable tax level which takes shape, must be regarded as a sort of friction, preventing the mechanism from functioning properly all the time. But, as we have already pointed out, it may be that a starting point based on individual utility functions of the kind we have employed above, is not particularly suitable for an analysis of what happens to public expenditure.

In Norway's case the official attitude to the question of the scope of public disposal of goods and services in the future is to be found in Parliamentary Report no. 54 (1960–1961): The general lines of the Norwegian tax policy. Here we read, *inter alia:* "As far ahead as it is relevant to see at present, it is assumed that the need will exist for a comparatively more rapid growth of collective consumption through public provision of services, in the form of education, health service, research, communications, etc., than in private consumption. Furthermore, this growth presupposes large-scale public investments in buildings and plant. Even though no similar rise in expenditure for defence purposes takes place, it is assumed that a reasonable extension of public activity will demand that an at least equally large percentage of the supplies of goods and services will be available for public purposes in future as in recent years."

After these remarks on the development that has taken place in the course of time, let us consider a comparison between different countries. In table 5 we have set out figures similar to those in table 4 for a number of European countries in 1957. As the national accounts are not set out on the same basis in all countries, many problems are involved in a comparison of returns for public consumption in relation to national product from one country to another. The figures in table 5, however, should in principle permit comparison, as they have been especially prepared for this purpose. On account of this standardisation of figures, returns for Norway in table 5 differ somewhat from the direct returns made on the basis of the Norwegian national accounts. For this reason it is not possible to make an entirely satisfactory comparison of the figures in table 5 with those in table 4.

Table 5

Public consumption shown as a percentage of gross national product, 1957

	Civilian	Military	Total
Sweden	12.6	5.0	17.6
United Kingdom	9.5	7.1	16.6
France	8.5	6.8	15.3
Netherlands	9.9	5.1	15.0
Austria	12.7	1.4	14.1
Western Germany	10.3	3.1	13.4
Greece	7.8	5.6	13.4
Denmark	10.0	2.8	12.8
Norway	8.8	3.4	12.2
Italy	7.8	3.9	11.7
Portugal	7.2	3.8	11.0
Belgium	7.0	3.3	10.3

Source: *Economic survey of Europe in 1959* (ECE, 1960).

In table 5, countries are listed according to the magnitude of total public consumption in proportion to gross national product. The order arrived at, however, is very greatly influenced by the amount of military consumption. This varies proportionately far more from country to country than the civilian share of public consumption.

Restricting ourselves to civilian public consumption, we clearly observe a certain tendency for countries with a high level of income to show a relatively higher public consumption in relation to the national product than is the case with countries with a lower level of income. There is, however, no rigid connection. Population density and geographical factors, and perhaps, too, the absolute size of the countries involved, are factors of importance to the need for public consumption. Similarly, historical and political circumstances will naturally be of considerable importance.

In the case of countries listed in table 5, investments in public consumption capital comprised something between 1.5% and 4% of gross

national product. Norway, with 2.5%, was fairly close to the average.
If we considered these figures side by side with the figures already shown
in table 5, there would be little change in the picture as far as comparison
between the countries is concerned.

Let us consider for a moment the composition of civilian public expenditure for goods and services. In table 6 the distribution of public
expenditure for goods and services for Norway, Sweden, and the United
Kingdom is shown. The figures show "current expenses" for Sweden
and the United Kingdom;

Table 6

Composition of public disposal of goods and services for consumption purposes

	Norway 1957	Sweden 1956	United Kingdom 1957
Administration	23	12	7
Police and justice	7	7	7
Education and research	34	31	28
Social services	6	9	4
Health	4	24	33
Roads, communications, water, sewerage	15	8	11
Church	2	5	⎰ 10
Miscellaneous	9	4	⎱
Total	100	100	100

Source: As for table 5.

in the case of Norway, figures for public consumption have been used.
This means that the figures are not entirely comparable, as the Norwegian
figures include wear and tear of public consumption capital, whereas the
figures for Sweden and the United Kingdom do not*. This difference
between the nature of the figures for Norway on the one hand, and for
Sweden and the United Kingdom on the other, will probably tend to
give undue weight to the items administration and roads, etc., in the

---

* In the publication from which these figures have been taken they have been listed
together, without any observations on the circumstances here mentioned.

figures listed for Norway, as compared with the two other countries.

In the figures listed there is a striking difference between the weight attached to the item Health for Norway and the two other countries. This is probably due to a difference in the definition of public undertakings: in the Norwegian figures the running of municipal hospitals is not included, as all such hospitals are in this context regarded as public enterprises, and therefore not included in the item Public Consumption*. On the other hand, it is a fact that public involvement in health, through the medium of the National Health Service, is more marked in the United Kingdom than in the Scandinavian countries.

On account of the circumstances here mentioned, the figures in the table do not provide a good basis for a comparison. It is therefore possible that the structure of public expenditure for consumption purposes is not so very different in the countries listed. If we add together administration, education and research, health, and roads, we shall include most of the public expenditure in all three countries. That administration should weigh more heavily in small countries than in large ones, appears reasonable, since a great many administrative tasks do not by any means increase proportionally with the size of the population. Similarly, geographical considerations would suggest that road expenditure in Norway should be comparatively higher than in many other countries.

A list similar to the one in table 6 could also be set up for public investments in consumption capital. We shall not reproduce these figures in detail here, but merely point out that investments in roads, communications, water and sewerage plus education and research, together account for approximately 70 % or more of total investments in public consumption capital in all three countries shown in table 6.

6.2.5. *Some concluding remarks on the satisfaction of collective wants*

As mentioned in the introduction to this chapter, in recent years the question has often been asked whether in the western countries too small a share of the supplies of goods and services is used to cover collective

---

* This problem, too, seems to be ignored in the publication from which the figures have been taken.

needs, and it is frequently felt that the answer to this question should be *yes*. We shall here make no attempt to answer this question, which incidentally requires to be formulated more precisely. We shall merely, on the basis of what has been said in the previous sections, suggest various factors which might help to explain why a tendency of this kind to sub-optimal allocation to the public sector could exist.

In the Lindahl theory we saw that one might achieve agreement on a Pareto-optimal public expenditure, provided one had arrived at a suitable distribution ratio $h = \bar{h}$ for the corresponding tax burden. The theory does not clearly state what will happen if one does not arrive at precisely this distribution ratio. But we can see in figure 2 that one of the parties will desire *less* expenditure than that which corresponds to the Pareto-optimal solution $G = \bar{G}$, no matter in which direction the actual distribution ratio deviates from $\bar{h}$. And it is possibly not an unreasonable assumption that the party which desires a small measure of public expenditure will have such phenomena as inertia and a propensity to retain the *status quo* on its side whenever there is disagreement.

The step effect we discussed with reference to Peacock's and Wiseman's investigations supports this line of thought, even though these authors place greater emphasis on another aspect than the one that is concerned with distribution. In their opinion the actual *level* of taxation becomes the object of an evaluation that is separate from the question of the needs for public expenditure, and traditional conceptions are formed of what taxation should be maximally. Both a "faulty" distribution of the tax burden and such traditional conceptions of the taxation level as indicated by Peacock and Wiseman are, however, expressions of the fact that one does not get the necessary connection between considerations of collective needs and the way of financing them.

This also emerged in the discussion of the system of majority decisions. In principle one should here arrive at optimal decisions, but only if one succeeded in considering simultaneously "all circumstances" – including the question of distribution.

The following might perhaps serve as an outline synthesis of the various approaches we have considered: one generalises the Lindahl approach to apply to cases involving many groups, instead of only two. One will then have to consider a number of distribution ratios $h_1, h_2, h_3, \ldots$, instead of merely one h. For longer periods at a time these distribution ratios will in the main be determined by the ruling tax system. An increase or decline in the total tax revenue will come partly automatically and partly by an adjustment in the tax rates without alteration in the actual structure. For this reason, when the annual decisions on expenditure are made, one can assume that the distribution effects of the tax system are more or less given. If in this case the actual distribution ratios correspond to "equilibrium values" $\bar{h}_1, \bar{h}_2, \bar{h}_3, \ldots$, we shall be able to get unanimity on the magnitude of public expenditure. If the distribution ratios deviate significantly from "the equilibrium values", a majority decision would have to be made. This can then give a non-optimal decision, and on account of inertia tendencies such as those mentioned above, generally produces too *low* expenditure. At certain intervals, perhaps especially in connection with extraordinary situations of various kinds, one may get an upheaval in the taxation system, which may also involve an adjustment of the distribution ratios $h_1, h_2, h_3, \ldots$. The combination of a recognition of the need for increased expenditure demanded by the extraordinary situation, and an adjustment of the tax system may then provide the basis for a "step" of the type described by Peacock and Wiseman.

Apart from these factors, any practicable tax form involves certain undesirable effects on the allocation of the economic resources of a country, effects which tend to be stronger, the larger the amounts to be collected. (We shall return to this in the next chapter.) This also prevents one from proceeding as far in taxation and public expenditure as a mere balance between personal needs and collective needs, *given a total supply of goods and services,* would warrant.

Finally, it should perhaps be mentioned that political considerations of the long-term development of the community loom large in determining public expenditure. These considerations may to a certain extent overshadow the balancing on purely economic and social grounds of the use of resources to satisfy personal and collective needs.

6.3. *Other public economic activity*

In the previous section we have examined the satisfaction of collective wants through the medium of public consumption and investment in public consumption capital. We shall now consider various forms of public economic activity which cannot naturally be grouped under this heading. Bearing in mind the survey of the public sector given in section 1.1, the sort of economic activity we are now going to consider will in the main be conducted through the medium of public enterprises of type 2A or 2B. We are thus concerned with activities in which the public sector produces goods and services which are sold to the citizens in the same way as a private firm sells its goods or services.

Since it is, as we have previously indicated, difficult to draw any hard and fast line between the satisfaction of collective wants and other wants, however, some of the circumstances we are now going to consider could also be examined from the point of view of the satisfaction of collective wants.

The starting point for most of our considerations is an economy of the type we have in Norway, where the production and sale of goods and services is in the main conducted through the medium of private firms. What we shall now discuss is mainly the question of what circumstances might *in special cases* be adduced as an argument in favour of a certain type of economic activity being carried out by public enterprises. We do not intend to discuss the more comprehensive political questions with regard to private or public ownership of the most important means of production in general.

6.3.1. *Production in cases involving decreasing average costs*

Let us assume that a commodity (or a service) is produced by a cost structure given by the total cost function $b(x)$, where x is the quantity produced. We know from the ordinary economic welfare theory that if purchasers of the commodity are quantity adjusters (i.e. they consider the price as given), the commodity ought to be sold at a price corresponding to the marginal cost. (This of course applies only when certain assumptions are made, which are discussed in books on welfare theory.) In order to achieve optimal production and satisfaction of needs for this commodity, we should accordingly have

$$p = b' = \frac{db(x)}{dx}, \tag{6.19}$$

where p is the price of the commodity, and b' is the marginal cost.

With a price fixation of this kind, the profit will be

$$\pi = px - b(x) = b'x - b(x).$$

This can also be written in the following form:

$$\pi = (b' - \bar{b})x, \qquad \text{where} \qquad \bar{b} = \frac{b(x)}{x}. \qquad (6.20)$$

From this it follows that the profit will be negative if marginal cost is less than average cost $\bar{b}$, viz.,

$$\pi < 0 \qquad \text{if} \qquad b' < \bar{b}. \qquad (6.21)$$

That marginal cost is less than average cost, is in turn the same as saying that the average cost curve is falling, since we have

$$\frac{d\bar{b}}{dx} = \frac{1}{x}(b' - \bar{b}). \qquad (6.22)$$

The above can be summed up as follows: If we have a case involving a falling average cost curve, a price fixation whereby the price is made equal to marginal cost will result in the producing enterprise incurring a loss. It is impossible to envisage a production and price fixation of this kind being maintained over a long period of time by a private concern. It will be forced to produce a smaller quantity than that corresponding to the solution above, and to maintain a higher price, so that a positive profit is obtained. On the other hand it is possible to envisage a public undertaking pursuing a price policy corresponding to (6.19), and thus helping to ensure that production is maintained at an optimal magnitude, over a longer period of time, on the assumption that the loss is covered by the public budgets. This is an important argument in favour of public enterprises in various branches of activity. Particularly in the case of transport and communications, where large fixed costs are involved, this argument carries great weight.

Let us consider a particular case, which will give us an opportunity of studying in greater detail some of the problems involved. In order to simplify matters, we shall base ourselves on very special assumptions, and carry out a more partial analysis than is strictly satisfactory. Conclusions corresponding to the ones we shall arrive at, may, however, be drawn in more general cases, and in the case of less partial models.

Let us consider the production of a commodity which is produced in a quantity x with a cost structure expressed by the total cost function

$$b(x) = \begin{cases} 0 & \text{when} \quad x = 0, \\ B + ax & \text{when} \quad x > 0, \end{cases} \tag{6.23}$$

where B and a are constants. Thus magnitude B expresses the fixed costs, and magnitude a the variable costs per unit of the product. For marginal cost and average cost we consequently have

$$b' = \frac{db}{dx} = a, \qquad \bar{b} = \frac{b}{x} = a + \frac{B}{x} \,(\text{when } x > 0). \tag{6.24}$$

Let us consider the utility of this good to the consumers. We first assume that the consumers' total utility can be written as follows:

$$U^* = F^*(x) + \textit{the utility of income used for} \\ \textit{other purposes than the good } x. \tag{6.25}$$

Here we have written the total utility as a sum of the utility of the good x and the utility of income used for other purposes. This presupposes that the want for the good x is independent of the other goods, an assumption which enables us to deal with the problem with a more partial line of argument than we should otherwise be allowed to do.

Let us furthermore assume that the good x in all cases only absorbs a relatively small share of the consumers' total expenses. We can then assume that the marginal utility of expenses for other purposes than x can be regarded approximately as a constant. Let this constant marginal utility of other expenses be λ. Furthermore, let y be the amount spent on things other than the good x, and let us assume that prices other than the price of the good x are constant, so that we have no problems with the price level for these other goods. We can then write (6.25) as follows:

$$U^* = F^*(x) + \lambda y + k,$$

where k is a constant. The marginal utility of expenses for other purposes than x is then equal to $\partial U^*/\partial y = \lambda$.

As the zero point and unit of measurement for utility have no bearing on the line of argument, we can further simplify things by transforming U^* into a new utility scale U by

$$U = \frac{U^* - k}{\lambda}.$$

This gives us the following simple expression:

$$U = F(x) + y, \quad \text{where} \quad F(x) = \frac{F^*(x)}{\lambda}. \qquad (6.26)$$

In (6.26) we can say that we measure the utility in terms of money. Magnitude y is measured directly in monetary units. For $F(x)$ we can consider the expression to the right in (6.26). Here the numerator $F^*(x)$ is given in terms of "utility units" according to the original scale which we introduced. The denominator λ is a marginal utility of something expressed in monetary units, and is therefore expressed as utility units per unit of money. Taken all round, the designation for $F(x)$ will then be units of money.

The reason why we are able to choose our scale so that we have the utility expressed in money, is that we have assumed the independence of the want for x and for what is included in y, and furthermore that we have constant prices for what is included in y, so that we can use the amount here as a gauge of volume, and finally that for the relevant range of variation we have a constant marginal utility of y.

Let us look at the conditions for an optimal use of the resources available for x and y. Let the total value available for x and y be R; then

$$R = \begin{cases} y & \text{if} \quad x = 0, \\ B + ax + y & \text{if} \quad x > 0. \end{cases} \tag{6.27}$$

In the following analysis we consider the magnitude R to be given. This means that we assume that the community has so to speak set aside and made available for y and x a definite amount of resources. To the extent that we shall consume the good x, a reduction will occur in the consumption of the good y, corresponding to the costs involved in the production of good x. (In this connection it may be noted that the basis for the cost function must be a set of prices which are the same as those which are used when we measure magnitude y.)

With this approach to the problem we must maximise the magnitude U under the condition contained in (6.27), when R is considered as given. It is easy to see that a necessary condition for a maximum of this kind is

$$\frac{\partial U}{\partial x} = \frac{\mathrm{d}F(x)}{\mathrm{d}x} = a \tag{6.28}$$

if it is clear that x is to be produced at all, i.e., if it is clear that we shall have $x > 0$. In other words, so much of the good x is to be produced that its marginal utility is equal to the marginal cost a. We get this simple form because we have selected a utility scale such that utility, like costs, is measured in terms of money.

Let us see what the result will be if good x is produced and sold to consumers at a price p, the consumers considering the price as given. From the consumers' point of view the situation is then that they have a certain income R^* at their disposal (earned income minus direct taxes), which we assume they consider given. Their budget condition will then be

$$R^* = px + y. \tag{6.29}$$

They will then maximise total utility U, under the condition given by the budget equation (6.29). This gives us the following condition:

$$\frac{\partial U}{\partial x} = \frac{\mathrm{d}F(x)}{\mathrm{d}x} = p. \tag{6.30}$$

We see that this gives the same result as optimisation in (6.28) if and only if the price p is equal to marginal cost a. In the case we are now considering this corresponds to (6.19) in the more general case. A price fixation whereby $p=a$ will result in the fixed costs B not being covered by the revenue accruing from the sale of x. If the good x is to be made available to consumers in a market where the consumers are quantity adjusters, however, a price fixation of this kind is necessary if an optimal use of resources is to be obtained.

A graphic presentation will throw more light on some of the problems raised in this connection, see figure 3. In this figure the amount of good x is measured along the horizontal axis. The curve marked $\mathrm{d}F(x)/\mathrm{d}x$ is the marginal utility curve for good x. This curve expresses at the same time the demand for x at various prices p when the consumers are quantity adjusters, cf. (6.30). The curve $\bar{b}$ is the average cost curve corre-

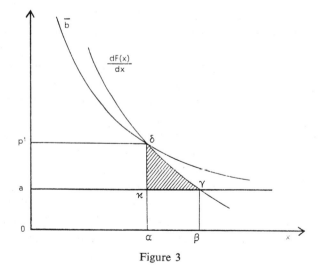

Figure 3

sponding to the formula on the right in (6.24). This approaches asymptotically the magnitude a, which represents the variable costs per unit of x. This magnitude is also marked off in the figure.

Optimal price fixation now corresponds to $p=a$. This will give an amount of the commodity expressed by $O\beta$ for x, corresponding to the demand when price is equal to a.

Let us now instead assume that good x is made available for consumers in a market at a price p, which is such that no loss is incurred in production. This price must be equal to the average cost $\bar{b}$. This is marked p^1 in the figure. It is determined by the point of intersection between the marginal utility curve and the average cost curve, as the price on the one hand must correspond to the marginal utility of the good when consumers are quantity adjusters, and on the other hand it must be equal to average cost, if no loss is to result from production and sales of the good. The corresponding amount of the good produced and sold will be $O\alpha$, which is less than the optimal $O\beta$.

On the basis of these assumptions, we can find an expression in the figure for the loss of utility that occurs with a price fixation of this kind which deviates from the optimal. This loss of utility will be a net magnitude which is arrived at in the following manner: With the production of x being $O\alpha$ instead of $O\beta$, the component $F(x)$ in total utility will decline in value, corresponding to the area of the trapeze-like area $\alpha\beta\gamma\delta$ in the figure (the integral from α to β of the marginal utility of x). On the other hand, y increases by $a(O\beta - O\alpha)$ when x is reduced from $O\beta$ to $O\alpha$, cf. (6.27). In the figure this is expressed by the area $\alpha\beta\gamma\kappa$. All told we have a utility decline corresponding to $\alpha\beta\gamma\delta$, and a utility increase corresponding to $\alpha\beta\gamma\kappa$. The net decline in utility will then correspond to the area of $\kappa\gamma\delta$, that is to say the shaded area in the figure. (Cf. the utility function (6.26).)

From this reference to the graph it is clear that, the more steeply the marginal utility curve falls in the relevant range, i.e., the more inelastic is the demand for the good in question, the less is the loss of utility suffered as a result of a price policy which aims to keep all costs covered. As an example in this connection may be mentioned radio licences. In this case we can say that the marginal costs to the producer of the services (i.e., broadcasting) caused by new listeners being added and enjoying the good, are equal to nought. The price, i.e., the radio licence, should consequently be made equal to nought, in order to satisfy the optimality requirement we have set up. On the other hand, in this case it is probably clear that very few people will give up listening to the radio on account of the licence price, as long as this comes within the range which has so far been current. That is to say, the demand for "radio services" is very inelastic as a function of the price. For this reason the loss of utility in the case of a price of this kind is hardly of any significance. (With the licence system we have for broadcasting, there is only a choice of two alternatives, viz., either to pay and secure the right to listen, or not to pay and thereby forego the right to listen. Strictly speaking the problems here involved can only be illustrated by means of the figure and formulae above, if one is willing to consider a utility function for the whole group of consumers, where the utility of "radio services" can be considered as a function of the share of the total number of consumers who have the right to listen.)

Similar observations might be made for various communications, such as railways, tramways, motorcoach services, etc. If we are dealing with a connection where there is no alternative passenger service, and where people *must* get through, the demand will be very inelastic and the triangle $\gamma\delta\kappa$ will be very small. That is to say, the loss of utility with a fare policy which provides cover for all costs will be small. If, on the other hand, we are dealing with a connection where people, at a certain level of fares, prefer to walk instead of being transported, the elasticity in the demand will be greater, and the loss of utility with a "mistaken" fare policy may be greater. (Where people choose between, e.g., a tramway and a private car, the demand elasticity for tramway services will be quite high, and the loss, as illustrated in the figure, will be comparatively great. In this case, however, the assumptions on which fig. 3 is based will hardly be fulfilled. In a case of this kind we should have to consider private car transport as part of magnitude y, and it could then hardly be regarded as want-independent in relation to magnitude x, which represents tram transport. A precise analysis in a case of this kind would demand introducing into the argument the actual want-dependence.)

In evaluating these problems it must always be borne in mind that whatever resources are not used in producing x, will benefit people through y. When we speak of loss, we do so not in the form of less goods *all in all,* but merely in the form of a poorer composition of consumption. When utility loss is small in the case of a "wrong" fare policy, where we have a highly inelastic demand, this is because the fare policy in this case is of little importance to the real composition of consumption.

So far the line of argument has been based on the fact that *if* the good x is to be produced and sold to consumers acting as quantity adjusters, then the price should be made equal to the marginal costs a. On the other hand, we have not raised the question of whether good x ought to be produced at all. This is a question which cannot be decided by means of a line of reasoning in purely marginal concepts. In principle we must here consider total utility. Furthermore, the fixed costs B now enter as a factor of significance, since B, of course, is variable in the sense that one avoids the costs B if one refrains entirely from starting the production of good x.

If we introduce y from (6.27) into (6.26), then total utility will be expressed in the following way, when $x>0$:

$$U = R + F(x) - (B + ax) \qquad (\text{when } x > 0). \qquad (6.31)$$

What we now have to do is to compare the maximum value we have for U in (6.31), that is to say, the value we have for U when (6.28) is fulfilled, with the value of U which we get when $x=0$, that is to say, with the value

$$R + F(0). \qquad (6.32)$$

If even the maximum value we can obtain for U in (6.31) is not greater than the value given in (6.32), then all in all it would not be "right" to start the production of x.

In a case like this various situations might be envisaged. The good x can, for instance, be an entirely necessary good, and we might express this by saying that $F(x)$ becomes negative and infinitely great in absolute value when x approaches zero. Then it would be quite clear that x should be produced, and from the above it then follows that the good should be supplied to consumers at a price corresponding to the marginal cost.

Next let us consider a case where we can say that $F(0) = 0$, and that

$F(x)$ rises for a rising x, but with a decreasing derivative. We have drawn-in a utility curve of this kind in fig. 4, together with the total cost curve $B + ax$. In this case the total utility one achieves, if x is not produced, will be equal to R. If the good x is produced, one will reach a utility which is equal to R plus the difference between the utility of x, $F(x)$,

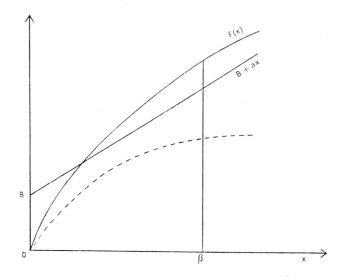

Figure 4

and the total cost $B + ax$. This means that the good x should be produced if any quantity exists where we achieve a positive difference between $F(x)$ and $b = B + ax$. In the figure we can see that this is possible when the functions have the forms that are drawn in there. We get the greatest difference between the total utility and total costs of production of x when $x = O\beta$. For this value of x the slope of the curve $F(x)$ is equal to the slope of the total cost curve $B + ax$. This is simply another expression of the solution we also found in fig. 3.

By way of comparison, an altenative shape for the function expressing the utility of good x (the dotted curve) has also been included in the figure. Here it is possible to find a point where the condition of marginal utility being equal to marginal cost can be fulfilled, but even with this adjustment of the quantity x, total utility will be less than if one refrained entirely from producing x^*.

The rule we have found for price fixation, once it has been decided that the good x is to be produced, may serve as a guiding line for price fixation for various forms of service which public enterprises or institutions sell to consumers. The magnitude that then has to be found is the marginal cost a. In principle, this should be possible with the help of accounting, statistical, and technical investigations. In practice, of course, many difficulties will crop up, especially in connection with the borderline between what should be considered variable and what should be considered fixed costs. Furthermore, difficulties may arise in cases where one is concerned with the production of several associated goods or services. However, the theory can be extended to make better allowance for such cases.

On the other hand, it is far more difficult to apply the rule relating to total utility, which should decide the question whether one should start

---

* The rules for marginal utility and total utility considerations which we have here presented, can be presented in an alternative manner by diagrams such as those below. Here, in an x, y graph, indifference lines corresponding to a utility function U have been drawn in. Furthermore, on the basis of (6.27) a curve showing possible combinations of x and y has been drawn in. If $x = 0$, then $y = R$. If $x > 0$, then $y - R - B - ax$. Thus the possibility curve starts at point $x = 0$, $y = R$, and then descends perpendicularly for a distance corresponding to B. It then continues with a slope of $- a$ when x increases. In the figure to the left below we then clearly have a case where it is not profitable (in a utility sense) to start production of x, while the figure on the right illustrates a case where this would be profitable. Once it is given that x is to be produced, the quantity should be determined in such a way that the indifference curve is tangential to the possibility curve, which corresponds to condition (6.28) in the text above.

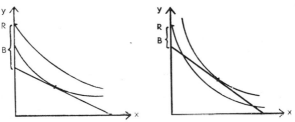

production of x at all. Here of course the total cost function may have been determined more or less accurately in advance, but it is difficult to imagine that the function $F(x)$ is known. A rule which might possibly be used is that no production should be started, unless there exists in any case one possible price, which would ensure that total costs of production were covered. (This should be understood hypothetically: optimisation would demand fixing a price equal to marginal cost, and not equal to the hypothetical price which would create at least a balance between total revenue and total cost.) In the case illustrated in our figures, prices exist which could produce a balance or a profit, viz. prices equal to p^1 or higher. These prices will result in a production of x which is equal to Oα or less. This rule, however, is not an absolutely valid rule, as it is possible to imagine cases where the marginal cost curve, throughout its course, lies beneath the average cost curve, so that it is impossible to find a price which would result in covering total costs, but where greater total utility can nevertheless be achieved by operating than by refraining entirely from producing the good in question. (This can easily be seen when it is considered that the total utility achieved through production and consumption of x, is measured by the area under the marginal utility curve, while total costs are expressed as a rectangle that can be formed from origin to a point on the average cost curve in fig. 3.)

As an alternative therefore a more complicated rule is suggested. For this, too, one imagines hypothetical price fixations in order to see whether it is conceivably possible to cover total costs. Here, however, we assume a more complicated price fixation than the simple one considered above. This price fixation would involve first setting a very high price, and selling what could be sold at this high price; then reducing the price somewhat, and satisfying the extra demand that resulted, and so on gradually down the scale. This would be continued until one had reached the point where the price was equal to marginal costs. If, with a price policy of this kind, one succeeded in making a surplus over total costs of production, it would be right to start production. Logically this rule is more satisfactory than the foregoing, and it is clear that it would enable a number of projects to "slip through", which would fail to pass the test which was first mentioned. It is, however, also clear that the rule which has here been explained is not easy to apply in practice. It can only serve to a certain extent as guidance or background for judgment decisions*.

A price fixation in agreement with the rule presented above will, as we have pointed out, produce a deficit in the producer's accounts. In the long run a price fixation of this kind cannot be followed by private producers, who can only operate when production yields a profit on a long-term basis. A cost structure with a falling average cost curve, a feature that is most marked in cases involving high fixed costs, can therefore by regarded as a factor in favour of public operation of the activity concerned. Any deficit could then be financed by public budgets. As an alternative to this, however, one might envisage a subsidy arrangement, in which private operation was maintained, but where the public authorities covered the deficit by subsidies. The actual arrangement would then have to be worked out in such a way that it induced the firm to fix its price in accordance with the rule we have set out above. To what extent one ought to choose public management or private management with subsidies, will depend on circumstances, some of which we shall return to below. Political considerations will, of course, also play an important role, and purely practical circumstances may often be of significance. In many countries, among them Norway, purely state-run enterprises and private firms with public subsidies (in addition to private without subsidies) are to be found side by side operating in the communications sector.

If what has been stated so far is in any way to constitute an argument in favour of public management, it is of course necessary that the public authorities, to a greater extent than private undertakings, should really

---

* The form of hypothetical price policy envisaged in this second rule means that through this price policy one succeeds in procuring for the producer a revenue corresponding to the entire utility that consumers enjoy from the good in question. For this reason this rule will correspond to the sort of total utility consideration which we have maintained is necessary to decide the question whether x should be produced at all. The first rule we mentioned, where we merely raised the question whether there exists *one* price that is such that a surplus will occur, provided that this price is fixed and retained, allows a so-called consumer's surplus to remain with the consumer. The income thus raised will not correspond to the total utility enjoyed by consumers, and for this reason this simple method gives no correct answer to the question of a comparison between total utility and total cost.

accept the consequences of the line of argument set out, and pursue a price policy more in agreement with the rule set out than private producers are prepared or can be induced to do. This does not always happen. A line of argument similar to the one above was set forth in a very precise form by the French engineer and economist J. Dupuit as far back as 1844. But it took a very long time before it was accepted and obtained any practical importance. In 1896 K. Wicksell published a major work on fiscal theory, where he strongly recommended that European state railways and other public enterprises should reduce their prices and rates, basing himself on a line of argument similar to the one presented above, and that they should cover their increased deficit with the aid of direct taxation. In this connection he wrote: "The size of the resulting deficit is immaterial in this connection, that is to say, it is irrelevant for the economic justification of the price reduction. It would of course be gratifying if the price reduction diminished the deficit or even led to an increase in revenue, since this would indicate a significant increase in use, which remains the thing of primary importance. At the same time this circumstance should give occasion for still further price reductions because, rationally, the deficit must always include the entire amount of the general costs and until this is so the enterprise has not reached its theoretical optimum utilization. Any surplus of revenue over cost would be even less acceptable. The existence of such a surplus as, for example, the spectacular profits of the Prussian State Railways, may be a shining testimony to the efficiency of the administration and to the prosperity of the industrial and commercial life of the country; but at the same time the surplus also indicates that the enterprise is far from its optimum degree of utilization both in national and in individual terms. The passenger and freight traffic of the Prussian State Railways would probably increase very considerably with an appropriate reduction in rates. Everyone would gain thereby and no-one need lose, provided only that the ensuing deficit be financed by taxes in a suitable manner" *.

The extent to which state railways and other public enterprises in various countries follow this rule today, is somewhat doubtful. In actual fact, state railways in most countries run at a deficit, which suggests

---

* Here quoted from *Classics in the theory of public finance,* eds. R. A. Musgrave and A. T. Peacock (London-New York, 1958).

that to a certain extent they follow the line set out in the argument above. At the same time, however, in most countries the official aim is to balance the accounts of such undertakings. Before pronouncing judgment on this aim, however, it must in every single case be made clear what is meant by "balancing the accounts". In Norway, for instance, certain fixed costs in the running of the state railways will be kept outside the accounts, and no attempt will be made to cover them by revenue. In Norway, as in other countries, one nevertheless most generally gets the impression that the deficit, e.g., in the state railways, is regarded as an inevitable evil, and not as the accepted result of a rational price or fare fixation for the services that are supplied.

Before drawing any final conclusions, it is also necessary to consider the following factor: a policy in agreement with the rules discussed above will produce a deficit which must be covered in another manner, that is to say mainly through taxation*. In the model we have considered in (6.23)–(6.32) and figs. 3 and 4, the deficit will exactly correspond to the fixed costs B. If consumers in the first instance have earned the entire income R, taxation must deprive them of the amount B, so that the disposable income R^* which appears in (6.29) will be equal to $u_\lambda + y$. If it were possible to find a form of tax such that the taxation itself did not in any way cause a deviation from optimality as far as the use of resources was concerned, this would not cause any fresh concern, and we could without more ado apply the line of argument adduced above. We shall return to this question in a subsequent chapter. For the time being it may be noted that no absolute answer can be given to the question whether or not the disadvantages resulting from taxation in some quarters will offset the benefit of its use in avoiding deviations in others, but that the objection here mentioned to the policy discussed above is in my opinion not decisive, if the tax involved is given the form of an income tax or a proportional sales tax. (Cf. in this connection the last words in Wicksell's statement quoted above.)

The last-mentioned question is equally relevant whether the price or rate policy discussed occurs in a state-run enterprise or in a private one subsidised through public budgets.

---

* In this connection I would remind the reader of the introductory remarks on the underlying assumptions in this chapter.

6.3.2.   Indirect effects in consumption and production

A private producer who determines the magnitude of his production and the combination of production factors, will take into account the sacrifices which are expressed as costs in production, and the utility created, to the extent that this affects revenue in the sales of the goods or services produced. Apart from the sacrifices and the utility thereby taken into account, however, sacrifices may be involved or utility created in more indirect ways in connection with the production, in such a way that no account is taken of them by the private producer in his decisions. In the same way there may be indirect effects in connection with consumption. When the private consumer determines the extent and composition of his consumption, he takes into account the utility he personally attains from such consumption. But it is conceivable that his consumption has effects for other members of the community, which are not taken into account in his decisions. The treatment of such "indirect effects" constitutes an important part of economic welfare theory. A detailed account of this would be out of place here. Mention of certain main features, relevant to the question of public management versus private management, will have to suffice.

One of the main conclusions of the ordinary welfare theory is that generally speaking, a system involving fixed-price quantity adjustment, both in production and demand, will not result in an optimal situation when such indirect effects which are ignored by individual private producers and consumers occur. Generally speaking it may then be said that in cases where *strong* indirect effects operate, a motive may exist for some form or other of state intervention.

Let us imagine a situation where a utility of the activity concerned operates beyond what accrues to the individual private purchaser of a good. If we have fixed-price quantity adjustment in production, the maginal cost in production will be equal to the price of the good. Furthermore, if we have fixed-price quantity adjustment on the demand side, we shall have an equilibrium of such a kind that the private marginal utility of the good, reckoned in terms of money (cf. above section, formulas (6.25)–(6.26)), is equal to the price. However, private marginal utility is less than the social marginal utility, because, as already stated, utility effects operate in the community beyond what accrues to the individual purchaser. With fixed-price quantity adjustment this will then produce the relationships:

Marginal cost = price = private marginal utility < social marginal utility.

$$(6.33)$$

Social optimality, however, demands that marginal cost shall be equal to social marginal utility. An adjustment such as that in (6.33) will then as a rule result in insufficient production of the good involved. Taking one's point of departure in a situation such as that in (6.33), and increasing production beyond this, will as a rule result in a diminishing social marginal utility. Whether marginal cost is constant, rising or diminishing, one will as a rule reach a point where equality is achieved between marginal cost and social marginal utility, and with production greater than what corresponds to (6.33).

An optimal adjustment in a case where private production, without special intervention, would give an equilibrium such as that in (6.33), might conceivably be achieved in the two following ways:

In the first place one might subsidise private production. One would then, so to speak, introduce two prices: one price that the producer receives, and a lower price that the private purchasers pay. The difference is the subsidy per unit of the good concerned. One would then get an equilibrium which can be described in the following way:

Marginal cost = price to producer > price for consumer =
            private marginal utility < social marginal utility.   (6.34)

With an appropriate degree of subsidising, it would be possible to create equality between marginal cost and social marginal utility.

In the second place one might envisage public management of the production involved. This would have to be carried out under a price policy in which the price is set at a lower level than marginal cost, so that the difference would correspond to the indirect utility of consumption of the good involved. One would then get a situation which could be described in the following manner:

Marginal cost > price to producer = price for consumer =
            private marginal utility < social marginal utility.   (6.35)

By setting the price at an appropriate level beneath marginal cost one would be able to achieve equality between marginal cost and social marginal utility.

Which of these two alternatives one should choose will naturally be a question of a similar kind to the one we discussed in connection with the case involving decreasing average cost.

The various approaches here suggested can be made to apply to a number of goods "produced" by public enterprises or institutions, such as for example education, health services, communications, etc. Indirect effects are in fact an important part of the argument in favour of having such undertakings operated by the Government rather than by private concerns. It must, for instance, be assumed that giving a citizen an education has utility effects for the community beyond the utility effect enjoyed by the individual person who receives that education. For this reason, education should be made available at a lower price to the individual citizen than the cost of giving him that education. More or less the same can be said of a great many health services. This emerges quite clearly in the case of an item such as vaccination. The individual person who is vaccinated receives a utility inherent in protection against disease. But in addition, there is the social utility that the person concerned, by virtue of having been vaccinated, will be less liable to spread infection, so that the vaccination of one person contributes to the protection of others as well. For this reason vaccination should be "sold" to individual citizens at a price lower than the actual costs of the vaccine, if citizens are to have a free choice of being vaccinated or not.

In addition to cost-benefit considerations such as these, it will of course often be possible to adduce arguments based on considerations of justice, when dealing with the question of how much the individual citizen should pay for benefits of the kind here mentioned.

Let us also consider a simple example involving transport problems. We shall choose an example which may not occur so frequently, but which clearly illustrates the point of indirect effects. Let us imagine a town situated at the very head of a fjord inlet; furthermore, let us imagine that the town is suffering from traffic problems, caused by narrow streets and a large number of cars. Through the town a considerable colume of traffic also passes between the west side and the east side of the fjord, traffic which has no connection with activities within

the town. It would be possible to set up a ferry service across the fjord
for cars wishing to pass from the west side to the east side, or vice versa,
without having any business in the town itself. If this ferry was run on
ordinary business lines, the fare per car would have to be such that the
costs of the ferry service would be covered, and if possible yield a surplus.
The individual motorists would then choose between using the ferry,
or driving through the town round the head of the fjord, taking into
consideration how much money they would save by driving through the
town, and thus avoiding the ferry, and what they might save in the way
of time and petrol, if instead they took the ferry. That is to say that the
individual motorists would compare the price of service here offered,
with the private utility this service offered them. Here, however, an
important indirect effect falls outside the comparison. For every car
which chooses to take the ferry across the fjord, instead of making the
journey through the town, the traffic situation in the town itself is eased,
and cars and other conveyances operating there can carry out their
activities more effectively. From a national economic point of view, if
one is to weigh these factors "correctly", the decision whether cars should
take the ferry from one side to the other, or drive through the town, should
naturally be made on the basis of an evaluation in which both the utility to
the individual driver using the ferry, and the indirect utility of easing the
traffic situation within the town for other road users, should be taken into
account. In order to obtain a "correct" adjustment in this case, one would
have to demand a lower price for ferry transport than one which would
cover the costs of this service. This could be achieved either by means of
public operation at a deficit or by subsidising private operation of the ferry.

The costs of the ferry service with which we are here concerned are
actually the marginal costs for every car that is ferried across. In this
example we actually have two factors that favour "running at a loss".
In the first place marginal costs will be lower than average costs, with
such implications as we saw in the previous subsection. In addition to
that we have the factor which we have just considered, viz., that one
ought to set the price lower than marginal costs, in order to take into
account the indirect effects on the traffic situation in the town.

Even though as a rule the overall picture is less transparent, similar
indirect effects will operate in connection with a great many communications projects.

One kind of indirect effect that is of great importance in connection with such things as the construction of railways, is the following: supposing we have a district where the economic structure is mainly based on activities involving low income, e.g., rather poor agriculture. Let us furthermore assume that if no railway were constructed to open up this district, and facilitate the transport of raw materials and finished products in connection with some industrial undertaking, people would remain living in the district, earning low incomes. If, on the other hand, a railway line were built serving this district, it would be possible to start an industrial undertaking where people were employed at higher incomes than they earned in agriculture. Furthermore, let us assume that these higher incomes correspond to the value of the marginal productivity of their work in this new undertaking. In that case we have an indirect effect which will not be reflected in the accounts of the private industrial undertaking, and for which the railway, too, would not be able to demand payment, viz., the increase in income earned by people in the district who are transferred from agriculture to industrial work. Here, too, it is conceivable that if the railway took freight rates that would cover the actual costs of freight (marginal costs), then from the private economic point of view the industrial undertaking would not be profitable. Nevertheless it may be profitable from the national economic point of view, when one takes into account the indirect effects that have been mentioned. Here various possibilities for achieving a social optimal adjustment are available: one might have private management of both the railway and the industrial undertaking on the spot, and subsidise one or both of these undertakings. Furthermore the railway might be run as a public undertaking, at low rates which produce a deficit, while the industrial undertaking was privately run. Finally, the railway might be privately run, at freight rates that would cover entire costs, while the industrial activity was state-run, at a deficit.

Considerations of the kind here mentioned have played an important role in shaping railway policy, e.g. in Norway, although the explanations are not always couched in the terminology here used.

As mentioned by way of introduction, we can also have cases in which a particular activity involves the community in indirect expenses which are not taken into account by private decisions. We can then distinguish between private costs and social costs for a given activity. With a behaviour involving fixed-price quantity adjustment, both on the supply side and on the demand side, we shall in a case of this kind obtain a result which can be described as follows:

Private marginal utility = price =
$$\textit{private marginal cost} < \textit{social marginal cost.} \qquad (6.36)$$

If no indirect utility effects are involved in the activity we are considering, social optimal adjustment will demand that private marginal utility (which would now be equal to social marginal utility) should be equal to social marginal cost. The adjustment described in (6.36) will then as a general rule involve unduly large production and unduly large consumption of the good concerned, as so much will be produced and used that private marginal utility will be forced down below the level corresponding to social marginal cost. The most immediate solution to the problem that here arises, would be to introduce a special tax on production or consumption of the good concerned. We shall then get a difference between the price paid by the consumer, and the net price obtained by the producer in the production and sales of the good concerned:

Private marginal utility = price for consumer > price to producer =
$$\textit{private marginal cost} < \textit{social marginal cost.} \qquad (6.37)$$

By setting the tax at an appropriate level, one can then ensure in this case that marginal utility will be equal to social marginal cost.

In a case like this, of course, one might introduce public management, in order to ensure a "correct" price fixation. This would then involve setting a price higher than the one which would produce equilibrium in a market with fixed-price quantity adjustment. This may be a concomitant argument in favour of the state, for instance, having a monopoly on sales of alcoholic liquor. Apart from the direct costs involved in the consumption of alcohol, occasioned by the production costs of the liquor, the consumption of alcohol often involves a series of social expenses over and above this, e.g., in the form of work to be discharged by the police and the law courts, an increase in the incidence of traffic accidents, and possibly, too, lowered working capacity of various kinds, etc., etc. These are expenses which private producers and retailers of alcoholic liquor would not include in the costs, if they were to operate according to the customary pattern of a private producer behaviour. As far as this special case is involved, a whole series of other considerations too, in addition to these purely utilitarian and economic ones, have of course played their part in establishing the policy that is pursued.

Otherwise, it is more difficult to find such striking cases where indirect costs are adduced as an argument in favour of public operation of various types of economic activity than to find cases where indirect utility effects have been adduced as an argument of this kind. As far as one is able to take into account any indirect costs which may have been established, this is more frequently done by means of excise taxes or through direct legislation.

6.3.3. *Other particular arguments in favour of public enterprise*

We shall mention briefly a few other factors which may play a certain role in deciding that certain types of economic activity should be carried out by public enterprise.

Preventing the creation of private monopolies. In the economic welfare theory it is shown that monopolistic behaviour may result in a price and a production level which does not correspond to the demands of social optimality. From other points of view, too, familiar arguments can be raised against private monopolies. In connection with economic activities where monopolies are particularly likely to arise, there are consequently strong factors in favour of public operation. This argument will apply to such sectors as telephone and telegraph services, postal services, various kinds of transport activity, and also a number of other types of economic activity. Frequently, though not always, this argument will apply to the same cases as those we dealt with under the heading "production in cases involving decreasing average costs". It is of course precisely in cases involving decreasing average costs that a large enterprise will have a pull over a smaller enterprise in the way of costs, so that we get a marked tendency towards concentration in one or a few large concerns; and in such cases a monopolistic price policy is necessary if a deficit is to be avoided.

Special long-term projects. In investment projects where capital is tied up for a long period, private producers will have to take into account various forms of uncertainty which the project involves. The same naturally applies to the public authorities, if they intend launching projects of this kind. But the nature of the uncertainty here involved need not be the same in both cases. Let us, for instance, consider the case of building electric power stations. Here, private producers pondering the question of establishing a power station may view the future with uncertainty, for the simple reason that they do not know how many other private producers might start similar production, thus tending to force the price of electricity down. If the production of electric power is reserved to the public authorities alone, this form of uncertainty will not arise and influence the decision. In such cases it may be that private activity will result in too little being invested in sectors where this kind of uncertainty occurs. This may be an argument in favour of public operation in these sectors – either in such a way that the public authorities have the sole right to engage in such activities' or that the public authorities start such undertakings side by side with private producers.

An alternative to public operation in such cases is a system of concessions, and other forms of agreement between public and private authorities, which eliminate or reduce the type of uncertainty arising from the fact that individual private producers do not know what other private producers may decide to do.

Apart from the development of power stations, this point of view can also be applied to the transport sector, and to whole regional development projects.

Effective management. In various cases considerations of efficiency of management have been used as an argument in favour of nationalising certain types of economic activity, e.g., mining, road haulage, and others. This consideration will occasionally coincide with what we have just said about the uncertainty involved in more long-term projects. For example, in connection with the nationalisation of mining, it has been maintained in some countries that private operation of mines has resulted in far less being invested than would have been socially optimal in mining, because private producers have felt a greater uncertainty for the future, and have therefore refrained from modernising and investing.

Above we mentioned the prevention of the formation of private monopolies as a motive for public operation. From the point of view we are now discussing, arguments in favour of public management can be found in the attempt to prevent competition *wherever this assumes particularly expensive forms.*

The comparative effectiveness of private or public operation in various situations is a question whose more detailed discussion lies outside the scope of this book.

Saving collection costs. In certain cases the costs incurred in collecting a price or fee for a service may constitute a fairly considerable share of the actual sums accruing through such price or fee. In such cases it may be maintained that the public authorities ought to operate the activity concerned and offer consumers the good free, in order to avoid the social expenses which the actual collection of the price or fee involves. This factor will hardly play any independent or decisive role in deciding on private or public operation in various cases. But it may play a certain role, as a concomitant factor, inter alia in connection with such things as the collection of tolls on roads and bridges. Here the actual expenses incurred in collecting dues, either in the form of plant and personnel for collection, and delays suffered by road users, may amount to sums which may be quite considerable, compared with the amount actually collected. A private bridge company could not in any case refrain from collecting dues if it were to cover the expenses involved in building the bridge. Public authorities, however, would be in a position to do so.

In this case, however, the decisive argument would be the one which we have already treated under the heading – Production in cases involving decreasing average costs. If we ignore wear and tear on the bridge due to the passage of cars, we shall here after all have a case involving large fixed costs and at the same time variable costs equal to nought. For this reason the price of the service, which in this case is access to driving across the bridge, should be fixed at zero. Any car which, to save the toll, chose another and longer route than the one leading across the bridge, would represent an unnecessary economic expense.

6.3.4.   Some data on public enterprises in Norway and other countries

In connection with the discussion above, we shall give some data on public enterprises in Norway and other countries – their total importance and the branches in which they operate. In this connection we shall define a public enterprise as one that is either directly subordinate to public authorities, or one in which the public authorities own more than fifty per cent, if the undertaking concerned is an independent legal entity, e.g., a joint-stock company. This line of demarcation will naturally prove somewhat arbitrary. How reasonable it will be in various cases depends inter alia on how the shares that are not owned by the state are distributed.

In order to illustrate the importance of public enterprises taken as a whole in some countries, let us first quote some figures for public enterprises' share of the total value added created in the country, their share in total employment, and in total gross investment. This has been done in table 7. The figures here and throughout this section have been taken from the already quoted *Economic Survey of Europe* 1959.

Table 7

The share of public enterprises in total value added, total employment, and total gross investment. 1957 or approximate years. (. . indicates that no figures are available)

Country	Percentage share of		
	Value added	Employment	Gross investment
Austria	. .	8	27
Sweden	13	7	15
United Kingdom	14	14	32
Norway	9	. .	14
France	10	7	25
Denmark	5	4	12
Belgium	. .	4	10

We can see here that the public enterprises' share of gross investment is greater than their share of employment and value added. This is due to the fact that public enterprises are largely to be found in activities demanding large capital outlay. In some cases, too, it is due to the fact that the state has taken over enterprises with the avowed object of carrying out far-reaching modernisation and reinvestment, in order to make an industry technically up to date. Finally, it is partly due to the fact that the state operates in branches which for technical and demand reasons expand more quickly than on the average is the case for the economy as a whole.

With regard to the question of what branches of activity are run by public enterprises, all the considerations previously mentioned in this section apply. Furthermore, more incidental circumstances will play a not insignificant role. In many countries, for instance, considerable German property was taken over by governments after the Second World War. This applied, inter alia, to countries such as Norway, France, and Austria. In certain cases this property has subsequently been sold to private companies or individuals, but in many cases the state has continued to operate the concerns on the basis of the property taken over at the end of the war.

Let us glance briefly at some of the sectors where we find the government most strongly represented in West-European countries.

In all these countries the *postal services* are a purely public activity.

In most countries the *telephone service*, too, is entirely dominated by the state.

The *transport sector*, especially railways and tramways, constitutes another sector in most of the countries concerned where government influence is strong or entirely dominant.

In a number of countries, among them Western Germany, The Netherlands, Belgium, Norway, Sweden, and Finland, the state and municipalities are strongly represented in *electricity* and *gas and water supply services*. In Italy a law has recently been passed for the nationalisation of electricity supplies.

Mining is more or less a state monopoly in Austria. Particularly in the case of coal mines, the state is dominant in Great Britain and France. The state also operates a large share of the mining industry in countries such as Italy, Sweden, Norway, Finland, and Western Germany.

In the production of *iron and steel* the state is entirely dominant in Austria, and also plays an important role in Italy, Sweden, and Norway. In Great Britain the steel industry was at one time nationalised, but was denationalised again after a number of years, so that recently the state has been responsible for only a fraction of steel production. However, it may now be nationalised again after the change of government, which took place in 1964.

In Norway and a number of other countries the state also plays an important role in the production of *aluminium*.

In addition, in a number of countries we also find the state operating, either on a large or dominant scale, in the production of *automobiles, aircraft, armaments, oil, alcohol, salt, tobacco, and matches*. In some countries, too, the state plays an important role in *forestry*.

If we compare the structure of state productive activities in Norway with the structure in other countries, one may say that in Norway it is comparatively widely distributed in a great many sectors. This is partly due to the factor we have already mentioned, viz., that after the Second World War the state took over a number of former German properties, and has subsequently to some extent continued to run these as state undertakings. In a number of other countries the state has acquired a complete monopoly of certain types of industry, while it has fewer undertakings distributed among other sectors.

Public undertakings are organised on somewhat different lines in the different countries. But as a general rule it would be right to say, as we have mentioned previously, that industries which do not represent natural competitors for private producers at home or abroad, and with which large and particularly important community interests are bound up, are often directly subordinate to a department or other state office, while activities run in competition with private producers in "traditionally private sectors", are frequently organised as state joint-stock companies or in some similar manner, so that they are given a larger degree of independence and freedom of action.

Forms of taxation and their effects

7.1. Why we have taxes

We have already discussed, in section 3.1, the aim and object of taxes in general. We pointed out that public expenditure in itself has an expansive effect. Consequently, if one has a limited production capacity or does not want imports to exceed certain limits, it will as a rule be necessary to counteract this expansive effect of expenditure to a greater or lesser extent, thus avoiding an inflationary development and/or a greater deficit in the balance of payments in foreign trade than is desirable. From the point of view of a macro consideration we may say that this is the aim of taxation.

Most countries, however, have many different kinds of taxation, and more than one type of tax. This applies not only if we consider the public authorities as one, but also if we consider different levels of government separately. Before taking a closer look at the various forms of taxation, we can therefore raise the question of why the different countries have come to operate with many different types of taxation. Several reasons can be given for this:

(a) In the first place there are many *historical reasons*. Previously one operated to some extent with different public treasuries for various purposes, and each of these levied its own taxes. Furthermore, public revenue has in the past often been founded on tax bases which would not be capable of providing the large amounts of taxation that have proved necessary in more recent times, even if they had been exploited to the maximum. At the same time it is often easier to retain an old tax and add a new, comparatively modest tax, than to change over and levy a heavy tax on an entirely new basis. For this reason the old taxes have not always been abolished when new forms of taxation have been adopted.

(b) *Considerations of equity*, too, often militate against a complete re-
vision of the system of taxation. Once a tax has been introduced, it
may often create unfair effects if it is subsequently abolished and
replaced by other taxes capable of producing a greater total revenue.

(c) In practice tendencies to *avoid taxes* or to *downright illegal tax evasion*
will always exist. (The borderline between these two categories need
not always be very clearly defined.) These tendencies, and the practical
effects of them, may often be greater for a particular tax, the higher
the rates for this particular tax. When the individual tax-payer considers the question of whether he should endeavour to evade a tax
he will probably weigh the disadvantage and unpleasantness he will
suffer if his attempt fails, against the financial gain he would enjoy if
the attempt succeeded. The unpleasantness will hardly increase proportionately to the amount involved; that is to say, it does not
increase proportionately to the rates of the tax involved. On the
other hand, the amount he stands to gain if his attempt succeeds
will often be proportional to the rates of taxation. For this reason
there will be a greater likelihood that his decision will be in favour
of an attempt to evade taxation when the rates are high. For this
reason it may be practical to operate with a great many taxes with
low rates, instead of a single tax with a high rate. A factor operating
in the same direction is that if one has many different taxes, the
income which escapes *one* tax will often be caught by another tax,
thus making it more difficult to achieve a large net evasion.

(d) Nowadays it is very natural to say that the reason for operating with
many different types of taxation is to enable the public authorities to
have *many policy instruments*. This enables the public authorities in
their economic policy to endeavour to achieve many different targets
at the same time. (Cf. in this connection the general discussion on
targets and instruments in Chapter 2.) We have already seen a few
examples of this in Chapter 3. In connection with model (3.27) we
saw how operating with both a direct tax and a sales tax made it
possible to include the market price level *side by side with* public
consumption of goods and services and employment as a variable for
which a target might be set up. The same circumstances were perhaps
more satisfactorily explained in model (3.68). In connection with model
(3.46) we saw that a system which includes special taxes on wage

incomes and on business profits might make it possible to operate with a target not only for the general level of activity, but also for the division of the national product into the two components consumption and investment. Using still more tax types, it is possible to operate with more detailed and specialised targets, e.g., with regard to the production or consumption of certain special goods. One can aim at influencing the distribution of disposable incomes among districts, types of family, etc. Taxation can also be used to achieve targets which are not in the first place economically motivated.

In this connection it should be recalled that not every tax can unconditionally be described as one instrument; cf. section 2.3.

Of the factors mentioned under points (a) to (d) above, the last-mentioned may be said to be so general that it could actually comprise all the preceding ones. The term target would then have to be interpreted so generally that it does not only indicate objectives of a kind that can be quantitatively described.

All the above would apply even if one had a dictatorial form of government. In a system comprising organs where there are representatives of groups with different interests, there would be a tendency to have several types of tax as a means of achieving sufficient agreement to enable decisions to be made. As we saw in Chapter 6, the "Lindahl mechanism" might involve separate financial arrangements for different components in public expenditure.

7.2. Survey of various tax forms

After these introductory remarks we shall give a brief survey of different forms of tax. We shall then consider in some detail problems involved in the shaping of income taxes and a general sales tax, which are the most important taxes in a country such as Norway. We shall subsequently deal with various problems in connection with the effects of various taxes. This will be done more or less in the form of examples, as so many problems can be raised within this field that a complete and systematic presentation would prove unduly lengthy.

The following survey will in the main be based on a division of taxes according to the tax base employed.

7.2.1. Head taxes

Head taxes differ from other taxes in that they have so to speak no other tax base than the actual existence of the individual. Head taxes are taxes levied as a fixed amount for every person (in most cases only males), irrespective of that person's income, consumption, capital, or other financial circumstances. Today taxes of this kind play hardly any practical role in economically developed countries. They have, however, a considerable theoretical interest. As the amount involved is not dependent on such matters as income, consumption of various goods, etc., a head tax will not exercise any influence on any of the marginal considerations that an individual undertakes in making his economic decisions. For this reason it differs from other taxes in a manner which is of great theoretical interest. We shall return to this in section 7.6.

7.2.2. Income tax

An income tax is a tax where the amount that the individual or concern has to pay depends on the person's or the concern's income in the current year, in a previous year, or over a longer period of time.

On a few occasions attempts were made to introduce income tax a very long time ago, but these attempts ran into very considerable difficulties. Income tax was not feasible until money economy had achieved its decisive breakthrough. In some countries income tax has been practised in something approaching the modern sense of the word since the time of the Napoleonic Wars. There was, for instance, an income tax in England as far back as 1799 based on a system of declarations and a tax percentage of ten per cent payable to the state. Exemptions could be made for various kinds of expenses, and there were tax-free exemptions in incomes for children and for life insurance premiums. Thus this tax comprised many of the features of modern income tax. The tax, however, was abolished fairly quickly, and all papers relating to it were burnt. In 1842 income tax was again introduced in England. It has been retained ever since, and on the whole the level of taxation has been raised every time England has been involved in a war, as mentioned in section 6.2. Originally the tax was proportional to taxable income, that is to say gross income minus legal exemptions as mentioned above. In 1909, however, a so-called "super tax" was introduced for large incomes, in addition to the ordinary proportional tax. This involved in reality a system of *progressive* income tax, that is to say a tax which takes a larger percentage of higher incomes than of lower incomes. (This super tax has subsequently been called a "surtax".)

No country can look back on such a long continuous period of income taxation as England. During the years before the First World War there was a large-scale introduction of income tax in other countries in Europe.

In the U.S.A. Congress passed a measure to introduce taxation of incomes as from 1894. This would bring in two per cent of incomes in excess of $ 4000. The tax, however, was declared illegal by the Supreme Court. The reason given was that setting a lower limit for taxable income involved a discrimination between citizens. From 1913, however, taxation of income was introduced.

In Norway income tax payable to the municipal authorities was made obligatory in 1882. Previously a number of municipalities had levied a tax, based on income, to cover special needs, e.g., poor relief. This had, however, not been compulsory prior to 1882. In taxation levied by the state, an income tax was introduced in 1892, and this became progressive from 1896. Norway, in other words, was comparatively early in the field, both in introducing a taxation on income and in making this progressive.

The taxation of income can be arranged as a *source taxation*, that is to say income is taxed "directly at source". An example of this is when one taxes interest income directly with the bank, deducting a certain share of a person's interest income, and paying it in to the public authorities, without involving depositors in any way. Another example is a wages tax, whereby employers make a deduction from wages, and pay this in to the authorities in the form of a tax, this constituting a final settlement of the taxation of the particular wage-earner in each case. In Norway we have had an at-source taxation of interest incomes for a number of years, and the taxation of seamen's wages has long functioned as a special wages tax. At present the possibility of introducing a similar tax for all wage incomes is being discussed.

Basing oneself entirely on a taxation at source of this kind, however, proves difficult if the aim is a taxation which is progressive with regard to the *total* net income of the individual income-earner. Suppose, for example, we compare three persons: A has only a wage income, B has only an income derived from interest, and C has a wage income as large as A plus an interest income as large as B. In other words, person C has a higher total income than either of the two other persons. If we now have a form of taxation which levies the same percentage on earned incomes and interest incomes, all three persons will have to pay a total tax amount constituting the same percentage of their total incomes. But if we operate with different rates for the taxation of wage incomes and interest incomes, the person who has the highest total income, viz. C, will have a tax which in relation to his total income will comprise a percentage lying between the percentage rate for wage incomes and the percentage rate for interest incomes. In this way he will bear a tax burden which constitutes a *smaller* percentage of his total income than is the case of one of the persons with lower incomes.

For this reason, if one wants a system of income tax where the rate of taxation is progressive in relation to a person's total net income, the tax, or at any rate a component of it, must be levied in relation to the earner's total net income (after various exemptions, such as those mentioned above, have been made).

If the tax the individual pays is to bear a certain relationship to his income, a periodisation must be carried out, in order to have time intervals in relation to which the income can be assessed. As a rule the period chosen is one year. As it is impossible to know what the individual has earned before the end of the year, an income-tax system of this kind must always be based on a tax assessment taking place after the period, during which the income is earned, has been concluded. For this reason the system in use has generally been that what a person pays in tax in the course of one year corresponds to the income which he earned during a previous period. However, it would be possible to envisage another arrangement: various methods might be tried to organise a system whereby a person in the course of one year pays approximately what corresponds to his income during the course of that same year. At the conclusion of the year an assessment of the total income earned must then be worked out, and the corresponding tax recalculated. If this differs from the provisional payment made, the difference has to be made good. If the system is a successful one, however, the discrepancies should not be particularly large. In Norway a system of this kind – the so-called "pay-as-you-earn system" – has been in force since 1 January 1957, as already mentioned in section 3.5. Various arrangements of a similar type have long been in use in several countries. As mentioned in the subsection dealing with automatic stabilisation in section 3.2, the question of which of these tax-payment arrangements is used has a bearing on the effect of taxes as automatic stabilisers.

7.2.3. *Net wealth tax*

A net wealth tax generally means a tax levied on gross wealth minus debts. In most countries taxation of wealth functions more or less as a supplement to income tax. In Norway it has also been introduced as an obligatory tax, side by side with the introduction of obligatory income tax to the municipalities.

The argument in favour of taxing net wealth, as well as income, has *inter alia* been as follows: in the first place wealth in itself is a reasonable object of taxation, in the sense that of two persons with the same income, but with different wealth, the one with the higher wealth will possess a greater "ability" to pay tax. In the second place, wealth tax may be regarded as a special tax on the income potentialities which wealth may provide. In some countries income derived from wealth has been regarded as a surer and more permanent form of income than earned income, and it has therefore been considered that a definite amount of an income of this kind provided a higher tax ability than a corresponding amount of other income, within a particular period.

On several occasions wealth tax has been introduced as an extraordinary tax, e.g., after wars, when states have been anxious to reduce their war debts, and where it has been considered reasonable that the population should contribute to this in relation to their wealth. Subsequently it may then have become permanent, though as a rule at a somewhat lower level than when it was introduced as an extraordinary tax.

Wealth tax may be proportional to net wealth, possibly after a certain tax-free allowance has been made, or it may be progressive with regard to net wealth, so that one pays a higher percentage of larger wealth than one would of smaller wealth.

In certain cases a tax is levied on *increase* of wealth over a certain period, as opposed to total wealth at a definite point of time. This has especially been the case after wars. It has been considered that an increase of wealth during a war has to some extent been "undeserved" income, and therefore justly liable to special taxation.

While income is a flow concept, liable to vary considerably from one period to another, wealth is a stock concept, which does not fluctuate so much in the short run. For this reason, wealth tax may offer special advantages to municipalities which are not in a position to pursue a fiscal policy with such aims as influencing the income level and cannot, to the same extent as the state, operate with a deficit in their budgets for long or short periods.

7.2.4. *Property taxes*

Property taxation can be designed either as a tax on certain kinds of property, generally real estate, or as a more general property tax which aims to include all objects which might have some sales value. An example of the last-mentioned type is the U.S.A.'s General Property Tax.

The tax can either be based on the value of the objects concerned (in certain cases market values, or in other cases values based on some system of assessment), or on so-called "objective criteria", such as, e.g., size measured in terms of area or volume, or the number of windows of a house, etc.

Property taxation is a very old form of tax. In rural areas it has given a fairly good idea of the income the owner could obtain, and it has therefore been useful as a tax corresponding more or less to the principle of "taxation according to ability". In urban areas the position has been much more difficult from this point of view, as there have been far more different kinds of income in towns that have not been correlated with property. For this reason many countries have introduced income and net wealth taxation in towns at an earlier stage than in rural areas.

Property taxation is now often regarded as an obsolete form of taxation. What may be said in defence of a tax of this kind, is that it provides a relatively stable tax base, and therefore offers advantages such as those mentioned above in connection with net wealth taxation. Furthermore, the base is often easier to assess than in the case of a tax based on net wealth, as mentioned in the preceding sub-section.

The objects of property taxation vary from one country to another.

In the United Kingdom this form of tax is levied mainly on houses. It is very important, since "rates" are the only form of local taxation in Britain. France has a special system of business taxes based on installed production equipment. In the U.S.A. the property tax has developed into a tax on practically every type of capital object, as mentioned above. In Denmark property tax is mainly levied on landed property.

In Norway there has been property taxation for several hundred years. Taxation of landed property has been based on a so-called *matrikkel*, which is a register of landed properties setting out details of ownership, cultivation, yield, capital value, etc., etc., as a basis for taxation. Both urban and rural municipalities have a system of regular assessment in order to establish a basis for levying property taxes.

Property taxes now play a relatively modest role in Norway, but in parliamentary report (Stortingsmelding) no. 54 (1960/61) the Ministry of Finance states that "it should be considered whether greater use should not be made of the property tax than is done today".

In connection with property taxes it would also be appropriate to mention a tax which has been discussed in a great many countries, viz. taxation of *increase in value* of real estate. Real estate often increases in value for reasons associated with the expansion and growth of an urban community, the construction of new communications, etc. In such cases an increase in value may be said to have been caused by the social development in general, and to have no particular connection with the owner's activity. It may then be considered reasonable to make this increase in value the object of a particular form of taxation. This factor has played an important role in various political movements in North America and Europe.

The varying role played by property taxation from one country to another is illustrated by the fact that whereas property tax per head of population per annum in Norway was some years ago as low as 14 *kroner*, the corresponding figure for the U.S.A. was 550 *kroner* and for Great Britain 240 *kroner*.

7.2.5.   *General sales tax*

By general sales tax is meant a tax which in principle is levied at the same rate on the sale of all kinds of goods and services.

General sales taxes of this kind are to be found in most European countries. However, the principle that this tax should be general is never enforced in its entirety. Certain exceptions are always made, either for practical or for social reasons. In several countries, for instance, food-stuffs are exempt from the sales tax. Furthermore, means of production are often wholly or partially exempt.

A general sales tax of this kind can be constructed in various ways: it might be levied only in the last stage of sale, that is to say the retail stage; only at the penultimate or wholesale stage, or at a still earlier stage. It might also be levied at several stages. We shall discuss this in greater detail in a later section.

In Norway a general sales tax payable to the state was introduced in 1935, levied at the rate of one per cent at all sales stages except sales from producer. In 1940 the tax was changed into a 10% tax on retail sales. In the years 1947–1951 the tax was reduced to $6\frac{1}{4}\%$, but it has subsequently been raised again to 10% and in 1964 to 13%. (The tax is calculated as 12% of sales value *inclusive* of the tax. A tax rate of 12% applied in this manner is the same as a tax percentage of approximately 13.6% levied on sales value *exclusive of* tax.) The reasons for introducing a sales tax are the general ones suggested in the introduction to section 1 of this chapter. A sales tax is comparatively easy to administer and supervise; it has the advantage that it can be changed at comparatively short notice, even within the ordinary budgetary periods, and it is productive of large yields without the rates being made too high, as a very large base exists on which to levy the tax.

The Norwegian sales tax applies as a principal rule to *sales of commodities*. At the same time, however, there are a great many labour services, extending from building and construction work, to ladies' and gentlemen's hairdressing, which are subject to taxation. The rules for a sales tax on work in connection with building and construction work have varied somewhat from time to time; most housing, however, has always been exempt.

The sales tax is most suitable as a source of revenue for the *state*, as different rates in different parts of the country might easily result in unfortunate trade disruptions. Furthermore, one trading centre might earn a great deal in the form of sales tax "at the expense of" surrounding country districts which might not belong to the same administrative unit.

For this reason, in most countries it will be found that the sales tax is used as a source of revenue to the state. In the U.S.A., however, sales tax is used by the individual federal states.

The importance of sales tax varies from one country to another. In Norway the sales tax is the state's largest source of revenue. The same applies to several other countries, but in the U.S.A., for instance, the federal authorities do not make use of a general sales tax at all, and Sweden did not introduce one until 1960.

7.2.6. *General expenditure tax*

As an alternative to taxing personal incomes might be envisaged taxing peoples' expenditure. A person's expenses could be calculated on the basis of income, with an addition for reduction in bank deposits and other claims, and deductions for increases in claims. Thus the aim would be to tax income minus net increases in claims. To what extent one should also deduct expenses in connection with purchase of a house or other kinds of fixed property, is a question whose solution might be envisaged in various ways.

Certain arguments can be raised in support of a tax of this kind, compared with an ordinary income tax – partly on the basis of consider-ations of equity, partly out of considerations concerning private savings, and partly out of considerations involving the effect of the tax on working incentive. The British economist Nicholas Kaldor is one of the leading advocates of this kind of tax*. There are, however, also counter arguments and it is difficult to decide conclusively what is best on a purely theoretical basis. So far expenditure tax has apparently only been tried on a major scale in India, where it did not prove entirely successful.

In connection with a tax of this nature one is tempted to ask: Why not levy a tax on expenditure through the medium of a sales tax, instead of levying the tax on the individual? The point here is that the amount a person pays in the form of sales tax will be proportional to his con-sumption, apart from certain effects which can be achieved by making exemptions from the ordinary sales tax for certain goods and possibly special taxes on other goods. By means of an expenditure tax for the

---

* See Nicholas Kaldor: *An expenditure tax* (London, 1955).

individual person, the tax can be made progressive in relation to his expenditure.

For *business undertakings*, too, an expenditure tax is feasible. Its advantages would primarily be that it would encourage a lowering of costs.

7.2.7. Investment taxes

For the purpose of stabilisation it may often prove useful to have a special form of tax on investments.

For this purpose two possibilities might be envisaged. In the first place one might levy a tax on *gross* investments, and in the second place an attempt might be made to tax only *net* investments.

The first type is undoubtedly the handiest from the administrative point of view, and it will serve the purpose of stabilisation just as well as the other type, because in this connection the actual investment activity will be decisive, and this can best be expressed by gross investment. But the objection can be made to taxation of gross investments that it will prove particularly damaging to production sectors operating with short-lived capital equipment, since gross investments compared to net investments would in such sectors be particularly high.

With regard to the actual organization of these taxes, two different types can be envisaged: in the first place the tax may be in the form of an excise on purchases of investment objects and the carrying out of investment work. It will then, in its actual form, resemble other special excise taxes. In the second place it can take the form of a tax on any increase in value of capital assets of investors. Of these two kinds, the first-mentioned is the handiest, as it involves fewer assessment problems – at any rate if the intention is to tax gross investments. A tax of this kind was used in Sweden for a number of years.

Something similar to what can be achieved through special investment taxes can be achieved by variations in the base for a general sales tax. When one wishes to stimulate investments, these can be exempt from the sales tax, and conversely when one wishes to put a brake on investment demand. With an arrangement of this kind, which has to some extent been practised in Norway, however, it is only possible to choose between tax rates which are either equal to nought or equal to the rate for the general sales tax. Using a special investment tax one can, if this is considered appropriate, choose rates lying between these limits, or higher than the general sales tax.

7.2.8. *Special excise taxes*

In several instances we have already touched on the form of tax which goes by the name of special excises, or simply excises. These are excises levied either on the production or the sale of certain specified goods or services. Excises of this kind have always played an important role, and are historically far older than general sales taxes. They are still playing an important role in most countries, including countries that have a general sales tax. In Norway the various excises together provide the state with a sum which is somewhat larger than the total revenue derived from the taxation of wealth and income, but less than the revenue derived from the general sales tax.

Historically speaking, one of the reasons for the great importance of excises has been that these are often easy to collect in practice.

Subsequently social considerations and considerations of equity have played an important part in shaping the system of excises. On the one hand has been the desire to tax luxury goods, and on the other hand the desire to limit the consumption of goods involving socially undesirable subsidiary effects, particularly alcohol.

Furthermore, the so-called "benefit principle" has played an important role in providing arguments in favour of certain excises. In principle this means that members of the community who to a particular degree benefit from certain aspects of public activity, should also contribute in a corresponding degree to the financing of such activities. An example of this line of argument is to be found in connection with the taxing of motor vehicles. It may be said that car-owners derive special benefits from public activities within the road sector, and that for this reason car-owners should make a particular contribution to the financing of these public expenses. This can then be done through special taxes either on the possession or use of a car, or on petrol, or on other accessories required in running a car.

Finally, special excises can be justified on the grounds that there is a desire to improve the allocation of resources through the tax system by taking into consideration indirect effects of various kinds, such as those discussed in the subsection on indirect effects in section 6.3.

In Norway the most important special excises are levied on objects associated with motor-car traffic, alcohol, and tobacco. A similar state of affairs exists in a great many West-European countries. In the U.S.A. taxation of motor vehicles and tobacco is on a considerably lower level than in most European countries.

In addition excises on gold and silver ware exist in practically all countries, and in many places there are excises on various objects associated with travelling, and amusements and entertainments.

For the same reason as in the case of general sales tax it is obvious that special excises are most suitable as a tax payable to the *state*.

7.2.9. *Customs duties*

Customs duties have played an important role for many hundreds of years. In the Middle Ages and the days of mercantilism, customs duties were as a rule the state's most important source of revenue. These were levied on export, import, and transit trade.

During the nineteenth century, as a result of the influence of liberalistic ideas, there was a marked trend towards a reduction in customs duties. Later on there was once again a development in the direction of protectionism. Customs duty was now levied only on imports, and the object was more frequently to protect domestic production against competition from abroad rather than to provide revenue for the state. Customs revenue has increased more slowly than other forms of state revenue, so that in recent times customs duties have constituted a comparatively small share of total state revenue in most countries. In more recent years, in connection with the establishment of customs unions and free trade areas, there has again been a tendency for customs revenue to decline also in absolute terms.

Technically speaking there are two main types of this tax. One is the specific duty, where the duty is calculated on the basis of the weight or quantity of the article or goods concerned, and the other is the *value* duty (*ad valorem* duty), where the amount to be paid is calculated on the basis of its value. Specific duty has the advantage that the actual base for calculating the duty can be established in an objective way. A specific duty is therefore frequently used where it is particularly difficult to establish values. On the other hand, a disadvantage of specific duty is that comparatively speaking it tends to penalise cheap goods more than expensive ones within the same category of goods. There is also a disadvantage in specific duty in that in periods of price fluctuation frequent changes in rates for the duty have to be made if it is to retain its real value unaltered. For these reasons the tendency in recent years has been in the direction of a greater degree of value (ad valorem) duty.

The question of which goods should be liable for high duties and which should be liable for lower duties, or even be exempt, is usually not considered to be a question of public finance.

7.2.10. Death duties

Early literature dealing with financial theory often contains a great deal on the subject of death duties. Two theoretical viewpoints are here represented: according to the first, death duty is to be regarded as "the *testator's* last tax", and according to the second point of view death duty is regarded as "the first tax of the *inheritor*".

According to the first viewpoint, the rates for a death duty should depend on the total size of the inheritance. According to the second point of view death duties should depend on the financial circumstances of the inheritor.

The question of death duty may pose different problems in the town and in the country. In connection with the running of a farm, death duty may not be natural, because a gradual transfer from father to son takes place, without the actual conditions of either of them being markedly changed. The position may be somewhat different in a town, where father and son each have their own household and each has his own job or runs his own business.

The sort of theoretical viewpoint mentioned by way of introduction above may have played some part in times past in shaping death duties. Nowadays other considerations emerge more strongly. In the first place considerations of equity are involved; in the second place one may ask how the various kinds of death duty affect savings. Finally, one may ask how the duties affect continuity in business life. It is, however, not easy to answer questions of this kind. For example, with regard to savings, it may be said that high death duties may well encourage people to save money, in order to ensure that there is enough for their descendants.

With regard to business life the view may be held that it is an advantage to ensure continuity, with son succeeding father, and that death duties should not be of such a kind as to prevent this. But on the other hand it may also be maintained that at certain intervals it would be an advantage to "inject fresh blood" into business life, and for this reason too much emphasis should not be placed on the factor just mentioned.

According to the first point of view mentioned above – death duties as "the testator's last tax" – death duty may in one way be regarded as a postponed wealth tax. On this basis one should expect a high death duty in countries with a low wealth tax and vice versa. To a certain extent this holds good. Britain and Sweden, for instance, have a low wealth tax, but on the other hand a comparatively high death duty. Norway, Denmark, and Germany have somewhat higher wealth taxes, and lower death duties, and in these countries the duty is calculated in relation to the portion of the estate which accrues to the various inheritors. In Norway the inheritor's wealth is also taken into account.

7.2.11. Other duties

In most countries there are also a number of duties payable to the state or local authorities, which according to ordinary terminology cannot be classified under any of the types previously mentioned.

We have, for example, a number of different types of duty which are imposed in order to promote special objectives within various branches of the economy. As these are determined by other considerations than those of public finance we shall not deal with them here.

Furthermore, there are a number of duties or premiums, associated with social insurance schemes. The rules for these duties will often be determined by various social considerations, which we shall not deal with here. Some of these duties, however, are so considerable that it is necessary to consider their *effects* in connection with fiscal policy. In Norway, for example, taxes and duties apart from social insurance premiums amounted in 1962 to about 10 000 million kroner, this being the total sum collected by the state and municipal authorities. Social insurance premiums amounted to about 2000 million kroner. Thus it will be seen that social insurance premiums comprise a considerable sum in relation to total taxation, and must therefore be taken into account in shaping fiscal policy.

In many insurance schemes the premiums for employees are paid in part by the employee himself, and in part by the employer. The relative proportion varies from one scheme to another, and there are also considerable variations if we compare one country with another. We shall not in detail investigate the questions this raises, but merely emphasise that the question of who *actually* bears the burden of insurance premiums cannot be answered without an analysis of how the actual insurance premiums affect the equilibrium position in the various markets. One would for instance have to answer the question of the extent to which the employers' share of insurance premiums affect demand for labour and prices of the products turned out by the firms or undertakings concerned.

The duties here mentioned do not as a rule figure in the state or municipal budgets.

7.2.12.   The importance of the various tax forms in Norway from 1875 to the present.

In the preceding sub-sections we have on various occasions briefly mentioned when the various types of tax were adopted in Norway, as well as adding a few remarks on the development in the importance of the various types of tax. Without commenting on this in any great detail, we shall illustrate the development below with the aid of figures, basing ourselves on a work by Kåre Amundsen*.

The first table below shows the importance of the various types of tax to the state during the period from 1875. The revenue accruing from the various types of tax is shown as a percentage of total state revenue on taxes and duties. (Whenever a budgetary year does not coincide with the calendar year, the year when the budgetary period *begins* is indicated in this and the following tables.)

The table clearly shows the transition that has taken place, first from customs duties as the most important source of state revenue, to income and wealth tax, and on to general sales tax. The marked change from 1910 to 1920 is due to two causes: in the first place the comparative isolation

---

* Kåre Amundsen: *Om skatter og skattepolitikk i Norge etter 1814* (Taxes and tax policy in Norway after 1814), Memorandum from The Institute of Economics at the University of Oslo of 22 February, 1960.

Table 8

The contribution of the various types of tax to total state tax revenues from 1875

Year	Income and wealth tax	General sales tax	Customs	Excises on spirits and beer	Other excises	Total tax revenue
1875	–	–	78.5	16.0	5.5	100
1890	–	–	72.6	20.2	7.2	100
1900	11.0	–	65.7	17.6	5.7	100
1910	11.9	–	73.1	7.6	7.4	100
1920	60.7	–	21.4	3.9	14.0	100
1930	26.8	–	34.9	16.9	21.4	100
1940	29.0	29.5	14.1	10.2	17.2	100
1950	34.8	21.8	6.6	14.0	22.8	100
1955	28.2	34.9	7.9	10.5	18.5	100
1961	22.8	38.0	8.2	8.7	22.3	100

caused by the world war, which resulted in a very considerable reduction in customs revenue, and in the second place the effect of the introduction of a new tax legislation from 1911, which *inter alia* introduced the obligation to make personal declarations. At the same time as customs revenue declined during the war, the need for state revenue increased, as we have suggested in a previous chapter.

In the column "Other excises" accruing to the state, taxes on motor vehicles account for a very considerable share.

For most of the last century it is difficult to get a clear view of taxation to the municipal authorities. As previously mentioned, there were originally different taxes for different purposes, such as schools, poor relief, etc. Legislature introduced in 1837 helped to regularise the position considerably, as the municipalities now became more clearly defined entities. The development of a money economy and of other industries than agriculture meant that landed property was no longer such a suitable basis for tax assessment as before. Income tax and wealth tax for this reason gradually superseded real estate taxes and special duties levied on various branches of production and trade. The municipalities were given a large measure of freedom, and for this reason the development varies considerably in the different parts of the country.

While the state was compelled to delay any introduction of income and wealth tax until the basis for it existed practically all over the country, the municipalities were thus in a position to start at different times, as conditions became more and more appropriate for such taxation in various parts of the land.

From 1863 income and wealth were no longer merely permitted as a basis for assessment of municpial taxation, but it was decided that at least half of a municipality's expenditure for poor relief should be financed by taxes levied on the basis of income and wealth. Initially fairly considerable emphasis was placed on wealth, in order to ensure that the transition from property taxes should not prove too sudden. In 1882 a new tax law was introduced, which increased the importance of income and wealth taxation, with greater emphasis now on income. In 1911, as mentioned above, new tax laws were again introduced.

Tables 9 and 10 below show the development of the importance to the municipalities of the various types of tax in the same way as table 8 illustrates the development for the state revenue. As development in towns and rural areas has been different, a table for each of these two types of municipality is given. On account of the circumstances mentioned above, the distinction between income tax and wealth tax is of considerable interest in connection with municipal taxation.

Table 9

The contribution of the various types of tax to the total tax revenue of rural municipalities from 1875

Year	Property tax	Net wealth tax	Income tax	Interest tax	Other taxes and duties	Total tax revenue
1875	35.6	22.7	32.8	–	8.9	100
1890	21.4	14.2	56.7	–	7.7	100
1900	11.6	17.7	64.5	–	6.2	100
1910	7.5	18.3	69.5	–	4.7	100
1920	1.5	10.5	86.5	–	1.6	100
1930	1.4	13.1	84.0	–	1.5	100
1940	1.0	9.1	84.1	4.8	1.0	100
1950	0.4	5.6	91.6	2.0	0.4	100
1955	0.2	5.1	93.4	1.1	0.2	100
1961	0.1	5.2	94.1	–	0.6	100

Table 10

The contribution of the various types of tax to the total tax revenue of towns from 1880

Year	Property tax	Net wealth tax	Income tax	Interest tax	Other taxes and duties	Total tax revenue
1880	24.3	10.6	57.0	–	8.1	100
1890	23.0	9.5	57.8	–	9.7	100
1900	24.5	8.8	60.0	–	6.7	100
1910	23.6	7.3	61.8	–	7.3	100
1920	22.8	26.3	42.2	–	8.7	100
1930	11.4	8.7	77.9	–	2.0	100
1940	10.5	6.0	78.4	3.2	1.9	100
1950	5.0	4.1	88.5	1.4	0.8	100
1955	4.0	3.6	90.3	1.5	0.6	100
1961	4.6	4.3	90.7	–	0.4	100

The tables clearly show the dominant importance to the municipalities assumed by income tax.

The interest tax included in tables 9 and 10 is the tax mentioned previously in connection with the discussion of taxation of income "at source".

There is also special taxation payable to counties. Here, property taxes originally played the dominant role. Subsequently the so-called "repartition" tax largely replaced it. The latter is a tax which counties raise from the municipalities.

7.3.   *Further observations on special problems in connection with income tax*

Many of the problems we shall deal with in this paragraph involve the definitions of various income concepts. Two of the central terms involved are the following:

$$
\left.
\begin{aligned}
\textit{Net income} \quad &= \textit{gros income} - \textit{expenses for earning, securing} \\
&\quad \textit{and maintaining the income.} \\
\textit{Taxable income} &= \textit{net income} - \textit{tax-free exemption dependent on} \\
&\quad \textit{family maintenance burdens.}
\end{aligned}
\right\} \quad (7.1)
$$

The definitions set out in (7.1), however, still leave many questions un-answered. There is a question of periodising income, the question of what types of expenses should be included under the concept "expenses for earning, securing and maintaining income" (the expression used in the tax law), questions concerning the form of various kinds of exemptions, and the question of how to deal with non-personal tax-payers.

Before attempting to answer these questions, however, it would seem appropriate to deal in somewhat greater detail with *progression* in the taxation of incomes, because the progression of income tax will have a considerable bearing on many of the other questions that arise in con-nection with the taxation of income.

7.3.1. *Progression in the taxation of incomes*

Let us first of all make a number of formal definitions, using the following symbols:

$$r = \text{net income}, \ s = \text{amount of tax}.$$

These magnitudes apply to a single tax-payer.

As per definition, in the case of income tax the actual tax will depend on the income. This we express by means of a function:

$$s = s(r). \tag{7.2}$$

In what follows we shall refer to this function as the (individual) *tax function*. We have expressed it here as a function of *net income*. We shall then have to take account of any possible tax exemptions in the functional form in (7.2). As an alternative, we might have envisaged the exemptions as deducted first, and then the tax expressed as a function of what in (7.1) is called taxable income. The starting point set out in (7.2), however, is the more convenient.

Many important questions in connection with the taxation of income revolve around the form of the tax function. In order to be able to discuss the form in greater detail we shall introduce the following concepts:

$$r - s(r) = \text{disposable income},$$

$$\bar{s}(r) = \frac{s(r)}{r} = \text{effective tax rate}, \qquad (7.3)$$

$$s'(r) = \frac{ds(r)}{dr} = \text{marginal tax rate}.$$

Thus what we have called the effective tax rate expresses how great a proportion of his net income a tax-payer pays in income tax. This is occasionally called average tax rate, but this expression is also used in other connections. The marginal tax rate expresses how great a proportion of an *addition* to the income will have to be paid out in increased tax.

In (7.3) we have expressed the marginal tax rate as a derivative of the tax function. Generally, when a tax is assessed, the income is rounded off downwards to the nearest round sum, e.g., to the nearest one hundred *kroner*. This means in practice that it would be more appropriate to express the marginal tax rate as follows:

$$s'(r) = \frac{s(r + 100) - s(r)}{100}.$$

However, in a discussion of principles, it would be most convenient to proceed as though the income liable for taxation may vary continuously, and the tax function is a continuous and differentiable function. As a rule it will be a simple matter to make the practical adjustment on the same lines as in the formula above.

In section 7.2.2 we have already defined a progressive tax as a tax which takes a larger relative share of the income, the larger that income is. In order to provide a more formal definition we can consider the derivative of the effective tax rate with regard to income, which will be

$$\frac{d\bar{s}(r)}{dr} = \frac{rs'(r) - s(r)}{r^2} = \frac{s'(r) - \bar{s}(r)}{r}, \qquad (7.4)$$

or we can consider the elasticity, which will be:

$$\text{el}\,\bar{s}(r) = \frac{d\bar{s}(r)}{dr}\,\frac{r}{\bar{s}(r)} = \frac{s'(r)}{\bar{s}(r)} - 1. \tag{7.5}$$

We can now proceed to define the terms progressive tax, proportional tax, and regressive tax as follows:

> Progressive tax: $\text{el}\,\bar{s}(r) > 0$, i.e. $s'(r) > \bar{s}(r)$
>
> Proportional tax: $\text{el}\,\bar{s}(r) = 0$, i.e. $s'(r) = \bar{s}(r)$ $\qquad$ (7.6)
>
> Regressive tax: $\text{el}\,\bar{s}(r) < 0$, i.e. $s'(r) < \bar{s}(r)$.

In the second case mentioned here, the one involving proportional tax, the tax function must necessarily be of the simple form $s = ar$, where a is a constant tax rate.

According to the definitions here given, there is nothing to prevent an income tax being progressive for a certain range of r, and regressive for another range of r. It might even be possible for the tax function to alternate several times between being progressive and regressive, or proportional, when we move from small incomes and up in the direction of larger incomes. In practice functions of this kind hardly ever occur in the case of taxation of incomes, if we ignore small "bulges" arising owing to the rules regarding rounding-off*.

Most income taxes are now arranged in such a way that a certain amount of income is entirely exempt from taxation; incomes in excess of this amount, and up to a certain limit, are taxed according to *one* marginal tax rate; incomes in excess of this limit and up to a new, higher limit are subject to a somewhat higher marginal tax, and so on. Thus in this way we have a system with a constant marginal tax rate within each income bracket, but increasing marginal tax rate from one bracket to a

---

* Another matter is that it is possible to investigate how the amount levied on a person in the form of various other types of tax may vary with that person's income. This may produce more complicated forms, with progression for certain income intervals and regression for others. However, this is not something specifically stated in the rules for these taxes, but a result of statistical co-variations.

higher one. The tax amount will rise piecemeal linearly, and the steepness will be greater, the greater the income. What we have called the effective tax rate will increase with income, but the increase will not be entirely even. If we suppose that we are studying the variation for increasing income, the effective tax rate will rise particularly rapidly as soon as one has just entered a new income bracket involving a higher marginal tax rate. The effective tax rate will then rise more and more slowly, as long as one is within the same bracket with regard to marginal tax rate, only to rise again more rapidly when we pass into a new and higher bracket.

A special case of the type of tax function we have here described is the case where incomes up to a certain amount – which we can call b – are exempt from taxation, whereas incomes in excess of this amount are taxed according to a constant rate, no matter how large the income is. A tax function of this kind can be indicated in the following manner, where a stands for tax rate:

$$s(r) = \begin{cases} 0 & \text{if} \quad r \leq b \\ a(r-b) & \text{if} \quad r > b. \end{cases} \tag{7.7}$$

The deduction b here corresponds to what in (7.1) is termed "tax exemption", and $r - b$ is the "taxable income".

For incomes in excess of b, we should, with a tax as in (7.7), get:

$$s'(r) = a, \qquad \bar{s}(r) = a\left(1 - \frac{b}{r}\right) \qquad (r > b).$$

We can see here that the marginal tax rate will be greater than the effective tax rate, so that the tax function (7.7) expresses a tax which according to the definitions in (7.6) is progressive. This special case of a progressive tax is often called a *degressive* tax. We can see that when the income r increases, the effective tax rate will approach the marginal tax rate a, so that the tax function can be said to approach a proportional tax when the income is large. The expression degressive is also occasionally used to describe a tax possessing this last-mentioned property, even though it does not correspond exactly to the form in (7.7).

In Norway the ordinary income tax payable to municipalities is formulated as a tax of the type shown in (7.7). Income tax to the state, on the other hand, is in the form of a progressive tax in the stricter sense of the word, viz., such that the marginal tax rate rises with rising income level even after the minimum limit for taxable incomes has been passed.

In a general debate on principles involving taxation of incomes, progression is often justified on a basis of social considerations of equity.

In the first place it is pointed out that it would not be reasonable to tax an income corresponding to "minimum subsistence level". This term is of course very vague, but the actual idea behind it affords a justification for exempting at least a certain amount of income from taxation as in (7.7).

With regard to the discussion on the form of the tax function, over and above the fact that a "subsistence minimum" should be exempt from tax, two different principles have been set forth in the textbooks.

First of all we have the so-called *benefit principle*. This lays down that the individual should pay taxes in proportion to the benefit he derives from public activities. Even without pursuing this line of argument in detail, most people will probably agree that it presents a very inadequate guidance to what a tax function should really look like. Whatever methods we try, it is difficult to establish who derives the greatest benefit from public activity. It is nevertheless possible that if public expenditure and the distribution of the corresponding tax burdens are determined as set out in Erik Lindahl's theory (see Chapter 6), then taxes will be distributed according to the benefit different groups derive from public activity. However, as shown in section 6.2, we are here concerned with a distribution according to *marginal* utility, and not total utility. Just as much or as little can be said about the fairness of the result this produces, as can be said about the fairness of the result produced by a market mechanism with regard to income distribution prior to taxation.

Secondly, we have the so-called *ability principle*. Roughly, this states that people should pay tax in accordance with their financial ability. Within this general frame of reference there are many different versions of the principle. Attempts have been made to define it more precisely with the aid of the concept of a utility function, e.g., by stating that all persons should accept an equally large absolute reduction of utility as a result of taxation, or an equally large relative reduction of utility, or that the total utility reduction for all tax-payers should be as small as possible. On the basis of various assumptions with regard to the form of the utility function (utility reckoned as a function of disposable income), different results can be deduced with regard to the form of the tax function*.

It is, however, difficult to believe that such a principle could provide an objective basis for establishing the form of the tax function. In the first place the familiar question of comparability of utility between persons arises in this connection too. This is, perhaps, not the most serious aspect of this matter, since any decision with respect to taxation must presumably be based, explicitly or implicitly, on a certain degree of comparison of utility as between persons (provided the taxation is not determined as a result of a downright struggle between groups, with every single group pursuing its aim quite selfishly). In the second place, independent of the first question, there is the problem of establishing the form of the utility function. Econometric investigations will go part of the way in this direction, but hardly far enough to provide knowledge of the form of the utility function for the whole of the income range such as one would have to know in order to deduce something about the form of the tax function for all actual income levels. In the third place – and this I consider the most important objection to the belief that it is possible with the help of the ability principle to make precise deductions about the tax function – great disagreement has existed among various champions of the ability principle as to how the principle should be more precisely defined, provided one knew the utility function. This is sufficient to show that not one of the various definitions of the principle contains any objective norm of equity.

In addition to these difficulties, in order to evaluate the fairness of a particular form of taxation, one ought to consider various *effects* of the tax, apart from the fact that it directly reduces the tax-payer's disposable income. There are some effects produced by the corresponding public expenditure (cf. the benefit principle above), and there are other effects operating through the price and income structure of the community. By such effects the tax burdens may be shifted onto other groups in the

---

* The most precise account of this is to be found in Ragnar Frisch: *New methods of measuring marginal utility* (Tübingen, 1932).

community than those on whom the taxes are formally levied. In such cases the fairness of a particular form of taxation cannot be assessed without taking this into account.

On the whole, therefore, I believe that the ability principle, in so far as attempts have been made to define and elaborate it with the aid of the theory of utility function, is mainly of abstract theoretical interest, and will not be able to play any significant role in the actual formulation of income taxation. A mixture of the following circumstances will probably be decisive:

1. An acceptance of the fact that "subsistence minimum" should not be taxed, together with a recognition of the fact that the public authorities must have considerable tax revenue at their disposal.
2. General considerations of fairness, which, however, cannot be defined precisely, as has been attempted, especially in connection with the "ability principle".
3. Conflicts between the economic interests of various classes or groups. The position here adopted will naturally colour one's attitude to considerations covered by 2 above. To a certain extent the formulation of the tax may play a role as a means of achieving agreement on expenditure increases, and thus bear the stamp of the preference structures of the various groups, cf. the Lindahl theory in Chapter 6.
4. Considerations on the more indirect effects of taxation, e.g. its effects on working incentives, savings, etc.
5. Considerations of practicability, and possibilities for and incentives to tax evasion.

In the various countries progression of income taxation has developed very markedly during the course of this century. In England the maximal marginal tax was at one time 19s 6d in the pound; in the U.S.A. marginal tax rates have been up to 91 %. In Norway the marginal rate in taxation of income to the state reaches a maximum of 55%, and in addition to this there is up to 19 % income tax to the municipal authorities, and up to 5 % tax distribution duty, which is the same as the former municipal surtax on higher incomes, and finally there is the $\frac{1}{4}$% special tax for development aid to other countries, producing a total of close on 80% as the maximal marginal tax rate. The level of income at which the maximum marginal tax is reached will of course vary from one country to another. It is lower in Norway than in most other countries.

It is, however, a very great question whether these highly progressive tax rates are really effective. In all countries there are various forms of excemption, special treatment of certain kinds of income, possibilities of splitting up incomes in various ways, apart from illegal tax evasions.

In the U.S.A., for instance, it is calculated that the tax actually paid amounts to 23% of income for incomes between 25 000 and 50 000 dollars, that the percentage then rises to 30% for incomes between 150 000 and 200 000 dollars, and that it then falls to 24% for incomes in excess of 1 000 000 dollars, in spite of the very sharp progression in the formal tax rates. These figures are set forth in a book by Louis Eisenstein, whose comment on tax rates is: "The rates bark more than they bite"*. (These figures are only mentioned as a pointer. A critical examination would demand a detailed examination of definitions, methods of calculation, and statistical material.)

The British economist Nicholas Kaldor maintains similar points of view as far as Britain is concerned**. He maintains *inter alia* that the high rates of income taxation are partly the result of a process in which the authorities have constantly replied to the inefficacy of taxation by raising the tax rates. He considers that this has produced a very unfair result, as in practice the various kinds of income offer very different opportunities of avoiding or evading the high rates.

In Norway the Tax Research Office of the Central Bureau of Statistics has carried out a comparison between income figures on the basis of tax statistics and on the basis of the national accounts, for various kinds of income. As far as the incomes of wage-earners and fishermen are concerned, no essential difference exists; in the case of agriculture, forestry, and "owners' incomes in other sectors" the figures shown in the national accounts are considerably higher than according to the tax assessment. The following comment to these figures is given by the Tax Research

---

* See Louis Eisenstein: *The ideologies of taxation* (New York, 1961), p. 181. See also R. A. Musgrave: Growth with equity, *The American Economic Review, Papers and Proceedings* (1963).
** See Nicholas Kaldor: *An expenditure tax* (London, 1955), pp. 27 and 46.

Office: "It may be debated whether tax assessment figures or national account figures give the best picture of actual incomes. For tax figures it may be maintained that our tax laws and assessment procedure tend to underestimate incomes where the assessment involves a certain degree of uncertainty. Relatively speaking, this operates to the disadvantage of the wage-earner. The result of the provisional examination of incomes statistics would appear to support this view. However, as nothing is known about the correctness of the national account figures, it is impossible to answer this question with any degree of certainty." *

Several of the problems of taxation of income with which we shall deal below are bound up with the progressivity of the tax function. Before proceeding we shall therefore show a general property of progressive tax functions which is important to some of these problems.

Let us assume that an income r consists of two components r_1 and r_2, so that

$$r = r_1 + r_2.$$

We are now interested in comparing the case when the income r is taxed as a single whole, and the case when the two components r_1 and r_2 are taxed separately. In the first case the tax will be $s(r) = s(r_1 + r_2)$, and in the second case it will be $s(r_1) + s(r_2)$.

According to the definition of effective tax rate in (7.3) we get:

$$s(r_1 + r_2) = (r_1 + r_2)\bar{s}(r_1 + r_2) = r_1\bar{s}(r_1 + r_2) + r_2\bar{s}(r_1 + r_2).$$

Now if both income components r_1 and r_2 are effectively positive, and if the tax function is progressive according to the definition in (7.6) for the relevant income range, we shall have:

$$\bar{s}(r_1) < \bar{s}(r_1 + r_2) \quad \text{and} \quad \bar{s}(r_2) < \bar{s}(r_1 + r_2).$$

---

* See Stortingsmelding (Parliamentary report) no. 54 (1960–61), Appendix 1.

If we use this in conjunction with the formula above, we get:

$$s(r_1 + r_2) > r_1 \bar{s}(r_1) + r_2 \bar{s}(r_2).$$

This can also be written:

$$s(r_1 + r_2) > s(r_1) + s(r_2). \tag{7.8}$$

Expressed in words, (7.8) means that, if the two income components are taxed jointly, the tax will be greater than it would be if one first calculated the tax applicable to the two income components separately, and then added the tax amounts together.

We shall also briefly give a formal expression of another property of a progressive tax function. This is concerned with the effect of a rise in the price level. Let us assume a tax-payer with a nominal income r. His real income can be defined as $r^{\text{real}} = r/p$, where p stands for price level. The nominal tax amount will depend upon the nominal income, as will follow from the tax function: $s = s(r)$. The real value of the tax amount is designated by s^{real}. We shall now consider a tax-payer who retains a real income unaltered, while the price level rises. The real value of the tax amount will then depend on the price level as follows:

$$s^{\text{real}} = \frac{s(pr^{\text{real}})}{p}.$$

From this formula we get

$$\frac{\partial s^{\text{real}}}{\partial p} \frac{p}{s^{\text{real}}} = \text{cl} \, \bar{s}(r),$$

where we have made use of formula (7.5). If we have a progressive tax function according to the definition in (7.6), the real value of the tax amount a tax-payer pays when he has an unchanged real income with a rising price level, will thus increase with the price level. The elasticity of the real tax amount, with regard to the price level, will simply be equal to the elasticity of the effective tax rate with regard to (nominal) income.

For the special case involving a degressive tax function as in (7.7), this effect will lie in the fact that the real value of the tax-free exemption b falls when the price level rises.

The importance this effect may have for the development of the share of a country's incomes at the disposal of public authorities, has already been touched on in Chapter 6. The effect indicated in the formula above is also of importance to the effect of the tax system as an automatic stabiliser when fluctuations are reflected in the price level.

7.3.2.   *The taxpaying unit. Maintenance burden*

In this section we shall only deal with the question of taxation of personal income-earners. The taxation of joint-stock companies will be dealt with in a subsequent section.

Let us first consider the question of the *taxpaying unit*. The main question here is whether we should consider the individual income-earner or the family as the unit, when several members of a family are in receipt of an income. We shall only consider the case involving a married couple where both husband and wife are in receipt of an income. More or less the same problem, however, will arise when there are grown-up children with incomes in the family.

Let the husband's and wife's incomes be respectively r_1 and r_2. Taxation could then be undertaken in many different ways.

In the first place we can choose the family as a unit of taxation, assessing the tax for the family as $s(r_1 + r_2)$. This may be called the joint tax principle, which was the dominant type in Norway until a few years ago.

In the second place we can choose the individual income-earner as a unit of taxation, with the result that the total tax that man and wife would have to pay is $s(r_1) + s(r_2)$.

It follows from the effect shown in (7.8), that with progressive taxation a higher tax on the family's income will result from joint tax than from separate taxation of each of the two income-earners. Which of the two principles will be more equitable is a matter of judgment which we shall not deal with here. Apart from the question of fairness, in making a choice between the two principles one must take into account to what extent one is interested in encouraging family members to seek employment.

If one chooses to tax income separately, the total tax levied on the family will depend on how the total income is divided among the individual income-earners within the family. (This does not apply to the special form of tax we have called degressive tax, when all the income-earners are above the minimum limit.) This may appear somewhat arbitrary in cases where the family actually has a joint household. In order to avoid this arbitrariness, without adopting the joint tax principle with the full effect mentioned above, one might levy on the family a tax equal to twice the tax for which one-half of the total income would be liable, that is to say, a total tax equal to:

$$2s\left(\frac{r_1 + r_2}{2}\right).$$

Thus the assessment is here made as if the total income were equally divided among the two income-earners. A system of this kind is in force in a number of countries, among them the U.S.A., where it is also used in cases where one of the incomes is equal to nought.

Let us compare the tax paid under the last-mentioned system with the tax one would pay if there were separate assessment of husband and wife on the basis of the income they had actually earned. First we re-write $s(r_1) + s(r_2)$ in the following manner, now using $r = r_1 + r_2$ and assuming that $r_1 > r_2$:

$$s(r_1) + s(r_2) = s\left(\tfrac{1}{2}r\right) + \left[s(r_1) - s\left(\tfrac{1}{2}r\right)\right] + s\left(\tfrac{1}{2}r\right) - \left[s\left(\tfrac{1}{2}r\right) - s(r_2)\right]$$

$$= 2s\left(\tfrac{1}{2}r\right) + \frac{s(r_1) - s\left(\tfrac{1}{2}r\right)}{r_1 - \tfrac{1}{2}r}(r_1 - \tfrac{1}{2}r)$$

$$- \frac{s\left(\tfrac{1}{2}r\right) - s(r_2)}{\tfrac{1}{2}r - r_2}\left(\tfrac{1}{2}r - r_2\right).$$

As we have:

$$r_1 - \tfrac{1}{2}r = \tfrac{1}{2}r - r_2 = \tfrac{1}{2}(r_1 - r_2)$$

this can be written as:

$$s(r_1) + s(r_2) = 2s(\tfrac{1}{2}r) + \tfrac{1}{2}(r_1 - r_2)\left[\frac{s(r_1) - s(\tfrac{1}{2}r)}{r_1 - \tfrac{1}{2}r} - \frac{s(\tfrac{1}{2}r) - s(r_2)}{\tfrac{1}{2}r - r_2}\right]. \quad (7.9)$$

In the square brackets two fractions appear; the first fraction can be taken to represent an average marginal tax for the income bracket from $\tfrac{1}{2}r$ to r_1. The second fraction can be taken to represent an average marginal tax for the income bracket from r_2 to $\tfrac{1}{2}r$. If the marginal tax was constant for the whole bracket from r_2 to r_1, the contents of the square bracket would be equal to nought. If, on the other hand, the marginal tax rises in this range, the contents of the square bracket will be positive. We then get:

$$s(r_1) + s(r_2) > 2s\left(\frac{r_1 + r_2}{2}\right). \quad (7.10)$$

Thus the principle in which one pretends that the total income is equally divided among husband and wife, results in a smaller total tax than the principle where husband and wife are taxed separately according to the income they have really earned.

The property which is expressed in (7.10) applies to tax functions which are progressive in the strict sense of the word, that is to say, such that marginal tax rises with income. This property is of as great importance to other problems as to the problem of taxation of husband and wife which we have here considered.

As a rule none of the three different principles we have here considered will be used without modifications. If, for example, the principle of joint tax is applied as a main rule, the fact that certain extra domestic expenses accrue from both husband and wife having gainful work outside the home is usually taken into account. This can be done by special exemptions when calculating taxable income. In applying the second principle explained above, problems often arise when husband and wife earn an income from the same activity, for example if both of them are working in a small enterprise owned by one of them. We shall, however, not deal in detail with these or similar modifications of the main principles.

Let us now proceed to consider how the family *maintenance burden* can be taken into account in assessing income tax. In this discussion we shall for convenience introduce a function $\sigma(r)$ to indicate the tax when no maintenance burden has been taken into account (nor the fact that the tax-payer maintains himself). Furthermore, let k represent the number of persons maintained. Apart from the tax-payer himself, k will then include husband or wife, unless assessed as a separate income-earner, plus children and any others regarded as maintained by the tax-payer we are considering. Finally, let $s_k(r)$ indicate the tax amount when the maintenance burden is k and the net income is r.

We shall distinguish between three main principles of taking the maintenance burden into account.

According to the first main principle a deduction in income is made depending on the size of the maintenance burden, such that the function σ will apply to the income thus reduced. Let $\Delta(k)$ be the exemption when the maintenance burden consists of k persons. According to the first main principle the tax will then be calculated as follows:

$$s_k(r) = \begin{cases} 0 & \text{if } r \leq \Delta(k) \\ \sigma(r - \Delta(k)) & \text{if } r > \Delta(k). \end{cases} \tag{7.11}$$

This principle is used in the assessment of income tax to the municipalities in Norway. The figures $\Delta(k)$ are listed in the so-called exemption tables. The difference $r - \Delta(k)$ is "taxable income".

A problem naturally arises as to how the figures $\Delta(k)$ are to vary with k. The answer to this question must depend on such things as how one assesses the expenses of maintaining large and small households, considerations of fairness, and perhaps also how the exemption structure will influence the development of family size. As an illustration we reproduce a table from the Norwegian exemption system in use for municipal income taxation:

Maintenance burden k	1	2	3	4	5	6	...
Exemption $\Delta(k)$ (*kroner*)	1600	3200	4900	6700	8600	10600	...
$\Delta(k) - \Delta(k-1)$ (*kroner*)	1600	1600	1700	1800	1900	2000	...

It will be seen that the exemption when $k=2$ is double the exemption when $k=1$. Furthermore, it will be seen that the additional exemption on the arrival of a new child will be greater, the more children one has in advance, as each figure on the bottom line of the table is 100 *kroner* greater than the preceding figure when $k \geq 3$.

Let us now consider a second main principle. Here the deduction is made in the actual tax instead of in the income prior to tax being calculated. In other words, the tax for which the tax-payer would have been liable, if he had no maintenance burden, is first calculated. A definite amount, depending on the size of his maintenance burden, is then deducted. If the result thus arrived at is less than nought, one might envisage the possibility of paying the "tax-payer" a relief. The usual procedure, however, is that in such cases the tax is assessed at nought*. This principle can be expressed as follows, using $D(k)$ to represent deduction in tax:

$$s_k(r) = \begin{cases} 0 & \text{if } \sigma(r) \leq D(k) \\ \sigma(r) - D(k) & \text{if } \sigma(r) > D(k). \end{cases} \tag{7.12}$$

While principle (7.11) was previously used for all income tax in Norway, in recent years principle (7.12) has been used in income tax to the state. To illustrate we reproduce the deduction amounts for income tax to the state for the year 1962.

Maintenance burden k	1	2	3	4	5	6	...
Amount deducted $D(k)$ (*kroner*)	400	800	1100	1500	2000	2600	...
$D(k) - D(k-1)$ (*kroner*)	400	400	300	400	500	600	...

The third main principle, which is, however, hardly fully applied anywhere, involves taking as the starting point the income per person in the

---

* But in Norway, as well as in many other countries, there is a system of family allowances independent of income. In Norway these allowances start with the second child. The system of such allowances must of course be considered in connection with the exemption rules in the tax system.

family or household to be taxed. We can then write:

$$
s_k(r) = \begin{cases} 0 & \text{if } \dfrac{r}{k} \leqq \varDelta \,. \\[2ex] k\sigma\left(\dfrac{r}{k} - \varDelta\right) & \text{if } \dfrac{r}{k} > \varDelta \,. \end{cases}
\tag{7.13}
$$

In this formula, the tax per person is a function of the income per person, after a tax-free amount $\varDelta$ has been deducted.

By differentiating the expression $k\sigma((r/k) - \varDelta)$ with respect to r, it will easily be seen that the marginal tax when $r/k > \varDelta$ is equal to the derivative of the σ function with respect to its argument, as for principles (7.11) and (7.12).

The argument in the σ function will, however, be different for these principles. This results in a marginal tax corresponding to (7.13) being the same for all families with the same income per person, whereas this does not apply in the case of (7.11) and (7.12).

Principle (7.13) is a generalisation of the last of the principles we mentioned for husband-and-wife taxation previously in this section.

In this principle one might possibly have used a sort of consumer scale, with one adult counting as unity, while children of various ages count as fractions of 1 in calculating the figure k. Something similar might also be envisaged in the case of the two other principles mentioned above, but this is not usual.

There are of course many factors involved in evaluating the principles here mentioned. One question which is often mentioned when such principles are evaluated is the question of what a tax-payer saves in tax when his maintenance burden increases by one. Let us consider this question a little more closely.

If the "tax-payer", prior to the increase in the number of persons he supports, is a zero-tax-payer, the question is naturally of no interest on the basis of the assumptions we have here made. If the tax-payer, prior to the increase in the number of persons he supports, pays a "positive" tax, but after an increase in his maintenance burden becomes a zero-tax-payer, the amount saved will be exactly equal to what he paid in tax before the increase in his tax burden.

In the discussion that follows we consider a tax-payer paying a positive tax both before and after the change in his maintenance burden.

Let us first consider the principle given in (7.11). If the maintenance burden here increases from k to $k+1$, while the income r remains constant, the tax amount for the tax-payer concerned will be reduced by

$$\sigma\left(r - \varDelta(k)\right) - \sigma\left(r - \varDelta(k+1)\right) = \left[\varDelta(k+1) - \varDelta(k)\right]\sigma', \quad (7.14)$$

i.e. by the marginal tax rate corresponding to the level for taxable income, multiplied by the increase in the exemption that occurs with an increase in maintenance burden. (The formula above only applies exactly if the marginal tax rate is constant for the range of variation for the argument in function σ here involved, or if σ' is the average value of the derivative of function σ, and thus the average marginal tax rate for the range mentioned.)

If one has a tax function with a rising marginal tax, (7.14) will mean that the person with a high income level will save more in tax when his maintenance burden increases than a person at a lower income level. This has often been adduced as an objection to principle (7.11), and is one of the reasons why this principle has been abandoned in Norway for income tax payable to the state. For ordinary taxation of income payable to the municipalities, however, the marginal tax is constant, and the effect we have just considered will consequently not apply there.

In the principle now used for assessing income tax to the state, viz. (7.12), the saving in tax with an increase in maintenance burden will simply be:

$$\left[\sigma(r) - D(k)\right] - \left[\sigma(r) - D(k+1)\right] = D(k+1) - D(k). \quad (7.15)$$

Thus here the saving in tax amount will be independent of the income level of the tax-payer.

Let us finally consider principle (7.13), where the income per person is taken as a starting point. We here get:

$$k\sigma\left(\frac{r}{k} - \varDelta\right) - (k+1)\sigma\left(\frac{r}{k+1} - \varDelta\right) = \frac{r}{k}\left[\sigma' - \frac{\sigma\left((r/k) - \varDelta\right)}{(r/k)}\right]. \quad (7.16)$$

(This formula applies exactly only if the derivative of the σ function is constant for the range from $(r/(k+1))-\Delta$ to $(r/k)-\Delta$ or if σ' is interpreted as an average marginal tax rate for this range.) This saving will be equal to the marginal tax rate multiplied by the amount deducted Δ, when the tax per person is proportional to taxable income per person. If the σ-function itself is progressive according to definition (7.6), the saving will be greater. However, the amount saved through an increase of the maintenance burden in (7.16) may show a different curve for increasing income, according to the precise form of the σ-function.

In evaluating principle (7.13) it is probably more convenient to evaluate directly the principle of calculating income and tax per person than to argue on the basis of (7.16).

7.3.3. *Fluctuating incomes*

The problem we shall now deal with is also associated with the progression of income taxation. Let us assume a person who for two successive years has incomes of respectively r_1 and r_2, and furthermore that the tax function is the same for these two years. For the two years together he will then have to pay a tax equal to $s(r_1)+s(r_2)$. (The size of his maintenance burden is now not of any particular importance, for which reason we shall not specify it with an index to s.) We shall assume that incomes r_1 and r_2 are different. Let us then consider another person who has a stable income, and who during the two years has earned a total income equal to that of the first-mentioned person. That is to say, he has an income of $\frac{1}{2}(r_1+r_2)$ for each of the two years. He will then have to pay a total tax of $2s(\frac{1}{2}(r_1+r_2))$ for the two years. Using precisely the same line of argument as in (7.9)–(7.10) we then see that the first person, that is to say the one with the variable income, will have to pay more tax for the two years than the other person, assuming that the marginal tax rate is rising for the income range that is here involved. The question is whether this is fair, when both persons have precisely the same total income for the two years in question.

The question of course also arises when we consider a longer series of years, during which one person has a fluctuating income and another has a more stable income, but with the same total income for the whole period.

In most countries marked results of this effect have been considered unfair, and attempts have been made to arrive at various arrangements in order to even out the difference.

One method used in a number of countries is *"average assessment"*. Instead of calculating the tax for a year on the basis of the income in the year concerned, the tax is worked out on the basis of an average income for a longer sequence of years, e.g., three or five years. In this way the particular effect on income fluctuating at brief intervals will be evened out. In Norway there is a rule for such average assessment of incomes from forestry. The reason for this is that in this industry incomes may vary considerably from one year to another, as a result of fluctuations in production due to natural or technical causes. Furthermore, a tax assessment based on one year's income might result in production being shifted in time, for fiscal reasons, in ways which would be unfortunate from the point of view of rational forestry.

Previously there was also average assessment for incomes in agriculture.

In other countries, too, similar rules for average assessment have generally only occurred in particular industries, where incomes for various reasons fluctuate markedly.

Another method of evening out the effect of fluctuations in income from one year to another is *"percentage assessment"*. This consists in establishing a norm in some way or another for what would be normal income in a particular activity, and then calculating the tax in relation to it, instead of in relation to the actual income in a particular year. In Norway this system was previously used in forestry (before the average assessment rule was introduced). The "norm" income was then gauged on the basis of the growth value of the forest.

The disadvantage of such systems as average assessment or percentage assessment is that the tax may be heavy in periods when actual income is low. This does not matter so much when dealing with natural fluctuations that can be foreseen by the individual. On the other hand it may prove more unfortunate when fluctuations are due to market conditions. If we want the tax system to contribute to an automatic stabilisation of income, systems such as those mentioned above are very unsuitable. Thus, in deciding to what extent such systems are to be used, various considerations must be weighed against one another.

Apart from such special assessment methods for industries where income may fluctuate for climatic or other natural reasons, in a number of countries special rules exist for the incomes of authors, artists, inventors, and others with similar kinds of income which may be highly concentrated on one or two years, whereas in other years they may have no income or a very small one. In Norway the rule exists that "the author of a work of art or literature or of a patent invention", when his income for one year exceeds his income for the two preceding years by a considerable amount, may claim to be assessed as though the income had been evenly spread over the three years concerned. In addition, in the case of income tax to the state, we have a special rule applicable to all types of income when the income one year exceeds the average income for the two preceding years by more than one-third.

The rules about the treatment of losses may be considered in the same context. Norway's tax laws contain a rule to the effect that in calculating the taxable income of a firm one may claim a deduction for losses resulting from business activity in the course of the ten preceding years. But for a rule of this kind, business activities which in some years show a loss and in others a considerable profit, would be in a worse position from a taxation point of view than businesses with a more even profit. Formally this is an approach of the same kind as the one used above, as we might also consider the tax function as being extended to apply to negative incomes. The marginal tax rate would then be nil for negative incomes, but positive when the income is positive or exceeds a certain positive minimum value. In this respect one has a rising marginal tax evoking effects such as those discussed above, when incomes fluctuate around this kink on the tax function.

A question of a similar kind to the one mentioned above, and one that has been discussed in recent years, is that of the shape of the life-time income curve in different kinds of activity. This question applies particularly to academic professions, which are entered upon later in life, owing to the protracted period of education and training. To make up for this, one often commands a somewhat higher income than the average for the period when one is actually in receipt of an income. If we then consider the entire career of a professional man, owing to the progression in taxation he will be somewhat more severely taxed than an income earner who has the same total income throughout his career, but has it distributed over a large number of years.

In this section it would also be appropriate to mention the British distinction between "earned income" and "investment income". Although there are many problems involved in drawing up a clear line of distinction, we can state as a main rule that earned income is an income from all types of activity, whereas investment income comprises incomes resulting from the ownership of property or estate. (A few years ago something in excess of 75% of taxable incomes in Great Britain were earned income.) The distinction was introduced into Britain's system of taxation in 1907, a lower rate being applied to earned income than to investment income. According to the system in force in recent years, $\frac{2}{9}$ of earned income, up to a certain level, can be deducted as a tax-free amount for income tax purposes. For incomes above this limit, $\frac{1}{9}$ can be deducted as a tax-free amount, up to a higher limit.

Originally the reason for favouring earned income for tax purposes as compared to investment income, was that the first type of income was more unstable or unreliable. To some extent earned income was regarded as more unstable because, in order to achieve it, one was dependent on health and working ability. In addition certain "life income" considerations played a certain part, as it was assumed that anyone relying on earned income would have to put aside something for his old age, whereas investment income would still accrue after one had become too old to continue in work and business. Subsequently other considerations have helped to strengthen the case in favour of continuing to maintain this distinction in the tax system. Among other things the need to encourage initiative has been adduced as an argument in support of fiscal favouring of income derived from activity (of which naturally income earned from work comprises a considerable share). It has also been pointed out that owners of capital enjoy certain tax advantages, owing to their opportunities of tax-free or favourably taxed income, of the kind generally described as "capital gains". The difference in treatment here mentioned can in part be regarded as a corrective to this.

The question of the taxation of capital gains will be dealt with in the section below.

7.3.4. Capital gains

The term capital gains comprises incomes which concretely speaking may be derived from fairly varied sources or causes. Common to all things called capital gains is the fact that they take the form of an increase in value of property. Generally, however, an increase in value of goods purchased and sold regularly as part of a business activity is nevertheless excluded from the term capital gains in the context of taxation.

Important examples of capital gains are a rise in the market price of stocks and shares and a rise in the price of land and other real estate.

Capital gains of this nature raise special problems in taxation of income:

1. In the first place the question may be asked whether such gains are really *income* in the same sense as other forms of income covered by income taxation.
2. Even if the answer to this question were yes, considerable difficulties often arise in an attempt to *establish the size* of the incomes assuming the form of capital gains. The value of a piece of real estate or a financial asset can perhaps be established fairly readily when it has to be sold, and the gains so to speak converted into cash. It is considerably more difficult to try to assess the values of capital gains that have not been realised. The difficulty is naturally least for the sort of objects for which a market exists, e.g., shares which are sold on the stock market. It is greatest for objects seldom sold, and not standardised in the same way as bonds or shares in a larger series.
3. Even if one accepts capital gains as income that should be taxed, one may raise the question *whether they are disposable* in the same way as other income. If capital gains cannot be disposed of just as easily as any other income, one might perhaps accept the idea that they should not be fully taxed either, just like any other income, as they provide less "tax ability".
4. Many questions may also be raised in connection with *the placing in time* of the income that takes the form of capital gains. From a practical point of view it is naturally handiest to proceed as though the entire income has been earned during the year a capital gain is realised, as it is then easiest to establish its size. But the same sort of objections can be raised to this as those we considered in the previous section in connection with fluctuating incomes, unless one has an opportunity of using one of the different types of averaging arrangements which were mentioned there. In order to tax capital gains as they accrue, one would, however, have to know the actual time course of the increase

in value for the various objects. Furthermore, taxation of this kind would be difficult, since this income is not easily disposable by the tax-payer until the gains have been realised. (In certain cases it might of course be envisaged that the tax-payer used the object as the basis for a loan, and that the size of the loan could be adjusted upwards at certain intervals. In this way the capital gain would be more disposable as it arises.)

We shall now revert for a moment to the question we first raised, viz. the question of whether capital gains are really incomes that should be subject to income taxation, side by side with other forms of income. On this subject highly varying opinions exist. We shall only consider some of the arguments adduced, without taking any final standpoint, as this can be done only when, apart from the more theoretical arguments, subjective evaluations are also included.

In discussing the question of whether capital gains are income on a par with other income, a distinction should be made between different types of capital gains according to their origin.

Let us first consider capital gains due to a *general rise in prices of all types of real goods*. There is no doubt here that anyone in possession of real assets which rise in price, can realise a nominal gain by selling them. But as long as the value of the assets a person possesses only increases in step with the general price-level, this increase in value will not result in the person being better off from the real (as opposed to nominal) point of view. The conclusion can therefore perhaps be drawn that a rise in value of real assets in step with a general rise in prices should not be regarded as income and be made the object of income taxation. However, the objection may be made to this point of view that a person possessing real assets that rise in nominal value will be more favourably placed than a person who has his fortune invested e.g. in bonds, which retain a more or less constant nominal value. This provides an argument for taxing the rise in value of real assets. As long as financial assets are not price-index-regulated in one way or another, so that they maintain their real value during a general rise in prices, these two considerations will be mutually opposed to one another, and no decision can be made except by evaluating on which one greater emphasis should be placed.

A rather different case is that of a more *partial rise in price*, that is to say a rise in the price of a particular asset or a particular type of asset, while the general price level remains fairly constant. This type of rise in price would in a real sense place the owner of such assets in a more favourable position than previously, as he can sell at a higher price and purchase more of other goods for the amount he gets than if he had sold the object concerned at an earlier point of time. A special case of this is a rise in the price of land in connection e.g. with development of communications or a growth in urban building. The rise in price this produces may be said to be due to the development of the community generally, and not to the initiative and efforts of the individual landowner. More or less historical coincidence may decide who owns the land that is rising considerably in value, and who owns land which is not rising in value. Consequently, for this type of capital gain an argument can be adduced for a special taxation, over and above a taxation according to the ordinary income tax. (We have previously mentioned this point).

Precisely the same line of thought can of course be used in a case where certain types of real assets rise in value at a *quicker rate* than what would correspond to the rise in the general price level. Here one might envisage calculating taxable rise in value by taking as a basis the rise in price of the various types of object compared with the rise in the general price index.

A rise in the market value of shares can to some extent also be considered from the same angle as a rise in the value of real assets. The value of a share can after all to some extent be said to reflect the value of the company's property. During a period of general rise in prices the nominal value of this property will increase, and then this will be reflected – with many deviations and delays – in the market price of the shares. In this connection the same arguments as those mentioned above can be made to apply.

A rise in the value of shares which does not reflect a rise in the general level of prices of this kind can be compared to a partial rise in prices of certain types of real assets.

The objection to taxing gains due to a rise in the value of shares is sometimes made that a rise in prices quoted for shares merely reflects expectations of increased dividends in future, and these future dividends will be taxed as income when they materialise. In my opinion this argument is not convincing. In the first place the person owning a share may choose to sell it instead of keeping it and waiting for his dividend. In this case he receives a real gain, and the objection made will not apply. But if the share-owner does *not* sell his share after a period of rising market quotations, then at any rate he may be said to have an *opportunity* for doing so, and his reason for not realising his share is probably that he considers it still more advantageous to keep it than to sell it and cash in on the gain. Incidentally, it might be relevant at this juncture to make a comparison with the general treatment of saved income under income taxation. The position is here that all ordinary income is taxed, whether it is spent or saved, even though it might be argued that savings are made in order to enjoy future advantages, and that for this reason it would be more appropriate to tax these advantages when they accrue, than tax the amount saved in the year the income is earned. In ordinary income taxation this line of thought is not accepted. The idea that a rise in the market prices of shares should not be taxed because it only represents an expectation of advantages in the future is of the same nature.

Let us now consider *gains from rising prices of bonds in connection with a fall in the interest rate*. If the owner of a bond chooses to sell his bond at the increased price, he will obtain a real gain, and it may be considered reasonable that this should be taxed like any other income. If he does not sell the bond, the position may possibly be said to be different; *inter alia* it may be pointed out that the annual interest payments which the bond gives are unchanged, despite the change in price. But on the other hand it may be maintained that when the owner of the bond chooses to hang on to it, instead of realising it at the increased price, then this must be due to the fact that he considers hanging on to the bond to be still more advantageous than selling it and cashing in on the higher price.

Let us now consider a few arguments in connection with the taxing of capital gains, arguments which are more independent of the special reason for capital gains.

The argument often adduced *against* the taxing of capital gains is that there is a logical connection between the taxing of capital gains and the right, when being taxed, to deduct capital losses from other income. The tax systems of most countries, however, do not permit such deductions for capital losses. Consequently capital gains, too, should be exempt. Formally this would appear an attractive argument on the grounds of symmetry, but there are many examples of similar claims being ignored in other sections of the tax system.

The fact that the right to deduct capital losses is only to a very small extent recognised in the legislation of various countries – and usually only against capital gains – is bound up with the fear that this right might otherwise often be exploited or abused to a marked extent by various groups, for the purpose of reducing their tax burdens. Another reason is probably the desire that the system of taxation should contribute to discouraging purely speculative business transactions. After all, the right to deduct capital losses would make it less risky to speculate.

Another argument adduced against the taxing of capital gains is that this kind of tax might hinder a natural and desirable turnover of capital objects – both real assets of various kinds and financial assets. This would be the case particularly when taxation of capital gains is carried out on the basis of *realised* capital gains, and of course for practical reasons the taxation of capital gains is generally carried out in this way. However, most types of tax have one or more undesirable subsidiary effects of this kind, and it is difficult to decide whether the undesirable subsidiary effects of capital gains taxation would be greater than the undesirable subsidiary effects of an alternative tax with the same yield.

Let us now turn to a few general arguments adduced *in favour of* taxation of capital gains.

The first argument is concerned with stabilization. As we have already mentioned, capital gains will in many cases reflect expectations for future income, and to this extent will not be countered by production during the period when the capital gains occur. They will generally occur in a boom period, when demand is already comparatively high for other reasons. If calculated capital gains likewise to a certain extent promote a demand for goods and services, they will represent an expansive element in a situation where this is not desirable. Consequently, out of a desire for a system of taxation which contributes to automatic stabilisation (cf. section 3.2.3), the taxing of capital gains might be considered highly appropriate.

Finally, one of the most important arguments in favour of the taxation of capital gains is the fact that the individual tax-payer will often, through his own dispositions, be able to choose whether a particular income is to appear as ordinary income or as a capital gain. If capital gains are exempt from taxation, people with opportunities for transforming their incomes into capital gains will naturally enjoy a particularly favourable position, compared with other earners of income. As the kinds of income that can be transformed into capital gains are almost exclusively to be found in the higher income brackets, this will contribute to a reduction in real progression in taxation. This is one of the most important reasons for discrepancies between actual progression and formal progression according to the tax tables, of which we gave a few examples in the subsection dealing with progression in income taxation.

The commonest way of transforming other income into capital gains is to retain profits within joint-stock companies instead of distributing a dividend. Profits that are retained in companies will result in the value each share represents increasing more than would be the case if a greater part of the profit had been distributed among shareholders. (If the entire taxation of the profits earned by joint-stock companies is carried out on company level, what has been stated above does not entirely apply. We shall return to the question of company taxation in a later sub-section.)

Naturally this transformation of income into capital gains will be a disadvantage to the individual income earner, in so far as such capital gains are not as easily disposable as regularly distributed dividends. However, the shareholder will generally have opportunities for selling some shares or using them as the basis for a loan.

A method common in many countries of making a profit available to shareholders in the form of capital gains, is for the company at regular intervals to issue new shares which old shareholders have a priority in purchasing, and which are available at a price lower than these shares would fetch in the open market.

A method that has been used a great deal in the U.S.A. is the following: A number of persons possessing bonds and shares set up a holding company, to which they transfer their shares. Dividends and interest on shares and bonds are not paid out to the founders of the company, but retained in the company and constantly re-invested in fresh holdings of bonds and shares. After a while the company is then liquidated, and what has been earned in the meantime will be available to the founders in a form that would be regarded as capital gains within the meaning of tax legislation. A new company could then be started again, and a new series of similar transactions set on foot. This method was also to a certain extent used by manufacturing firms, especially in the film industry. The procedure would be to establish a separate company for every new film that was going to be made. When the film had been completed, and could be released, the company would be dissolved and the film taken over by the founders of the company. The value of the film would then be calculated on the basis of the expected revenue it would bring in when it was released. The difference between this value and what had been invested in the company was considered as capital gain, and was therefore not taxed as ordinary income. As the film was shown, its value would be written down, so that no taxable net income would occur, unless the film happened to bring in more than had been expected when its value was registered immediately after the company had been dissolved.

Similar methods have also been used in other countries. When such practices have become widespread, the legislative authorities have generally endeavoured to frame rules aimed at preventing precisely this kind of abuse. Experience, however, has frequently proved that once a hole in the law has been plugged, new ones will be found which will enable people to transform ordinary income into capital gains, thus avoiding taxation of incomes in countries where capital gains are not liable for taxation.

In a book already mentioned, *An expenditure tax*, Nicholas Kaldor attaches great emphasis to the question of capital gains in his argument for expenditure tax instead of income tax. The main point is that with an expenditure tax there is no need to decide which of various types of capital gains are income in the ordinary sense of the word: "Thus if capital gains are taxed to the extent that they are actually spent, there is no need to inquire how far they are fictitious; it is left to the individual recipient of these gains to sort these things out for himself, in deciding how far he is justified in treating them as spendable gains." In addition, those opportunities for tax evasion and avoidance will be closed which exist in any income-tax system that does not endeavour to deal with every type of capital gains, realised or not realised, in the same way as all other incomes.

There are probably just as many different methods of treating capital gains as there are countries with income tax. A survey of the various systems is out of place here. Generally, only realised capital gains are taxed; as a general rule, too, capital losses can be deducted only from capital gains, but not from ordinary income, when income is taxed.

Furthermore, it is fairly general for capital gains realised on objects held for a very short period to be taxed in full, just like any other income, while capital gains realised on objects held over a longer period of time are not taxed, or are at any rate not taxed in full. A distinction is also often made between the taxation of capital gains from various kinds of financial assets and various kinds of real assets.

Up to 1965 Great Britain was one of the countries that went furthest of all in exempting capital gains from taxation, ordinary types of capital gains being wholly exempt from taxation. In the U.S.A. capital gains have been taxed according to special rates, the maximum rate varying somewhat from year to year, but generally being somewhere in the neighbourhood of 25%. This means that the maximum rate for the taxation of capital gains has been far below the marginal tax rate for regular incomes earned by persons in the upper income brackets.

In Norway capital gains are generally subject to taxation when they are part of the taxpayer's business activity. Furthermore, capital gains from the sale of "building lots" are subject to tax, according to certain definitions. There is furthermore a general rule that capital gains from the sale of assets that have been owned for less than ten years are taxable; but this rule does not apply to capital gains from the sale of shares and bonds. In the Storting report no. 54 (1960–1961) mentioned above, however, this question is raised by the Government, which states that "the Department (of Finance) is of the opinion that the reintroduction of taxation of gains from the sales of shares and bonds should now be considered". Furthermore, the report mentions that "in the opinion of the Department there are grounds for considering the question of tax liability for other capital gains outside business, as well".

In business capital gains will often result from stocks of goods rising in price. Such capital gains (or losses, in the case of a drop in prices) will be visible to a greater or lesser extent in the income shown in a firm's accounts, depending on *the principles for inventory valuation*. The same types of consideration adduced above in connection with capital gains generally will also apply to the question of evaluating stocks in hand in connection with business taxation. This, however, also raises many special questions of business accounting and administration, which we shall not deal with here.

7.3.5. *Depreciation*

In any productive activity where capital equipment is used, this equipment will in time suffer wear and tear and depreciate. Today this is regarded in every country as part of production costs, and depreciation – calculated in one way or another – can be deducted from gross income when net income is worked out for the purpose of tax returns.

Per se it is quite feasible to have income tax without a deduction for depreciation. In England, for instance, it was not until 1878 that the right to deduct depreciation was introduced, and at that time income tax had already been in force for quite a long time. However, a system which does not include deduction of depreciation would result in considerable discrimination as between branches of business activity. It would prove an advantage to firms operating with little capital equipment in proportion to gross income, and would be a disadvantage to those operating with large capital equipment (if we suppose that tax rates are adjusted in such a way that in both cases the same total tax yield is obtained from firms). In order to avoid this discriminatory effect, which would undoubtedly prove undesirable in most cases, the right to deduct depreciation has to be introduced.

In most countries which adopted income taxation later than Britain, the right to calculate depreciation for tax purposes was generally introduced immediately. As a rule, however, this originally applied only to physical wear and tear of capital equipment. Not until later has the right to make depreciation allowances corresponding to what is now called obsolescence been incorporated in tax rules.

Even though the decision has been made to introduce depreciation allowances, many questions still remain with regard to the actual formulation of the rule.

In the first place we have the question of whether the firm itself shall have the full right to decide the time form of depreciation for tax purposes, or whether the tax rules are to establish certain norms which firms must observe. Both systems have been practised. In Sweden firms have enjoyed considerable freedom in this respect. This, however, has subsequently been changed, and in most other countries, too, more or less fixed norms for depreciation are laid down in the tax rules.

Various considerations from the point of view of the individual firm may support the freedom of the firm to determine the time form of its calculated depreciation. In Sweden, those in favour of this right emphasised *inter alia* that they believed this would result in a stabilisation of dividends, since businesses would make large depreciations in the periods when they had large earnings, instead of allowing the distributed dividend to follow profit fluctuations proportionately. It is, however, perfectly possible that businesses might use one set of depreciation rules – as laid down in the law or in tax rules in connection with the law – when returns of taxable income have to be made, and make decisions on investment, dividends, etc., on an entirely different basis. To the extent this occurs, the argument mentioned carries less weight. More purely fiscal considerations would then have to decide whether free or fixed depreciations should be allowed in the tax rules.

An argument against free depreciations, then, is that this freedom might be exploited by businesses and firms to speculate in changes in the tax percentage. In Sweden, for instance, many enterprises made very high depreciations during the war, as they expected a marked reduction in the tax rate after the war was over. They consequently aimed at small taxable incomes during the war, even though this meant rather larger taxable incomes after the war. Speculation of this kind can, of course, also work when changes in the opposite direction are expected. All this may result in an instability which would generally be considered unfortunate. Free depreciation also creates uncertainty for the authorities when the tax yield for a subsequent year is to be estimated.

Another factor is that when firms have the full right to choose for themselves the time schedule for depreciations, for given tax rates they will be able to distribute their taxable income in such a way that total tax over a longer period of time is lower than it would have been if the firms had not had this freedom to determine depreciations themselves. For this reason, other things being equal, a system with free depreciations must be combined with higher tax rates than a system involving fixed systems of depreciations.

A factor which in recent years has weighed heavily, is the importance of the public authorities' possibility of influencing investment activity in the country. If a government-determined time schedule for depreciations exists, one can use *alterations* in this schedule as a means of influencing investment activity. We shall return to this below.

The considerations here mentioned have resulted in most countries adopting systems in which the time schedule for depreciations is more or less precisely laid down in tax legislation or other tax rules.

The next question we shall mention concerns the actual amount that can be written off. The main question here is whether depreciation can be carried out merely on the basis of the historical cost of acquisition of the real object concerned, or on the basis of the current price of replacement. Most countries use historical cost as the basis for depreciations, but at the same time in most countries the point has been raised whether it would not perhaps be more appropriate to use current replacement cost as the basis.

The principle of depreciation on the basis of replacement cost can furthermore be interpreted in two different ways:

(a) The principle can be formulated in such a way that the firm can each year make a depreciation comprising a fixed percentage of the re-placement value of the real object in that year.
(b) The principle can be formulated in such a way that the total depreci-ations over the entire life of the real asset is exactly sufficient to re-acquire a new real asset of the same kind at the price obtaining when the first real asset has served its time.

The three principles we have now mentioned (historical acquisition price and two different formulations of the system of replacement price) are illustrated by a simple example in table 11. Here we consider a real asset which is acquired at price 90 in the first year (representing, e.g., 90 000 *kroner*). The asset has a life of three years, and the price of a new asset of the same kind rises to 120 in the second year and to 150 in the third year. The table shows what depreciations should be undertaken every year according to each of the three principles, and furthermore the total amount of depreciation for the whole period. (We have set out table 11 to illustrate a case involving rising prices, as this would probably be most realistic. An exactly corresponding table could of course be drawn up to cover a case of falling prices for the real asset involved.)

The figures in the line showing depreciation amount according to his-torical price of acquisition do not need further explanation, apart from the fact that we have assumed that depreciations of the same amount will

Table 11

	1st year	2nd year	3rd year	Total depreciation amount
Current price of a new asset	90	120	150	—
Depreciation according to the historical cost of acquisition	30	30	30	90
Depreciation according to the replacement cost, formulation (a)	30	40	50	120
Depreciation according to the replacement cost, formulation (b)	30	50	70	150

be carried out every year. In a period of rising prices the total depreciation amount for the whole period will here naturally not amount to what is necessary to replace the real asset at the conclusion of the period, viz. 150.

The figures in the line for depreciation according to formulation (a) of the replacement cost are simply calculated as one-third of the value of a new real asset of the same type every year. The sum of the depreciation amounts calculated in this manner will likewise not amount to what will be required to re-acquire a new asset at the conclusion of the whole period. The position might have been different if during an intermediate year – here the second year – we had had a peak in the price development, so that the value of a new asset in this year was particularly high.

The figures in the line for depreciation amounts, according to formulation (b) of the replacement cost principle, should perhaps be explained in more detail. During the first year a third of the value of the asset is written off according to the prices that year, i.e., an amount of 30. In the second year the value of a new asset of this kind has risen to 120. In the course of the first and second year together one should have written off two-thirds of the value of the asset. If we take the price in the second year as our basis, then in the course of the first and second year together we should have written off two-thirds of 120, viz. 80. Now in the first year we have already written off 30; for this reason, in the second year we should write off 50, so that the sum of the first and second year is 80. In the third year the position is this, that for the first, second, and third year together we should have written off as much as is necessary to re-acquire a new asset at the price obtaining in the third year, viz. 150. We have previously written off $30+50=80$; consequently we write off $150-80=70$ in the third year. In this way of course we achieve the object of what has been defined above as formulation (b).

In debating the question of depreciation principles in relation to taxation it is often maintained that the actual aim of calculating depreciations must be for the firm to be able to replace a real asset, when it has been scrapped, and that a depreciation principle must therefore be selected which makes this possible. This should then result in choosing the principle which we have called above formulation (b) of depreciation on the basis of replacement cost. Accepting this point of departure, the conclusion is undoubtedly right, if one is dealing with a firm which is stationary, in the sense that it merely makes replacements, but no new investments. The problem may be different for a firm which also undertakes new investments, so that its machine plant is steadily increasing. We shall consider this in greater detail, using a simple numerical example.* Let us consider a firm which acquires a machine in the year 0, and then makes a new investment of one machine every fifth year. Furthermore, let us imagine that all the machines have a working life of ten years, after which they are all immediately replaced. For the time being we shall assume that prices are constant, and for simplicity that a new machine always costs 100 *kroner*. Depreciation is carried out with equal amounts every year, viz., 10 *kroner* annually for every machine owned by the firm. Furthermore, we assume that all amounts written off are allocated to a particular fund, and that replacements are financed by drawing on this fund, whereas new investments are financed from other sources. The first 26 years in the history of this firm can then be described as in table 12. (We are assuming that all machines are acquired at the beginning of a year, and that depreciation starts in the same year as the machine is acquired.)

---

* Based upon A. R. Prest, *Public Finance* (London 1960), p. 311.

Table 12

Year	0 1 2 3 4	5 6 7 8 9	10 11 12 13 14
New acquisition	100	100	100
Replacement			100
Total machine plant	1 1 1 1 1	2 2 2 2 2	3 3 3 3 3
Depreciation	10 10 10 10 10	20 20 20 20 20	30 30 30 30 30
Depreciation fund	10 20 30 40 50	70 90 110 130 150	80 110 140 170 200

Year	15 16 17 18 19	20 21 22 23 24	25 26 ...
New acquisition	100	100	100
Replacement	100	200	200
Total machine plant	4 4 4 4 4	5 5 5 5 5	6 6 ...
Depreciation	40 40 40 40 40	50 50 50 50 50	60 60 ...
Depreciation fund	140 180 220 260 300	150 200 250 300 350	210 270 ...

In this table only the last line needs a more detailed explanation. We are assuming here that in every column we shall record the depreciation fund *at the end* of the year involved, viz., after money has been drawn from the fund for financing replacements in years when this is carried out, and after depreciations in the year have been undertaken and the amounts have been added to the fund. The last line of table 12 can then be constructed by cumulating the penultimate line, making a deduction in years when replacements are made. That is to say, in year 10 we draw 100 *kroner* from the depreciation fund, in year 15 we likewise draw out 100 *kroner*, in year 20 we draw out 200 *kroner*, corresponding to the replacement of the two machines acquired in year 10, and in the year 25 we draw out 200 *kroner*, corresponding to the replacement of the two machines that were acquired in year 15. Similarly table 12 could be further developed.

What is of interest now, is that in the case of this firm there will always be *more* than enough in the depreciation fund to finance replacement investments. We see that at the conclusion of year 9 we have 150 *kroner* set aside in the depreciation fund, whereas at the beginning of year 10 we actually need only 100 *kroner* for replacement. Furthermore, when replacement has to be undertaken in year 15, we have 200 *kroner* on the replacement fund from the preceding year, whereas replacement now requires only 100 *kroner*. In year 20 we have 300 *kroner* on the depreciation fund from previous years, whereas replacement requires only 200 *kroner*. And finally, in year 25 we have 350 *kroner* from the preceding year on the depreciation fund, whereas replacements now likewise require only 200. If we continue to extend the table, it will easily be seen that we shall always have an amount in the depreciation fund greater that that required for replacements.

We have here considered a case which does not involve a rise in prices, so that it actually makes no difference which of the already mentioned principles for depreciation we make use of. Let us imagine, however, that there is a certain rise in price for the type of machine here involved, and that we employ depreciation on the basis of historical acquisition price. Since in the example reproduced above we accumulated a surplus in the depreciation fund in excess of what was required for making replacements, it is immediately clear that, using the same depreciation principle, one would be able to meet a certain rise in price of machines, without the depreciation fund becoming too small to enable replacements to be financed. This can easily be illustrated in greater detail by numerical examples in the same way as the example used above.

From this the following conclusion can be drawn: The premise that the depreciation fund should always be sufficient to finance replacements, need not automatically lead to the conclusion that replacement cost must be used as a basis for calculating depreciation.

Let us now choose another starting-point, viz., the very definition of income, to see whether it will lead to more positive conclusions. With this starting-point, the question of depreciation will be closely connected with the question of capital gains dealt with above.

As our first definition of income let us choose the following: Income in a period of time is the amount that could be used for consumption during the period, without the *nominal* value of capital going down. Lct us now, in order to explore the consequences of this definition, consider a person running a business activity, who in the course of a period of time earns an amount E before depreciations have been taken into account. Let us furthermore assume that the nominal value of the capital equipment used in production is K_0. If no changes in price occur in the course of this period, we assume that this capital will be reduced in value to K_1. (This statement implies a number of problems which we shall not go into here.) Meanwhile the price of the kind of capital equipment we are here dealing with changes in the course of the period. We shall use P to represent the price level for capital equipment obtaining at the conclusion of the period. The price level P is expressed in relation to the price level at the beginning of the period.

According to this the nominal value of the capital will have been reduced from K_0 to PK_1 in the course of the period. (If the price level has risen sufficiently, we can of course have $PK_1 > K_0$.) Consequently, of the amount E, $K_0 - PK_1$ must be "set aside" in order to retain nominal capital unchanged. The rest, i.e.

$$r = E - (K_0 - PK_1), \tag{7.17}$$

can be consumed without nominal capital being reduced. According to the income definition we started with, (7.17) should then indicate the income to be used as a basis for taxation. It is illuminating to rewrite (7.17) as follows:

$$r = E + (P - 1)K_1 - (K_0 - K_1). \tag{7.18}$$

"Correct income", according to the definition we have now taken as our starting-point, consists in other words primarily of earned income prior to depreciations (E) and a capital gain $(P-1)K_1$. The factor $(P-1)$ is a measure of the rise in price during the period. Capital gain is calculated by multiplying this price-increase factor with the capital amount left at the end of the period. (It would of course be unreasonable to calculate capital gains on that part of the capital which is "worn out" in the course of this period.) From this gross income an amount corresponding to the reduction in value one would have had on the capital, if no change in price had taken place, is then subtracted. We can interpret this as depreciations calculated without taking into account the rise in price that has taken place during the period.

Let us now as an alternative take the following definition of income as our basis: Income in a given period is the amount that can be consumed in that period without the *real value* of capital falling.

Calculated in prices obtaining at the beginning of the period, the decline in the value of capital, as a result of wear and tear and of obsolescence, will be $K_0 - K_1$. When the price of the capital has increased from 1 to P, an amount $(K_0 - K_1) P$ must be set aside in order to offset this. According to the last-mentioned definition the income will then be:

$$r = E - (K_0 - K_1) P. \qquad (7.19)$$

This corresponds to taxing the earned income without any addition for capital gains, and with a depreciation on the basis of the price ruling at the conclusion of the period we are considering.

If this method of depreciation is used for several consecutive periods, the amount set aside will not necessarily be equal to what is required to replace the real capital asset after it has been completely written off, as was shown in the simple numerical example at the beginning of this section. This may be said to be due to the fact that we have not taken the full and entire consequences of the second definition of income which we have submitted. If we imagine a lasting rise in price, and furthermore assume that the amount written off each year is accumulated in a fund and, for instance, deposited in a bank, the real value of what is written off in any particular year will sink in the following years (when prices are rising). If we also include this when we apply the last-mentioned definition of income, we shall arrive at a depreciation principle corresponding to what we called formulation (b) of the replacement cost principle in the numerical example at the beginning of the section.

The two definitions we have here mentioned lead us, as we have seen, to different conclusions. In choosing between these definitions one is faced with the same kind of problems that we faced in connection with the question of capital gains. If we compare our owner of real capital with owners of financial assets, and if in the taxation of the latter we do not take into account changes in the real value of their assets, it would be reasonable to take as our point of departure the first of the above-mentioned definitions of income. Not taking into account changes in the real value of financial assets, as far as the owners thereof are concerned, in fact implies that we have for this particular group applied the first of the definitions of income we have mentioned. The first definition of income may also appear reasonable if we are concerned with an isolated rise in prices for the type of real capital involved, as an unchanged nominal capital will then have an unchanged real value in all *other* ways apart from purchase of this type of real capital.

In a similar way we may say that if we compare a taxpayer who uses real capital in his business with other owners of real assets, and taxation of these owners takes no account of changes in the nominal value of their real assets, then it is reasonable to apply the second definition of income as a basis for taxation of firms or persons who use real capital in their business.

The arguments here adduced in connection with formulae (7.17)–(7.19) are only intended as a simple illustration of how the question of the basis of depreciation can be approached through an attempt to choose a "correct" definition of income, and how the question of depreciation will then be closely connected with the question of capital gains. For a complete treatment of the question in this way, it would be necessary to introduce financial assets explicitly in the considerations, and likewise to distinguish between prices for the types of real capital used in production and the general price level for other goods.

Before leaving the question of the basis for depreciation, we shall briefly mention a point of view which has achieved some prominence in this debate in various countries. This is concerned with the development of trade cycles. It has been maintained that the use of a historical cost of acquisition as a basis for depreciation results in businesses overestimating profits in boom periods, when prices are rising, and that this tends to increase the instability of the development. For this reason historical cost should not be used as a basis for depreciation, if the intention were to organise the system in such a way that it would help to damp trade cycles. The objection that is raised to this is, that the use of the historical cost value does of course lead to businesses having to pay larger tax in boom periods, since this principle will result in smaller depreciation amounts than the use of replacement cost when prices rise. This is true enough, but it would not entirely outweigh the first-mentioned effect, as the tax of course takes only *part* of an increase in income. The question, however, is whether businesses permit themselves to be "fooled" by nominal values, as assumed at the beginning of this line of argument. If businesses constantly bear in mind the distinction between nominal values and real values, and provided they are motivated in their decisions by real values, then from the point of view of stabilisation it would be best to apply the historical cost principle, as the decisive factor would then be that this principle results in taxes increasing more in a boom period than would be the case if the replacement cost was used as a basis for depreciation.

We shall now consider a final question in connection with depreciation, viz. the question of the *time form* of depreciation. Here many considerations of a business-administrative kind, which we shall not deal with here, can be raised. We shall only consider what is significant for the use of depreciation rules as an instrument for promoting national economic objectives.

In most countries the so-called straight-line method has been used for depreciation, when incomes are to be calculated for taxation. This consists in writing off every year an equally large proportion of the total basis for depreciation, which may be the historical cost of acquisition of the real asset or the replacement cost of the object. It is the straight-line method which is used in the numerical examples set out above.

In England another system is used, viz. such that depreciation of a real asset is annually fixed at a definite percentage of the *remaining* value of the asset, after depreciations in previous years have been deducted. In this way depreciation is large in the first year, after which it gradually diminishes. When the asset is taken out of service, a final sum is written off, corresponding to the remaining value, minus any scrap value.

In most countries, however, modifications of the actual basic principle have been made, providing opportunities for undertaking specially rapid depreciation in the first few years that an asset is being used. Historically this has in some places been introduced during periods when the price level was particularly high, and where it was expected that prices in subsequent years would again return to the "normal level". It has then been prompted by the idea that during a period of high prices businesses should undertake large depreciations, so that they would not be "burdened" when prices and incomes, nominally speaking, returned to a lower level.

Another reason for modifications of the basic principle has been that businesses undertaking large investments often have a strained liquidity in the first few years after investments have been made – partly because investments are costly, and partly because incomes from investments do not immediately reach the level at which they are expected to settle in the long run. In order better to adapt the time form of taxation to the time development of a firm's state of liquidity and income, the depreciation rules have therefore often been modified in the direction of higher depreciation in the first few years ("accelerated depreciation"). Finally, in a great many countries, temporary modifications of the time form of depreciations have been used in economic policy for the purpose of influencing investment. Extraordinarily fast depreciation has been allowed when there has been a desire to stimulate investment, and this has in turn been withdrawn when the desire has been to put a brake on investment. There are even examples, in the last-mentioned situation, of such drastic steps being taken as a refusal to allow *normal* depreciation. Thus in Canada, in 1951, when there was a desire to put a brake on rising prices, it was decided that in calculating income for taxation no depreciation whatever should be allowed during the first four years after a real asset had been acquired.

The experience of a number of countries suggests that such alterations in depreciation rules are among the better methods of influencing investment activity. This is due in part to the fact that such changes have different effects on the acquisition of real assets and the acquisition of financial assets. If one attempts to stimulate activity by granting general tax relief in the form of a reduction in the tax percentage, then this advantage will accrue to an investor whether he invests in real capital or financial capital. If, on the other hand, tax relief is granted in the form of accelerated depreciation, an investor can only exploit this relief by investing in real capital. A corresponding effect applies in the case of contractive actions.

In connection with *permanent* systems of accelerated depreciation compared to ordinary business accounting principles, it has often been debated whether such arrangements only offer businesses a temporary postponement of tax or whether they entail a lasting advantage. We shall consider this question in greater detail.

It is immediately clear that in the case of a firm which undertakes an investment and plans to operate only for a limited period of time, accelerated depreciation will merely mean a postponement of tax (a "tax credit"), and in this way a form of interest gain. The case of a firm continuing to operate and investing throughout the foreseeable future is more complicated. Let us imagine a firm of this kind undertaking gross investment with a time rate $J(t)$, so that in a small (mathematically infinitesimal) period of time, from point of time t to point of time $t + dt$, it undertakes a gross investment $J(t)dt$. We assume that $J(t)$ grows at a rate q per unit of time, i.e.

$$J(t) = J(0)e^{qt}. \tag{7.20}$$

With regard to ordinary depreciations – as this is mathematically simplest – we now assume that these are determined as a fixed percentage $100a$ of the remaining, not depreciated, capital value at all times. Let the ordinary depreciations during a small interval of time dt be $A(t)dt$. We then have

$$A(t) = aK(t), \tag{7.21}$$

where $K(t)$ is the remaining capital value at point of time t. (We are ignoring periodisation into complete financial years, proceeding as though depreciations were taking place continuously.)

We assume that accelerated depreciation is formulated as a system involving "initial depreciation allowance", i.e., that the investor, whenever an investment is made, can immediately write down a fixed fraction h of the gross amount invested. This means that in a small period of time dt he can undertake initial depreciations amounting to $H(t)dt$, where

$$H(t) = hJ(t). \tag{7.22}$$

In a time interval dt the non-depreciation capital value will increase by an amount dK, which must be equal to the gross investment in this period of time, minus the depreciations that take place in the same period, viz.

$$dK = J(t)\,dt - A(t)\,dt - H(t)\,dt.\qquad(7.23)$$

On the basis of the assumptions now made, we can determine the time functions for the variables that have been introduced. If we insert from the previous formula in (7.23), we get a differential equation for the development of K:

$$\frac{dK}{dt} = J(0)(1 - h)e^{qt} - aK(t).\qquad(7.24)$$

This gives the following solution (if we assume $q \neq -a$):

$$K(t) = \frac{1 - h}{q + a}J(0)(e^{qt} - e^{-at}),\qquad(7.25)$$

where we have assumed that $K(0)=0$. We can interpret this either as an assumption that we are considering a newly started firm, or as an expression of the fact that we are only considering the development of the capital, with appurtenant depreciations, that is invested after point of time $t=0$.

On the basis of (7.25) we can now find an expression for the total depreciations that the business can undertake per unit of time, i.e. for

$$D_h(t) = H(t) + A(t) = hJ(t) + aK(t).\qquad(7.26)$$

The index h to the symbol representing total depreciation indicates that we are considering the total depreciation when initial depreciations can be carried out with a fraction h.

If we insert from (7.20) and (7.25) in (7.26), we get

$$D_h(t) = \frac{a(1 - h)}{q + a}J(0)(e^{qt} - e^{-at}) + hJ(0)e^{qt}.\qquad(7.27)$$

If $h=0$, that is to say, if initial depreciations are not allowed, the depreciations will show the following time function:

$$D_0(t) = \frac{a}{q+a} J(0)(e^{qt} - e^{-at}).$$ (7.28)

What is now of interest is to compare the development of the total
depreciations in a case involving initial depreciation allowances, and in
a case without initial depreciation. If we ignore the possibility that the
business may have periods with a deficit, this comparison will also show
how the current tax advantage afforded by initial depreciation develops
through time. If one has proportional taxation, what is saved in tax
by depreciations would simply be proportional to the depreciation
amounts. (We are assuming that the firm always achieves a large enough
gross income to be able to "exploit" depreciations fiscally.)

If we consider $D_h(t)$ relative to $D_0(t)$, we get

$$\frac{D_h(t)}{D_0(t)} = 1 + h\left[\frac{q+a}{a} \frac{1}{1 - e^{-(a+q)t}} - 1\right].$$ (7.29)

Providing h and $q>0$, this expression will always be greater than 1.
This means that the total depreciation in a case involving initial depreciation will always be greater than the depreciation when only ordinary
depreciation is allowed. When $t\to\infty$, the expression in (7.29) will approach a limit:

$$\frac{D_h(t)}{D_0(t)} \to 1 + \frac{hq}{a} \quad \text{when} \quad t\to\infty.$$ (7.30)

This formula is valid when $a + q > 0$.

We can now consider various cases.

Let us first assume that we are dealing with a firm with constantly
growing gross investment, i.e., a firm with $q>0$. Initial depreciation allowances will in this case lead to a permanent current advantage, since the
limit value (7.30) for a firm of this kind will be greater than 1. If we

assume, for example, that the firm increases its gross investment by 10% annually, that ordinary depreciations are 10% of the remaining capital value, and that there is at all times a 30% initial depreciation allowance, we can insert $q=0.10$, $a=0.10$, and $h=0.30$ in the formula (7.30). We then get the value 1.30. In this case, in other words, the total depreciation, when initial depreciation is allowed, will converge to a level 30% higher than if initial depreciation had not been allowed. It is clear, then, that in the case of this firm the current tax will always be less than if there had been no initial depreciation allowance (assuming that this allowance is not counterbalanced by a higher tax percentage).

Let us now consider a firm which undertakes equally large gross investment every year, that is to say a case where we have $q=0$. In this case the proportion in (7.29) will first be greater than 1 and then converge towards the value 1 when $t \to \infty$. The proportion will never be less than 1 in value. This means that a firm of this kind, with stationary gross investment, will enjoy a gradually decreasing benefit per year from the initial depreciation allowances. As time passes, the position of the firm will be such that current depreciations will be of the same amount as they would have been if initial depreciation allowances had not been introduced. The advantage one has enjoyed, however, is never lost as a result of ordinary depreciation at a later stage being reduced on account of previous initial depreciations. Though we may say that initial depreciation allowances merely involve a postponement of tax, this postponement will in fact persist *ad infinitum*.

Let us next consider a firm starting with relatively large gross investments, but in which the gross investment per year gradually decreases, i.e., $q<0$. We shall then have to distinguish between two different cases. Let us first assume that we have $0 < -q < a$, so that we continue to have $a+q>0$. In this case (7.30) will still apply. The development will then be that initial depreciation will to start with lead to greater total depreciations than would have been enjoyed without this allowance, but after a certain time total depreciations, with a system of initial depreciation, will be less than they would otherwise have been. Thus initial depreciation allowances would then result in the tax burden after a certain time being greater than it would otherwise have been, and it can therefore now only be said to represent a postponement of the tax for a finite period of time. Even in this case the system of accelerated depreciation would of course result in a reduction of the *present value* of the firm's total tax burden.

If finally $-q>a$ so that $a+q<0$, (7.30) will then no longer apply. We shall then have

$$\frac{D_h(t)}{D_0(t)} \to 1 - h \quad \text{when} \quad t \to \infty . \qquad (7.30')$$

Otherwise there will be no essential changes in the conclusions we have just drawn.

We shall not elaborate the special case $q = -a$.

Thus we find that initial depreciation allowances in the long run are a particular advantage to expanding firms – expanding in the sense that investments per year are growing. This is occasionally used as an argument in favour of a permanent system of initial depreciation allowances, as branches with increasing gross investments will often be "expansion sectors", which are believed to show a "promising future" and should consequently be assisted in their development. This point of view has been very much to the forefront *inter alia* in the U.S.A. In my opinion the problem is not quite so simple. Frequently investments in certain branches, e.g., in connection with new types of durable consumer goods, will tend to grow more rapidly than a balanced market development would warrant. In such cases an extra stimulus, provided by a system permitting initial depreciations, might result in greater market instability.

The above analysis of the effect of accelerated depreciation is based on a work by E. D. Domar*.

7.3.6. *Some observations on company taxation*

In the standard literature on company taxation two principal points of view are to be found with regard to the taxing of companies' income.

The first point of view adopts the attitude that all private income in the community can in the last resort be said to be income accruing to physical persons, and that these should therefore be considered as the only final

---

* See essay VIII in E. D. Domar: *Essays in the theory of economic growth* (New York, 1957). (Originally printed in *The Quarterly Journal of Economics* (1953) under the title: The case for accelerated depreciation.)

taxpayers. The most apparent conclusion to be drawn from this point of view might perhaps be that one ought only to tax the income of companies to the extent that it is distributed in the form of dividends to physical persons. However, this would hardly be satisfactory: it might lead to a constant accumulation of wealth in joint-stock companies, without the income producing it being registered anywhere as taxable income*. Joint-stock companies would perhaps only declare dividends to the extent shareholders wished to use their income for consumer goods, while the rest of the company's income was retained and accumulated in the company. Taxation merely of the dividend declared would then correspond more or less to taxation of consumer expenditure. To compensate this one might levy some tax on the company itself. But according to the fundamental viewpoint mentioned above, this could only be a substitute for taxing the personal taxpayers. Thus a consequence would be that one should avoid so-called "double taxation". In the last resort, all income within the community according to this view accrues to physical persons, and "the same income" should not be taxed at company level and at the level of the personal taxpayer.

According to *the second point of view*, a joint-stock company is regarded as something with its "own identity", and therefore as a natural taxpaying unit, side by side with personal taxpayers. According to this point of view the company is considered more or less as part of the environment to which the individual physical person adjusts himself in the way he finds economically most profitable. In taxing the individual person, it is then irrelevant how the company is treated fiscally. Accordingly the concept of "double taxation" would be rejected.

The first of these points of view is perhaps the most natural, when one is dealing with small joint-stock companies intimately associated with a limited number of physical persons. The second point of view is maybe more appropriate when we are speaking of large joint-stock companies that survive individual persons, and having shares that are bought and sold in the stock market.

----

* To the extent that retained profits are reflected in stock-market quotations, one might have them registered in the names of physical persons by including the corresponding capital gains – realised or unrealised – at all times in their income. We shall return to this point.

According to the first point of view considerations of equity will necessarily play a considerable role, as this involves endeavouring to adapt taxation in relation to joint-stock companies in such a way that a reasonable burden is borne by the "final taxpayers", i.e., the physical persons. In the second point of view considerations of this kind are not involved in taxing a company. Instead, purely practical considerations with regard to the effect of the taxes in various other respects will be more important.

We shall now consider more closely what consequences these two points of view entail in the formulation of the tax system.

If we follow the first main point of view, several alternatives can be envisaged.

(a) One could tax the entire income of the company at company level, and not at shareholder level. This would be a case of what we referred to previously as taxation at source. This system is used in Norway in taxation to the municipalities. It raises no particular problems in that connection, because ordinary income tax to municipalities is proportional to incomes, over and above certain minimum incomes. In the case of income tax which is progressive in the stricter sense, however, problems arise in taxing incomes at company level. Within the individual company there will be shareholders with a varying number of shares, and also with varying incomes from *other* sources. With progressive income taxation they should be taxed at different rates. It is also possible that one company with a certain income has shareholders with fairly low incomes, and that another company with the same income has shareholders with a fairly high income. If the income of a company is to be taxed at company level (and calculated solely on the basis of returns from the company, and not on the basis of the incomes of individual shareholders), this cannot be taken into account, as should be done with progressive taxation when personal taxpayers are regarded as "final taxpayers".

(b) In order to take this factor into account, one might, instead of taxing at company level, levy a tax on the dividend paid out at shareholder level. At least as far as this portion of the company's income is concerned, one will then be able to take into account the incomes of the individual shareholders, and tax them correspondingly. In income tax to the state in Norway, dividends on shares paid out are taxed at shareholder level (as well as being taxed at company level). However, problems arise here with regard to that part of the company's income which is not paid out in dividends to shareholders. Various possibilities might be envisaged for this.

(b_1) This part of the company's income might be taxed at company level. This means that for this portion of the company's income, the attempt to tax according to progression in personal tax rates is abandoned. One resorts, in fact, *partly* to the principle mentioned under (a).

(b_2) It might be possible to credit each shareholder in the accounts with a share of the company income that has not been paid out in dividends, and levy an income tax, payable by the shareholder, on an amount which would then consist of income from other sources, share dividend plus the proportional share of the company's non-distributed profit. This would make it possible to apply progressive taxation throughout. However, this method might prove unfair to shareholders who receive small incomes from other sources, and who cannot exercise any decisive influence on the company's allocations, since the portion of the company's income that is not distributed in dividends cannot be freely disposed of by the shareholder in the same way as other income.

(b_3) The larger the portion of its income a company refrains from distributing as dividends, the greater the actual capital backing for each share. Sooner or later this will generally lead to the shares in the company concerned rising on the stock market. If an effective capital gains tax is in operation, it will be possible, by means of it, to take into account to some extent the retained profits in the company when taxing shareholders. The retained profits, however, are only very imperfectly reflected in share prices, as these will also be influenced by many other circumstances. Even the fact that not very much is distributed in dividends will *per se* often help to keep share quotations down over a short period. Just which trends will exert the greatest influence will then depend *inter alia* on how far into the future the market "looks", when the various shares are evaluated.

If the second main point of view mentioned above is used as our basis, tax levied on the company will not really be considered as taxation of shareholders. Emphasis will then be placed on the consideration that if the shareholders prefer to place their capital otherwise than in shares, then they are at liberty to do so. On this basis one can tax the whole income at company level, as well as the dividend at shareholder level. This is done in income tax to the state in Norway. In addition to this one might possibly have a tax on capital gains on shares.

Once one has dissociated taxation of joint-stock companies from the principles for taxation of personal income-earners in this way, purely practical considerations will, as already mentioned, bulk larger in the formulation of the tax system with respect to companies.

For this reason most countries, as a general rule, have a proportional taxation of a joint-stock company income. In some countries a mild progression is applied, e.g., in Norway, through the so-called tax distribution duty. In practice it would be impossible to apply a steeper progression for total income in taxing company incomes, since a company would then easily be able to avoid the effect of the progression by formally splitting up into several smaller companies. (Below we shall, however, return to a special form of progression which can be used for companies.)

Even though proportional taxation has been maintained as a main rule for companies, different rates have nevertheless been used in a great many countries for that part of the company's income which is distributed in the form of dividends, and that part which is retained. In some countries importance has been attached to the argument that companies should be encouraged to consolidate by restricting their dividends. In other countries more importance has been attached to the argument that a distribution of dividends might be an advantage in the sense that it would entail less freezing of capital in particular companies and branches, and greater opportunities for establishing new firms and developing new branches. Thus, in England distributed profits were for many years more severely taxed than retained profits in a company, while in Norway we have had the opposite arrangement in the case of taxation carried out at company level. Now in both these countries, as is the case in the USA, both parts of the company's income are subject to the same tax at company level.

Denmark has up to recent years practised a special form of progressive taxation of joint-stock companies. However, tax rates applicable to a company's total profits cannot be made unduly progressive, as this would result in a split-up of companies of the kind mentioned above. Instead, tax rates have been made dependent on the company's income, *considered in relation to the paid-up share capital*. This makes possible a form of progressive taxation which the company is not in a position to avoid by splitting up into a number of smaller companies. Sweden at one time had a similar arrangement.

We shall finally mention two special problems which have been the subject of discussion in Norway in recent years.

The first involves the comparison between the taxation of joint-stock companies and the taxation of business people running their own personal firms. According to the system at present in force in Norway, joint-stock companies pay proportional income tax both to state and municipal authorities (apart from the tax-distribution duty), while personal (unincorporated) enterprises pay a tax to the state according to the ordinary progressive scale in force for personal taxpayers. The point at issue is whether this results in unfortunately discriminatory effects between branches or between firms operating in the same branch. I do not consider that one could expect serious effects, as a personally owned firm can of course as a rule be converted into a joint-stock company, if this is considered advantageous. As a rule this can be carried out in such a way that the owner of the firm and his family continue to retain full control. If a firm continues on the basis of a personal firm, even though it is subject to severer taxation than a joint-stock company with a similar income level, this must be because the owners consider the advantages this entails greater than the fiscal advantages they would gain by converting their firm into a joint-stock company. Traditional and legal grounds undoubtedly make for a *certain* rigidity of structure, as far as forms of ownership are concerned, and consequently the arguments here adduced are not *entirely* sufficient to dispose of the problem raised. The question has been discussed in Norway of amending tax rules for owners of personal firms so that the portion of their income which may be said to derive from their business activity will be taxed in accordance with the rules applicable to the taxation of company incomes.

The second problem is concerned with the choice between different methods of financing investments in a joint-stock company. According to the rules which were in force in Norway until recently, the position was as follows: If a joint-stock company financed an investment by raising a loan, the interest on this loan was considered as expenditure which could be deducted when taxable income was calculated. If, on the other hand, the company financed extensions by issuing new shares, the dividend distributed on these shares was not regarded as expenditure for the company, but was taxed as part of the company's income. In the long run this would sometimes result in a marked increase in companies' debts, in proportion to their equity capital. This was considered unfortunate, and a rule has now been introduced to the effect that on certain conditions dividends payable on newly issued shares are exempt from income tax at company level. In this way increases of equity capital are brought fiscally more in line with the raising of loans for financing investments.

7.4. *Further observations on the formulation of a general sales tax*

The question with which we are here primarily concerned, is at which stage or stages in the distribution system a general sales tax should be levied. The problem has already been touched on in section 2, but we shall here deal in somewhat greater detail with the most important considerations that apply.

  The most important factors that should be considered in comparing the various types are probably as follows:

1. The effect on the price *level* in sales to the final consumers of the goods concerned.
2. Effects on *relative* prices.
3. Effects on the distribution system ("integration effects").
4. Possibilities for discriminating between different goods, especially with regard to exempting certain goods from taxation.
5. The question of whether it is necessary for imports and exports to be accorded special treatment.
6. The control and administrative demands which the system involves.
7. Possibilities of effecting rapid changes in the rates in force, as an element of stabilisation policy.

We shall consider these factors in connection with various types of sales tax. We shall distinguish between two main types, viz. single-stage taxes and multiple-stage taxes.

7.4.1. *Single-stage taxes*

By single-stage tax is meant a sales tax which is imposed only at one stage of the distribution system. It may be imposed on the sale from producer to wholesaler, *or* on the sale from wholesaler to retailer, *or* on the sale from retailer to the consumer. Finally, there may be several wholesale stages, and there must then be rules stating at which stage the tax is to be levied.

Let us first consider the effect on price level. For the purpose of our argument, we shall proceed as if only one type of goods is produced. For the moment we shall assume that we have to choose between alternative types of tax which will bring in the same amount, with a view to ensuring that in all cases demand is maintained at the same level. We shall later on reconsider this assumption.

Let us assume that a cost structure exists in production which can be described by a cost function $b(x)$, where x is the amount of the good produced. The producers' behaviour is assumed to be such that the price they obtain will be equal to marginal costs in production, which we term b'.

We also assume that we have a wholesaler stage and a retailer stage, and that traditional trade margins – which we shall call a_w for wholesalers and a_r for retailers – are adhered to at these stages. (Closer analysis will of course show that these margins are determined by economic mechanisms. Economic theory, however, is not particularly well developed with regard to explaining margins in the trade sector, and we shall therefore not deal with this in any greater detail here.)

If we alternatively impose a tax with the rate of t_p, t_w or t_r respectively on sale from producer, wholesaler, or retailer, then the price the final consumer pays will be:

$$
\begin{aligned}
P(t_p) &= b'(1 + t_p)(1 + a_w)(1 + a_r), \\
P(t_w) &= b'(1 + a_w)(1 + t_w)(1 + a_r), \\
P(t_r) &= b'(1 + a_w)(1 + a_r)(1 + t_r).
\end{aligned}
\tag{7.31}
$$

We have assumed here that the tax is fixed as a fraction of the price before the tax has been included.

In the case involving tax on sales from producer, the wholesaler will buy the goods at a price equal to $b'(1 + t_p)$. To this he will add a trade margin of a_w, and finally a trade margin of a_r will be added at the retail stage. Similarly for the other formulae in (7.31).

Let us consider the tax *yields* which the three different types of sales tax bring in. In the same order as in (7.31) we get:

$$T^{ind} = b't_px,$$
$$T^{ind} = b'(1 + a_w)t_wx, \qquad\qquad (7.32)$$
$$T^{ind} = b'(1 + a_w)(1 + a_r)t_rx.$$

If we apply a sales tax on sales from producer, the tax rate will apply to an amount which is equal to the value of the sales price from the producer, and this will be $b'x$ before the tax has been added. If we have a sales tax on sales from the wholesaler, the tax rate will be applied to an amount which also includes the trade margin at the wholesaler level. Finally, if we have a tax which is imposed on sales from the retailer, the tax rate will be applied to an amount which also includes margins at the retailer level.

It will be seen from (7.32) that if the tax yield is to be the same in all three cases, we must have

$$t_p > t_w > t_r. \qquad\qquad (7.33)$$

It then follows from (7.31) that

$$P(t_p) > P(t_w) > P(t_r). \qquad\qquad (7.34)$$

If a particular tax amount is to be raised, we shall in other words get the greatest increase in the price level at final purchase when the tax is levied at the first stage in the distribution system. We shall get the smallest rise in the price level when the tax is imposed on retail sales.

The explanation of the effect here described is that taxes imposed at an earlier level in the distribution system will be multiplied in turn with trade margins at later stages of sale. A tax at an early stage leads in this way to higher incomes per unit sold in the later stages of sale, provided the amount sold is unchanged (or marginal cost b' is constant, despite changes in the amount sold x). In the long run, it may perhaps be considered unlikely that trade margins in the later stages could be maintained unchanged. The increased income which results from calculating trade margins on taxes imposed at an earlier stage, may lead to an influx of new businesses, owing to higher returns than in other branches. This cannot, however, result in the inequalities in (7.34) being entirely eliminated, since tax at an earlier stage also increases the need for circulating capital in the later sales stages. The increased profits there will not therefore occur without an increase of capital demanding returns.

On the basis of the above it may be said that considerations of the effects on the price level favour imposing the sales tax at the last level of sales.

Let us next consider the effects on *relative* prices. Formulas similar to that in (7.31) can then be applied to each single good. It will then easily be seen that relative prices will not be "distorted" by any of the single-stage taxes we are here considering. This holds good, even with a different number of levels in the distribution system for different goods, and even though there are different trade margins, provided only that these remain unaffected by the sales tax. For this reason relative prices need not be considered when a choice has to be made from among the tax forms we are now dealing with

The effects on the *distribution system* is a consideration that has to be taken into account in the choice between single-stage taxes and multiple-stage taxes. We shall consider this in greater detail below.

As previously mentioned, there is hardly any country in which a sales tax applies to all goods bought and sold. For social, cultural, or other reasons there is as a rule a desire that *certain goods should be exempt*. This consideration favours placing the sales tax at a stage in the distribution system, where the goods have not yet been mixed to any considerable extent. If, for instance, the sales tax is placed on the retail level, ordinary country stores, provision merchants in towns, and other shops, too, will to a large extent sell goods of various kinds, so that from the administrative and supervisory point of view it will be very difficult to make any discrimination. If the sales tax is on the wholesale level, it will be easier to administer an arrangement in which certain goods are exempt from the tax.

The question of *the treatment of imports* is often of great importance in connection with sales taxes. If a sales tax is levied at the retail stage, imported as well as home-produced goods will be subject to the same treatment. If the sales tax is imposed at an earlier level, imported goods will in certain cases be able to circumvent this stage, and proceed to the retail stage, where they are sold to the consumer without being subject to sales tax. This factor will operate more strongly, the earlier the stage in the chain at which sales tax is imposed. For this reason, if any "favouring" of imports in undesirable, the tax must either be imposed at the retail stage or else special steps must be taken to ensure that imported goods are also included. There are also problems in connection with *exports*. Generally sales tax will not be levied on goods that are to be exported. If the tax is imposed at the retail stage, exports will automatically be exempt from sales tax (apart from retail sales to tourists). If the sales tax is imposed at an earlier stage, it may be necessary to introduce certain refund arrangements in cases where a good which has already been subject to sales tax is to be exported.

With regard to *supervision and administration* it is obviously an advantage to have the tax imposed at a stage where there are comparatively few firms and where each firm stocks a comparatively narrow range of goods. This would suggest the advantage of having a tax at an earlier stage than the retail stage.

Finally, we have to consider the possibility of carrying out *rapid changes in the tax rates*. This would suggest the advantage of levying the tax at the ultimate level. With taxes at earlier levels, difficulties are apt to arise when changes are made, since businesses will be in possession of stocks purchased at prices corresponding to earlier rates of tax. With a tax imposed on the last stage, no businesses will have stocks of goods that have already been subject to tax.

7.4.2. Multiple-stage taxes

Let us now consider multiple-stage taxes. Of these, there are two main types: the first is the *cumulative multiple-stage tax*. This is a sales tax which is imposed at all stages of sales, and on the full value of the sale at every stage.

Let us consider a tax of this kind in the case where we have three stages, as in (7.31). The producer will then receive a price b' for himself; the wholesaler will purchase the good at a price $b'(1+t_c)$, where t_c is now the rate for the cumulative tax. He adds the margin a_w. In addition, a tax must also be added at this stage, so that the retailer buys the good at a price $b'(1+t_c)(1+a_w)(1+t_c)$. He adds the margin a_r, and furthermore a tax must be paid once again, at a rate t_c, before the consumer can finally obtain the good. The price will then have reached a total of

$$P(t_c) = b'(1 + a_w)(1 + a_r)(1 + t_c)^3. \qquad (7.35)$$

The tax yield that accrues will be

$$T^{\text{ind}} = b't_c\left[1 + (1 + a_w)(1 + t_c) + (1 + a_w)(1 + a_r)(1 + t_c)^2\right]x. \qquad (7.36)$$

Here an amount $b'xt_c$ accrues from the first sales stage, i.e., in sales from producer to wholesaler. In sales from wholesaler a tax amount $b'x(1+t_c)$ $(1+a_w)t_c$ accrues. Finally, from the retail stage an amount $b'x(1+t_c)$ $(1+a_w)(1+t_c)(1+a_r)t_c$ accrues. If these are all added together, we get (7.36).

If a cumulative tax is to bring in the same amount as a single-stage tax, it is of course sufficient to use a much lower rate. *The increase in price level*, however, will be greater than it would be with a tax levied only at the retail level and bringing in the same amount. This is because the tax imposed at an earlier stage is included in the basis on which the trade margins for subsequent stages are applied ("pyramidisation"). Considering the effect on price level, a single-stage tax on the last stage will therefore be preferable to a multiple-stage tax bringing in the same amount. Certain "psychological advantages" with the low *rate* of a cumulative tax, compared with a single-stage tax, may possibly be indicated, but it is difficult to make any final pronouncement on this subject*.

With regard to the effects on *relative prices*, a cumulative tax will result

---

* The fact that the price-raising effect is greatest with a cumulative tax can formally be shown as follows. The condition that the same tax yield is to be produced by imposing a single-stage tax on the last stage as by using a cumulative tax gives us

$(1 + a_w)(1 + a_r)t_r = t_c[1 + (1 + a_w)(1 + t_c) + (1 + a_w)(1 + a_r)(1 + t_c)^2]$.

This is arrived at by requiring equality between the expressions from the last line in in distortions if the various goods pass through a different number of stages on the way from producer to consumer, since the tax will render relatively more expensive the goods that pass through a large number of stages.

This is closely bound up with the effects on *the organisation of the distribution system*, or what we have called above "integration effects". The fact that a good is made more expensive by taxation at every stage, results in a tendency to attempt to "skip" certain stages in the traditional chain. In the long run this may lead to business activity being integrated, in the sense that stages previously operating as consecutive links are merged in one. In certain cases this would undoubtedly mean a rationalisation of distribution, and in this respect may be regarded as a favourable effect of the cumulative tax. This was one of the reasons why, when sales tax was first introduced in Norway, this particular form was chosen.

With regard to the possibilities of *discriminating between various goods*, the cumulative tax is less convenient than any of the single-stage taxes, as it of course involves discriminating at every stage in the distribution process. In the treatment of *imports and exports*, too, a multiple-stage tax of this kind is relatively unpractical. From the point of view of *administration and supervision* it is obviously a disadvantage of this tax that there are so many businesses which have to make payments and to some extent have to be supervised. In cases where the same firm runs e.g. both a

------

(7.32) and from (7.36).

We can rewrite this as follows:

(A) $$t_r - \left[\frac{1}{(1 + a_w)(1 + a_r)} + \frac{1 + t_c}{1 + a_r} + (1 + t_c)^2 \right] t_c .$$

By developing the expression $(1 + t_c)^3$ it is easy to see that we have the following identity:

(B) $$(1 + t_c)^3 - 1 \equiv [1 + (1 + t_c) + (1 + t_c)^2] t_c .$$

Since both a_w, a_r, and t_c are positive magnitudes, the right side in (A) will be less than the right side in (B). Consequently we get:

$$1 + t_r < (1 + t_c)^3 .$$

If we then compare the last line in (7.31) with (7.35) we get:

$$P(t_c) > P(t_r) .$$

wholesale and a retail trade, however, this system does offer certain advantages, for with a cumulative tax, all sales from this firm will be subject to tax, irrespective of whether they are wholesale or retail sales. With a single-stage tax supervision problems arise in the case of firms with mixed trade operations of this kind.

The second main type of multiple-stage tax is the *value-added tax*. This involves imposing a tax at each stage only on the increase in price or value which takes place at the stage concerned.

Let us consider once again a case where we have one producer stage, one wholesale stage, and one retail stage. We might also have considered the case involving a tax imposed on the raw-material stage and the inter-mediate production stages. In practice this is very important, particularly perhaps for a comparison with income tax on enterprises. For simplicity in a comparison with other general indirect taxes we shall, however, ignore it, and assume that the good is taxed for the first time when it leaves the producer. The procedure is thus as though the entire value of the good when it leaves the producer has been created at this stage. The wholesaler will then purchase the good at a price of $b'(1+t_v)$, where t_v represents the rate of the value-added tax. At the wholesale stage a value is added which is the trade margin a_w applied to the price $b'(1+t_v)$. At this stage the tax is the tax rate multiplied by this added value, i.e., $b'(1+t_v) a_w t_v$. The retail trade will then purchase the good at a price of $b'(1+t_v)[1+a_w(1+t_v)]$.

We proceed in precisely the same way for the retail stage. We then arrive at a final price which will be

$$P(t_v) = b'(1 + t_v)[1 + a_w(1 + t_v)][1 + a_r(1 + t_v)]. \qquad (7.37)$$

It is seen that this tax has the same effect as though the production costs and all the trade margins had been raised $100\, t_v$ per cent.

The total amount this tax brings in will comprise the following com-ponents: $b'xt_v$ from the sale from the producer, $b'(1+t_v) a_w xt_v$ from the sale from wholesaler, and finally $b'(1+t_v)[1+a_w(1+t_v)] a_r xt_v$ from sale from retailer. This makes a total of

$$T^{\text{ind}} = b't_v\{[1 + (1 + t_v) a_w][1 + (1 + t_v)a_r]\} x. \qquad (7.38)$$

It may be said that, using this value-added-tax, every part of the total value of the product is taxed only once. It is therefore natural to compare it with the single-stage tax imposed on the retail stage, as the last-mentioned tax also only taxes the entire value of the product once. For this reason, too, it is reasonable to suppose that the tax rates with which one has to operate using the two types of sales tax, must be of the same order of magnitude if the aim is to raise the same amount. If we compare formula (7.38) with the last line in (7.32), however, we see that the value-added-tax brings in a greater amount than the single-stage tax levied on the retail stage, when $t_v = t_r$. This is because a tax on value added at earlier levels is included in the calculations of trade margins at later stages, thus increasing the value added which is taxed at these subsequent stages.

If we compare the *effects on price level*, on the assumption that the tax yield should be the same, we find that the value-added tax results in a somewhat greater rise in the price level than a single-stage tax at the retail stage. This is due to the circumstances already mentioned, viz. that at a later stage in the sales process margins are calculated on amounts which include the portion of the value-added tax that has been levied at earlier stages*.

---

* Formally what has been stated here can be proved in the following way. By comparison between the last line in (7.32) and (7.38), we saw that the value-added tax brings in the greatest amount if $t_v = t_r$. In order to obtain the *same* yield in the two cases, we must consequently have $t_r > t_v$. To be more precise, we must have

(A) $(1 + a_w)(1 + a_r)t_r = [1 + (1 + t_v)a_w][1 + (1 + t_v)a_r]t_v$.

Let us compare the expressions for the price level in the two cases, i.e., the last line in (7.31) and (7.37). If we use (A) we can write the expression for price level in the case of a value-added tax as

(B) $$P(t_v) = b'(1 + t_v)(1 + a_w)(1 + a_r)\frac{t_r}{t_v} .$$

If we now compare this with the last line in (7.31), we get

(C) $$\frac{P(t_v)}{P(t_r)} = \frac{t_r/(1 + t_r)}{t_v/(1 + t_v)} .$$

When $t_r > t_v$, this gives us

$$P(t_v) > P(t_r) .$$

If various goods pass through the same number of sales stages, and if the structure of trade margins is the same for all goods, a value-added tax will not result in any distortion of the *relative prices*. If the number of stages is the same for all goods, but the structure of trade margins different, the result may be a certain distortion. But this will be so small that it will hardly play any practical role. If the number of stages is different for different goods, various cases may be imagined involving a certain distortion of relative prices, but under normal conditions distortion will here, too, be so small that it will hardly play any practical role, and in any case it will be less than the distortion of relative prices one is liable to get with a cumulative tax when the number of sales stages varies from one commodity to another.

The fact that the number of stages plays a less important part in a value-added tax than in a cumulative tax means that the value-added tax does not tend so strongly to effect an *integration in trade* as a cumulative tax.

With regard to *opportunities for exempting certain goods* from taxation, a value-added tax is about on a par with a cumulative tax. That is to say that the opportunities are less favourable than for a single-stage tax imposed, e g , on the wholesale stage.

If a country has value-added tax and imports goods that have not been liable for taxation of this kind in the exporting country, a special treatment of *import goods* is necessary if a "distortion of the competition" between import goods and home-produced goods is to be avoided. If, on the other hands, import goods have been liable for value-added taxation at the stages through which they passed in the land of origin before being exported, this kind of special treatment of imports would not be necessary. This in particular is the reason why the member countries of the European Economic Community, in their efforts to harmonise indirect taxation, are likely to choose the value-added system. Furthermore, the individual member countries will presumably be permitted to impose a last-stage sales tax with rates varying from one country to another, as a last-stage tax of this kind does not result in a distortion of competition as between foreign and domestic goods.

With regard to *supervision and administration* with a value-added tax there are the same number of units where tax has to be collected, and if necessary supervised, as with a cumulative tax. The actual calculatison and supervision will be somewhat more complicated with a value-added tax, since the value added is a more complicated concept than gross sales value. On the other hand the system will entail some built-in mutual control between successive stages of distribution.

As we can see from the above survey, the various systems of general sales taxation all have their particular advantages and disadvantages. In every country the choice must be made after weighing the various considerations that must be taken into account, and the actual choice has differed from one country to another. All types of tax mentioned above are to be found or have been used in some countries. As an example it might be mentioned that, apart from Norway, a tax on the retail stage is to be found in Sweden and the U.S.A., on the wholesale stage in England (as a "purchase tax" with differentiated rates and many goods exempted), and at several stages in West Germany, the Netherlands, and France. In the last-mentioned country it appears in the form of a value-added tax.

7.4.3. *Further observations on the basis for a comparison between various types of sales tax*

In the above subsections we have compared various types of sales tax, on the assumption that they were to bring in the same amount. We shall now consider this assumption more closely. For this purpose we shall pursue a simple, macro-economic line of argument.

Let us assume that a fiscal policy aims to achieve a definite production, the volume of which is indicated by x. Furthermore, we shall assume that the public authorities aim to dispose a certain share G of this production, so that $x - G$ will be available for private disposition. The fiscal policy will then aim to ensure that the volume of private demand is exactly equal to $x - G$.

The production x will be sold to the consumers at prices which we shall express by means of the price level P. The sales value, at the last stage, will then be Px. This sales value includes sales tax amounting to T^{ind}. Furthermore, we have direct taxation bringing in an amount T^{dir}. The disposable income of the private sector will then be

$$R^* = Px - T^{\text{ind}} - T^{\text{dir}}. \tag{7.39}$$

Let us assume that the total private demand depends on the private disposable real income, and that this dependence can be expressed by the function f. The aim of fiscal policy will then be to adjust taxation in such a way that this demand is equal to $x - G$, i.e., so that the following condition is fulfilled:

$$f(R^*/P) = x - G. \tag{7.40}$$

When a certain target is fixed for x (for example, based on the target of full employment) and it is desired that a volume share G of this shall be allocated to the public sector, then this is tantamount to endeavouring to achieve a definite value for the private disposable real income R^*/P. This in turn means that one must aim at a definite value for $(T^{\text{ind}} + T^{\text{dir}})/P$, as we have

$$\frac{Px - T^{\text{ind}} - T^{\text{dir}}}{P} = x - \frac{T^{\text{ind}} + T^{\text{dir}}}{P} \tag{7.41}$$

where x is given on the basis of the target for production.

If we use this as a background for our comparison of various systems of indirect taxation, we shall find that it is not in fact the nominal tax yield that ought to be the same for different types of taxation, but the nominal tax yield divided by the market price level that arises. This means that the form of tax resulting in the highest market price level should also bring in the greatest nominal yield, if the effect on real demand is to be as desired.

This involves no qualitative modification of the conclusions arrived at above. The conclusion in (7.33), for example, will on the basis of (7.34) apply to an even more marked extent, on the basis of observation we have now made, than on the baiss of a comparison where we assume that the nominal tax yield should be the same in all cases.

Apart from what has here been mentioned, the effect of taxation on the liquidity situation might be considered. In a certain sense this factor will tend to suggest a return to the basis of comparison we first used, viz. the nominal tax yield. For if we take the effect on liquidity into account, a tax resulting in a considerable rise in the price level, and which consequently evaluated on the basis of the line of reasoning in connection with

(7.41) should also bring in a large nominal tax amount, will have a more contractive effect than what can be expressed merely with the help of a demand function of the kind considered in (7.40). In the first place a tax of this kind will result in a considerable withdrawal of liquid assets from the private sector, and in the second place the rise in prices will in itself reduce the real value of the remaining liquid assets in the private sector.

7.5. *Partial analyses of the effects of various types of tax*

In Chapter 3 we analysed the macro-economic effects of ordinary income tax and general sales tax. We shall now consider in greater detail the effects of various types of tax. The analyses we shall here present will in various respects be partial and incomplete. In principle, of course, they should form parts of all-embracing models, in which all mutual effects are taken into account. To construct such comprehensive models would however be beyond the scope of this presentation.

The partial analyses we shall present can be interpreted in two different ways.

In the first place they can be interpreted as *approximations* to the answers one would get if one used a comprehensive model. The question of when partial analyses will provide a useful approximation, belongs to more general economic methodology. In general it may be said that partial analyses are permissible as an approximation when we consider a market which is small in relation to the whole, so that the effects of what happens in this market on the entire economy, and thence the feed-backs to this same market, are so small as to be negligible.

In the second place, partial analyses may be regarded as "bricks" which can later be fitted into a more complete model. Many of the partial effects we shall discuss below can, for example, be regarded as shifts in functions of the kind pertaining to the macro-economic models in Chapter 3. In the macro-models we can then, if we so desire, analyse the effects of such shifts throughout the entire economy, and possibly also feed-back effects upon magnitudes which we temporarily considered as given in the partial analyses.

As we have previously seen, there are a great many different kinds of taxes, and for every type of tax it would as a rule in turn be possible to imagine very many ways of working them out in detail. It might be possible for us to investigate the effects of each of these on a whole series of different circumstances. There is for this reason hardly any limit to the number of questions one might pose with regard to the effect of taxes. For this reason, the following analyses should be regarded more as a sample of examples, even though it has been our intention to select some of the more interesting ones.

We have included below some points which will be familiar from general economic theory. In such cases we have attempted to make the presentation as brief as possible.

7.5.1. *Effects of an excise duty on the price and sale of a single good.*

The problem with which we shall deal here, is a classic example of analysis of tax shifting. This expression derives from the fact that the problem has often been posed in the following manner: Supposing an excise duty is imposed on the production or sale of a particular good. To what extent can the producers or the sellers then shift this duty on to the buyers?

Let us first consider the question of a case where we have perfect competition in the market for the good concerned. We shall tackle the problem merely with the aid of comparative statics, i.e., we shall only study the market equilibrium before and after the duty has been imposed. In a case of this kind it cannot be said in any concrete and denigratory sense that one party transfers the burden of duty to the other. With this type of a market, the conditions for market equilibrium will of necessity involve certain adjustments in price and sales, and the direction and scope of these adjustments will depend on the shape of the cost and demand curves.

Let the price which the purchasers of the good pay be P, and let the demand curve be given by

$$x = f(P), \qquad (7.42)$$

where x is the quantity sold. (As we shall here all the time assume market equilibrium, we need not make any distinction in symbol between the quantity demanded, the quantity supplied, and the quantity sold.) This demand curve is a result of an aggregation of the individual functions.

Let the price the sellers get for the good be p. The quantity supplied will depend on this price:

$$x = g(p). \tag{7.43}$$

This supply function is the result of an aggregation of the supply functions for the various firms producing the good involved.

The difference between the price which the purchasers pay, and the price which the sellers get, will be equal to the excise duty per unit of the good. Assuming that the duty (t) is expressed as a definite number of *kroner* per unit of the good sold, we get:

$$P = p + t. \tag{7.44}$$

When the excise rate t is given, these equations will determine the prices P and p and the quantity sold x.

By implicit differentiation in this system we can find how a change in the excise rate will affect prices and quantity. Taking f' and g' respectively to indicate derivatives of f and g, and assuming that the demand curve is falling ($f' < 0$) and the supply curve is rising ($g' > 0$), we get:

$$\frac{dP}{dt} = \frac{g'}{g' - f'} > 0 \tag{7.45}$$

$$\frac{dp}{dt} = \frac{f'}{g' - f'} < 0 \tag{7.46}$$

$$\frac{dx}{dt} = \frac{f'g'}{g' - f'} < 0. \tag{7.47}$$

The price that purchasers pay (the market price) will accordingly rise when the duty increases, while the net price to the seller after the duty has been paid, will fall when the duty increases. The quantity sold will also decrease.

In such tax incidence analysis it has been customary to consider the ratio between the increase in price "suffered" by the purchaser and the decrease in price "suffered" by the seller. This ratio will be

$$\left|\frac{dP}{dp}\right| = \left|\frac{g'}{f'}\right|, \tag{7.48}$$

in other words simply the ratio between the slope of the supply curve and the slope of the demand curve. The more suppliers react to a change in price, and the less demanders react to a change in price, the greater the share of the excise duty that will in this sense be carried by the purchasers.

In the deduction above we have strictly speaking only considered an infinitesimal change in the excise rate. If the demand and supply curves are linear, f' and g' will be constant. We can then use (7.45)–(7.48) as well for finite changes in the tax rate, i.e., *inter alia* for a comparison between a situation involving a tax rate and a situation without tax.

If we wanted to, we could easily rewrite (7.48) using supply and demand elasticities. The result could then be expressed in the following manner: the more elastic the supply is, and the less elastic demand is, the greater share of the excise will purchasers have to bear in relation to sellers.

Above we have taken t to represent an excise, i.e., $t > 0$. Precisely the same analytical procedure can of course be used if $t < 0$, i.e., when we in reality have a subsidy on a good. Instead of the question of who is most severely burdened by the duty, we shall then have the question of who enjoys the greatest advantage from the subsidy.

Formula (7.48) does not of course give any complete picture of how the burden of a duty is shared among the two parties. Strictly speaking we should investigate how the change in a duty affects the producers' profits and the purchasers' utility. If we imagine the utility for the consumers expressed in terms of money, as we did in section 6.3, however, (7.48) will apply as a first approximation to this more complete approach*.

---

* Let us first consider the producers. Their profits will be

$$\pi = px - b(x)$$

where $b(x)$ is the cost function. When there is perfect competition, price will equal marginal cost, so that $p = b'$, where b' represents marginal cost. (This establishes the

It might also be of some interest to consider how the tax revenue changes with the tax rate. Let T^{exc} represent the amount produced by the excise duty. We then have

$$T^{\text{exc}} = tx \qquad (7.49)$$

which gives us

$$\frac{dT^{\text{exc}}}{dt} = x + t\frac{dx}{dt}. \qquad (7.50)$$

---

supply function $x = g\,(p)$.)

The differential of the profit π is

$$d\pi = p\,dx + x\,dp - b'\,dx\,.$$

But when $p = b'$, this is reduced to

$$d\pi = x\,dp\,.$$

Let us now consider consumers' utility and assume that it is expressed in a similar manner as in formula (6.26)

$$U = F(x) + y\,.$$

Utility maximisation, given the budget condition $R^* = Px + y$ where R^* is taken as given, yields

$$dF(x)/dx = F' = P.$$

The differential of U is

$$dU = F'\,dx + dy\,.$$

When changes dx and dy occur for a change in P, while R^* remains constant, we have

$$dy = -P\,dx - x\,dP$$

and consequently

$$dU = F'\,dx - P\,dx - x\,dP\,.$$

Furthermore, since we have $F' = P$, this reduces to

$$dU = -x\,dP\,.$$

Finally, if we consider the ratio between the reduction of utility for the consumers and the reduction in profits for the producers, we get

$$\frac{dU}{d\pi} = -\frac{dP}{dp}\,.$$

We are thus back to a comparison between the burden borne by the consumers and producers of the kind we used in (7.48).

If we consider a change on the basis of a situation where we have no duty, i.e., where $t=0$, this simply gives us $dT^{exc} = x\,dt$. As a first approximation to the tax revenue produced by a small excise duty, we can, in other words, simply multiply the quantity sold by the duty imposed per unit. If the duty is further increased, we must, however, take into account the fact that the quantity sold decreases when the duty increases, i.e., we must take into account both parts of (7.50) where dx/dt is given in formula (7.47). This term is negative on the assumptions we have made.

On the basis of (7.50) and (7.47) we could deduce rules for establishing a tax rate of such a kind that the revenue produced would be as large as possible. This, however, is seldom a relevant way of posing the problem, and need therefore not detain us here.

The simple theory presented in (7.42)–(7.48) is familiar from general economic theory. It can be applied wherever we have a market for a good which constitutes a small share of the demanders' total budget, and where furthermore there is no special dependency between this and other markets, so that what takes place in this market affects prices in other markets, and these prices in turn affect the demand or supply in the market where excise duty is imposed. Furthermore it is naturally conditioned by the assumption of perfect competition and that the dynamic adjustment to a state of equilibrium takes place so quickly that equilibrium solutions are of practical interest.

Next let us consider for a moment the effect of the same type of duty when there is a monopoly on the supply side. It is then convenient to consider the demand function (7.42) rewritten in such a way that we have the price expressed as a function of the quantity sold:

$$P = P(x). \tag{7.51}$$

The concept of a supply curve ceases to be relevant when there is a monopoly on the supply side. For this reason we must now return to the cost curve $b(x)$. The producer's profit, after excise duty has been paid, will now be

$$\pi = P(x)x - b(x) - tx. \tag{7.52}$$

If we assume that the monopolist exploits his position fully, we get the following condition:

$$P(1 + \check{P}) = b' + t \qquad (7.53)$$

where $\check{P}$ is the price flexibility corresponding to (7.51) and b' represents marginal costs in production.

On the basis of (7.53) we get the following formula for the effect of a change in the tax rate with regard to the quantity sold:

$$\frac{dx}{dt} = \frac{1}{2P' + P''x - b''} < 0. \qquad (7.54)$$

Here, P' and P'' are the first and second derivatives of function (7.51) and b'' the derivative of the marginal cost function b'. From (7.54) and (7.51) we get the following formula for the effect on the price that purchasers have to pay:

$$\frac{dP}{dt} = \frac{P'}{2P' + P''x - b''} > 0. \qquad (7.55)$$

On the basis of the second order condition for profit maximum it can be shown that the denominator in (7.54) and (7.55) must be negative. Thus, as in the competitive case, we get the amount sold being reduced when the duty increases, and the price purchasers pay will rise. In (7.55), however, it is theoretically possible (though this would hardly occur with any frequency in practice) that the price P will increase by *more* than the increase in the excise duty rate, and that in this way the price accruing to the seller will also increase as the duty increases. An effect of this kind would not be possible in a case with perfect competition, cf. (7.46).

If both demand curve and cost curve are linear, we shall have a particularly simple case. Then p'' and b'' in (7.55) will vanish, and we get

$$\frac{dP}{dt} = \frac{1}{2}. \qquad (7.56)$$

Thus in this case the purchase price will increase by half the excise duty, and the other half of the duty will have the effect of a reduction in the price accruing to the seller. This is a classical result in the tax shifting theory.

In the case of perfect competition it made no essential difference if the duty had the form of a fixed number of *kroner* per unit of the good sold, or as a fixed percentage in relation to the sales value. In the case of a monopoly, this question will play a somewhat greater role. The monopolist will in fact in his price policy take into account the effect a rise in price will have on the duty, when this is stipulated as a percentage rate in relation to sales value. For this reason, if a markedly price-raising effect of duty is undesirable, it may in a monopolistic situation be an advantage to specify the excise as a percentage rate in relation to sales value*.

We have assumed above that the monopolist fully exploits his position. This is an extreme assumption; frequently a monopolist will, of course, maintain a lower price than the monopoly price theory pure and simple might warrant. This may be due partly to consideration for public opinion and a desire to avoid intervention by the authorities, and partly because the monopoly may desire to maintain a somewhat lower price than short-term profit maximisation would warrant, in order not to tempt others to endeavour to break its monopolistic position. In a situation of this kind, with a monopolistic situation not fully exploited, the result of imposing an excise may often be that the price to purchasers is raised corresponding exactly to the rise in duty.

A reaction of this kind on the part of the monopoly will be easy to explain and defend *vis-à-vis* customers and the authorities, while at the same time it will prove more advantageous to the monopolist than a less than full shifting. (If the monopoly was previously just short of full exploitation of its monopoly position, cases may of course be envisaged where it would not pay the monopolist to shift the whole excise on to purchasers.)

Finally, if for a moment we consider intermediary cases between monopoly and competition, there are many different possibilities. We shall only briefly mention a couple of these.

---

* A more detailed analysis of various sides of the effects of excise on a good where a monopoly exists on the supply side is to be found in Ekskurs 11 in *Notater til økonomisk teori* (Notes on economic theory) by Ragnar Frisch (Oslo, 1947).

Let us imagine a situation involving a small number of unorganised producers, where the price is on a level such that the producers together could earn more if the price were raised, but where at the same time none of the producers dare take the initiative in raising the price, as each of them is afraid that the other producers will not follow suit. In a situation of this kind, the imposition of an excise or an increase in the already existing excise may act as a signal to the various producers, such that each of them would now expect the other producers too to want to raise their prices. What would probably happen here would be that the price would be raised corresponding exactly to the increase in the duty, as each producer would expect all the others to do precisely this, and would wish to conform.

If the various producers, prior to the increase in duty, were of the opinion that the price was far below what would be most advantageous, but none of them dared to raise it, for fear that the others would not conform, a shifting of more than 100% of the duty would of course be possible. The difficulty, however, would be that the individual polypolist would not know how far the others would go, and this would create a tendency to hold back.

We have envisaged here a situation in which the polypolists were not bound by any agreement. If they have an agreement with regard to establishment of prices, the position would probably be rather more like the one we described as a not fully exploited monopoly position.

On the whole we might perhaps draw the conclusion that while the shape of the cost and demand curves determine the degree of shifting in the case when we have either perfect competition or a fully exploited monopoly, in the various intermediate cases a shifting of exactly 100% will more frequently result. This will probably apply particularly on a short-term basis. In the long run here, too, adjustments to an equilibrium situation, dependent on cost and demand conditions, will probably be the result.

7.5.2. Capitalisation of tax

If we are to analyse the effect of a duty imposed on ownership of various types of capital objects, we cannot simply use an analytical tool of the kind used in the preceding subsection. In such cases a particular effect, which is described by the expression *capitalisation of tax*, will occur.

As an example let us consider a security or a real asset which yields income for an unlimited future. The price of this capital object will be the discounted value of the future incomes which the object is expected to yield. Let us assume that these incomes are $a_1, a_2, \ldots$, or generally a_τ for the year τ. If the discount factor is r, the value of the capital object, when there is no tax, will be

$$P_0 = \Sigma a_\tau (1 + r)^{-\tau},$$

where the sum covers all years in the future.

Let us next assume that a tax is introduced. This tax may be related to the yield a_τ, or it may be related to the actual ownership of the capital object, and possibly depend on its value. We need not specify this in greater detail, but simply let the tax vary according to time, so that anyone owning the object in year τ will have to pay a tax of s_τ.

We assume that the capital objects to which the tax applies can be realised in a market. Any possible purchasers of such capital objects will then take into account the tax which is now imposed on the ownership of the capital objects or their yield. The price of the capital objects will then be reduced to the present value of the *net* yield of the capital objects, i.e., the present value of the yield minus the tax for all years. The price will therefore be

$$P_1 = \Sigma (a_\tau - s_\tau)(1 + r)^{-\tau}.$$

From these formulae it will easily be seen that the fall in price will be equal to the present or capitalised value of all future taxes imposed on the capital object:

$$P_0 - P_1 = \Sigma s_\tau (1 + r)^{-\tau}. \tag{7.57}$$

This result shows that even if it is the future owners of the object who will have to pay the taxes s_τ, the person who owns the object at the point of time when the tax is imposed and announced, will have to bear the entire burden of the tax, as the value of the object will be reduced instantaneously by the entire capitalised value of all future tax imposed on the object concerned. Thus, this applies even if he chooses to sell the object immediately after the tax has been announced.

We have here assumed the existence of a market which reacts instantaneously, and fully reflects the tax for all future time. In practice, perhaps, the effects will not be so marked, as it will not always be assumed that the tax will be permanent. But there is no doubt that a certain degree of capitalisation often occurs in connection with taxes associated with the ownership of capital objects or their yield. It may not always seem fair to introduce taxes that can be capitalised in this way; and once taxes of this kind are introduced, it may seem wrong to abolish them later on, as the entire gain corresponding to the capitalised tax relief for all future time will accrue to those who, for more or less casual reasons, are in possession of the object at the precise moment when the tax relief is announced.

7.5.3. *The effect of a profit tax on a firm's behaviour*

Let us approach the problem in a general way and consider a firm which aims to maximise a profit which we shall call π. The size of this profit will depend on a set of variables $x,y,z,\ldots$ by

$$\pi = \pi(x, y, z, \ldots). \tag{7.58}$$

Furthermore, let us assume that $x,y,z,\ldots$ can be freely varied, apart from the restrictions that, e.g., quantities and prices cannot be negative.

Let us next introduce a tax function $s(\pi)$. The disposable profit will then be $\pi - s(\pi)$. It is now reasonable to assume that the firm will aim to maximise this disposable profit. If we assume that the tax rises with the profit, but that the marginal tax rate is less than 100%, i.e.

$$0 < \frac{ds(\pi)}{d\pi} < 1,$$

we get the following simple conclusion: The greater π is, the greater the disposable profit $\pi - s(\pi)$ will be. Consequently, the values of $x,y,z,\ldots$ which maximised π, will also give a maximum for the disposable profit

$\pi - s(\pi)$. Briefly this means that the firm's decisions with respect to $z, y, z, \ldots$ are unaffected by the profit tax s.

This constitutes a useful point of departure for a discussion of the effects on the behaviour of a firm of a tax levied on the firm's profit. But nevertheless it will probably be felt that the matter is not quite as simple as this result suggests, and that various modifications are therefore necessary. We shall here point out some of these which perhaps play a certain practical role. It is difficult to arrive at any unambiguous conclusions here, since economic theory has so far not proved particularly fruitful with regard to this field of problems, and because empirical investigations are rendered difficult by the fact that so many different quantitative and qualitative factors are at work simultaneously that it is difficult to sort out the various cause and effect relations.

1. If the profit earned in various businesses is taxed in different ways, the line of argument above would be too simple. If we imagine a particularly severe taxation of the profit in a particular kind of undertaking, the net profits in the severely taxed type of businesses in relation to capital will be less than the net profits in relation to capital in other types of business. In the long run, this will result in capital being withdrawn from the severely taxed branch and flowing into less severely taxed branches, even though the conclusion above applies to the momentary adjustment at every point of time with the capital equipment as given.

Now there will not be many cases in which a tax on profit is specially formulated for individual branches. As a rule the tax on profit will be an application of the general income-tax rules for personal businesses, or an application of general tax rules for joint-stock companies to businesses organized in this particular form. The rules can, however, be applied differently to different types of business, and for other reasons too it may have a different *effect* on different branches. One example of this might be the one we considered in section 7.3.5 on depreciation, viz. that access to particularly rapid depreciation was in a certain sense an advantage for more rapidly expanding branches, and for this reason to a certain extent discriminated in its effect between branches, even though the same rules might apply to all branches.

What has here been mentioned is basically only an example of the fact that the conclusion we drew in connection with (7.58) is of limited validity because it is based on a *static and partial* argument.

2. In practice, of course, a business must make its decisions on the basis of its *expectations* as to the effects different decisions will produce. These expectations, then, will provide the basis for the function $\pi(x,y,z,...)$ which determines the business's decisions. In this situation it might easily happen that a change in the tax on profits would change these very expectations, thus leading to changes in the business's decision with respect to inputs, outputs, investments or prices.

It might, e.g., be possible for the business to interpret the changes in taxes as an indication of the trade-cycle trends in the nearest future, and that this will affect its decisions. It is naturally difficult to establish any empirically verifiable relationships of this kind; the effect can only be taken into account by the fiscal authorities on the basis of their evaluation.

3. Changes in expectations may also enter in, and prove significant in a more special way when the decisions of one enterprise are partly determined by its conjectures about the decisions of other enterprises. If, for example, one has a polypolist situation in which all producers would gain from a rise in price, but none of them dares take this step, as they do not expect the others to follow suit, an increase in the tax on business profits might have a precipitant effect, in a similar way as the one we described in the subsection dealing with the effects of a tax on production or sales. We might then get a shifting of the profits tax to the purchasers of the product. In the case of a not fully exploited monopoly, too, a shifting of this kind might arise for the same reasons as the ones we have dealt with in the subsection just mentioned.

The shifting possibilities here mentioned may be termed *forward* shifting. The possibility of a *backward* shifting can also be envisaged, i.e., a shifting whereby the business pays lower prices for some of its production factors because of the tax. Important in this connection is the question of the effect on wages. If a tax on business profits is increased, this might effect the result of wage negotiations in such a way that the resulting wages are lower than they would otherwise have been since the disposable profits in the businesses are probably often a factor to which considerable weight is attached in negotiations of this kind.

In the U.S.A. especially attempts have been made to investigate statistically and econometrically to what extent a shifting of tax on businesses' profits actually takes place. For reasons just mentioned it is difficult to arrive at precise conclusions, but the results available appear to support the hypothesis that a considerable degree of shifting takes place.*

These considerations provide part of the background for the remark on p. 67 in the macro-economic analysis in Chapter 3, to the effect that changes in the tax of a business's income need not always affect the disposable income in "quite such a way as might at first appear" (cf. also section 7.7.4 of this chapter).

4. The simple line of argument above assumes that the income concept providing the basis for taxation coincides entirely with the profit concept motivating the business's decisions. As a rule this will not be so in every detail. Generally speaking we can assume that there is a utility function

$$U = U(x, y, z, ..., s) \tag{7.59}$$

which motivates the business's decisions. In this utility function we have included all the variables at the disposal of the enterprise, and in addition the tax s, as arguments. As a special case of this, it might be envisaged that the enterprise was maximising a disposable profit

$$\bar{\pi}(x, y, z, ...) - s(\pi(x, y, z, ...)) \tag{7.60}$$

where $\bar{\pi}$ indicates the profit concept at the base of the business's motivations and decisions, while π expresses the income concept used as a basis for assessing the tax. If there were no tax, the business would maximise $\bar{\pi}$. When there is a tax, the business will maximise (7.60), and this could now produce a different result for $x, y, z, ...$ than maximisation of $\bar{\pi}$.

An example of the approach symbolised by (7.59) is to be found in the question of the so-called "business luxury" which a great many people believe to be stimulated by high business taxation. By "business luxury" is meant the sort of measures which, either from a prestige or a welfare point of view, are of value to the undertaking or the management, that

---

* Cf. M. Krzyzaniak and R. A. Musgrave: *The shifting of corporation income tax* (Baltimore, 1963).

is to say measures accorded a value beyond the effect they might have on profits. This utility value is not expressed in the profit concept π on which taxation is based. At the same time, perhaps, the pertinent outlay can be partly or entirely deducted as expenses. In cases of this kind the existence of tax might distort the firm's allocations more in the direction of "business luxury". (Whether this is to be regarded as an unfortunate effect is, naturally, a matter of judgment.)

Another example of a difference of this kind between what motivates an undertaking and what provides a basis for taxation, has already been dealt with above, viz. the treatment of returns on equity capital in a business. From the point of view of the enterprise a normal return on equity capital can be regarded as a cost item, but from a taxation point of view it is not deductible. In this respect part of the tax – viz. what corresponds to tax on the calculated normal return on equity capital – has an effect corresponding to an increase in capital costs. As previously mentioned, this may affect the forms of financing, and there may also be certain shifting effects in so far as it contributes to raising the cost curve from the point of view of the individual firms. This type of shifting effect will make itself felt even if there are no special market forms of the kind we mentioned under point 3 above.

This argument is essentially an opportunity cost consideration. The importance of the argument may therefore depend on the coverage of the tax, i.e. to what extent it leaves some types of return unaffected.

In the following subsection we shall deal in greater detail with other effects which can be attributed to what is symbolised in (7.60). These are more specially concerned with the effect of taxation on a firm's investments.

5. The argument which led to the conclusion that a firm's decisions are not affected by a tax on its profit, was based on the assumption that the magnitudes $x,y,z,\ldots$ could be freely varied, quite independently of the actual disposable profit which is left in the firm after the tax has been paid. In a perfect market with regard to financing, this might perhaps be permissible. However, in actual fact the position will be such that the financing possibilities of the individual firm for the purpose of expansion will depend to a certain degree on its own disposable profit – partly because this profit can itself be used for financing investments, and partly because it may influence the business's possibility to obtain credit. If in such a case financing possibilities limit a business's investments, a tax on

a firm's profit will naturally, over a longer period of time, influence the actual development of the firm. This corresponds with the effect we have shown in macro in section 3.3.1: "Effects via disposable profits". To what extent these effects will make themselves felt will depend, as already mentioned, on the scope for shifting of tax.

7.5.4. *Further analysis of the effects of a profit tax on a firm's investment calculations*

When applied to the question of a firm's investment calculations, the general conclusion at the beginning of the preceding subsection means as follows: Assuming that a firm carries out all the investments which according to its calculations will provide a profit, a tax will reduce this profit, but cannot change the profit into a loss when the tax percentage is less than 100. Consequently all investments yielding a profit *before* tax, will do so *after* tax has been taken into account, and the tax should not prevent otherwise profitable projects from being carried out.

This argument assumes that no financing difficulties prevent the carrying out of profitable projects, i.e., we are ignoring the considerations dealt with under point 5 in section 7.5.3.

The conclusion here recorded is modified, however, when we consider in greater detail how *depreciations* enter into the picture. They introduce a difference between what motivates the firm's decisions and what provides the basis for the calculation of tax, viz. a modification of the type symbolised more generally by (7.60).

Let us assume that we are considering an investment project consisting of an outlay K at a point of time 0, which is "today". In one year's time there will be an in-payment a, in two years' another in-payment a, and so on, up to and including an in-payment a which will take place n years after the actual investment has been made.

The amount K is assumed to be spent on acquiring a real asset, which is worth zero after n years.

If we now calculate the present value of this investment with its appurtenant stream of in-payments, we get:

$$V = a\left(\frac{1}{1+r} + \frac{1}{(1+r)^2} + \ldots + \frac{1}{(1+r)^n}\right) - K, \qquad (7.61)$$

where r is the calculation rate of interest. For brevity's sake we shall write this

$$V = a\beta_n - K,$$

where

$$\beta_n = \frac{1}{1 + r} + \frac{1}{(1 + r)^2} + \ldots + \frac{1}{(1 + r)^n}.$$

First we shall assume that there is no tax in connection with this investment. The project will then be carried out if $V > 0$. An investment where

$$V = 0, \quad \text{or} \quad a\beta_n = K,$$

is exactly on the margin of being profitable, i.e., it is what we call a "marginal investment project."

If the tax were now calculated as a certain percentage of V, the tax would not affect the decision whether to make the investment or not. If, and only if, the investment calculation gives $V > 0$ before the tax has been taken into account, would there also be a positive present value left after the tax had been calculated. Furthermore, an investment project which was marginal *prior to* tax being taken into account, would continue to be marginal *after* the tax had been taken into account.

In actual fact, however, tax is not calculated in this way. The tax for each year is calculated as a fraction of the income in the current year, and this is calculated by subtracting from gross income a a depreciation on the investment amount K. Let us assume that the depreciation is carried out according to "the straight line method" over the entire lifetime of the project, which is n. The depreciations will then each year be equal to K/n, taxable income each year will be equal to $a-(K/n)$, and the tax each year will be equal to

$$s = \left(a - \frac{K}{n}\right)\bar{s}, \tag{7.62}$$

where for simplicity's sake we are assuming that $\bar{s}$ is a constant tax rate.

Every year from year 1 to year n the net income after tax has been paid will be

$$a - \left(a - \frac{K}{n}\right)\bar{s}.$$

The present value of the entire project, when tax has been taken into account, will consequently be

$$V^* = \beta_n\left[a - \left(a - \frac{K}{n}\right)\bar{s}\right] - K.$$

If we compare with the formula for V, we shall see that this can be written in the following form

$$V^* = V - \beta_n\left(a - \frac{K}{n}\right)\bar{s}. \tag{7.63}$$

For an investment which is profitable before tax has been taken into account, $na > K$, that is to say the total income is greater than the capital outlay necessary to launch the project. When $\bar{s} > 0$, then we shall always have $V^* < V$. If we consider especially an investment project which is marginal when the tax is not taken into account, i.e., a project where $V = 0$, from (7.63) we get $V^* < 0$, that is to say that the project is unprofitable when tax is taken into account. Furthermore, we see that even though $V > 0$, it is possible that the tax will result in $V^* < 0$. Thus it is now possible that a project that was profitable and would have been carried out if no tax had been levied, would be unprofitable and would not be carried out when tax is taken into account.

In order to consider more closely what this is due to, we shall consider specially the investment that was marginal before the tax was taken into account. For this investment we have $V = 0$ and $a\beta_n = K$. We can then write (7.63) in the form of

$$V^* = -\left(K - \beta_n\frac{K}{n}\right)\bar{s}. \tag{7.64}$$

Here, $\beta_n K/n$ in brackets expresses the present value of all the future depreciation allowances discounted at a rate of interest r. This will be smaller than the capital outlay K. This is intuitively obvious; formally it follows from the definition of β_n that $\beta_n < n$.

When an investment which is marginal before tax is taken into account is unprofitable when tax enters into the calculations, we can in other words say that this is due to the fact that the present value of the depreciation allowances allowed in tax assessment is less than the capital outlay made at the beginning of the project period.

If taxation is desired which does not affect investment calculations in this manner, there are two different methods that might be devised. (The "if" in this connection should be emphasized, since the purpose of taxation generally is to reduce total demand.)

The first consists of allowing depreciations which are such that the present value of all depreciations together comprises the initial capital outlay. If one added up the depreciation amounts without any discount, one would then arrive at a greater total than the initial capital outlay. In this sense one would then have to permit depreciation allowances of a greater sum than what was invested.

The other arrangement consists in allowing the entire investment amount to be immediately written down. The present value of the project when the tax has been taken into account will then be

$$V^{**} = a\beta_n - K - \bar{s}a\beta_n + \bar{s}K.$$

Here the first term, $a\beta_n$, indicates the present value of the future income from the project. From this the initial capital outlay is subtracted. Furthermore the present value of future tax payments, viz. $\bar{s}a\beta_n$, is subtracted. Finally, we have added what is saved in tax by an immediate depreciation of the entire capital outlay K. It is here assumed that there are other incomes, so that the whole of this depreciation allowance can be utilised. On this assumption V^{**} can be written in the form of

$$V^{**} = (1 - \bar{s})(a\beta_n - K) = (1 - \bar{s})V. \tag{7.65}$$

Here, V^{**} will always have the same sign as V, and we shall have $V^{**} = 0$

when $V=0$. A tax permitting this kind of depreciation will thus not affect the choice of investment projects which are considered profitable and are carried out.

The above-mentioned method can moreover be regarded as a special case of the one we mentioned first, since it enables one immediately to write off the entire amount K, and then the "present value" of the depreciation allowance will be exactly equal to K, which was the requirement of the first method.

Let us now return to a consideration of the effect of a tax with the customary form of depreciation. Once again we shall consider the case involving a marginal investment prior to taxation, i.e., the case where we have $V=0$ and V^* given by (7.64). V^* is then negative, and we can regard $-V^*$ as an expression of the amount by which the tax has reduced the present value of the project. We shall investigate how the effect of the tax depends on the length of time n that the project lasts. We shall then first rewrite (7.64) as

$$\frac{-V^*}{K} = \left(1 - \frac{\beta_n}{n}\right)\bar{s}. \tag{7.66}$$

Using the definition of β_n given above, it will be seen that β_n/n is smaller, the greater n is*. It then follows that the value of the expression

---

* If we write down the expression for β_{n+1} in a similar way as for β_n, and divide, we shall get

$$\frac{\beta_{n+1}}{\beta_n} = 1 + \frac{\dfrac{1}{(1+r)^{n+1}}}{\dfrac{1}{1+r} + \cdots + \dfrac{1}{(1+r)^n}}.$$

As the numerator in the fraction on the right is here smaller than each of the terms in the sum of the denominator, we get

$$\frac{\beta_{n+1}}{\beta_n} < 1 + \frac{1}{n} = \frac{n+1}{n}.$$

From this it follows that

$$\frac{\beta_{n+1}}{n+1} < \frac{\beta_n}{n}.$$

in (7.66) is greater, the bigger n is. From this we can draw the following conclusion: If we compare marginal investment projects of different durability, the tax will lead to the greatest reduction of the present value of the project in relation to the initial capital outlay for the projects that last longest. In this sense the effect of the tax we have here considered may be said to discriminate against long-term investments.

The discriminatory effect we have arrived at here involves the calculations determining the demand with regard to investments. To what extent taxation will in fact reduce the realised amount of long-term investments more than the amount of short-term investments, cannot be decided by a partial analysis of the demand side alone. The supply side for various types of capital would also have to be included. The problem is of the same kind as the question of the effects of interest changes for long-term and short-term investments respectively*.

In the discussion above we have assumed that the calculated rate of interest r is independent of changes in taxation of the profit produced by the project. This may be realistic if we are dealing with the financing of a project from one's own savings, and one "demands" a definite rate of interest on the amount invested before one is willing to forego consumption. Furthermore this may be realistic if, for instance, we are dealing with investments through a joint-stock company, and the taxation we are discussing is taxation of income from joint-stock companies, which may be varied independently of the taxation of other forms of income. In other cases, however, the assumption of a given rate of interest to be used in the calculations may make the above analysis less relevant. In principle the calculation rate of interest should reflect the interest one could get on capital invested in alternative ways to the project we are considering. If then the tax (or any changes in it) covers both incomes from this project as well as incomes from all alternative uses of the capital, the calculation rate of interest will in principle be affected by the tax. This would demand a more complicated analysis than the one we have here given**.

Pursuing the macro-economic implications of such effects as we have

---

* In this connection see Bjørn Thalberg: Om renteendringers virkninger for langsiktige og kortsiktige investeringer (On the effects of changes in the rate of interest on long-term and short-term investments), *Ekonomisk Tidskrift* (1957).

** For a more detailed discussion of this question, see Sven-Erik Johansson: *Skatt-*

here considered could be done with the aid of a model of the kind we used in subsection 3.3.4, "Effects via the rate of interest" in chapter 3. There, in equation (c), in model (3.60), we assumed that private investments were dependent on the rate of interest. This dependence is derived from considerations of calculations of the type fundamental to the argument in this section, as it is assumed in the model that profitability considerations, and not the opportunities for financing, determine investment demand. The effect of taxation we have now considered would have to be introduced into model (3.60) as a shift in function g contained in equation (c). When a shift in this function occurs, there will of course generally speaking be a feed-back effect on the interest level r.

As mentioned in connection with model (3.60) in Chapter 3, there will as a general rule be considerable uncertainty with regard to the effects of changes in the interest level on investment demand. To the same extent there will probably be uncertainty with regard to the actual power of such effects in the investment calculations as we have discussed in this section.

We have above mentioned one possible discriminatory effect of taxation of the income of enterprises, viz. the discrimination between long-term and short-term investments. Without going through the various arguments, it should be mentioned that other discriminatory effects, too, may arise. Possibly of particular importance will be effects unfavourable to investments involving high risks and favourable to expenses for sales promotion, compared with physical investments*.

7.5.5. *Income tax and supply of labour*

The ordinary theory of the relationship between income tax and supply of labour is treated in most economics textbooks. We shall here merely add a few observations.

---

investering-värdering (Taxes-investments-valuation) (Stockholm, 1961), especially pp. 72–84. The analysis presented above is based particularly on an article by E. Cary Brown: Business-income taxation and investment incentives, in: *Readings in the economics of taxation,* eds. R. A. Musgrave and C. S. Shoup (London, 1959).

* The first point is closely associated with the discussion of fluctuating incomes in section 7.3.3. In connection with the second point raised, the reader is referred to Ole Hagen: "Den skattemessige behandling av investering i markedsposisjon", (Tax treatment of investment in market position), *Statsøkonomiske Tidsskrift,* 1963.

In discussing the effects of a change in income tax on labour supply, it is important to define what sort of changes one has in mind. Let us take as our point of departure the existence of a tax function $s(r)$, of the kind we introduced in section 7.3.1. Furthermore, let us consider an income earner who is on a certain income level r_0. We can then distinguish between two types of changes in tax function, defined for the given income r_0:

Pure marginal rate increase: $s_1(r_0) = s(r_0)$; $\quad s_1'(r_0) > s'(r_0)$.

Pure level increase: $\quad\quad\quad s_1(r_0) > s(r_0)$; $\quad s_1'(r_0) = s'(r_0)$.

$$(7.67)$$

Here $s_1(r)$ is the tax function after change. In the case of the pure marginal rate change the tax amount corresponding to income level r_0 will be the same for the new tax function as for the old, whereas on the other hand the slope of the tax function, that is to say the marginal tax rate in point r_0, has increased. With the pure change in level for the tax function, the tax amount corresponding to income level r_0 is higher according to the new function than according to the old, whereas on the other hand the marginal tax rate is the same.

If we assume that the supply of labour is determined by the maximisation of the utility of disposable income over and beyond the disutility of work, one can draw conclusions as to how the two types of tax-change defined in (7.67) influence the supply of labour from the wage-earner who is initially on the pre-tax income level r_0.

With pure marginal tax rate increase, the actual utility enjoyed at the point where adaptation takes place under the tax function $s(r)$ will be unchanged when a change is made to tax function $s_1(r)$. On the other hand, situations involving a somewhat smaller amount of work, and thus a somewhat smaller income than r_0 before tax, will now appear more advantageous than they did when the tax function was $s(r)$. For this reason an increase in the marginal tax rate with unchanged tax level at r_0 will lead to a reduction in the supply of labour. Correspondingly, a reduction of the marginal tax will result in an increased supply of labour from wage-earners at this income level.

On the other hand, a pure increase in the level of tax with marginal tax rate at r_0 unchanged, leads to an increase in the marginal utility of money, and this will induce increased work effort. Correspondingly, a reduction in the tax level will result in reduced work effort.

Other types of tax change may be regarded as combinations of changes in level and changes in marginal tax rate. This applies, for instance, to changes in the tax rate for a proportional income tax, since raising the tax rate would then result both in raising the marginal tax rate and raising the level of tax corresponding to a given income. The former would involve a tendency to reduced work, and the latter a tendency to increased work. The net effect would depend on the flexibility of the marginal utility of money, as demonstrated in the ordinary theory of labour supply.

The discussion above involves changes in the tax function at a given income level, corresponding to the point of adaptation of a given wage-earner before the change in the tax function. It is often maintained in a debate on taxation that high marginal tax rates result in an unfortunate reduction in labour supply, and that for this reason marginal tax rates should be reduced. We shall not here try to formulate any definite opinion as to the desirability of a change in tax which would stimulate increased labour supply, but it is important to draw attention to a point which complicates the matter, even when it is accepted that a higher labour supply would be desirable. The point is that *it is impossible to achieve a change in marginal tax rates without at the same time having a change in the level of taxation for some taxpayers*. In order to illustrate this in greater detail, let us compare a progressive tax function with a proportional tax*.

Let s_0 be the tax function for proportional tax and s_1 be the tax function for the progressive tax, and let us assume that the two tax functions are to bring in the same total revenue. For taxpayers in the lower income groups both the amount of tax and the marginal tax rate will be lower with the progressive tax than they would be with proportional tax. The lower tax amount would pull in the direction of reduced work, and the lower marginal tax rate in the direction of increased work. Thus, the net effect cannot be determined by purely theoretical considerations. In somewhat higher income groups there will be taxpayers who have the same marginal tax rate whether the proportional

---

* I am basing myself here on Richard A. Musgrave, *The theory of public finance* (New York, London, 1959) p. 244.

or the progressive tax function is used. At the same time, the amount they will have to pay in tax will be lower with progressive than with proportional tax. For this reason these taxpayers will offer less work with progressive taxation than with proportional taxation. In a still higher income category there will be taxpayers who will both have to pay a lower tax amount and will have a higher marginal tax rate with progressive tax than proportional tax. In the case of these taxpayers, both factors will operate in the direction of a lower labour supply. In the higher income categories there will be taxpayers who will both have to pay a higher tax amount and will have a higher marginal tax rate with the progressive tax function than with the proportional one. Once again, in the case of these taxpayers, the net effect will be ambiguous.

Considering the population as a whole, then, it cannot definitely be said what the net effect of a change from proportional to progressive tax will be on supply of labour. The same will apply in the case of a change from a *somewhat* progressive to a *more* progressive tax function. There is, however, a group of taxpayers in an income group which we might roughly describe as being somewhat above the average, of whom – according to this theory – it might be said with a large measure of certainty that they are influenced in the direction of reduced work with progressive taxation, as compared with proportional taxation.

This theory is based on the assumption that the individual can determine his own amount of work. This means that the theory is perhaps not particularly relevant in the present situation, where many institutional arrangements reduce the individual's choice. There is, however, a certain flexibility, *inter alia* with regard to the following points: The individual can choose what *profession* he would like to aim at, through his education, training, and in other ways. The choice here might well be one between vocations involving hard work and high remuneration, or less strenuous work and lower pay, and it is possible that the tax situation may influence this choice. In a family one may choose *how many members of the family are to seek paid work*. The individual employee can to a certain extent determine *how much overtime* he is prepared to work, and for some people there may be a *choice between full-time and part-time work*. There may also be a choice with regard to the *intensity of work* during actual working hours, especially where piece work is in force or systems involving production bonuses, etc. Finally, a great many categories have an opportunity of doing *extra work*, in addition to their ordinary occupation.

Particularly for people in the liberal professions or running their own businesses, several of these alternatives will be available. At the same time they will perhaps frequently be people in what we called above the "above-average income group". These are perhaps above all the groups most affected by the question of tax and work effort. On the other hand many motivating factors for work effort are here involved, apart from the actual remuneration of the work concerned. These include such factors as prestige considerations, and the social pressure operating to maintain a definite consumer standard, professional interests, etc., etc., which tend to make the assumption of a *homo oeconomicus* less realistic.

Various attempts have been made to investigate empirically the effect of taxes on labour supply*.

On the basis of these investigations no clear tendency for tax progressiveness to result in a reduction in work can be shown. A British commission which studied the question in great detail arrived at the following conclusion**: "Such rates are criticised as tending to repress effort and to discourage the taking of risks. Probably they do, to some, though quite an unascertainable, extent. All heavy taxation may be said to have this repressive effect, just as, though again to an unascertainable extent, it tends to stimulate effort by diminishing the individual's disposable income. But if we are asked to infer from this that the heavy rates have any special disincentive effect upon the receivers of the higher levels of income, so as to justify a shifting of the existing weight of taxation from these ranges to lower levels of income, we are bound to reply that we see no evidence that the higher income earners are specially affected by disincentive. Probably it is still too early in the history of our social development to form a just appreciation of the effects of very high taxation on the activity of the professional man, the salary earner and the individual producer. These effects can only be studied properly when a generation has grown to maturity which has never known a régime in

---

* Several are mentioned in E. R. Rolph and G. F. Break, *Public finance* (New York, 1961) pp. 153–56.
** See *Royal Commission on the Taxation of Profits and Income, second report* (Her Majesty's Stationary Office, London, 1954). At that time, as previously mentioned, tax progression was very high in Britain.

which high earnings are not largely absorbed in tax. But in the meantime we should not conclude, either from our own observations or from such evidence as we could extract, that the high managerial post, for instance, is declined because its rewards are not thought worth obtaining or that the artist or the professional man abates his energies because tax has made it not worth while that he should exercise them to the full. What influence high taxation has on this sort of activity seems to us to lie mainly in making a man disinclined to take on a casual engagement or something out of his usual course and less in affecting the vigour with which he pursues his ordinary calling."

To be on the safe side it should perhaps be mentioned in conclusion that the question of tax progressiveness cannot be decided merely on the basis of the considerations of the effect on supply of labour. If it is discovered that progressive taxation exercises an unfortunate effect on work input, then this effect must be balanced against other considerations which the tax aims to take into account, first and foremost, of course, its effect on income distribution and the living conditions enjoyed by various groups of people.

7.5.6. *Income tax and saving*

Let us first consider personal saving. The structure of an income tax may influence this in two different ways:

1. It may influence personal saving via the distribution of disposable incomes.
2. It may influence the individual income-earner's motivations for saving.

Let us first consider the effects via income distribution. On this point a certain lack of clarity often exists, as it is often maintained that since people with high incomes save a large proportion of their income, and people with low incomes only save a small proportion, the more unequal the distribution of incomes is, the greater total saving. This is a truth with some modifications. The objection to the contention in this form will be clearly seen if we consider a case in which all persons have the same linear consumption function

$$c_i = a(r_i - s_i) + b. \tag{7.68}$$

Here, c_i is person no. i's income, r_i his income before tax, and s_i the amount of tax person no. i has to pay. The coefficient a is the marginal propensity to consume, and b a constant. If $b>0$, then (7.68) means that people in the higher income groups would tend to consume a smaller proportion and save a greater proportion of their disposable income than people in the lower income groups.

On the basis of (7.68), by addition, we get the following total personal saving:

$$Total\ personal\ saving = \Sigma r_i - \Sigma s_i - \Sigma c_i = (1 - a)(\Sigma r_i - \Sigma s_i) - Nb.$$
$$(7.69)$$

The sum here includes all income-earners, and the number of income-earners is N. As we can see, the total saving is independent of how the total tax amount Σs_i is distributed among individual income-earners. The point here is not to confuse the average and the marginal rate of saving. Even though the average rate of saving for the higher income categories is higher than in the lower income categories, income distribution need not – as we have seen – in any way influence total saving. *It is only when the marginal rate of saving varies with income level that income distribution and thus the distribution of tax has any influence on total saving.* For this reason, it is intuitively easy to overestimate the actual quantitative significance for total saving of the structure of income taxation. But there is hardly any doubt that there is *a certain* curvature of the saving function, and thus *a certain* negative effect on total saving as a result of tax progression (for given incomes before tax and a given total tax revenue).

With respect to motivations for saving it is theoretically and empirically difficult to determine the effect of taxation. It is possible to bring a great many theoretical arguments to bear, but it is difficult to arrive at any convincing conclusions. We shall therefore only refer to Bent Hansen's book, which deals with these problems in great detail*. Bent Hansen here shows that the question of the effect of taxation on saving is closely bound up with the well-known question of the effect of interest

---

* See Bent Hansen: *The economic theory of fiscal policy* (London, 1958), especially chapter VIII.

on saving. A comparison between the effect of an income tax and a tax on consumer expenses clearly illustrates the existence of this connection. Income tax first of all taxes income as a whole during the period it is being earned, and secondly taxes the incomes which saved-up capital yields in future. An expense tax merely taxes that portion of income which is being spent now, and income which capital yields in future is also taxed only to the extent it is spent. A comparison between the two cases clearly poses a problem which has a great deal in common with the problem of the effect of a change of interest on saving, and in this case, as is generally agreed, no definite answer has been supplied by general economic theory or by econometric approaches.

In this connection a warning should be issued against unduly simplified reasoning. Let us assume that the expense taxation is organized as a sales tax on consumer goods. In this connection one often comes across the simple idea that since the sales tax directly affects consumption and not saving, it must encourage saving to a greater extent than an income tax. This would be correct if the tax were *temporary*. The effect of a *permanent* sales tax, however, would be to reduce the real value of the amount saved up as well as of the sum expended on consumption, that is to say it would reduce the basket of real goods one can procure for the amount saved up, should one subsequently wish to spend the money.

Furthermore, there are probably grounds for observing that the debate on the effect of taxation on saving has possibly concentrated unduly on personal saving. During several of the postwar years, when very large investments have taken place, company saving has been equally important as personal saving*.

There appears to be a tendency in many countries for company saving to be residually determined after tax has been paid and a more or less traditionally determined dividend is distributed. In such cases a shift between taxation of personal incomes and company incomes will influence total saving (with the reservation we have already made with regard to the possibility that company taxation can be shifted through prices and in other ways). This point is the basis for the model in the subsection 3.3.1 on Effects via disposable profits.

To the extent that a high total investment is desired in a country, and

---

* Cf. the footnote on pp. 32 33.

taxes at the same time have a tendency to reduce private saving because they have to be structured in such a way that they also serve other targets, e.g. a desire to obtain a more equal distribution of disposable income, the conflict between the various objectives can partly be eliminated by high public saving. This thinking has played a great role in forming Norway's fiscal policy in the postwar years. For this reason Norway has had relatively high public saving. Other saving, too, has, however, been fairly high in Norway, so that the public share of total saving has not actually been exceptional in an international context.

Figures listed below show the average porportion, for the years 1950–1958, of total gross saving accounted for by public gross saving in a number of European countries (Source: *Economic Survey of Europe 1959*, ECE, 1960):

Finland	45%	Denmark	22%
Austria	35%	Sweden	22%
West Germany	27%	United Kingdom	18%
Norway	26%	Italy	18%
The Netherlands	23%	France	13%
		Belgium	4%

Comparisons for subsequent years arc hard to get hold of, but there is no doubt that public saving in Norway in some of the years after 1958 was on the average higher than in the period 1950–1958.

7.6. *Considerations of forms of taxation from the viewpoint of economic welfare theory*

The choice between various forms of tax is one of the fields where the economic welfare theory is most frequently invoked.

One of the main precepts in the welfare theory is that the marginal rate of transformation between goods in production must be equal to the marginal rate of substitution between the same goods in the consumer's want structure. The main conclusion, when the welfare theory has been applied to tax questions, has been that one should not employ tax structures whose effect is to upset this marginal correspondance.

Before making a more detailed evaluation of the relevance and significance of this line of approach, we shall show more precisely what it involves, by carrying out the analysis on the most simplifying assumptions.

Let us assume that there are only two goods which are being produced and consumed in the community we are considering. Let the amounts of these goods produced be X and Y, and let us assume that a technical transformation function exists, which we can express as follows:

$$f(X, Y) = 0. \tag{7.70}$$

We assume furthermore that it has been decided that the government is to use amounts x_0 and y_0 of the two goods*. The rest of production is used by the private sector. Taking x and y to express the private consumption of goods, we then get

$$x + x_0 = X, y + y_0 = Y. \tag{7.71}$$

The possibility curve for private consumption of goods will then be represented by

$$f(x + x_0, y + y_0) = 0, \tag{7.72}$$

where x_0 and y_0 are to be regarded as given magnitudes.

We assume that private preferences can be expressed by a preference or utility function $U(x,y)$. We shall arrive at the most important conclusions by pretending that there is *one* representative consumer who acts

---

* In textbooks on the subject we are now dealing with, it is often assumed in discussions of this kind that government is to collect a definite tax revenue. This presupposition is somewhat unfortunate, as to a certain extent contact with considerations of real resources and their allocation is lost. I have therefore chosen to introduce the assumption that the government has to obtain certain amounts of the two goods, even though this may make the analysis somewhat more complicated than it would be if we supposed that the government had to collect a definite revenue in taxes. It would have been still more satisfactory to link the analysis here with the question of an optimal determination of public consumption on the lines we developed in chapter 6.

as demander of the goods, but we could also carry out a more general analysis, in which we explicitly accounted for the presence of many consumers. We should then have to introduce welfare theory concepts of a Pareto nature.

We shall get the conditions for maximum welfare by maximising the utility function U under condition (7.72). This gives us:

$$\frac{U_x(x, y)}{U_y(x, y)} = \frac{f_X(X, Y)}{f_Y(X, Y)} \qquad \text{(maximum welfare)}, \qquad (7.73)$$

where function symbols with indices signify derivatives.

Formula (7.73) expresses the main precept, mentioned above, that the marginal rate of transformation in production should be equal to the marginal rate of substitution in consumption. Thus, this precept is still valid, even though the public authorities are to have definite quantities of the amounts of the two goods produced.

Let us now consider the behaviour that will result when we have private production and private disposition of incomes arising from production, for purchase of the two goods. Let the income accruing to producers be

$$R = pX + qY. \qquad (7.74)$$

That is to say, the amounts produced are X and Y, and these are sold partly to the government and partly to private purchasers. Prices p and q express what is left after any sales taxes or excise duties have been paid.

As producers, private persons will maximise this income under the constraint given by the transformation function (7.70). This gives us the following condition

$$\frac{f_X(X, Y)}{f_Y(X, Y)} = \frac{p}{q} \qquad \text{(producer adaptation)}. \qquad (7.75)$$

As consumers, private persons will have at their disposal an income which is R reduced by the income-tax amount T^{dir}. We assume that they use all this disposable income in purchasing the two goods we have specified. The budget condition for consumers will then be

$$Px + Qy = R - T^{\text{dir}}.$$ (7.76)

Here, P and Q are the prices purchasers of the goods must pay. These include any sales taxes and excises on the two goods. The tax per unit of each of the two goods being respectively t_x and t_y, we get:

$$P = p + t_x, \qquad Q = q + t_y.$$ (7.77)

If the tax rates t_x and t_y constitute the same proportion of the price for both goods, we can talk of a general sales tax. If not, we may talk of special excise duties.

Before continuing it might be useful to check the accounting relationships which are implied by the above. If for the prices P and Q we make insertions in (7.76) from (7.77), we get

$$px + qy + (t_x x + t_y y) = R - T^{\text{dir}}.$$

What is here contained in brackets expresses the total tax revenue from the private sector through duties on sales to private purchasers. We can indicate this by T^{ind} (indirect tax). If we furthermore express the total tax by T, we then get

$$px + qy = R - T^{\text{dir}} - T^{\text{ind}} = R - T.$$

From (7.74) and (7.71) we get

$$px + qy = R - px_0 - qy_0.$$

If we now compare the last two formulae, we obviously get

$$T - T^{\text{dir}} + T^{\text{ind}} = px_0 + qy_0.$$ (7.78)

The total tax revenue is thus here equal to public expenses for the purchase of the amounts x_0 and y_0 of the goods*. At the bottom of the
transformation function (7.70) lies a presupposition that given amounts
of resources are taken into use. We have therefore implicitly assumed that
problems of the "Keynesian type" do not arise.

On the consumption side we shall have a maximisation of the function
$U(x,y)$ under the condition (7.76), as we assume that the consumer
considers the prices and the disposable income as given magnitudes under
this adaptation. We then get

$$\frac{U_x(x, y)}{U_y(x, y)} = \frac{P}{Q} \qquad \textit{(consumer adaptation)}. \qquad (7.79)$$

If we now compare (7.75) and (7.79) with condition (7.73) for maximum welfare, we shall see that the producer and consumer adaptations
we have here described will satisfy the condition for maximum welfare
if, and only if:

$$\frac{p}{q} - \frac{P}{Q}, \qquad (7.80)$$

i.e. that indirect taxes must not cause any distortion of the relative prices
facing consumers compared with the relative prices facing producers.
This is fulfilled if, and only if, the indirect taxes constitute the same
fraction of the price for each of the two goods, as is seen by the following
transformation:

$$\frac{P}{Q} = \frac{p + t_x}{q + t_y} = \frac{p(1 + t_x/p)}{q(1 + t_y/q)}.$$

---

* We have here in T^{ind} only included duties on goods which private persons purchase.
Correspondingly, we have calculated public expenses according to prices, excluding
duty. We could, of course, without in any way changing the actual facts, have calculated on the basis that a duty was also paid on sales to the public authorities, and
correspondingly that public expenses would correspond to the value of x_0 and y_0,
calculated at prices inclusive of duties.

Without running counter to condition (7.73) for maximum welfare, we can thus use two forms of taxation: We can use direct taxes, and we can use a sales tax which levies the same percentage of the value of the two goods. On the other hand, a special excise duty on one good, or special duties on the two goods but with different rates, would lead to the realisation of a solution corresponding to a lower utility level than can be achieved on the basis of the production conditions described by the transformation function (7.70).

For a graphic illustration in greater detail of what the result arrived at above entails, see fig. 5. Here in the first place axes for the produced quantities X and Y are drawn. In this coordinate system a transformation

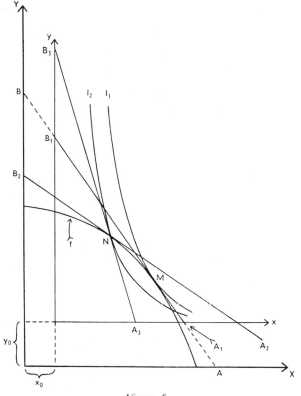

Figure 5

curve is drawn-in, corresponding to formula (7.70). In the figure this curve is marked f. Next, a new coordinate system has been drawn-in for measuring private consumption of the two goods, i.e., for x and y. In this system we can draw in indifference lines as I_1 and I_2, representing the function $U(x,y)$.

Here it will easily be seen that the welfare maximum would be represented by point M, where the transformation curve is touched by an indifference line. This point will be achieved by adaptations (7.75) and (7.79), provided (7.80) is fulfilled. From the producer's point of view the iso-revenue lines would then be represented by lines parallel to AB in the diagram, while at the same time the budget line for consumers would have the same slope and thus be represented by the line A_1B_1. The transformation curve's tangency with AB would represent adaptation (7.75), and the indifference line I_1's tangency with A_1B_1 would represent consumer adaptation (7.79). The transformation curve and indifference line will at the same time be tangential to one another, since they are tangential to the same straight line at this point, so that the optimum condition (7.73) is fulfilled.

Let us now instead imagine that a special excise duty t_x is imposed on the consumption of one good, while no excise is imposed on the other. The adaptation conditions (7.75) and (7.79) could then produce a result such as N in the diagram. At this point we have

$$\frac{P}{Q} = \frac{p + t_x}{q} > \frac{p}{q}.$$

This means that the consumers' budget line will now decline more steeply than the iso-revenue lines for producers (7.74). In the figure, A_3B_3 represents the budget line for consumers, to which the indifference line I_2 makes a tangent at point N. This tangency expresses condition (7.79). At the same time A_2B_2 is an iso-revenue line for producers. This is tangential to the tranformation curve at the same point N. The last-mentioned tangency expresses producer adaptation (7.75).

Because the tax t_x results in the budget line A_3B_3 and the revenue line A_2B_2 not coinciding, but cutting one another at point N, the optimum condition (7.73) will not be fulfilled in the point we have now reached.

Correspondingly we see in the figure that the indifference line I_2 through point N corresponds to a lower utility level than the indifference line I_1 through point M.

A loss of welfare (an "excess burden") of this kind occurs with taxes that distort relative prices, provided there is a transformation curve on the production side and indifference lines on the demand side showing "ordinary" curvature, as in figure 5. It is, however, of a certain interest that no such loss occurs in two extreme cases. This is illustrated in figs. 6 and 7.

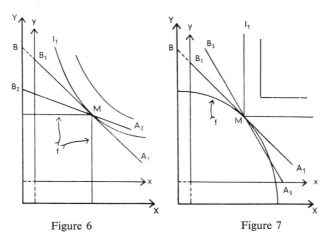

Figure 6   Figure 7

In fig. 6 we have, as an extreme case, imagined the transformation line *f* assuming a right-angled shape instead of the previous curved shape. This means that a definite amount of each good can be produced, and increased production of one good cannot be achieved by reducing the production of the other. In this sense there is now no substitution possibility in production. In this case adaptation will result in point M, no matter what taxes are imposed (provided only they satisfy the demands we have previously mentioned, so that demand is precisely large enough to absorb supply). The prices that consumers pay will here always stand in a proportion corresponding to the slope of the tangent to the indifference line through point M. Non-proportional taxes on the two goods will distort the slope of the iso-revenue lines for producers, e.g., as shown by line A_2B_2 in fig. 6. However, this has no bearing now on the composition of production, since no substitution possibilities in production exist. For this reason, too, there is no loss in welfare as a result of a taxation of this kind which distorts the relative prices faced by producers.

We might see this in the light of the treatment in section 7.5.1 of the effects of a special excise duty on a single good. From formulae (7.45)–(7.47) we see that if the supply is entirely inelastic ($g' = 0$), the price consumers pay will be unaffected by the excise. Furthermore the price producers get will be reduced to the full extent of the duty, and, finally, the amount sold of the good will not be affected. This agress with what has just been said in connection with fig. 6.

In fig. 7 we have retained the same shape for the transformation curve as in fig. 5, but we have assumed that the two goods in the want structure are completely complementary. The indifference lines are then represented by a family of right-angled curves such as I_1. In this case adaptation too will result in point M, no matter what excise duties may be imposed on the two goods. The prices obtained by producers will now always stand in proportion to the slope of the tangent to the transformation curve at point M. Duties that do not impose the same percentages on the two goods will distort the budget line for consumers in relation to this slope, as for example to A_3B_3. This does not, however, affect the composition of consumption, nor the utility level arrived at.

The case we have just considered can also be further clarified by formulas (7.45)–(7.47). The assumptions on which fig. 7 is based correspond to the existence of an elastic supply, while at the same time there is no substitution in consumption resulting in elasticity on the demand side when the tax changes are always adjusted in such a way that there is no "income effect". This corresponds in (7.47)–(7.49) to the case $g' > 0$ and $f' = 0$, i.e., a case where the entire excise duty is reflected in the price which the purchaser pays, while at the same time the quantity sold remains unchanged.

A comparison of this kind is bound to flag somewhat when in fig. 7 we consider both goods at the same time, while (7.47)–(7.49) is based on a partial consideration of one good. Nevertheless, we have seen that there is correspondence between the conclusions drawn.

The line of argument in connection with figs. 6 and 7 appears to support the classical rule in the theory on excise taxes that one ought to tax goods which are either completely inelastic in supply or completely inelastic in demand. In order to explain this rule in greater detail, however, it is necessary to consider a case involving at least three goods, as in a case involving two goods the situation would either be such that both goods are inelastic or both are elastic, whether we are dealing with the supply side or the demand side*. Let us therefore now imagine that we have three goods which are produced in quantities X, Y, Z and furthermore that quantities x_0, y_0 and z_0 are to be made available to the government sector. Let us first assume that production offers substitution possibilities, so that we now get instead of the transformation function (7.70)

$$f(X, Y, Z) = 0. \tag{7.81}$$

However, on the demand side we assume that the new good we have added is an absolutely necessary one, of which a definite quantity $\bar{z}$ must be consumed. The utility function will then continue to be $U(x,y)$, but this now being conditioned by a quantity $\bar{z}$ of the third good being consumed.

In order to determine maximum welfare we can now proceed as though total utility U declines beyond any limit as soon as the consumption of the third good is less than $\bar{z}$. On the other hand utility will remain constant if consumption of this good increases beyond the quantity $\bar{z}$. In order to maximise utility it is therefore obvious that a quantity $Z = z_0 + \bar{z}$ of this good should be produced, as a smaller production would result in an infinite fall in total utility, and larger production could only take place at the expense of the two other goods, thereby reducing total utility.

All in all maximum welfare will then be determined by

$$\frac{U_x(x, y)}{U_y(x, y)} = \frac{f_X(X, Y, Z)}{f_Y(X, Y, Z)} \tag{7.82}$$

which now replaces (7.73). Furthermore, of course, the transformation function (7.81) must be satisfied, and in addition the conditions

$$x + x_0 = X, \qquad y + y_0 = Y, \qquad \bar{z} + z_0 = Z. \tag{7.83}$$

---

* In the interpretation given above, cf. the remark on "income effect".

Let us now consider the producers' and consumers' adaptations when we have prices which can be influenced by the existence of indirect taxes. Let the price producers get for production of the third good be v, so that instead of (7.74) we now get

$$R = pX + qY + vZ. \qquad (7.84)$$

Instead of (7.75) producer equilibrium will now be determined by:

$$\frac{f_X(X, Y, Z)}{p} = \frac{f_Y(X, Y, Z)}{q} = \frac{f_Z(X, Y, Z)}{v}. \qquad (7.85)$$

Let us assume that the duties on the two first goods are still given as t_x and t_y; furthermore, let the duty per unit of the third good be t_z, and the price consumers pay for this good be V. Then instead of (7.77) we now get

$$P = p + t_x, \qquad Q = q + t_y, \qquad V = v + t_z. \qquad (7.86)$$

Instead of (7.76) the budget condition for consumers will now be

$$Px + Qy + Vz = R - T^{\text{dir}}. \qquad (7.87)$$

Utility maximisation for consumers will now have to consist of consumption of the third good being $z = \bar{z}$, while the income disposable after this quantity has been purchased, i.e., $R - T^{\text{dir}} - V\bar{z}$, is divided among purchases of goods x and y in such a way that $U(x,y)$ is maximised. Instead of (7.79) we then get the following:

$$\frac{U_x(x, y)}{P} = \frac{U_y(x, y)}{Q}, z = \bar{z}. \qquad (7.88)$$

If the adaptations (7.85) and (7.88) are to satisfy condition (7.82) for maximum welfare, the necessary and sufficient condition will then be the same as in (7.80), whereas it is immaterial what the price of the third good, which is entirely inelastic in demand, may be in relation to other prices.

Expressed in another manner we then get the following conclusion: If we are to have duties on goods which are elastic in demand, the duties on these goods must be proportional. In this sense we should in fact not have any *special* excise duties on such goods. On the other hand we can have any rate of special excise on the good for which a definite quantity is demanded, irrespective of the price, viz. the good which is entirely inelastic in demand. The conclusion can be understood on the basis of the following reasoning: A special duty on the good which is entirely inelastic in demand will find its complete outlet in the price consumers pay for the good. As this will not cause consumers to vary their demand for this good, the effect of the duty will be precisely the same as for a reduction in his disposable income through the medium of direct taxation.

A similar argument can be pursued if we have a good of which a definite amount is produced without any substitution relationship to the other goods in production. We shall likewise outline the argument that applies in this case.

We now describe production by stating that amounts X, Y, and Z are produced of the three goods, in such a way that a transformation function $f(X,Y)$ exists between goods X and Y, whereas we always have $Z = \overline{Z}$, where $\overline{Z}$ is a given figure.

On the demand side, however, we now assume that all three goods appear in the ordinary way as substitutable goods in a utility function $U(x,y,z)$.

The consumption of the third good will now be given by $z = \overline{Z} - z_0$.

For the constellations which it would be of any interest to compare, we assume that all three goods have positive marginal utilities. This means that there will never be occasion to use less of the third good than what is set out in this condition, since giving up the use of this good will not result in any greater consumption of the other two goods, as there are no substitution possibilities between this good and the other two goods in production.

In addition to the transformation function in production and the accounting equations with $\overline{Z}$ as a given magnitude, the maximum welfare will then be determined by

$$\frac{U_x(x, y, z)}{U_y(x, y, z)} = \frac{f_X(X, Y)}{f_Y(X, Y)}. \tag{7.89}$$

Producer adaptation will be determined by

$$\frac{f_X(X, Y)}{p} = \frac{f_Y(X, Y)}{q}, Z = \bar{Z}. \tag{7.90}$$

Consumer adaptation will be given by

$$\frac{U_x(x, y, z)}{P} = \frac{U_y(x, y, z)}{Q} = \frac{U_z(x, y, z)}{V}. \tag{7.91}$$

Now, too, we can see that condition (7.80) is necessary and sufficient for these adaptations to satisfy the requirement (7.89) for maximum welfare, whereas the relationship between the price for the third good, which is now entirely inelastic in supply, and the prices of the first two goods, is irrelevant. The conclusions as to what kinds of duty are "permitted" if one is to avoid an "excess burden" will, in fact, be exactly as in the former case, where we assumed that there was no elasticity in the demand for a third good.

In the last case we have considered, a special duty on the third good will always affect the price the producer gets for the good, to the full extent of the duty. It will therefore not affect the relative prices consumers face when they determine their consumption. On the other hand, it will not affect the producers' choice of composition of production either; here it will only act as a reduction in the price of the fixed quantity $\bar{Z}$ of the third good produced, and therefore in the same way as if incomes had been reduced through the medium of direct taxation.

It is not difficult to generalise the results we have here arrived at, to cover cases involving several goods of both the elastic and the inelastic type. The results agree with the classical rule mentioned above, which, e.g., has been expressed by Ursula Hicks as follows: "If any important commodity can be found whose supply or demand is completely inelastic, it will minimize loss of surpluses to raise all, or as much as possible, of the revenue by means of it."*

It is more difficult to demonstrate the correctness of the extension of this rule, as formulated by Ursula Hicks: "As long as either of the elasticities is very low, although not absolutely zero, it will still be advisable to tax the commodity concerned heavily, if it is desired to raise a given revenue from outlay taxes." It is naturally tempting to draw a conclusion of this kind for the case involving goods which are *almost* completely inelastic in supply or demand, when we know that the rule is exactly valid for goods that are entirely inelastic, but it is far more difficult to provide clear proof for the correctness of the rule in this extended form. In my opinion the traditional proofs for the rule in this form are too partial to be entirely satisfactory.

The result developed above is *inter alia* used as an argument for special taxation of land or the use of land, as it must be assumed here that the supply is inelastic.

Any attempt to apply these rules, however, will often result in a collision with *other* considerations than those expressed in the line of argument above. If, for instance, one wishes to follow the rule that taxes should be imposed on goods that are entirely inelastic in demand, then these will often be goods that count heavily in the budgets of families or social groups in relatively low income brackets. Taxation of this kind will therefore often have distribution effects which are not acceptable. This has not been taken into account in the line of argument above, where we have pretended that we had *one* representative consumer. If we had carried through our argument with several consumers, each with his own particular utility function and share of the total income involved, we would obtain the conclusion in the following form: Taxation according to the rule that special duties should be imposed on goods that are entirely inelastic in demand would not contradict the conditions for optimum in the Pareto sense. But among all the Pareto-optimal points it might lead to one which from the distribution point of view was not acceptable. On the basis of a welfare evaluation where distribution considerations also are

---

* See Ursula K. Hicks, *Public finance* (London and Cambridge, 1948) p. 171.

included, one might well prefer special taxes on goods that were elastic in demand, even if this did not result in a Pareto-optimal point, since one may well, on the base of a comprehensive evaluation, consider a non-Pareto-optimal point with an equitable distribution preferable to a Pareto-optimal point with an inequitable distribution.

Of course the best thing would be if one could find goods that were of such a kind that the rule for taxation of goods that are inelastic in supply or demand would not conflict with the distribution considerations one is anxious to take into account. Many authors have considered the above-mentioned taxation of land to be a case of this kind.

If one cannot find goods of this nature, the above arguments suggest that one should either utilise direct taxation or a proportional taxation of all goods, viz., a form of general sales tax that does not distort relative prices*.

Precisely the same arguments we have here been through for taxes can, of course, be applied to subsidies. All the formulas above will also apply when we allow negative values of t_x, t_y, and t_z to represent subsidies. The argument would then suggest that, if one wishes to carry out an equalisation of living conditions through subsidy arrangements, one should preferably subsidise goods that are inelastic in demand (while at the same time they must, of course, weigh heavily in the budget of families or groups one is anxious to support). On the basis of this line of argument, the subsidising of necessary foodstuffs or arrangements involving exemption from ordinary sales tax for certain necessary foodstuffs, may be said to conform closely with the results we have reached above. But to the extent that a certain elasticity of demand operates in the case of these goods, too, it would of course be still more in conformity with the argument above to carry out an equalisation by means of direct subsidies**.

In the line of reasoning set out above, we have ignored any indirect effects in consumption and production. Furthermore we have assumed that both producers and consumers consider prices as given. If these assumptions are not fulfilled, then there may be – from welfare-theoretical con-

---

* Cf. the factor mentioned as no. 2 in the introduction to section 7.4.
** In the next section we shall consider more closely methods of calculating distribution effects of taxes, duties, and subsidies.

siderations – grounds for imposing taxation in such a way that relative prices are affected. Various factors in this connection are dealt with in the subsection "Indirect effects in consumption and production" and the subsection "Other particular arguments in favour of public enterprise" in section 6.3. In view of these circumstances, the rules we have adduced above, to the effect that taxes that interfere with relative prices should not be applied, should be given a more moderate form: one should not use taxes that interfere with relative prices unless one has a consciously recognized *reason* for doing so. Such reasons may be the desire to "correct" for indirect effects which "the market does not take into account", or to achieve distribution effects which are considered more important than any disadvantages the arrangements may involve for allocation, and which one does not believe could be achieved in other ways with less unfortunate subsidiary effects.

We have above implicitly assumed that a definite productive input is made, irrespective of the structure of taxation. This assumption is the basis for the use of such transformation functions as we have utilised, where the productive input is not explicitly expressed. If we introduce the productive input – which may in the simplest cases be a measure of labour input – as a variable, the analysis will be somewhat more complicated, and the effects of the tax we have designated as T^{dir} – viz. direct taxation – will also have to be critically examined.

Let us sketch the line of argument, without carrying out a detailed analysis. If the work input were a variable quantity, it would have to be included in the transformation function, side by side with the quantities of the various goods that are produced. Furthermore, it would be reasonable to allow the work input to enter as an argument in the utility function, side by side with the consumption of the various goods. Maximum welfare would then be achieved when one had a certain marginal balance between the various goods, as analysed above, and in addition a certain marginal balance between what the work yields in the form of production and what it (partially viewed) involves in the form of disutility. If then supply and demand for labour are determined according to traditional theory, an income tax would prove a distorting factor, preventing the achievement of maximum welfare in the same way as non-proportional excise duties prevent the achievement of maximum welfare in the analysis carried out above. One would then be left with the conclusion that only one type of tax would be compatible with the demand for maximum welfare, viz. a tax independent of everything except possibly the size of the family – i.e., a head tax*. On the basis of distribution considerations, however, this is not a very acceptable tax**. This highly unsatisfactory and not easily applicable conclusion has resulted in many people rejecting the welfare theory as a useful instrument for analysing taxation questions. Personally, I do not agree with this negative view of the welfare theory. The fact that the theory leads to such an "impracticable" solution when one pre-supposes substitution possibilities and free adjustment of all variables both in production and demand, shows the dilemma one faces in formu-lating taxation. That this dilemma exists is not "the fault of the welfare theory", but is an expression of real circumstances. It shows that, as far as one has to have public expenditure which must be financed in some form or other by calling in revenue from the private sector, it is impossible to avoid arrangements which do not involve unfortunate subsidiary effects. The very system of organisation in existence makes it impossible to achieve the maximum welfare which *per se* should be possible within the technical or physical limitations to which the community is subject. The problem then is to arrive at arrangements which, within the narrower set of possibilities that the system of organisation permits, is the best, from an over-all evaluation. In my opinion, despite the arguments we have just adduced, income tax then constitutes a relatively efficient form of tax. This is due *inter alia* to the fact that the actual supply of labour is hardly such a free variable in adjustment from the point of view of the individual as, e.g., the composition of private consumption. We have already dealt with this question in section 7.5.5 above. In determining work effort,

---

* Cf. I. M. D. Little, Direct versus indirect taxes, *The Economic Journal* (1951). Also printed in *Readings in the economics of taxation,* eds. R. A. Musgrave and C. S. Shoup (London, 1959).

** One might imagine a form of head tax structured in such a way that to a certain extent it had an equalising effect, if one could find a criterion for income-earning *ability* which the individual person himself could not influence. One might then levy the tax in relation to this *ability*, thus achieving a defensible distribution of the tax, without disturbing and interfering with marginal considerations which welfare-theoretical arguments point to. Elements of this have existed in earlier forms of tax-ation, and it may be practical to endeavour to work out something of this sort in future.

groups enjoying a particularly large measure of freedom in this respect will often be motivated by a great many other factors apart from the purely economic. This point was also touched on in section 7.5.5.

We shall not raise here the question of more fundamental changes in the system of organisation.

7.7 On the effects of the tax system on income distribution

We have previously, on several occasions, mentioned the question of the effects of a tax system on income distribution. In several of the subsections in this chapter we have touched on aspects of the problem, involving weighing against one another the desire to exploit the tax system for income equalisation and other aims considered desirable in connection with taxation, to the extent that the various wishes or aims may possibly conflict with one another. In weighing these considerations it is naturally important to have a certain quantitative measure of what is achieved. For this reason, it has long been customary to carry out calculations in an attempt to establish how strong an effect the taxation system has on income distribution. The main purpose of this section is to clarify more closely the nature of such calculations and the assumptions on which they are based.

It has of course not *always* been one of the aims of taxation to contribute to income equalisation. The classical view was that the competitive mechanism ensures that everybody is rewarded according to his ability and efforts, and that for this reason the structure of taxation should be as neutral as possible with regard to income distribution. In practice this meant as a rule a preference for proportional income taxation.

The German economist Adolf Wagner was one of the first writers on public finance to advocate the use of taxation for the purpose of income equalisation. In a work from 1890 he wrote: "Besides the 'purely financial', immediate purpose of taxation, it is possible to distinguish a second purpose, which belongs to the realm of social policy. Taxation can become a regulating factor in the distribution of national income and wealth, generally by modifying the distribution brought about by free competition." But it is quite apparent that this idea encountered strong opposition at that time. In connection with what is quoted above

Wagner adds: "I stand firmly by this conception, against all polemics" *.

We shall here restrict ourselves to the effect of taxes on the distribution of *personal* incomes. It is this aspect of the question that has stimulated the greatest interest in recent decades. Previously, on the other hand, the interest in the effects on *functional* income distribution was almost as great, or even greater, taking precedence in the debates on tax problems waged by the physiocrats and classics. Frequently, however, this involved forms of taxation which play a minor role today, at any rate in countries such as Norway.

The effects of taxation on the industrial and geographical distribution of incomes are also of considerable interest. However, we consider these questions of less central importance in the sphere of public economics, and as belonging rather to the sphere of industrial economy and industrial policy.

7.7.1. *Posing the problem*

Calculations previously carried out with regard to the effect of the tax system on income distribution have been based more or less explicitly on the idea of endeavouring to compare the distribution of disposable real income under the tax system in force with the situation in which no taxes existed at all. This is a somewhat unsatisfactory way of posing the problem, as a situation involving no taxation is not a feasible alternative to the existing tax system (as long as one envisages an economic system where the bulk of incomes at first hand is earned privately).

A more satisfactory way of posing the problem is to make a comparison between the distribution of disposable real incomes under the tax system in force, and the distribution that would occur under a different tax system. One's choice of a basis for comparison would then depend on the particular aspects one is most interested in investigating. It might, for instance, be of interest to compare income distribution under the system in force with the distribution one would get under a number of alternative systems that have actually been proposed. For the purpose of investigating the effects of the tax system on income distribution for more general

---

* The above quotations have been taken from *Classics in the theory of public finance*, eds. R. A. Musgrave and A. T. Peacock (London and New York, 1958) p. 8.

purposes, the most natural basis for comparison would probably be a tax system based exclusively on proportional income taxation. Many people would probably regard a system of this kind as a *neutral* tax system from the distribution point of view. Basing ourselves on the reasoning above, we should, however, have to consider this as a *definition* of a neutral tax system, since according to this line of reasoning there is no meaning in saying in any absolute sense of the word that a system based on mere proportional income taxation does not influence income distribution.

In order to carry out an investigation of the type we have here outlined, we should in principle require a model involving production conditions, demand conditions, and income-earning fully specified in the model. One could then, within the framework of this model, compare the solution in the case involving the actual tax system in force with the case involving a proportional income taxation as the only tax. Obviously the best thing would be if one could here compare the *utility levels* which the various persons or groups achieve in the two cases involved.

In practice it is hardly possible to carry out a complete analysis of this kind. The first step in the direction of simplifying the issue would be to decide to compare disposable real incomes occurring in the various cases, while assuming that the utility levels are determined by these incomes. In the subsection below, in which we shall select a comparatively general starting point, gradually making the analysis more specific, we shall display the other assumptions and simplifications which will have to be adopted, if we are to arrive at simple calculation formulae of the type used for investigations in this field.

In carrying out such investigations the question naturally arises as to which fiscal instruments should be included in the analysis. When we speak of the effects of the "tax system", it goes without saying that all direct taxes should be included. The question of wealth taxes might perhaps be raised, and it might be said that since these are levied in proportion to wealth, they are irrelevant to the question of income distribution. This might perhaps be true if income and wealth were uncorrelated magnitudes. But in point of fact, people with high incomes are also on an average people with considerable wealth, while people with low incomes as a rule have little or no capital. A wealth tax might therefore have a considerable effect on the distribution of disposable incomes.

Furthermore, it is no doubt obvious that a general sales tax should be included in the analysis. One might perhaps assume in advance that a general sales tax has no bearing on the aspect from which we are now considering the tax system, as it will probably correspond precisely to a form of proportional taxation. In point of fact, however, as mentioned earlier, certain goods will always be exempt from a sales tax, so that it will not cover all types of expenses to which a person may be subject. In addition we must consider the questions that arise in connection with the fact that the entire income is not spent in the purchase of goods and services, but that some of it is saved in monetary forms.

As far as excise taxes are concerned, various questions may arise in deciding which of them should be included in the investigation. There is hardly any doubt that taxes on luxury goods should be included. Taxes of this kind, after all, are often levied on luxury goods out of consideration for income distribution. The same applies to a number of other taxes imposed out of fiscal considerations. In the case of car taxes and petrol taxes it might be possible to defend the viewpoint that these should be excluded, as they meet the needs of services that the State grants car-owners and car-users by building and maintaining roads and communications. It might then be argued that anyone who has large car expenses and therefore has to pay large car taxes will also receive in return large services from the State, so that one cancels out the other, and that it cannot therefore be said that this sector of taxation affects income distribution.

On the other hand, it is difficult to state with any accuracy what proportion of car taxes corresponds to the services which the State grants income-earners in relation to the use they make of their cars, and what proportion is of a purely fiscal nature. Usually car taxes are included in the investigation on an equal footing with other taxes.

Customs duties on various goods may be considered in the same light as excise taxes. Previously customs duties played a very considerable role in investigations of the effects of the tax system, and duties were often imposed on goods of such a kind that, from the distribution point of view, it had a regressive effect in relation to incomes.

Company taxes come in a special category. Here various solutions can be chosen, according to one's views on the taxation of companies, cf. the arguments set out in subsection 7.3.6 on company taxation. Certain investigations include company taxation in the analysis, endeavouring in various ways to distribute among shareholders the taxes of various kinds levied on the company. Other investigations exclude company taxation from the analysis.

It may also be debated whether public expenses should be included, to the extent they may be said to affect income distribution. If we consider the Norwegian tax system, it is clear that subsidies should at any rate be included in the analysis, since the very object of these is frequently to influence income distribution in particular directions. To a certain extent they constitute a conscious corrective to taxes and duties which are considered to have unfortunate effects from the distribution point of view. If taxes were included in the analysis, but not the "corrective", the picture would be incomplete. It would also be natural to include in our analysis a public expense such as family allowances in Norway, as this has a definite distributive purpose. Formally speaking, subsidies and allowances of this kind may be regarded as negative taxes.

Examples are also to be found of attempts to calculate the distributive effects of other types of public expenses, e.g., expenditure on education. However, this is not generally done, and it is obvious that this is bound to involve considerable difficulties and highly hypothetical arguments.

There is, of course, no reason why one should not attempt to calculate the distributive effects of every single element in the tax system, imagining in every single case that the element in question has been replaced by a corresponding proportional income tax. The total effect of the tax system as a whole would then emerge as a sum of the effects of the various elements. This naturally provides a great deal more information than a mere calculation of the total effect, and would prove of far greater use when considering possible changes in the tax system.

7.7.2. *Methods of calculation*

The formulae that are often used for calculating the effects of the tax system on distribution of income could be written straight down and a comparatively acceptable justification for them could be given. Here, however, we shall take a more general starting-point, with a view to seeing what presuppositions will have to be made *en route* if we are to arrive at the simple methods of calculation of the kind generally used. For this purpose the most practical approach is to assume that for the moment we are considering a definite income-earner and the taxation to which he is subject. The necessary concepts are set out in table 13. Here are first of all listed the income and price concepts which apply, under the tax system actually in force. Next follow the corresponding magnitudes under a system involving merely proportional taxation of income. In the table this is referred to as "the hypothetical tax system". The magnitudes applying under the hypothetical tax system are marked with an asterisk. (On various previous occasions we have used an asterisk when dealing with income symbols in order to show that we are dealing with disposable income. In this section, however, the asterisk is used exclusively to show when we are dealing with magnitudes applicable to the situation under the hypothetical tax system.)

We could have shown that all magnitudes apply to a definite income-earner by using an index i, but no difficulty should be involved if, for the sake of simplicity, we omit the use of this index.

The symbols in the first three lines of table 13 are the same as those we introduced at the beginning of section 7.3.1.

In the fourth and fifth lines are shown the prices of the various goods which the income-earner purchases, and the quantities he purchases. In

Table 13

	The actual tax system	The hypothetical tax system
(1) Nominal income prior to taxation	r	r^*
(2) Direct tax	$s = \bar{s}r$	$s^* = \bar{s}^* r^*$
(3) Disposable nominal income	$r - s = (1 - \bar{s})r$	$r^* - s^* = (1 - \bar{s}^*)r^*$
(4) Prices	$P_1 \ldots P_n$	$P_1^* \ldots P_n^*$
(5) Consumption	$x_1 \ldots x_n$	$x_1^* \ldots x_n^*$
(6) Price level	$P = 1$	$P^* = \dfrac{\Sigma P_j^* x_j}{\Sigma P_j x_j}$
(7) Disposable real income	$\dfrac{r - s}{P} = r - s$	$\dfrac{r^* - s^*}{P^*} = (r^* - s^*) \left/ \dfrac{\Sigma P_j^* x_j}{\Sigma P_j x_j} \right.$

line (6) we have shown the price level. The convention we have used is to set the price level at 1 under the actual tax system, and to calculate a price index P^* which shows what the price level would be under the hypothetical tax system when we use the consumed quantities under the actual tax system as weights. It would of course be possible to adopt different procedures on this point.

This price index is used to deflate nominal income, so that in line (7) we get disposable *real* income. By the method we have chosen to express the price levels in the two situations, the disposable real income in line (7) will express the income *calculated in kroner under the actual tax system*. This is probably the most practical approach, since it is easier to evaluate the results when they are expressed in this way than if they had been expressed in *kroner* under the hypothetical tax system.

Our aim is to compare disposable real income for the income-earner under the actual and under the hypothetical tax system. This comparison can be carried out in various ways. We have chosen here to endeavour to find an expression for the *difference* between the disposable real income under the actual tax system and under the hypothetical tax system:

Δ = *disposable real income under the actual tax system minus*
     disposable real income under the hypothetical tax system.   (7.92)

If this magnitude is positive, the income-earner we are considering will enjoy an advantage from the actual tax system compared with the hypothetical one. If Δ is negative, it means that the income-earner is more unfavourably placed under the tax system in force than he would have been under a system with merely proportional income taxation.

Before proceeding to develop a formula for Δ, it is convenient to introduce a simplified way of writing the price index. We have

$$P^* = \frac{\Sigma P_j^* x_j}{\Sigma P_j x_j} = 1 - \frac{\Sigma (P_j - P_j^*) x_j}{\Sigma P_j x_j}.$$

This can be written in the following form

$$P^* = 1 - q, \quad \text{where} \quad q = \frac{\Sigma (P_j - P_j^*) x_j}{\Sigma P_j x_j}. \qquad (7.93)$$

We can then write Δ as

$$\Delta = (r - s) - \frac{r^* - s^*}{1 - q}. \tag{7.94}$$

The ideal solution would be if we could carry out our calculations on the basis of this formula, as it now stands. This would demand the use of the kind of comprehensive model we mentioned by way of introduction. The calculations carried out in practice in various countries have been based on a long series of simplifying assumptions. We shall now gradually introduce assumptions of this kind, and see how the expression for Δ will become amenable to comparatively simple practical calculations. In order to avoid an unnecessarily protracted deduction, detailed discussion of the various assumptions will be postponed till the next subsection.

We shall first rewrite (7.94) in the following form

$$\Delta = \frac{1}{1 - q}[(1 - q)(r - s) - r^* + s^*] =$$

$$= \frac{1}{1 - q}[(r - r^*) + (s^* - s) - q(r - s)]. \tag{7.95}$$

We then assume that the income prior to direct taxation is the same under both tax systems:

$$r^* = r \qquad \text{(assumption)}. \tag{7.96}$$

(7.95) can then be simplified as follows:

$$\Delta = \frac{1}{1 - q}[(s^* - s) - q(r - s)]. \tag{7.97}$$

In the first bracket in (7.97) we now have the difference in the amount for direct tax in the two cases involved. This is a comparatively simple magnitude to calculate. It will be equal to $(\bar{s}^* - \bar{s})r$ when $r^* = r$. The magnitudes r and $\bar{s}$ can be observed under the system in force. The question which is likely to involve a certain measure of difficulty is what tax rate $\bar{s}^*$ should be utilised for proportional income tax under the hypothetical tax system. It might be chosen in such a way that the total tax revenue accruing from all taxpayers will be the same under the hypothetical tax system as under the one actually in force, or alternatively one might endeavour to proceed in a more subtle manner, and choose a tax rate such that the contractive effect of taxation was the same in the two cases. Whichever choice one makes, however, will not be of particularly great importance to the conclusions arrived at with regard to the effects on income distribution, since the rate $\bar{s}^*$ has to be the same for all income-earners, so that the tax amount $s^* = \bar{s}^* r$ will be proportional with income prior to taxation for the individual taxpayers. The choice of tax rate $\bar{s}^*$ has some bearing on the "zero point" for the measuring of the advantage or disadvantage to the individual taxpayer under the system in force, but is less important in a comparison *between various taxpayers*.

The magnitude q in the formula (7.97) still presents certain problems. We shall return to the definition of q in the formula (7.93) in order to consider more closely what assumptions may be made in order to facilitate the calculation of factor q. The problem is, of course, how high the prices P_j^* would be under the hypothetical tax system. We shall make the presupposition that the prices under the alternative tax system would be equal to the prices under the tax system at present in force, minus the taxes imposed on various goods. This means that we are assuming "complete shifting" in the sense that every tax placed on a good is reflected fully in the price the purchaser pays for that good. If we now calculate taxes as proportions of price including tax, and use θ_j to express the rates, we then get

$$P_j^* = P_j(1 - \theta_j) \qquad \text{(assumption)}. \qquad (7.98)$$

Magnitude q could then be written as follows

$$q = \frac{\Sigma \theta_j P_j x_j}{\Sigma P_j x_j}, \qquad (7.99)$$

and (7.97) could be written as follows

$$\Delta = \frac{1}{1-q}\left[(s^* - s) - \frac{r-s}{\Sigma P_j x_j}\Sigma\theta_j P_j x_j\right].$$
(7.100)

All the terms are now in principle known when s^* is fixed, as discussed above. The magnitudes s, r, P_j, x_j, θ_j are observable under the tax system actually in force, and q can be calculated from (7.99).

The sum $\Sigma\theta_j P_j x_j$ in (7.100) can be interpreted as the amount the income-earner pays in indirect taxes when he makes his purchases. In the formula this amount is multiplied by a factor $(r-s)/\Sigma P_j x_j$, which may differ from 1 in value, but which will be of this order of magnitude. For the moment let us assume that it is equal to 1, and then later on discuss this assumption in greater detail:

$$\frac{r-s}{\Sigma P_j x_j} = 1 \qquad \textit{(assumption)}$$
(7.101)

(7.100) then becomes

$$\Delta = \frac{1}{1-q}\left[s^* - (s + \Sigma\theta_j P_j x_j)\right].$$
(7.102)

We have thus arrived at a formula which is very close to the ordinary method for calculations of this kind. What is most frequently calculated is (sometimes with the opposite sign) what is contained in the square bracket in (7.102), viz.,

$$(1-q)\Delta = s^* - (s + \Sigma\theta_j P_j x_j).$$
(7.103)

This is actually the advantage accruing to the taxpayer we are considering, under the tax system in force, *expressed in the krone value which would obtain under the hypothetical tax system:* according to the definition,

$\varDelta$ is this advantage expressed in the current value of the *krone*, and in (7.103) $\varDelta$ is multiplied by a factor $(1-q)$, which is the price level under the hypothetical tax system as compared with the tax system in force.

Normally $q>0$, so that $1-q<1$, since the system in force involves indirect taxes which are replaced by direct taxes under the hypothetical tax system.

As already mentioned by way of introduction, it might prove most convenient to express the results of the calculation in terms of the ruling value of the *krone*, since this is a *krone* value to which one is accustomed, and which therefore makes it easiest to evaluate the results.

As previously mentioned, the actual tax under the hypothetical system s^* is relatively unimportant for a comparison between the various income-earners, since s^* is proportional to income prior to taxation. For this reason, it is frequently sufficient to present results for the contents of the brackets on the extreme right in (7.103)*. It is simply the sum of the direct and indirect taxes which the taxpayer we are considering may be said to pay under the system in force.

In principle, q will differ for different people, since the x's in (7.99) represent the individual person's consumption of various goods. (The prices and tax rates for indirect taxation, on the other hand, will be common to all persons.)

In concrete calculations every individual taxpayer cannot, of course, be considered. As a rule taxpayers are grouped according to size and composition of family on the one hand, and according to size of income prior to taxation on the other. Within each group the average family can then be considered, and one can work out its income, direct taxation, and the composition of its consumption, with the help of household surveys

---

* Earlier calculations, merely presenting what corresponds to the terms in the bracket to the right of (7.103), have not been based on the same kind of reasoning on which we have here based ourselves.

Instead of calculating the effect of the existing tax system, as compared with a hypothetical tax system, one has proceeded as though one were comparing a situation involving tax and a situation involving no tax. With all the simplifying presuppositions that have been made in order to arrive at (7.103), the difference between these points of view will not be particularly great, as far as the nature of the calculations to be carried out is concerned, but it will still be of importance to the interpretation of the calculations.

or other statistical methods. Furthermore, when the prices that are paid are known, and the rates of the various types of tax (which may be negative figures, if subsidies are involved), it is easy to work out the value of Δ according to (7.102) or of $(1-q)\Delta$ according to (7.103).

7.7.3. Discussion of the assumptions forming the basis for calculations of the effects of taxes on income distribution

In the preceding subsection we deduced a simple method of calculating the effect of a tax system on income distribution. In deducing the final formulae (7.102)–(7.103) we made a series of assumptions which at that stage were not discussed in detail, in order not to break the continuity of the presentation. We shall now return to these assumptions and discuss them in greater detail.

The first assumption we made, after deciding to take our starting-point in the concept of disposable real income for the purpose of comparison, was assumption (7.96), to the effect that nominal income prior to taxation would be the same under the hypothetical tax system as under the system actually in force. There would be no difficulty in pointing out cases where this assumption *might* be false. Members of certain groups within the community, for instance, might be in a position where they are capable of direct negotiation with regard to their own incomes, and can ensure themselves a definite income *after taxation* in connection with various types of work or services. This might apply to various kinds of work by artisans; it might apply to various kinds of consultant work; and it might apply to various kinds of positions – especially in the higher income brackets – where income and other conditions cannot easily be standardised for a large group. In cases of this kind there will be a factor tending to make income *after* direct taxes has been paid – viz., what in table 13 is called disposable nominal income – constant, instead of nominal income *before* taxation. It is, however, difficult to establish empirically how great the significance of this would be. Conditions of this kind, in so far as they exist, are probably somewhat special, and should be the object of special investigations rather than being included among the assumptions in calculations concerning the effects of taxes on income distribution generally.

For major groups of income-earners, one might discuss to what degree the existence of various types of tax influences the results of negotiations, e.g., in the case of wages, the prices of agricultural products and of fisheries products, or other factors of importance to incomes. Naturally one should not confine oneself to investigating what is actually adduced in the form of arguments in negotiations, but consider what really lies behind the "official" arguments. The whole set-up is then bound to be somewhat speculative, and it is difficult to propose any assumption which is patently better than what is expressed in (7.96).

If one has a system involving high excise duties for certain goods, incomes in the sectors producing these goods would naturally be affected if the duties were replaced by a system involving only proportional direct taxation. In some cases, however, effects of this kind might prove some-what temporary, as production factors would probably gradually be transferred from other branches if incomes rose appreciably in a particular branch or a few branches. These factor movements would tend to even out again the effects on income distribution which would occur immediately after the change in the tax system. On this basis assumption (7.96) can be defended.

A similar line of thought can be adopted with regard to subsidies. In the case of groups such as farmers and fishermen in Norway, however, there are weighty arguments in favour of an attempt to base one's calculations on other presuppositions than (7.96). Among other things, there is not the same degree of mobility as, e.g., between manufacturing industries or service industries.

If one wanted to include in the analysis the effects of taxation on the income of joint-stock companies, this could be included in connection with (7.96). Instead of assuming equal incomes prior to taxation for the various personal income-earners under the two systems, one would have to introduce a difference which would represent the effect of company taxation on the dividends accruing to personal shareholders. In order to carry this out, it would be necessary to know how the share capital is distributed among income-earners in the various income-groups.

The next assumption we shall consider is (7.98), where it is assumed that all indirect taxation is shifted in its entirety on to the final purchasers of goods.

The magnitude θ_j in the above may be imagined to consist of a general sales tax plus any excise duties on various goods.

We shall first consider the component consisting of general sales tax. We can then discuss the shifting assumption on the basis of the model in section 3.6. It will easily be seen from equation (b) in (3.68) that if employment under both the existing and the hypothetical tax systems is to be the same, and if the nominal wage-level is unchanged, the sales tax would be reflected fully in the market price level. As a general rule one can therefore accept an assumption of this kind for the sort of calculations we are here discussing. The actual details in the calculation may well prove more complicated, depending on what type of sales tax is involved. Some goods will always be exempt from a sales tax, and as a result of the various structures a sales tax may be given, the tax may not fall equally heavily on all goods (cf. section 4 of this chapter). This could, however, be taken into account by considering deviations from the general or average level of the sales tax in the same way as in the case of excise duties or subsidies.

In considering the shifting assumption for excise duties (including subsidies considered as negative duties), the situation is undoubtedly more complicated. The discussions in section 7.5.1 show what factors should be taken into consideration. In principle one should, of course, proceed still further than what is set out in section 7.5.1, where the line of argument was of a partial nature.

On the other hand, if one accepts partial arguments of this kind, then in the case of goods produced in markets where there are reasons to assume that free competition exists, and when one is only interested in the situation after it has readjusted itself following a change in tax structure, one should be able to calculate the changes in prices that take place with the aid of formulae such as (7.45). One would then have to base oneself on estimates for elasticities or derivatives of supply and demand functions.

In section 7.5.1 we saw that an excise duty will affect more strongly the market price for the good, the more elastic the supply curve is. In the case of many goods sold in a country such as Norway, the assumption that supply is completely elastic can be defended on the grounds that this is an approximation to the actual situation. We have, *inter alia*, many imported goods where the price is determined by the world market and hardly influenced by Norwegian demand. Furthermore we have a whole series of goods which are partly produced domestically, and partly imported. Here, too, total supply could be highly elastic.

In the case of a large proportion of the goods produced in manufacturing industry, processing costs more than the raw materials. Here too we might assume a very elastic supply – at any rate in the long run, when production plant can be expanded.

In the case of goods to which none of these factors apply, resulting in a sufficiently elastic supply curve to warrant presupposition (7.98), there may be grounds for supplementing the analysis from section 7.5.1 with a consideration of the income effects on demand for the individual good.

In fig. 8 we have drawn-in a demand curve $f_j(P_j)$, and a supply curve $g_j(p_j)$, where the index j marks a specified good. The diagram here corresponds entirely to the analysis in section 7.5.1. The distance between p_j and P_j comprises the excise tax per unit of the good, which with the symbols we have used in this section can be written $\theta_j P_j$.

The assumption made in (7.98) expresses the fact that the price for good j falls from P_j to p_j when the duty θ_j is eliminated, or to express it in another way: $P_j^* = p_j$. However, from the diagram it will be seen that if the duty θ_j is removed, the new P_j^* will be determined by the point of intersection A between the supply curve and the demand curve, and will thus come to lie *between* P_j and p_j. In other words, in applying assumption (7.98) we are exaggerating the effect of the removal of the duty on the market price of the good.

Here, however, a new factor, as compared with the analysis in section 7.5.1 comes into play. Under the hypothetical tax system taxation by excise duties is to be replaced by proportional income tax. We have previously assumed that incomes prior to taxation are unchanged by a change in the tax system. When an excise duty is removed, and is replaced by a proportional income tax, the disposable nominal incomes will as a result be somewhat reduced. In fig. 8 this will effect a shift towards the left in the demand curve, provided the good in question has a positive income elasticity. The new demand curve is shown in the broken line in fig. 8. It will be seen that the point of intersection with the supply curve (B) will now lie lower than the old point of intersection, and the market price of the good we are considering will thus drop somewhat more than would have been the case if we only based ourselves on an analysis of the kind used in 7.5.1. All in all, we shall therefore approach somewhat more closely to a result corrsponding to the assumption made in (7.98), but in the great majority of cases this would not reduce the new market price right down to the price which the producers receive under the actual system in force.

Even though we have now exceeded the bounds of what is set out in section 7.5.1, there are in principle a great many other complications which should be introduced into the line of argument in connection with fig. 8.

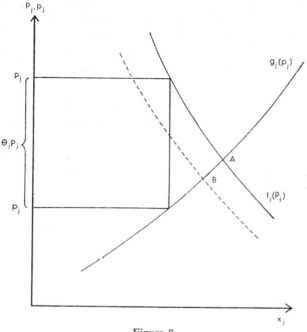

Figure 8

Actually we ought to take into account how all other changes in the tax and duty system taking place simultaneously with the change we discussed in connection with the figure, work in this market. In general nothing definite can be said about the direction in which the net effect of all these other changes will tend. But it is probable that they will cause a further reduction in the market price of the good we are considering, as they will evoke a substitution effect in demand, working to the disadvantage of the good we are considering.

On the basis of such arguments it is clear that we also ought to regard price effects for goods on which no duty has been imposed, but which at the same time are not completely elastic in supply. In their case, the removal of duties on *other* goods (and their replacement by direct taxes) will produce a negative shift in demand, and thereby at the same time a certain reduction in price.

Summing up, then, we reach the following conclusions: In the case of goods where the supply curve is completely elastic, assumption (7.98) will be fulfilled. In the case of other goods on which excise duties are imposed we shall generally have a higher market price under the hypothetical tax system than what we should expect in view of assumption (7.98), but at the same time a lower price than what would correspond to a direct application of the partial analysis (7.42)–(7.47). On the other hand, as a result of substitution effects, the market price will also be somewhat lower for tax-free goods under the hypothetical tax system than under the system in force. In (7.98) these prices are assumed to be the same under both tax systems.

All this applies to market conditions with free competition. As mentioned in section 7.5.1, given other market conditions one may find good reasons for assuming that a shifting of 100 per cent will occur, that is to say a shifting corresponding to the assumption made in (7.98).

Although there are undoubtedly cases where attempts should be made to base oneself on other assumptions than (7.98), it should be possible to conclude from the discussion above that this assumption is not so unrealistic as to render calculations based on (7.102)–(7.103) meaningless or valueless.

Finally, let us consider the assumption contained in (7.101). The numerator in the fraction (7.101) is the disposable income of the income-earner. The denominator is his purchase of goods and services. The difference between these magnitudes will comprise the income-earner's savings in the form of money*. On this basis we can re-write (7.101) as follows:

$$\frac{\Sigma P_j x_j + \text{monetary savings}}{\Sigma P_j x_j} = 1 . \qquad (7.104)$$

It will be seen that condition (7.101) will be fulfilled provided that monetary savings are equal to zero. If in fact monetary savings are not equal to zero in the case of the income-earner we are considering, the

---

* If magnitudes $x_1 \ldots x_n$ merely include purchases of goods and services for consumption, the difference between $r - s$ and $\Sigma P_j x_j$ will also include saving in real assets.

factor $(r-s)/\Sigma P_j x_j$, which will then differ from 1, should be taken into account in calculating Δ. This factor is connected with the choice of the disposable real income under the two different tax systems as our basis of comparison. This implies that we have also deflated the proportion of the income which is not used for the purchase of goods and services, using a price index, cf. the last line of table 13. In the case of an indirect taxation which is expected to be permanent, this would appear reasonable, taking the view that a sum which is saved in monetary form will then have its real value in future use influenced by the price effects of taxation. In most calculations that have been carried out with regard to the effect of taxation on income distribution, this factor has not been taken into account, and the approach has been to proceed as though indirect taxation merely affects amounts which an income-earner actually uses for current purchases of goods and services*.

We have now discussed in greater detail the various assumptions which were made in order to arrive at (7.102)–(7.103). As already mentioned, these formulae express the method of calculation most in use, but it will emerge from the discussion here that it would in principle be better to base the calculation on (7.100) than on (7.102)–(7.103). Furthermore, it would of course be still better if one could employ a more subtle approach than one based on assumption (7.98). This would involve calculations on tax shifting, of the kind we discussed in connection with fig. 8, and one would have to work out factor q on the basis of the definition in (7.93) instead of (7.99). It would then be possible to calculate Δ on the basis of (7.97). The most satisfactory solution would, of course, be if one could also abandon assumption (7.96), and instead carry out well-founded estimates for the difference between income before taxation under the two tax systems. We could then use formula (7.94) for calculating Δ.

7.7.4. *Some illustrations*

The most recent investigation in Norway on the effects of the tax system on

---

* An exception is an investigation by the Tax Research Office of the Central Bureau of Statistics of Norway, which we shall return to in the following subsection. The question raised in connection with (7.104) has been discussed theoretically on previous occasions by Mr. Arne Øien of the Tax Research Office.

income distribution was carried out by the Tax Research Office of the Central Bureau of Statistics of Norway in connection with the Ministry of Finance's Parliamentary Report no. 54, 1960–1961 on the general lines of the Norwegian tax policy. An account of the Tax Research Office's investigation is printed as Appendix I to this report.

To illustrate the argument in the foregoing section we shall here briefly mention some of the main features borne out by this investigation.

The investigation is based on income statistics and household accounts from 1958, but aims in principle to show the effects of the tax rules in force as of 1 July 1960 (with certain minor exceptions). The taxes included in this investigation are income and wealth taxes, compulsory insurance premiums, general sales tax on goods and services for private consumption, excise taxes on goods and services for private consumption, allowances from compulsory health insurance, old age insurance and family allowances (negative direct taxes), price subsidies for milk and milk products and for flour (negative indirect taxes).

Generally speaking, the investigation is based on assumptions of the kind we have mentioned and discussed in the two preceding subsections, even though in actual calculations other procedures have in part been used than those corresponding to the formulae we have examined.

Direct taxes naturally showed a considerable progression with respect to incomes, and at the same time weighed less heavily on families with a large number of children than on families with few or no children.

On the other hand social insurance premiums showed a notable regression with regard to income level, and no marked dependence on size of family.

The "negative direct taxes", that is to say direct allowances, naturally accrued primarily to income-earners in the lower income brackets, and to a greater extent to families with many children than families with few children.

In the case of general sales tax, alternative calculations have been made based on somewhat different assumptions. In the main alternative the effect of sales tax is calculated on the assumption we adopted with our starting-point in table 13 above, viz. that indirect taxes also affect saved income, in the sense that the real value of these saved amounts is reduced when indirect taxes effect a rise in market prices. On the basis of this assumption general sales tax, with a few exceptions, had the same effect as a tax which is proportional with income and independent of family size, i.e. it has no redistributive effect compared with a proportional income tax. Since not all goods and services are covered by sales tax, however, it constitutes a fraction of incomes which is lower than the formal tax rate.

If as an alternative one chooses the assumption that sales tax only affects income-earners to the extent that they purchase goods and services that are taxed, sales tax has a regressive effect with regard to income. Whereas for married couples with two children in an income bracket between 4–8 000 *kroner* it constituted 11.8% of income, in the case of families of the same type with incomes above 32 000 *kroner* it constituted merely 5.2% of income. That is to say, compared with a proportional income tax it worked to the disadvantage of families in the lower income brackets and to the advantage of families in the higher income brackets. This effect is naturally connected with the fact that saving is relatively higher in the higher income brackets. At the same time the sales tax according to this alternative calculation presses more heavily on larger families than on single persons or married couples with no children.

Taken as a whole, excise taxes have a progressive effect for the income categories comprised by the investigation. At the same time they affect small families and unmarried persons more severely than families with a large number of children. On the whole it may thus be said that the system of excise taxes, compared with proportional income tax, works to the advantage of income-earners in the lower income categories and with larger families.

Similarly, price subsidies (negative indirect taxes) worked in favour of income-earners in the lower income brackets and in favour of larger families.

The results for the different kinds of taxes have also been added together so that it is possible to see the effects of the tax system as a whole. Compared with a system involving only proportional income taxation (with no regard for the breadwinner's burden), the tax system in force was favourable to income-earners in income brackets below 4000 *kroner* as far as single persons were concerned, whereas single persons with higher incomes would have benefited from a transition to a system of proportional income taxation. In the case of married couples without children the tax system in force proved an advantage in the case of incomes below 12 000 *kroner*, whereas childless married couples with incomes in excess of 12 000 *kroner* would have benefited from a transition to a system involving merely proportional taxation. In the case of married couples with two children, the borderline was around 20 000 *kroner*, and for larger families somewhat higher. Using the alternative method of calculation, in which no account is taken of the effect of indirect taxes on the real value of saved income, the borders would be somewhat different from those here specified.

A classical investigation of the effects of a tax system on income distribution is one undertaken in 1948 by Richard Musgrave, in cooperation with a number of other economists, for the United States*.

In principle, it is based on assumptions such as those we have analysed above, leading to formulas such as (7.103). On certain points, however, it is based on somewhat different assumptions, and it also includes various factors which have not been introduced into an investigation such as the Norwegian one just referred to. I shall here mention briefly some of the special features of Musgrave's investigation.

In the first place it may be mentioned that Musgrave includes in his investigation the effects of company taxation. With regard to the shifting possibilities for the tax levied on the company's earnings, he envisages three alternatives:

(a) In this alternative it is assumed that one-third of the tax on company income is shifted on to consumers through higher prices for the products sold by the company. In addition it is assumed that one-eighth of the tax on company income is shifted back on wage-earners through lower wages than would otherwise have been the case. The remainder is then calculated to be absorbed as a reduction of the company's disposable income. This alternative is the main alternative, that is to say the one which the authors consider the most realistic of the alternatives presented.

(b) In this alternative it is assumed that the whole tax is shifted forward onto consumers through higher prices on products.

(c) In this alternative it is assumed that the whole tax acts as reduction in the company's disposable surplus.

---

* Richard A. Musgrave *et al.*, Distribution of tax payments by income groups, *The National Tax Journal* (1951).

Alternatives (b) and (c) were included in order to illustrate the effects of such extreme assumptions. As already mentioned, the authors consider alternative (a) the most realistic.

The non-shifted tax that falls on company income is regarded as consisting of two components: a tax on that portion of the profit which is distributed in the form of share dividends to personal income-earners, and a tax on the retained profit. The first of these components is assumed to reduce the distributed dividend, and this affects personal income-earners in various income groups according to how large a share these various groups have of the total distributed dividends. For this reason the tax on this component of companies weighed particularly heavily on income-earners in the high income brackets.

In the case of that portion of company tax falling on non-distributed profit, two alternatives were considered:

(1) With this alternative the tax falling on the non-distributed profit is ignored, and is considered to have no bearing on personal income distribution.
(2) With this alternative it is assumed that the tax on the non-distributed component of company income affects private shareholders in relation to their shareholdings. Then this tax too will affect the various income categories in the same way as the tax levied on the distributed portion of company income.

Of these two alternatives the authors consider (2) as the main alternative, but they consider all combinations of alternatives (a), (b), and (c) mentioned above, and alternatives (1) and (2) for dealing with the non-shifted tax which falls on the non-distributed company income.

That portion of the company tax which is assumed to be shifted on to consumers according to alternative (a) and alternative (b), is largely distributed among the various income brackets in relation to their share of total consumption. Some, however, was also distributed according to consumption of special goods. That portion of the company tax which is assumed to be shifted back onto wage-earners is distributed among the various income categories in relation to their share of total wage income.

In the U.S.A. property taxes play a greater role than in Norway, and it is therefore more important in an American investigation than in a

Norwegian one to provide detailed treatment of these taxes. Musgrave divides property taxes up into various components, and also considers shifting possibilities for some of them.

In the case of social insurance premiums, the general position was that one-third was paid by employees and two-thirds by employers. The one-third paid by employees was assumed to act entirely as a burden on employees. The portion paid by employers was dealt with in various alternatives. In the main alternative it was assumed that one-third of the employer's share was shifted back onto the employees in the form of lower wages than they would otherwise have had. The remainder of the employer's share was assumed to be shifted onto consumers through higher prices.

The economics of local authorities

8.1. Local self-government

Norway is divided up into a large number of municipalities enjoying a certain measure of self-government or autonomy. A similar situation exists in most of the other countries in Europe, even though the measure of self-government is very frequently less than in Norway.

A municipality may be defined as follows: "An area which forms a separate legally constituted community subordinate to the State, and invested with the authority to decide its own administrative affairs wholly or partly by means of its own government organs."*

In Norway the basis for municipal self-government was established by legislation in 1837. This has subsequently been revised on various occasions, but the main principles of what is called municipal self-government have remained the same ever since that date. Generally speaking these may be summed up as follows:

(1) Before the Act of 1837 municipalities had been governed by civil servants appointed by the State. After 1837 municipalities received their own government bodies representing the citizens in the municipality.

(2) The State has no right to make any imposition on municipalities unless this State right is explicitly established by law.

(3) Municipalities may themselves freely start and maintain any activity they might consider desirable, provided this is not explicitly forbidden by law.

---

* See K. M. Nordanger and Arnljot Engh, *Kommunal kunnskap* (Oslo, 1960) p. 23.

The last-mentioned point is a very important element of municipal self-government. It implies that the delineation of a municipality's sphere of activity is negative. This guarantees greater freedom of initiative on the part of the municipalities than would have been the case if there had been a *positive* delineation of the municipalities' sphere of activity, that is to say an arrangement whereby municipalities are only allowed to promote matters which the law explicitly states they may promote.

Apart from the points of principle mentioned above, a municipality's facility for financing its activities will in practice play an important role in the exploitation of the formal self-government enjoyed by the municipality. We shall subsequently discuss in greater detail the methods whereby municipal activities can be financed, and at this juncture merely mention that in all countries the State exercises a decisive influence in this respect.

In Norway, through the medium of tax legislation, some right to tax has been delegated to the municipalities. However, fairly narrow limits for this taxation have been laid down. If, on the one hand, through legislation, the State orders the municipalities to carry out a whole series of measures of various kinds – cf. point (2) above – and on the other hand gives municipalities limited facilities for financing their activities, the municipalities may find themselves in a position where the entire revenue at their disposal is spent in carrying out the measures which the law enjoins on them to carry out. In such cases municipal self-government is naturally in practice not particularly great, even though the principles set out above apply formally. In Norway this situation is keenly felt by a large number of municipalities with a comparatively weak revenue basis.

The reasons for desiring a certain measure of municipal self-government are primarily as follows:

(a) It is considered an important part of a democratic social and institutional set-up.
(b) In the case of a great many problems which have to be tackled on a collective basis, there is little need to carry out a standardised solution for the whole country, as needs and wishes may vary from one district to another. It is, of course, possible *per se* for a central authority to make decisions which do not involve standard norms for the whole country but instead meet local demands and wishes in various ways.

On the other hand, the chances for local needs and desires to count are much greater if decisions are made locally. In this connection the reader is also referred to the arguments set out in section 6.2.3 on the majority principle as a means of making decisions.

(c) Finally, the administration of a great many projects can be carried out more cheaply and more effectively if one bases oneself on a decentralised system of authority and a decentralised administration than if complete centralisation existed. It is not only possible to cut down on the number of channels through which various matters have to pass, but increased efficiency can also be achieved by utilising knowledge of local conditions.

There are naturally limits to how far one can go in decentralising the authority to take economic-political decisions, even though these limits can in no way be precisely established. We discussed some of the questions in connection with decentralisation of the use of policy instruments in subsection 2.1.4. It was there pointed out quite generally that it is possible to decentralise where instruments exist which are selective with regard to a "target variable", and where at the same time this target is not strongly influenced by other instruments. As a concrete example we might consider the question of water supply to various areas. We then have a whole series of target variables, viz. goals for providing water to every single area. The instruments involved are the damming of rivers, etc. If what is done in one area to secure water supplies within the area has little bearing on other areas, every area can be entrusted with the task of arranging its water supply without any interference from above. But this is of course not always the case. It will then be seen that the question of the possibilities of decentralising decisions without producing results which are unreasonable, seen from the point of view of the entire community, is dependent on concrete circumstances.

8.2. *Size and sphere of action of municipalities*

In discussing the question of the size of municipalities, it is natural to take as one's point of departure the reasons mentioned for having municipal self-government. In principle these reasons often suggest that municipalities should be very small. On the other hand, a great many factors must be taken into account which point to certain limits for *how* small municipalities should be. The most important factors are possibly the following:

(1) A municipality must always have a certain administration. Offices must be set up, and personnel appointed. If the population of a municipality is too small, the administrative organs will have some difficulty in utilising their entire capacity, and for a given standard of administrative quality and efficiency the administration will then prove comparatively expensive per resident within the minicipality. In small municipalities, too, every single administrative organ will tend to deal with matters of highly differing kinds, with the result that there will not be much degree of specialisation.

   In about 1950 the position in Norway was this, that the actual administrative expenses per inhabitant were greater in the large municipalities than in the small. This might appear to contradict what has just been said. On the other hand, there is no doubt that the standard of administration was higher in the large municipalities than in the small. At the same time the large municipalities were relatively wealthier, so that they undertook a greater number of tasks. They therefore had "more things" to administer. Finally, in the small municipalities relatively more administrative work was carried out by elected representatives.

   These factors were studied by the Municipal Divisions Committee, which came to the conclusion that it was "remarkable" how high administrative expenses per inhabitant were in the smallest municipalities*.

(2) Similar observations to those mentioned above apply to a great many other activities carried out by municipalities. In Norway, as in a great many other countries, the school system is to a large extent under municipal jurisdiction, and municipalities are obliged by law to satisfy certain minimum requirements with regard to the scope and form of instruction given. Irrespective of how many school pupils there are in a municipality, the school must be divided up into a certain number

---

* Report no. 2 of the Municipal Divisions Committee, p. 33. (Printed in 1952.)

of grades, and must have at its disposal classrooms and teachers for the various grades. If the municipality is very small, and the number of pupils consequently small, teaching will be expensive per inhabitant or per pupil. If a school is organised on the basis of the minimum permitted number of classrooms and specialist rooms, and the minimum permitted number of teachers, who will consequently not be able to specialise to any degree, then the quality of the teaching may well be low.

(3) A municipality enjoying self-government must always have a certain number of elected officials. If the municipality is very small, one will frequently have elected officials who work more or less as "factotums". In larger municipalities it is possible to employ the services of elected officials who have particular qualifications in various spheres.

(4) If a country is divided up into a great many municipalities, some of these municipalities are bound to be comparatively very poor areas. If the municipalities are larger, there will be a greater chance that an area which is particularly poor will be included in a municipality together with other areas enjoying a better economic basis. In the municipal budget a certain form of equalisation can then take place between areas within the municipality, whereby the municipality provides services to citizens which will be on a higher level than the poor area could have provided on its own, and at the same time maybe at a somewhat lower level than the wealthier parts of the municipality could have provided if these had constituted a municipality on their own. To what extent this consideration should count in determining the municipal boundaries, will depend on the extent of which it is possible to carry out an equalisation between municipalities on a State basis or through associations of municipalities such as exist in the counties. If an arrangement exists, through the medium of State organs or counties, for equalisation between municipalities, the factor here mentioned will play a less important role in establishing the extent of a municipality.

Apart from these more general considerations, concrete geographical and population factors will naturally help to determine the size of a municipality. For many reasons municipalities ought, after all, to constitute what is loosely called a "natural entity".

The question of municipalities' extent and boundaries has been an important political problem in Norway during the postwar period.

In 1837 the country was divided up into 355 rural municipalities and 37 urban municipalities. At that time the boundaries were drawn up largely on the basis of ecclesiastical subdivisions. During the years that followed cases sometimes occurred of municipalities being merged, but there was a far stronger tendency to split up the original municipalities into several new ones. This proceeded at a comparatively even rate right up to the years between the two world wars. As a result of this, by the beginning of the 1950s there were as many as 680 rural municipalities and 64 urban municipalities. In size rural municipalities varied from a few hundred inhabitants to 30 000 inhabitants, while urban municipalities ranged from units with less than 1 000 inhabitants to the capital, Oslo, with over 400 000 inhabitants. Changes in local economy and the development of transport and communications had rendered many of the old municipal boundaries somewhat unpractical and fortuitous. On the basis of the findings of the above-mentioned Municipal Divisions Committee a large number of cases have subsequently occurred of municipalities being joined together in larger units, and this process is still continuing. As a result, the number of municipalities is being reduced, and the average size of municipalities is on the increase.

During the investigation into the problems of municipal divisions, use was made in part of a Swedish analysis, which had investigated in turn each of the various spheres of activity of municipalities, and on this basis calculated the optimum size of municipalities. As a general rule the Norwegian committee found that for administrative reasons municipalities should have a minimum size of 2 500–3 000 inhabitants. There is nevertheless bound to be a very considerable divergence in the size of municipalities.

Even though a municipal division is arrived at which satisfies the new economic, communication, and population factors, there will always be a number of problems which have to be solved on a wider social basis than that of the individual municipality, and which at the same time it would be impractical for the State to deal with. For such purposes we have in Norway counties which comprise associations of individual municipalities, and there are also many forms of inter-municipal *ad hoc* cooperation.

As far as the municipalities' sphere of activity is concerned, in most cases it naturally follows from the reasons already mentioned why it is desirable to have municipalities with a certain measure of self-government. This sphere will include areas where there are no particularly strong grounds for aiming at standard solutions on a national scale, but where there are strong grounds for taking local needs and desires into account, and utilising local knowledge in finding the best solution.

As already mentioned, municipalities have various degrees of freedom in determining their activity in various fields. One may distinguish between four systems:

(a) In a number of fields it is clearly laid down in law that the municipalities *shall* carry out certain definite measures or maintain certain types of activity. In such cases, there is no freedom of choice for municipalities in deciding *whether* these things have to be carried out, but there will of course always be a certain degree of freedom in deciding in detail as to *how* such measures are to be carried out, what people should be appointed for this purpose, and so on.

(b) More generally than what is mentioned above, it is laid down by law that municipalities shall maintain a certain *minimum* number of activities or services in a particular field, while at the same time municipalities may decide whether they will offer more than the minimum laid down by law.

(c) In other fields the situation is this, that the laws do not lay down any municipal duty, as in the paragraphs above, but the laws lay down that to the extent a municipality decides to undertake certain tasks, it may receive state grants in carrying out these tasks, *provided it adheres to certain standards laid down by law*. Thus in such cases municipalities are in principle free both in deciding whether to take on a task and also in the manner of carrying it out, but State grants are conditional on such tasks being carried out in a particular way.

(d) Finally, in conformity with the principle that the municipal sphere of activity is negatively delineated, there are a great many fields where the municipalities themselves take the initiative and carry out various tasks, without the authority of any law and without any intervention or support on the part of the State.

There is no need to present here a concrete review of the various fields of activity in order to illustrate which of these principles is applied. We need only mention that an examination of the legislation dealing with schools, roads, and social insurance will disclose examples of all the principles under points (a) to (c) above. With regard to tasks which municipalities undertake, but of which there is no mention in any law, examples can be found within the cultural sphere, in sport, municipal baths, etc., as well as a large number of more markedly economic undertakings. A considerable development in the municipal field of activity has taken place since municipalities became independent organs with their own budgets, e.g., in the days when the budget for the municipality of Baerum, just outside Oslo, amounted to 41 specie dollars and 10 shillings, and the largest item on the budget was bonuses for shooting lynx. (It should, however, be mentioned that in those days many municipal activities were run on the basis of special funds which were not merged in a joint budget for all municipal activities. This would apply, for instance, to municipal poor relief.)

Even though considerable development in municipal activity has taken place, taking the long-term view, and basing ourselves on the *total* expenses of municipalities, we shall find that it has grown more slowly than State activity. Whereas municipal expenses at the turn of the century lay somewhere between 80 and 90% of State expenses, in the last decade they have been about one-half of State expenses. This comparison, however, includes all sorts of transfers. If we confine ourselves to considering expenses for the purchase of goods and services, we shall find that the rate of development municipally has been about the same as that of the State. This applies as an average over a long period. However, it conceals considerable unevennesses in development. The tendency to step-wise increase in public expenditure which we discussed in section 6.2.4, with reference to the book by Alan T. Peacock and Jack Wiseman, is especially applicable to State expenses. As a result, these stepped increases tend to distort the relationship between State and municipal expenditure. Among other factors, this is expressed in the figures below, which show municipal expenditure for goods and services in relation to State expenditure for goods and services for some selected years. (The figures are based on returns from the Central Bureau of Statistics. They are calculated on a gross basis, in the sense that payments received by the public authorities for some of their services have not been deducted.)

1900	1905	1910	1915	1920	1925	1930	1935	1939
0.82	0.98	1.12	0.87	1.28	1.67	1.60	1.56	1.17

1946	1948	1950	1952	1954	1956	1958	1960	1962
0.59	0.94	1.08	0.85	0.81	0.98	1.02	1.03	1.02

In their studies of the development of public expenditure in Britain Peacock and Wiseman point out, in addition, the displacement effect, which is an expression of what we have called step-wise increase of public expenditure, something which they call a *concentration process*. This is a tendency towards concentration of expenditure in the hands of central organs, instead of local bodies: "It is concerned not so much with changes in the total volume of public expenditures as with changes in the responsibility for such expenditures. In many societies, the functions of government are shared between a central authority and other (state and local) authorities whose powers may be protected by statute (as in legal federations) or conferred by the central government. In such countries local autonomy usually has many defenders, and its preservation is frequently a matter of political importance. At the same time, economic development produces changes in the technically efficient level of government, and also produces demands for equality of treatment (e.g., in services such as education) over wider geographical areas. These opposing pressures are reflected in the relative evolution of the expenditures undertaken at different levels of government. Clearly, this evolution is distinct from the displacement effect, since the forces just described operate in normal as well as in disturbed times."

A concentration process of this kind can hardly be said to have taken place in Norway. It will be seen from the figures above that the scope of municipal activity increased considerably, in proportion to the State, from the turn of the century to the interwar years. (The large municipal expenditure in the period around and after the First World War was based partly on loans, which resulted in municipalities undergoing a protracted crisis of debt, especially during the period of restoring the gold parity value of the *krone*. During the period after the Second World War municipal expenditure, as compared with that of the State, has on the whole been lower than in the interwar years, but – as already mentioned – it was still on a level with what it had been in the years prior to the First World War.

Below are shown, for a number of European countries, the percentage share of local bodies in total public expenditure on goods and services. These figures apply to the year 1957 and have been taken from the *Economic Survey of Europe* for 1959, of which use has previously been made. (While the above figures for Norway give municipal expenditure in relation to that of the State, the figures below give municipal expenditure as a proportion of the total. But even apart from this, they will not be entirely comparable with the figures we have used for Norway above. On the other hand, the figures in the table below should provide a basis for comparison between themselves.)

Sweden	55	Italy	35
Netherlands	48	United Kingdom	33
Norway	46	France	25
Austria	39	Greece	19
Belgium	38		

As will be seen, figures vary considerably, Norway being among the countries where municipalities play a comparatively large role within the public sector as a whole.

8.3.   Financing municipal activity

In various countries many different principles are in use for the financing of municipal activity. We can distinguish between the following main types:

1. *Transfers from the State.* Under this system, the State is the only authority to collect taxes. Some of the revenue the State collects through taxation is then distributed among the municipalities. It is possible in this connection to distinguish between two different methods of transfer:

   (1a) *Conditional transfers.* These are transfers of the kind we have already mentioned in connection with the question of municipal self-government. In such cases transfers are not in the form of

lump sums, which the municipality may use as it thinks fit, but
are conditional on the municipality carying out certain measures
or activities, and in many cases carrying them out in a particular
way.

(1b) *Unconditional transfers*. Under this system every municipality
receives a definite sum which it may use as it thinks fit. Naturally,
certain principles are necessary to determine the distribution of
the total amounts transferred to the various municipalities. In
this respect population in the various municipalities is a primary
factor. In many cases, however, other and more complicated
"distribution keys" are used apart from population, besides dis-
cretionary appraisal.

2. *Sharing taxes with the State*. Under this system there is a joint tax
   system for the whole country. Rules and rates must then be determined
   by the State authorities. The tax revenue accruing from taxpayers in
   a particular municipality, however, is divided between State and municipality according to pre-arranged rules, e.g., it may be decided that
   the State is to have a certain percentage and the municipality the rest
   of the total amount collected.

3. *Taxes on the same bases as the State, but with rates laid down on a
   municipal basis*. An example of this kind of arrangement is when the
   State levies income tax, and the taxpayers in the municipalities in
   addition to this tax to the State also pay a tax to the municipality
   calculated on the same tax base, but according to rates determined by
   the municipal authorities. In such cases total taxation may vary from
   one municipality to another. From the purely administrative point of
   view, an arrangement of this kind can, of course, be carried out in
   various ways, with a greater or lesser degree of integrated administration and collection.

4. *Municipal taxes on separate bases*. Under this system the State and
   the municipalities have, so to speak, divided the various types of tax
   bases between them, so that a particular tax base is exploited either
   solely by the State or solely by the municipality.

In addition to these forms we naturally have *loans* as a method of
financing municipal activity.

No country has concentrated entirely on a single one of the principles mentioned above. When, for example, one of the principles (2) to (4) is utilised, a municipality's income will depend on the level of prosperity among the population in that municipality. This could easily result in considerable inequality as between the various municipalities with regard to the level of services that the municipal bodies are capable of giving their citizens. For this reason, in utilising these principles, it has in most countries been found necessary to carry out a number of direct transfers from the State to less prosperous municipalities. This is the case *inter alia* in Norway, where principle 3 constitutes the basic method for financing municipal activity: municipalities tax income and net wealth according to rates they themselves determine, within certain limits, while at the same time the State, too, taxes the same sources of revenue. Besides this, municipalities receive a whole number of conditional transfers in connection with schools, roads, etc. Furthermore, they receive unconditional transfers through grants made from the *Tax Distribution Fund*. This was established in 1936, and originally financed by the so-called interest tax (tax on interest on bank deposits). This arrangement was abolished in the 1950s, since when the Tax Distribution Fund has been financed by a special tax on higher incomes (now called the "Tax Distribution Duty"). In addition to this, the State has in some years made grants to the Tax Distribution Fund directly via the State budget.

The system mentioned above under (4), viz. municipal taxes on special bases, now plays a less important role in Norway. As an example we have property tax, but as mentioned it no longer plays such an important role in the total budgets of municipalities. In a great many countries, however, the position is different. In some countries also sales or excise taxes on certain goods exist as a special tax for authorities on a lower level than central government. This is true, *inter alia*, of the financing of the federal states in the U.S.A.

In Great Britain, apart from property taxes, principle (1b), unconditional transfers from the State, plays a very important role.

In the Netherlands and Belgium a system of shared taxes with the State is used. The proportions according to which this division is made are specially fixed for each single year. The same principle also plays an important role in Austria and West Germany, but here the proportion is fixed for several years at a time.

In Belgium and France a pure form of the principle mentioned as no. 3 above at one time played a certain role. First the State determined a tax on land and other property, and then the individual municipalities fixed so-called "centimes additionels" as an addition to the rates enforced by the State. The revenue accruing from these additional rates went to municipal budgets.

Finally, let us consider a few points which are important for evaluating the various methods of arranging the financing of municipal acticvity.

From the point of view of *municipal self-government* the system involving sharing taxes with the State alone is clearly not a particularly good principle. This system gives the municipality no control over the actual extent of its activity, since the level of joint taxation is centrally determined. In the same category may be placed transfers from the State which are also centrally determined. Within this system, conditional transfers in turn provide a lesser degree of independence for the municipalities than unconditional transfers. If systems of this kind are combined with a certain degree of municipal taxation, however, it will be possible to arrive at practical systems which at the same time uphold the principle of municipal self-government. There is, however, no country in which one goes as far as to allow municipalities to undertake any kind and any extent of taxation merely on the basis of their own judgment. In Norway the tax laws lay down upper and lower limits for the tax percentage municipalities may use in levying income and net wealth taxes, and there is also a limited scope in the choice of the exemption tables for family maintenance. There are various reasons for these limits. One is that complete freedom for municipalities to decide the tax rates might result in considerable variations in the taxation level from one municipality to another. This might result in capital and labour being attracted to municipalities with a low level of taxation, which in turn would make it possible for these municipalities to lower the tax level still further, while at the same time municipalities starting on a relatively higher tax rate would have to increase their rates still further. This would result in a development which would tend to increase the inequalities in the level of prosperity which already exist as between municipalities. Another factor applicable to a country such as Norway, where the work of tax assessment was previously carried out by municipal bodies, is the following: If municipalities had a free hand in levying as high tax rates as they wanted, municipal assessment officers might tend to assess incomes and capital at a low level, in order to prevent too much money from the municipality passing into the State treasury, while at the same time the municipality could maintain its own tax revenue by raising the tax percentage. For many reasons a trend of this kind would have unfortunate results.

As far as the desire for *simplicity and efficiency* in taxation are concerned, generally speaking it may perhaps be said that systems involving the greatest degree of limitation in municipal self-government will frequently be the simplest. In particular, an arrangement involving sharing a tax with the State could be worked out in a simple, handy manner. Nevertheless, in this system too it is difficult to avoid a certain amount of controversy in deciding the municipality of origin of a tax amount, and consequently to what municipalities some of it should be returned.

An arrangement, involving taxation on the same bases as the State, can also be worked out with comparative simplicity. In Norway this potential simplicity has not been fully exploited, as there are certain discrepancies in income and net wealth tax between the definition of taxable income and wealth for municipal taxation and for State taxation. As we have already mentioned in passing, this applies to the treatment of shares and share dividends.

With regard to transfers from the State to the municipalities, there are grounds for assuming that unconditional transfers are simpler than conditional transfers. This need, however, not always be the case. As already mentioned, unconditional transfers must also be decided on the basis of certain criteria, such as population figures, possibly the income level in the municipality, and possibly, too, with various special needs of different kinds in view. The fact that they are "unconditional" only means that they are not conditioned by certain ways of spending the money. An arrangement involving State grants for such matters as municipal road-building or schools, according to certain standard rules, could quite possibly prove just as simple and automatic in its execution as an arrangement involving unconditional transfers.

One ought also to take into account how the various systems influence the *direction and efficiency of the exploitation of resources* in the country. There is no need here to repeat the various considerations previously made regarding the effects of the various forms of tax in this respect. We shall merely point out that with regard to the two different forms of transfer from State to municipality that we have mentioned, unconditional transfers would, as a general rule, prove preferable because such transfers do not interfere with municipal evaluation of the relative costs of the different projects involved. On the other hand, when certain types of activity are automatically supported by the State, while other types are not, an efficient municipal administration will naturally take account of this in its decisions, and adapt its dispositions towards activities of the kind that receive State grants. This is no decisive argument against various forms of conditional transfer, but it does suggest that arrangements of this kind should be used circumspectly, and preferably when, from the point of view of the State, there are obvious reasons for attempting to induce municipal dispositions in certain directions*. An example of the latter is when the State makes special grants for municipal construction work which takes place during the months of the year when there would otherwise be seasonal unemployment.

From the same point of view we might also consider such effects on localisation of economic activity and housing as we mentioned above in connection with the question of allowing municipalities complete freedom to decide their own taxation. Regional movements of business and people caused by differences in tax level between municipalities will often be found to prove inefficient if we consider the country as a whole.

As a rule a certain *equalisation* between municipalities, with regard to living conditions and social welfare standards, is desirable. We have already touched on this point above, and it is obvious that any arrangement in which the financing of municipal activity is exclusively based on the taxable potential present in the actual municipality itself, will result in inequalities. In such cases municipalities will either be forced to accept highly varying tax levels, or highly varying levels in the quality and scope of the municipal services available to citizens. In a country such as Norway both these circumstances exist. Municipalities with the weakest economic basis as a general rule maintain taxation at the maximum permitted rates, and even so are not in a position to give their citizens as wide a range of services as municipalities maintaining lower taxation rates. This in spite of the fact that not inconsiderable arrangements to promote equalisation

---

* See Kjeld Philip: *Det offentliges finanspolitik og den økonomiske aktivitet* (Fiscal policy and economic activity), especially chapter XXVI.

exist, through the medium of various forms of transfer already mentioned.

The desire to equalise living conditions as between municipalities may to some extent clash with the desire for the most efficient population distribution and localisation of economic activity, from the point of view of the country as a whole. The various considerations must in such cases naturally be evaluated on a political basis.

Finally, the various systems can be evaluated on the basis of the possibilities they offer for carrying out an *effective fiscal policy*. It must be assumed that, by the dispositions they themselves freely decide, municipalities cannot be expected to make any contribution to a fiscal policy with country-wide targets. For example, if a municipality, where the need exists to stimulate economic activity, were to make certain tax concessions for this purpose, the bulk of the increased demand which would result would be directed towards products produced outside the municipal boundaries. Pursuing a fiscal policy for stabilization purposes is therefore in the main bound to be a task of central government. For this reason, systems in which the municipalities themselves are responsible for a large proportion of taxation, would not be very efficient. To a certain extent this applies to conditions in Norway, where a very considerable proportion of income taxation, which might have provided the most important fiscal instrument of policy in regulating total demand, is in the hands of the municipalities. A large proportion of the population pay income tax only to their municipality. In changing the tax rates for income tax to the State there are therefore limited potentialities in influencing demand.

For a more detailed analysis of how municipal dispositions affect the problem of influencing total demand through fiscal policy, we might make a simple extension of the small model (3.13) in Chapter 3. We shall now in particular consider

G_s = State purchases of goods and services,
G_m = total municipal purchases of goods and services.

Correspondingly, let us distinguish between tax payable to the State and tax payable to the municipalities:

T_s = tax revenue to the State,
T_m = total tax revenue to the municipalities.

We shall assume that tax to the municipalities is a linear function of national income R:

$$T_m = t_m R + h_m,$$ (8.1)

where t_m and h_m are constants. We now assume that the municipalities always will (or must) balance their budgets, not endeavouring to influence demand by means of a deficit or surplus budget:

$$G_m = T_m.$$ (8.2)

In the case of the State, we shall consider both expenditure G_s and the tax revenue T_s as instruments of policy. If we consider private investment demand I_P as autonomous, and assume the following consumption function:

$$C_p = a(R - T_s - T_m) + b,$$ (8.3)

we shall then get the following solution for the national product:

$$R = \frac{1}{(1-a)(1-t_m)}[G_s - aT_s + I_p + b + (1-a)h_m].$$ (8.4)

From this solution we can draw two conclusions. In the first place it will be seen that the amount of State tax or State expenditure needed to compensate a definite shift in, e.g., private investments, is uninfluenced by the tax function for municipal tax. In the second place, it will be seen that if G_s and T_s are maintained constant, a certain shift in, e.g., private investments will lead to a greater reaction in R, the greater t_m is, since the multiplier in (8.4) is bigger. In this sense, municipal taxes and municipal expenditure as determined by (8.2) have a *destabilising* effect. The municipalities are here in fact carrying out a policy of the kind we discussed in subsection 3.2.4.

We shall also see what the solution of the national product will be when we consider State tax yield as a function of national income, while at the same time State expenditure G_s continues to be regarded as autonomously determined. We then get for State tax

$$T_s = t_s R + h_s, \tag{8.5}$$

where t_s and h_s are constants, and we get the following solution for the national product:

$$R = \frac{1}{(1-a)(1-t_m) + at_s} [G_s + I_p + b - ah_s + (1-a)h_m]. \tag{8.6}$$

Let us, on the basis of (8.6), express the degree of automatic stabilisation we achieve, just as we did in the case of formulae (3.41)–(3.42) in Chapter 3. We get

$$\gamma = \frac{\dfrac{1}{1-a} - \dfrac{1}{(1-a)(1-t_m) + at_s}}{\dfrac{1}{1-a}},$$

which can also be written as follows:

$$\gamma = 1 - \frac{1-a}{(1-a)(1-t_m) + at_s}. \tag{8.7}$$

It will here be seen that the degree of stabilisation is greater, the greater t_s is, but smaller, the greater t_m is.

We can thus say that the State, which maintains its expenditure un-influenced by tax revenue, contributes to automatic stabilisation, whereas the municipalities, which allow expenditure to follow income, contribute to *destabilisation*.

It might be of interest here to ask when the total stabilising effect will be equal to nought. We get the condition required for this by making $\gamma = 0$. This gives us

$$t_m = \frac{a}{1-a} t_s. \tag{8.8}$$

If as a numerical example we put $a=0.75$, the automatic stabilising effect of State and municipal behaviour will thus be equal to nought if the macro marginal tax rate in municipal taxes is three times as high as the macro marginal tax rate in taxation to central government.

On the basis of this numerical example, it should be possible to conclude that the tax conditions in Norway as a net effect will give a certain positive automatic stabilisation, even though municipalities may pursue the pattern we have presupposed in our discussion above. In actual fact, changes in municipal expenditure demand some planning in advance and a great many items of expenditure are also predetermined. For this reason a change in tax revenue will not cause such an automatic reaction in the level of expenditure as we assumed in (8.2). Furthermore, by regulating municipal permission to raise loans, and by regulating transfers, the State would to a certain extent be in a position to influence municipalities, for the purpose of stabilisation. Nevertheless, our discussion ventilates an important problem in connection with fiscal policy, in an economy where municipal budgets, as a total, constitute a very considerable amount, compared with that of the State, and where they finance their activities by means of their own tax revenues.

As part of a selectively planned fiscal policy, conditional transfers to municipalities might prove a practical instrument. State grants for extraordinary public works projects on a municipal scale, a common feature in Norway, may be considered from this angle. The same applies to subsidies, of the kind already mentioned, for municipal construction work set on foot during those months of the year when considerable seasonal unemployment might result, if no special steps were taken to prevent this. In practice, the State will also as a rule be in a position to influence municipal dispositions to a certain extent by laying down certain guiding lines of policy or by making recommendations.

Index